ONE WORLD ARCHAEOLOGY
Series Editor: P. J. Ucko

THE EXCLUDED PAST
Archaeology in education

Edited by

Peter G. Stone
Regional Education Officer, English Heritage

Robert MacKenzie
School of Social and Historical Studies, University of Portsmouth

London and New York

First published by Unwin Hyman Ltd in 1990

First published in paperback 1994
by Routledge
11 New Fetter Lane, London EC4P 4EE

Simultaneously published in the USA and Canada
by Routledge
29 West 35th Street, New York, NY 10001

Typeset in 10 on 11 point Bembo by Computape (Pickering) Ltd,
Pickering, North Yorkshire
Printed in Great Britain at Redwood Books, Trowbridge, Wiltshire

British Library Cataloguing in Publication Data
   The excluded past: archaeology in education
   (One world archaeology: 17)
   1. Educational institutions. Curriculum subjects.
   Archaeology
   I. Stone, Peter   II. MacKenzie, Robert   III. Series 930–1 107

Library of Congress Cataloging in Publication Data
   The Excluded past: archaeology in education/edited by Peter Stone, Robert
   MacKenzie.
          p. cm. – (One world archaeology: 17)
   Includes bibliographical references.
   1. Archaeology – Study and teaching. 2. Educational anthropology.
   3. Minorities – Education. 4. Education – Developing countries.
   5. Race awareness – Study and teaching. 6. Developing countries – History –
   Study and teaching. I. Stone, Peter. II. MacKenzie, Robert. III. Series.
   CC83.E93 1989 930.1–dc20 89–22441

ISBN 0–415–10545–5

List of contributors

Alex Barlow, Australian Institute of Aboriginal Studies, Canberra, ACT, Australia.

John Blacking, Department of Social Anthropology, the Queen's University of Belfast, Northern Ireland, UK.

Shirley Blancke, Concord Museum, Massachusetts, USA.

Dilip K. Chakrabarti, Department of Archaeology, University New Delhi, India.

Heather Devine, Archaeological Survey of Alberta, Edmonton, Canada.

Clare Fawcett, Department of Anthropology, McGill University, Montreal, Canada.

Len Garrison, The Association of Caribbean Families and Friends, Nottingham, UK.

Stephen Gawe, African National Congress, London, UK.

Junko Habu, Faculty of Science, University of Tokyo, Japan.

Manfred Hinz, Namibia Project, Universität Bremen, Germany.

Luke Holland, Survival International, London, UK.

Alice B. Kehoe, Department of Anthropology, Marquette University, Milwaukee, USA.

Elizabeth Khawajkie, Division of Equality of Educational Opportunity and Social Programmes, Unesco, Paris, France.

Robert MacKenzie, School of Social and Historical Studies, University of Portsmouth, UK.

Stefano Mammini, Società Cooperativa Archeologia, Rome, Italy.

Francis Meli, African National Congress, London, UK.

★Andrzej Mikołajczyk, Muzeum Archeologiczne i Etnograficzne w Łodzi, Poland.

Godfrey Muriuki, Department of History, University of Nairobi, Kenya.

★Nwanna Nzewunwa, Faculty of Humanities, University of Port Harcourt, Nigeria.

Cjigkitoonuppa John Peters Slow Turtle, Massachusetts Commission on Indian Affairs, Boston, Massachusetts, USA.

Philip Planel, Independent researcher, Die, France.

Nadezhda Platonova, Leningrad Institute of Archaeology, USSR.

Irina Podgorny, Museo Municipal Alte. Brown, Ranelagh, Argentina.

Wendy Richardson, Education Department, Hampshire County Council, Winchester, UK.

Mario Sanoja Obediente, Academia Nacional dela Historia de Venezuela, Caracas, Venezuela.

Paul Sinclair, Department of Archaeology, The University, Uppsala, Sweden.

Karolyn Smardz, Archaeological Resource Centre, Toronto, Canada.

Peter G. Stone, Education Service, English Heritage, London, UK.

Iraida Vargas Arenas, Departamento de Arqueología y Etnografia, Universidad Central de Venezuela, Caracas, Venezuela.

Simiyu Wandibba, National Museums of Kenya, Nairobi, Kenya.

Lilla Watson, Department of Social Work, University of Queensland, Australia.

★ Deceased.

Foreword

This book is one of a major series of more than 20 volumes resulting from the World Archaeological Congress held in Southampton, England, in September 1986. The series reflects the enormous academic impact of the Congress, which was attended by 850 people from more than 70 countries, and attracted many additional contributions from others who were unable to attend in person.

The *One World Archaeology* series is the result of a determined and highly successful attempt to bring together for the first time not only archaeologists and anthropologists from many different parts of the world, as well as academics from a host of contingent disciplines, but also nonacademics from a wide range of cultural backgrounds, who could lend their own expertise to the discussions at the Congress. Many of the latter, accustomed to being treated as the 'subjects' of archaeological and anthropological observation, had never before been admitted as equal participants in the discussion of their own (cultural) past or present, with their own particularly vital contribution to make towards global, cross-cultural understanding.

The Congress therefore really addressed world archaeology in its widest sense. Central to a world archaeological approach is the investigation not only of how people lived in the past but also of how, and why, changes took place resulting in the forms of society and culture which exist today. Contrary to popular belief, and the archaeology of some 20 years ago, world archaeology is much more than the mere recording of specific historical events, embracing as it does the study of social and cultural change in its entirety. All the books in the *One World Archaeology* series are the result of meetings and discussions which took place within a context that encouraged a feeling of self-criticism and humility in the participants about their own interpretations and concepts of the past. Many participants experienced a new self-awareness, as well as a degree of awe about past and present human endeavours, all of which is reflected in this unique series.

The Congress was organized around major themes. Several of these themes were based on the discussion of full-length papers which had been circulated some months previously to all who had indicated a special interest in them. Other sessions, including some dealing with areas of specialization defined by period or geographical region, were based on oral addresses, or a combination of precirculated papers and lectures. In all cases, the entire sessions were recorded on cassette, and all contributors were presented with the recordings of the discussion of their papers. A major part of the thinking behind the Congress was that such a meeting of many hundreds of participants that did not leave behind a published record of its academic discussions would be little more than an exercise in tourism.

Thus, from the very beginning of the detailed planning for the World Archaeological Congress in 1982, the intention was to produce post-Congress books containing a selection only of the contributions, revised in the light of discussions during the sessions themselves as well as during subsequent consultations with the academic editors appointed for each book. From the outset, contributors to the Congress knew that if their papers were selected for publication, they would have only a few months to revise them according to editorial specifications, and that they would become authors in an important academic volume scheduled to appear within a reasonable period following the Southampton meeting.

The publication of the series reflects the intense planning which took place before the Congress. Not only were all contributors aware of the subsequent production schedules, but also session organizers were already planning their books before and during the Congress. The editors were entitled to commission additional chapters for their books when they felt that there were significant gaps in the coverage of a topic during the Congress, or where discussion at the Congress indicated a need for additional contributions.

Quite exceptionally, as mentioned in the Preface, it was decided to postpone proceeding towards the publication of a book on archaeology and education for one year, to allow an unusual number of new chapters to be commissioned. This decision reflected the paucity of in-depth case studies and carefully considered viewpoints at a time when the essential nature of the interrelatedness of archaeology and education had been little examined. This intervening year saw the publication of the *Archaeological Review from Cambridge*, whose Autumn 1987 edition was devoted to 'Archaeology as education' (and see below).

One of the main themes of the 1986 Congress was devoted to 'Archaeological "Objectivity" in Interpretation', where consideration of the precirculated full-length papers on this theme extended over four and a half days of academic discussion. The particular sessions on 'Archaeological "Objectivity" in Interpretation' were under my overall control, the main aim being to focus attention on the way that evidence of the past – including archaeological evidence – has been used and viewed by particular groups (whether local, regional or national) at different times. Essential to this aim was the exploration of the reasons why particular interpretations might have been chosen, or favoured, by individual societies and traditions at specific points in their development, or at certain stages in their activities. The whole theme attempted, therefore, a unique mix of critical assessment of the basis of archaeological methodology with critical awareness of the social contexts of the use (and possible manipulation) of the evidence of the past.

Central to this re-evaluation of the strengths and weaknesses of archaeological approaches to the interpretation, and indeed 'display', of the past – whether through academic articles or by means of formal or informal curricula, or through museums or site presentation – is an assessment of the methodologies and approaches to the significance of material culture. This has long been a core issue in archaeological discussion, but it badly needed re-examination. Throughout the history of archaeology as a discipline material culture, or at least the repetitive association of distinctive material culture objects, has been taken to reflect activities of specific social groups or 'societies' whose physical movements across a geographic stage have often been postulated on the basis of the distribution patterns of such objects, and whose supposed physical or ethnic identity (see also *State and society*, edited by J. Gledhill, B. Bender & M. T. Larsen) has often been assumed to correlate with such artefactual groupings. More recently archaeologists have been forced to recognize, often through lessons gained from ethnography, that a distinctive material culture complex may represent the activities of a vast variety of social groupings and subgroups, and that archaeological classification may often serve to camouflage the more subtle messages of style and technique (see also *Animals into art*, edited by H. Morphy, and *Domination and resistance*, edited by D. Miller, M. J. Rowlands & C. Tilley) which probably symbolize complex patterns of behaviour, as well as individual aspirations, within any society.

If the very basis of the equation between a material culture complex and a social grouping is ambiguous, then much of archaeological interpretation must remain subjective, even at this fundamental level of its operations. Whenever the archaeological data of material culture is presented in museums, on sites, in literature, in schools or in textbooks, as the evidence for the activities of 'races', 'peoples', 'tribes', 'linguistic groups' or other socially derived ethnic amalgamations, there should be at least scepticism if not downright suspicion. In a large number of such cases, what we are witnessing is the none-too-subtle ascription of racial/cultural stereotypes to static material culture items.

The overall theme therefore took as its starting point the proposition that archaeological interpretation is a subjective matter. It also assumed that to regard archaeology as somehow constituting the only legitimate 'scientific' approach to the past needed re-examination and possibly even rejection. A narrow parochial approach to the past which simply assumes that a linear chronology based on a 'verifiable' set of 'meaningful' 'absolute' dates is the only way to tackle the recording of, and the only way to comprehend, the past completely ignores the complexity of many literate and of many nonliterate 'civilizations' and cultures. However, a world archaeological approach to a concept such as 'the past' focuses attention on precisely those features of archaeological enquiry and method which archaeologists all too often take for granted, without questioning the related assumptions.

Discussions on this theme during the Congress were grouped around seven headings, and have led to the publication of five books. The first subtheme, organized by Stephen Shennan, Department of Archaeology, University of Southampton, which lasted for almost a day, was concerned with 'Multiculturalism and Ethnicity in Archaeological Interpretation' and the second, under the control of Ian Hodder, Department of Archaeology, University of Cambridge, which occupied more than a day, was on 'Material Culture and Symbolic Expression'. The fourth subtheme, 'The Politics of the Past: Museums, Media, and other Presentations of Archaeology', was organized by Peter Gathercole of Darwin College, Cambridge, and also lasted for more than a day. Each of these subthemes has led to a separate book: *Archaeological approaches to cultural identity* (edited by S. J. Shennan), *The meanings of things* (edited by I. Hodder), and *The politics of the past* (edited by P. Gathercole & D. Lowenthal, of the Department of Geography, University College London). The fifth subtheme, on 'The Past in Education', was organized by Robert MacKenzie and discussion of this topic (which lasted formally for half a day at the Congress and informally throughout the week by means of displays and educational events) has been expanded into this book under his and Peter Stone's editorship. David Bellos of the Department of French, University of Manchester, was responsible for a short discussion session on the sixth subtheme 'Mediations of the Past in Modern Europe', and contributions from this subtheme have been combined either with those from the third on 'Contemporary Claims about Stonehenge' (a short discussion session organized by Christopher Chippindale, of the Department of Archaeology, University of Cambridge), or with those from the seventh subtheme on 'Indigenous Perceptions of the Past' which lasted for almost a day. Robert Layton of the Department of Anthropology, University of Durham, was in charge of this seventh topic and has also edited the two resulting books, *Conflict in the archaeology of living traditions* and *Who needs the past?* The former also incorporates several contributions from a one-day discussion on 'Material Culture and the Making of the Modern United States: Views from Native America', which had been organized by Russell Handsman of the American Indian Archaeological Institute, Washington, and Randall McGuire of the Department of Anthropology of the State University of New York at Binghamton.

The whole of the 'Archaeological "Objectivity" in Interpretation' theme had been planned as the progressive development of an idea and the division of it into subthemes was undertaken in the full knowledge that there would be considerable overlap between them. It was accepted that it would, in many ways, be impossible, and even counter-productive, to split for example, education from site presentation, or literary presentations of the past from indigenous history. In the event, each of the books resulting from this overall theme has its own coherence; they also share a concern to make explicit the responsibility of recognizing the various ways of interpreting humanly-created artefacts. In addition they recognize the social responsibility of archaeological interpretation, and the way that this may be used, consciously or unconsciously, by others for their own ends. The contributions in these books, directly or indirectly, explicitly or implicitly, epitomize the view that modern archaeology must recognize and confront its new role, which is to address the wider community. It must do this with a sophisticated awareness of the strengths and the weaknesses of its own methodologies and practices.

A world archaeological approach to archaeology as a 'discipline' reveals how subjective archaeological interpretation has always been. It also demonstrates the importance that all rulers and leaders (politicians) have placed on the legitimization of their positions through the 'evidence' of the past. Objectivity is strikingly absent from most archaeological exercises in interpretation. In some cases there has been conscious manipulation of the past for national political ends (as in the case of Ian Smith's Rhodesian regime over Great Zimbabwe, or that of the Nazis with their racist use of archaeology). But, apart from this, archaeologists themselves have been influenced in their interpretation by the received wisdom of their times, both in the sort of classificatory schemes which they consider appropriate to their subject, and in the way that their dating of materials is affected by their assumptions about the capabilities of the humans concerned. Nowhere is archaeological explanation immune to changes in interpretative fashion. This is as true of Britain as of anywhere else – Avebury and especially Stonehenge have been subjected to the most bizarre collection of interpretations over the years, including all sorts of references to them having been constructed by Mycenaeans, Phoenicians or Romans. Although, at first sight, it is tempting to assume that such contentions are different from attempts by politicians to claim that the extraordinary site of Great Zimbabwe was constructed by Phoenicians using black slaves, the difference is not very easy to sustain.

Realization of the flexibility and variety of past human endeavour all over the world directs attention back to those questions that are at the very basis of archaeological interpretation. How can static material culture objects be equated with dynamic human cultures? How can we define and recognize the 'styles' of human activity, as well as their possible implications? In some contexts these questions assume immense political importance. For example, the archaeological 'evidence' of cultural continuity, as opposed to discontinuity, may make all the difference to an indigenous land claim, the right of access to a site/region, or the disposal of a human skeleton to a museum, as against its reburial.

All these factors lead in turn to a new consideration of how different societies choose to display their museum collections and conserve their sites. As the debates make clear about who should be allowed to use Stonehenge or 'develop' Avebury – and how these two World Heritage sites should be displayed – objects or places may be considered important at one time and 'not worth bothering about' at others. Who makes these decisons and in what contexts? Who is responsible, and why, for what is taught about the past in schools or in adult education? Is such education based on a narrow local/regional/national framework of archaeology and history, or is it oriented towards multiculturalism and the variety of human cultural experiences in a worldwide context? What should the implications be for the future of archaeology?

The particular events leading to the production of this book have been alluded to above, and have also been detailed in its Preface and elsewhere (Ucko 1987, pp. 150–1ff.). It has seemed worthwhile to do so because, despite several published general statements of intent, and considerable practical work in schools, there has been an absence of attempts to confront the relationship between education and archaeology, except in the most superficial manner, prior to 1986. The unusual step of widening debate about the role of archaeology to include its position and effect within the spheres of both informal and formal education in itself constituted a significant learning experience. Previously, one suspects, most archaeologists had simply assumed that any education that incorporated material about the past must be a positive education. Certainly, most Western archaeologists, just like other Westerners, normally have no appreciation of the fact that, in many countries and cultures, an imposed education is seen to be one of – and perhaps *the* – most serious threat to liberty and cultural self-determination. It is difficult for many involved in the educational professions to recognize that, to others, they are agents of alienation, simply contributing to the production of mere societal 'tools' suitable for employment. As an Australian *Aboriginal* contributor demonstrates (Ch. 8), things may be so bad that any Aboriginal child claiming to have done well within the White education system may be regarded with suspicion, or even as a failure, by other Aboriginal people. As an Australian *White* educator admits (Ch. 7), the primary aim of the Australian education system towards Aborigines is to remove their 'Aboriginality', which is still seen by the majority of the population to be a bar to so-called progress. Teaching about Aborigines is often a battleground, involving accusations about the appropriation of a people's heritage, and the fact that dominance is being asserted through control of knowledge, via non-Aboriginal authored books and archival manuscripts (Ucko 1983, Allen 1988). As *The excluded past* demonstrates, these are not experiences unique to Australia (e.g. Breunig 1975, for the Hopi Indians of North America), and, in some cases, they may have a profound effect on the teachers concerned. It is part of the complexity of the situation that one of the few perceived ways towards advancement (other than sporting prowess) in many societies is through an existing imposed education system, and that it is the discipline of education itself that has attracted many of the 'successful', 'Fourth World', individually known 'personalities' of Australia, Canada, etc. 'Education' is a subject about which we all not only feel strongly, but about which most of us also have a 'view'. Meanwhile, as Trigger (1989) has put it so forcibly, those who are afraid to confront the real issue – that is, the issue of who is to be given powers of executive decision-taking and decision-making about the control of a people's past (whether in museums or through education) – are bound to lose out in the long term. In addition, if they delay, they will be seen to be responsible for the dismemberment of archaeology and anthropology.

The excluded past (and see chapters and introductions in *State and society*, edited by J. Gledhill, B. Bender & M. T. Larsen, and in *The politics of the past*, edited by P. Gathercole & D. Lowenthal) includes several chapters that document how the specific absence of any content about the past within the educational syllabus may negate the whole existence of a people and of whole cultures – even, it is argued, facilitating genocide (e.g. Chs 9 & 11). Other chapters demonstrate how, even when particular cultures are indeed incorporated within the formal education system of a region or state or nation, the only vision of that culture that is promulgated is one formulated by the dominant society (e.g. Chs 5, 10, 17, & 19). *The excluded past* forces one to realize the essential connection between the control and exercise of power, and education.

Many of the pages of this book are concerned with the varying ways in which the exercise of such power – through education – have been effected, as well as the specific nature of the use of interpretations of the past within such power politics. As one reads through *The excluded past* it becomes abundantly clear that what is being demonstrated is often not only the simple exclusion of whole parts of a society's past, but many other subtle manipulations as well. In many contexts, education involves choices about the use of the language(s) of instruction, choices which, in themselves, are often seen as dictatorial, imperialist, or even racist (e.g. Ch. 14, and see Kishani's chapter in *Conflict in the archaeology of living traditions*, edited by R. Layton). In others, the examples used to illustrate archaeological techniques or interpretations may be inappropriately chosen and result not only in incomprehension (Ch. 12) but may also act as continuing reminders of the foreign origin and development of archaeological enquiry. In an important chapter by Hinz (Ch. 6) the point is stressed that de-colonialization must include not only the writing of new histories of the country or region by those previously excluded, but also the rewriting of colonial history to recognize, explicitly, the role of the colonialists in disenfranchising from their own pasts the very people for whom they had assumed responsibility.

Realization that inclusion or exclusion from a curriculum may be part of the politics of power also focuses attention on the way that nations have made use of teaching about the past in their attempts to create the kind of national image best suited to their own particular political philosophy. In two important contributions, Sinclair (Ch. 12) and Fawcett & Habu (Ch. 18) demonstrate how changing forms of nationalistic development within a particular country may modify attitudes towards, and research and edu-cation about, the past. Such nationalistic aims may even lead to results in the conservation field, influencing what is destroyed, what is conserved as it is, and what is restored (Ch. 22). Several chapters examine the educational basis and results of the insistence by those who control education in some countries that history only really begins with literacy (and, therefore, that everything preceding such a 'stage in development' is irrelevant), and reject both its basis and its implications (and see *Who needs the past?*, edited by R. Layton). New nation-building may choose either to make use of the evi-dence of the past or to adopt a strategy that denies the relevance of the past to the future of the new nation. In the former case, there are significant choices to be made, particularly when the current situation – as in Papua New Guinea (Ch. 13) – is one of cultural diversity, between allusions to the archaeological evidence for the recent, or the remote, past. Several chapters in this book demonstrate why some nations teach that literacy is only one of several mechanisms whereby history may be communicated and transmitted. The other mechanisms include spoken language and oral history.

Such mechanisms should, of course, also include archaeology. However, archaeological interpretation may often be seen as contrary to the evidence of oral history, and the relationship between the two is often full of tension. This book highlights the fact that, in many countries, archaeology is also seen to be an elitist occupation and, in recently independent countries, an activity explicitly linked to former subjugation. In such a context the future of archaeological investigations is far from assured.

The excluded past is a book whose major concerns are with the nature of archaeological enquiry itself. Implicit in many of the discussions about the role of the past within educational systems are questions concerning the fundamentals of archaeological investigation, including the university discipline of archaeology. A central feature is the relationship between archaeology and other disciplines, predominantly history, but also geography and anthropology. In this book the nature of archaeology within different tertiary educational systems in different parts of the world is treated as a matter of crucial importance.

It is therefore staggering to realize that in the 33 or so British universities that taught some kind of archaeology a few years ago only four taught an obligatory component of World Archaeology. (Optional courses on World Prehistory only existed in a further four universities, on African Archaeology in only one university, and New World Archaeology in two universities.) British 'world archaeological' endeavour is almost exclusively focused on Europe and based on a few British Schools of Archaeology in places such as Athens, Rome and Ankara. Archaeology in Britain, in its university teaching and its interpretive base, is under serious risk of becoming merely parochial. In several other parts of the world, archaeology is seen as a Western academic preoccupation of little relevance to the country concerned. Indeed, *The excluded past* reveals some of the strange bedfellows that have been associated with archaeological enquiry – from land rights cases (Ucko 1983, Allen 1988) to opposition to the Christian Church.

In a delightful chapter (4) based on personal experience, and echoed in several other contributions, Wandibba describes why prehistory is often considered to be a particularly difficult subject at university and why, as a result, it has to struggle to maintain its existence as a subject independent of history. Such practical considerations may influence what is taught as archaeology, and this assumes great importance when it is realized that only certain kinds of archaeological interpretation are really suitable for responding to the interests of those who, exceptionally, wish to stress the existence of 'history' in nonliterate times (Reece 1987, p. 180). The apparently unresolvable debate regarding what is, or should be, the relationship between the disciplines of archaeology and history continues. While this tension exists, little of the sophistication of the debate about the role of history in the school appears to rub off on those who are concerned with archaeological enquiry (Slater 1984).

Education at primary and secondary levels is a process of selection and, often, simplification, as it is also, in part at least, at tertiary level. The so-called 'processual' and 'postprocessual' archaeologies which are taught and applied within several universities, particularly in the Western world, may appear at first sight to be far removed from 'historical narrative' and to be intelligible only to those who are highly numerate and who have some understanding of systems theory. Such 'modern' approaches to the past also seem far removed from the sort of archaeology that was concerned with the history of technology, an approach that can be so successfully introduced into all kinds and levels of education (Richardson, Ch. 24, Tuniq Project 1988, Ucko 1989a). *The excluded past* documents the enormous gap that may exist between the expectations and knowledge of school teachers as compared with some university researchers and teachers, and discusses the problems inherent in such differential access to knowledge and interpretive models. Similarly, there is little to suggest simplicity in those current archaeological discussions that derive their main emphases from scientific analyses of fauna or from anthropology – not even when tackling a favourite subject such as relations between humans and animals (*The walking larder*, edited by J. Clutton-Brock; *Signifying animals*, edited by R. G. Willis). Questions such as how the flow of information to educators can be assured, whose responsibility it really is to produce textbooks, and the social significance and role in general of studies of the past, are all considered in this book for the first time within a worldwide context.

It is a chastening experience to learn from *The excluded past* how little research has been directed towards the understanding of the underlying philosophies of education with regard to the past. In many ways, whether or not the past is taught at all at any level of a formal education system, the nature of any past that *is* taught, and whether adequate resources are also supplied, seem to be almost matters of chance, depending on each individual situation. At the same time there can be no doubt that what is, or is not, taught can have the most profound effect on the self-respect, or otherwise, of living communities, not least within the context of multiculturalism (*Who needs the past?*, edited by R. Layton). The situation in the United Kingdom as perceived by Black people in Britain is vividly presented in Chapter 19.

In the context of the education of our children, those parts of the past that are not excluded are often based on stereotypes deriving from preconceptions about prehistoric communities which themselves are often hangovers from Western assumptions about a hierarchical development from the simple to the complex, assumptions that are all too easily transferred from the past to the modern nonliterate or noncentralized society (and see Smith 1983). *The excluded past* makes it clear that many such stereotypes are also sexist and racist (and see Burtt 1987).

In the context of educating the adult public, in addition to similar stereo-typical distortions through film and TV, there is the added problem of the existence of subjects that are not communicated at all. Even in tertiary-level archaeology there is often ignorance about the nature and variety of existing legislations concerning the past (*Archaeological heritage management in the modern world*, edited by H. F. Cleere), including the relatively new concept of a 'world heritage'. The events of 1988 and 1989 regarding the World Heritage site of Avebury (Ucko *et al.* in press) appear to demonstrate that a concept such as the ownership of the past by a world community has little or no appeal – or, at least, is not understood – when concerned 'locals' are confronted by representatives of a world heritage on the one hand, and representatives of the 'enterprise society', the latter fully endorsed by government, on the other. The concept of a 'world heritage' will only be a success if education – in its widest sense – achieves the necessary influence to promote it. Currently (Ucko 1989b, 1990), the concept of world ownership of rights in the past is an ill-defined one. World heritage, in the hands of an organization, Unesco, which itself comprises national representations and interests, often appears to the public of a particular country to bring with it uncaring foreign interference in local development plans (e.g. in the case of an archaeological site, such as Avebury, in close association to a living village), or attempts to remove effective control from the very cultural groups who think of themselves as actual descendants of those who origi-nally created the particular sites under consideration (*WAB* 1989). All this closely mirrors the experience of Australian Aborigines, who have had to confront the realities of an outside community that has effectively appro-priated the very sites and land with which they identify, in the name of a newly defined 'common cultural heritage', as expressed through imposed foreign forms of legislation (Allen 1988, pp. 86–9). Not surprisingly, perhaps, the legislation that is applied can only be understood within 'the context of the growing power of central and local government that was . . . characteristic of nineteenth century Europe' (Hunter 1981, p. 25). Without close analysis of the basis of concepts such as 'world heritage', and without any clear awareness of the possible relationships between politics and legisla-tion about the past, and without clear public presentational and educational programmes, knowledgeable debate about the nature of the cultural heritage – which is so necessary for an appreciation of both identity and its potential role in the context of attitudes to future development – will not be able to take place.

Despite the shortcomings of much university archaeology education, it is probably still true that it is in this sphere that innovations are most likely to take place. It is therefore important to note that legislation affecting archaeo-logical materials (*Archaeological heritage management in the modern world*, edited by H. F. Cleere), as well as the 'heritage industry', are now beginning to feature within university curricula, at least in parts of the Western world. It is obviously urgent that discussions and research should focus on the question whether the concept of an undifferentiated past 'owned' by the

world at large – and as assessed by national politicians – is compatible with
the aims of multicultural education, which attempts to promote respect for
the individuality of all human cultures and their right for continued self-
determination. A 'pan' (world-ownership) approach leads, in part, to educational generalizations; but it could also lead to an appreciation of the
multicultural nature of all nations and regions. The decolonialization process
necessarily involves the rewriting of history by those who are newly
independent and who, as reported in this book, have every reason to assume
that what has been written about them by their erstwhile rulers was biased.
It is for future consideration to determine how the concept of a 'world'
interest and ownership of the past may, or may not, fit in with the
aspirations of those who wish to make use of the evidence of the past as part
of their very own, and unique, cultural heritage.

Successful education of adults and children about the past will presumably
lead to further increases in visits – they are already increasing by 5 per cent a
year – to museums, monuments and sites. In Britain, more than 3 million
people are interested in archaeology, and over a million visitmore than 10
sites a year. Overall there are more than 70 million visits a year to archaeological and historical sites by UK residents (information from David Keys,
the Archaeology Correspondent of the *Independent*). By and large archaeologists have not yet accepted that they should be responsible for the
production of materials suitable for such visitors, let alone for the production of teaching materials for children before they are taken on such field
trips (Burtt 1987, p. 172). Some might well argue that this is a good thing,
given the fact that few archaeologists are trained to be educators, and that
the production of materials for different age groups is a highly skilled
activity (Ch. 25). Exceptions do occur, as was the case with special guides
for the prehistoric site of Avebury in southern England, originally in the
1930s under the inspiration of Alexander Keiller (Chapman 1939) and in
recent times through an English Heritage Study Pack for Teachers (Coupland 1988). In these cases it is striking that such works have either chosen to
report new archaeological 'finds' or have had to carry out their own
synthetic research in order to present a rounded picture of the evidence
under consideration. Whereas the 1939 'guide' (which reached its 13th
impression in 1968) attempted to cater for adults and children via a set of
'typical' questions and answers, the English Heritage Study Pack for Teachers on *The Avebury monuments* (Coupland 1988) represents one of several
new attempts to identify levels of explication and knowledge suitable to
different age groups. Even in such an exemplary case, however, the differing backgrounds of urban and rural British children are not explicitly
catered for. Although Avebury is one of only 11 sites in the United
Kingdom to have been listed as a World Heritage site, and can therefore
presumably anticipate increased overseas visitors, nothing exists at the site
or in educational materials or in the form of guidebooks to accommodate the
special needs of such visitors.

It is clear that educating about the past is a complex and still relatively

Table   Percentages of readers of selected British national daily newspapers who visited archaeological sites, historic houses and castles, and museums between April 1987 and March 1988.

	Archaeological sites	Historic houses and castles	Museums
Independent (992 000 circulation)	20.4	45	53.4
Times (1 170 000)	13.9	43.4	51.5
Guardian (1 403 000)	19.2	43.4	56.5
Sun (11 324 000)	3.1	14.9	19.6
Express (4 392 000)	6.5	27.8	30.1

Source: Target Group Index, British Market Research Bureau, 1988.

underdeveloped field of endeavour. Despite the huge numbers of people in the UK referred to above who are interested in archaeology, it should not be assumed that *all* Britains are naturally interested in the past. The figures available for Britain for the period from April 1987 to March 1988 show the complexity of the situation (see Table). It is likely that different presentational and educational materials would be appropriate for different groups of British visitors.

A new awareness of the problems of presenting the past as part of general education also serves to highlight how little is still understood of the potentials and limitations of childrens' understanding of chronology and time-depth at various ages. The revelation in this book regarding the positive potential within primary education of archaeological experiment and interpretation should be coupled with the question of what can be expected of children on an actual excavation. It may be as a result of the long-standing British involvement of amateurs in archaeological investigation, and the current problems that exist there between such untrained would-be excavators and professional archaeologists, that the serious involvement of children in important excavations is extremely rare. Yet, as *The excluded past* reveals, this is far from being the case in some other countries. In the USSR, for example, voluntary excavation experience, included as part of childrens' club activities (Ch. 20), has led to a situation where, for example, in 1989 eight members of the professional excavation team at the Neolithic site of Jeitun in Turkmenia came up through such school clubs. Alternatively, of course, in a country such as India, the excavator is often a labourer, while the archaeologist acts only as supervisor (Ch. 2).

Some of these matters are also undoubtedly related to underresearched questions concerning comparisons of the excavation methods used in different countries. However, they also involve ethical questions posed by the source and nature of the financing of archaeological investigation in any given situation. In the UK, for example, there is no legislation to enforce archaeological investigation prior to development (except in special circumstances), and much archaeology is therefore dependent on the 'goodwill' of the developer. In some cases such a 'voluntary arrangement' has resulted in the production of attractive information brochures (e.g. Hawkes & Jenkins 1989), but the suspicion must remain that the position of independent, commercially-based archaeological units will inevitably, one day, be compromised by their financial dependence on the very people who may refuse to heed the lessons to be learnt from archaeological investigation.

Myths create another set of problems that are raised in this book. The first aspect of this is the teaching of myth, whether the teachers be archaeologists or trained educators and irrespective of whether it be the myth of past or present cultures (Chs 10 & 18). Once taught in school or university, the myths of 'another culture', whatever their nature, are all too often likely to appear as fiction and, thereby, to be contrasted to 'history'. The educational consequences of such a result can be presumed to be immense.

A second aspect involves myth-making by those taught about the past, and the consequences of this when it is spread through the world by the media. Thus, *The Times Educational Supplement* (10.6.88) recently carried an article about Australia entitled 'Football scuffle kicks off call for separate schools' which reported that

> Aboriginal Malu Bellear, aged 15, dressed in an anti-bicentennial T-shirt, told more than 800 students: 'We remember that like the Jews who suffered at the hands of Nazi Germany, our people too have suffered a great Holocaust. They were tortured, massacred and herded like animals on to reserves, denied the right to live by their laws, speak their language or practice their religion . . .'

The article then put this into an educational context:

> Last year, the Sydney College of Advanced Education held an early graduation ceremony for six Aboriginal students who did not want it to take place during the bicentennial year, a 'time of mourning for all Aboriginal people'.

As education about the past spreads within a community, and as its involvement grows in the actual recovery of archaeological material, so the question arises again as to the 'orthodoxy', or otherwise, of the information offered to it in available literature. *The excluded past* provides several worrying examples of the kinds of problems that may obtain in this regard. It is not only specific questions about how to ensure that such publications are regularly updated, or how to avoid overt forms of stereotyping in them, that are important. At a more general level, this book points to the fundamental problem, which appears to exist in countries as far apart as Canada, Kenya and Venezuela, that educational publishing is often in the hands of private (and often foreign) commercial publishing companies, whose primary aim is to produce only what will sell, and sell at a significant profit. For educational works, such an arrangement is clearly far from desirable, but government-subsidized printing is also unacceptable, being a recipe for imposed orthodoxy of view. The degree to which the 'authorized' textbook version of the past may develop is exemplified by Chapter 18's analysis of the postion in Japan.

Many other problems are raised in this book which are of immense importance to both educators and archaeologists, and which need concerted action for their resolution. One involves the whole question of management of sites, even in those cases where it is simply assumed (but without evidence) that there is real interest in site ownership on the part of an educated public. Greeks, for instance, are now given free access to the Acropolis in Athens. However, it is not simply the question of who should pay for the right to visit such sites – belonging to the 'world', to the region, to the nation, or to those who can claim to be the cultural heirs to the ancient cultures that created them – but also of who may be allowed to 'despoil' or modify them. Many countries have site-management problems deriving from the popularity of site visits because they have to balance protection versus income from tourists. Meanwhile, Australian Aborigines are demanding the right to 'update' rock art sites which, to the average Australian, are remnants of the past to be preserved unchanged and unchanging through European-derived legislation (*Archaeological heritage management in the modern world*, edited by H. F. Cleere; *The politics of the past*, edited by P. Gathercole & D. Lowenthal; Mowaljarlie *et al.* 1988). These are complex issues about which the majority of the public remain more or less ignorant. Many contributors to *The excluded past* stress that it is only by being made aware of such problems at school that the protection of sites, through a real appreciation of their significance for identity and pride, will ever be accomplished (and see Pretty 1987, p. 118).

The whole nature of this book belies any easy assumption that interest in the past, and therefore in archaeology, is a convenient natural condition of the public at large (Prince & Schadla-Hall 1987). This is not to deny that, in a country such as the United Kingdom, the past is of great public concern and the heritage industry big business. The British pay some £75 million a year (excluding travel) for visits to historic monuments. Some figures even suggest that heritage visits in Britain by UK residents are now more popular than trips to the cinema, art galleries, football or rugby matches, and even the seaside – only walking, pubs, restaurants, dancing, and bingo are more popular (information from the General Household Survey). It is for this very reason that informal and formal education about archaeology and the past is so important. It is not only ignorance, which clearly has to be tackled, but also those attitudes that derive in other regions of the world from such an abundance of richness in monumental remains that they have become culturally undervalued, ceasing to be 'seen' by those whose daily life is carried out in and around them (Ch. 22). In such situations the task of the educators is to sensitize local populations to their own heritage.

The excluded past should serve as a vital landmark in the future development of archaeology as a subject. 'The relationship between archaeology and education is such that it should be impossible for archaeologists to utter or write a word in public without considering the educational implications of that word . . . archaeologists have the potential to contribute to society' (Holman & Burtt 1987, p. 111). This book is exceptional because it attempts to meet not only this challenge but also that of Ferro's (1981) conclusion that the control of knowledge about the past is a prerequisite for the social control of the present. Only by continuing and extending the kinds of analyses presented in these pages will we be able to understand, let alone influence, those who do indeed exercise control over the ways that knowledge of the past enters into the wider arena of education.

P. J. Ucko
Southampton

References

Allen, H. 1988. History matters – a commentary on divergent interpretations of Australian history. *Australian Aboriginal History* 2, 79–89.

Breunig, R. G. 1975. Schools and the Hopi self. In *The new ethnicity: perspectives from ethnology*, J. W. Bennett (ed.), 51–8. St Paul: West Publishing Co.

Burtt, F. 1987. 'Man the hunter': bias in children's archaeology books. *Archaeological Review from Cambridge* 6 (2), 157–80.

Chapman, D. E. 1939. *Is this your first visit to Avebury?* Basingstoke: Her Majesty's Stationery Office.

Coupland, L. 1988. *The Avebury monuments*. Study Pack for Teachers. London: English Heritage.

Ferro, M. 1981. *The use and abuse of history or how the past is taught*. London: Routledge & Kegan Paul.

Hawkes, J. & V. Jenkins 1989. *The past in progress: the archaeology of the Thames Valley Business Park*. Salisbury: Trust for Wessex Archaeology.

Holman, N. & F. Burtt 1987. Theme editorial: archaeology as education. *Archaeological Review from Cambridge* 6 (2), 110–14.

Hunter, M. 1981. The preconditions of preservation: a historical perspective. In *Our past before us. Why do we save it?*, D. Lowenthal & M. Binney (eds), 22–31. London: Temple Smith.

Mowaljarlie, D., P. Vinnicombe, G. K. Ward & C. Chippindale 1988. Repainting of images on rock in Australia and the maintenance of Aboriginal culture. *Antiquity* 62, 690–6.

Pretty, K. 1987. Archaeological education for everybody. *Archaeological Review from Cambridge* 6 (2), 115–18.

Prince, D. R. & R. T. Schadla-Hall 1987. On the public appeal of archaeology. *Antiquity* **61**, 69–70.

Reece, R. 1987. Teaching archaeology as perpetual revolution. *Archaeological Review from Cambridge* **6** (2), 175–80.

Slater, J. 1984. The case for history in school. *The Historian* **2**, 13–16.

Smith, A. B. 1983. The Hotnot syndrome: myth-making in South African school textbooks. *Social Dynamics* **9** (2), 37–49.

Trigger, B. G. 1989. A present of their past? Anthropologists, native people, and their heritage. *Culture* **8** (1).

Tuniq Project 1989. *Newsletter*, No. 8, 11 May. Canada: Sanikiluaq, NWT.

Ucko, P. J. 1983. Australian academic archaeology. Aboriginal transformation of its aims and practices. *Australian Archaeology* **16**, 11–26.

Ucko, P. J. 1987. *Academic freedom and apartheid: the story of the World Archaeological Congress*. London: Duckworth.

Ucko, P. J. 1989a. In conclusion: some problems and questions. *CBA Education Bulletin* **6**, 40–3. London: CBA.

Ucko, P. J. 1989b. Foreword. In *Archaeological heritage management in the modern world*, H. Cleere (ed.) ix–xiv. London: Unwin Hyman.

Ucko, P. J. 1990. Foreword. In *The politics of the past*, P. Gathercole & D. Lowenthal (eds). London: Unwin Hyman.

Ucko, P. J., M. Hunter, A. J. Clark & A. David in press. *Avebury in plan and prospect: changing perceptions*. London & Devizes: Royal Anthropological Institute & Wiltshire Archaeological Society.

World Archaeological Bulletin No. 3. 1989. Oxford: Oxbow Books.

Contents

Preface

The concept of the 'excluded past' – and hence this book – has assumed a significance far greater than originally anticipated by the organizers of the 1986 World Archaeological Congress in Southampton. In the Revised World Archaeological Congress Second Announcement (1986), 'education' was placed within the session on 'The Politics of the Past: Museums, Media, and Education', within the overall theme 'Archaeological "Objectivity" in Interpretation'.

From such a humble origin 'The Past in Education' emerged as two complete sessions under the overall organization of Robert MacKenzie. We are grateful to Peter Lee and Denis Shemilt who co-chaired the session 'Young People and the Past', and to Taka Mudariki, who co-chaired with Robert MacKenzie the session 'The Past beyond School'. We would also like to record here our thanks to the contributors who produced 20 precirculated papers on education, and the participants who shared in the lively but all too short discussion that these presentations provoked.

Not only were there two formal sessions on education within the Congress, but there was also a programme of informal events that was organized to coincide with, and supplement, the official Congress programme. Peter Stone, Kate Wilson-Barnes (both of the Southampton University 'Archaeology and Education Project') and Robert MacKenzie, collaborated in organizing a major series of 'Archaeology and Education Open Events'. These daily events consisted of multimedia displays, films, and discussions, and an Open Forum on the final Saturday to discuss 'The Future of the Past in Education'. The overall aim of these events was to provide a bridge between the formal Congress sessions and more general educational concerns, and to attempt to demonstrate the relevance of archaeology to people for whom it is not a professional consideration (Ucko 1987, pp 149–50, WAC Programme 1986, pp. 121–4). Clearly, consensus for a wider role for archaeology in education had emerged (Ucko 1987, p. 39).

Thus, from an unexalted beginning, the promotion of the important relationship between education and archaeology grew into a major enterprise. This publication is part of this pioneering development.

We should perhaps make it clear that only 7 of the 27 chapters (7, 9, 18, 19, 22, 23, 24) contained in this book originated from papers given at the 1986 World Archaeological Congress. This is because we were determined to counter the initial domination of contributors from the West, and we wanted to commission work on ideas suggested during discussion in the Congress sessions. We thus obtained the agreement of the Series Editor and Unwin Hyman to delay publication until we had commissioned more chapters. We hope that a good book has resulted.

The two formal sessions, and the Open Events mentioned above, have led to several significant developments. At the Plenary Session of the Congress a resolution was adopted that had been formulated in the Education Open Forum. It read:

> Archaeology has an essential role to play in formal and nonformal education, and henceforth [education's] interests will be fully represented in the present international archaeological forum, and in any future world body concerned with the furtherance of sciences related to the study of the past.
>
> (*World Archaeological Bulletin* 1987, p. 38)

Since then education has been designated as the very first item on the list of topics to be discussed at the Second World Archaeological Congress which is to be held towards the latter part of 1990.

Two other important meetings have taken place since 1986. The 1987 'Archaeology Meets Education' conference in Southampton (Richardson 1989) was the first of a series of meetings, jointly attended by archaeologists and educators, that have begun in Britain and elsewhere. In addition, it was agreed in January 1989 at the First Joint Archaeological Congress in Baltimore that a newsletter entitled *Archaeology and Education* would be established to develop such links.

These developments are encouraging, and we hope that this book will contribute to the process of forging links between archaeologists and non-archaeologists, to enable a balanced and concerted effort to be made towards the understanding of the central importance of the past. In this attempt, with all its imperfections, we have tried to demonstrate the plurality of views, the complexity of issues, and possibilities for future action. At long last, through the World Archaeological Congress, we appear to have begun the dialogue that is necessary with the wider community, a dialogue that will hopefully ensure that momentum is maintained.

If this book reflects a freshness and optimism, then we are glad. But a cautionary note should be sounded. Strong forces perpetuate the exclusion of many pasts. If this book does nothing else, it should contribute to a better understanding of the origins and nature of the 'excluded past'.

The book does not pretend to identify or cover every aspect of 'the excluded past'. Only passing mention is made of the role of adult and continuing education in a few of the following chapters. Much further work needs to be done in these and other aspects of the excluded past. We had also hoped to include more contributions from indigenous authors, and our failure to achieve this is only partially compensated for by a number of non-indigenous contributions from, for example, Barlow (Ch. 7), Blacking (Ch. 13), Sinclair (Ch. 12) and Holland (Ch. 11). Watson (Ch. 8) and Blancke & Peters (Ch. 10) fill part of this 'indigenous' gap, but a more extensive and detailed discussion of indigenous views on the teaching of the past needs to be high on any list for future publications in this field.

We may not necessarily agree with all of the points made in the following chapters. However, we consider that the wide spectrum of views presented combine to make an important contribution to a new aspect of a continuing debate.

We should like to record our thanks to the *Journal of Indigenous Studies* for permission to reproduce the article by Watson (Ch. 8). We owe Jane Hubert an enormous debt for much help on earlier drafts of various chapters, and thanks go to Rosemary Groube for information about Papua New Guinea. We would also like to thank Genevieve Wheatley and Jill Regan. Genevieve provided invaluable translation and typing services, and both Genevieve and Jill gave us incalculable support during an extended and sometimes trying period.

Finally, we cannot let this opportunity pass without acknowledging the role of Peter Ucko, the Series Editor. His foresight, skills and energy have been instrumental in elevating the status of education in the eyes of professional mediators of the past, and in urging educators to come to grips with the complexity, and importance for their work, of the archaeological discipline.

Robert MacKenzie
Peter G. Stone
Southampton

References

Richardson, W. (ed.) 1989. *Education Bulletin* No. 6. London: CBA.
Ucko, P. J. 1987. *Academic freedom and apartheid: the story of the World Archaeological Congress*. London: Duckworth.
World Archaeological Bulletin, 1, 1987.

Preface to the paperback edition

There have been numerous developments throughout the world since *The Excluded Past* was first published. Contributors have had the opportunity to make minor changes to their chapters, but the extensive revision needed to bring all the chapters fully up-to-date has not always been possible. Thus, for example, Philippe Planel's and Wendy Richardson's contributions have been superseded by the introduction of a National Curriculum in England. However, many of the underlying ideas in these chapters still raise relevant and important educational issues irrespective of any particular national context. On re-reading the book we are again struck by the uniformity and passion of argument common in all chapters that enabled us originally to identify the reasons for, and existence of, 'the excluded past'. Many of the same arguments are taken up and expanded in chapters in *The Presented Past: heritage, museums and education* (Stone & Molyneaux 1994) to which we refer readers interested in the continuing debate over the interpretation and presentation of the past within formal and informal curricula around the world.

We note with sadness the deaths of three contributors (John Blacking, Andrzej Mikołajczyk, and Nwanna Nzewunwa).

Peter G. Stone
Robert MacKenzie
Southampton, 26 May 1994

Introduction: the concept of the excluded past

ROBERT MACKENZIE & PETER G. STONE

Background

Although recognition of the concept and existence of a past 'excluded' from education is not new, the processes of exclusion have only recently been clearly isolated. Such 'exclusion' is most common in the area of the curriculum often referred to as the 'humanities', where content and methods of teaching geography and history in schools have long been the focus for discussion and debate between educationalists and subject specialists.

In 1874, in his *Short history of the English people*, Green attempted to shift the emphasis away from an elitist 'drum and trumpet' view of history towards the lives of ordinary people (Samuel 1989). In the USA, at the turn of the century, part of the debate between the educational establishment and the Progressive movement focused on which version of the past should be taught, and how (Dewey 1899, Mayhew & Edwards 1936). In 1919 Clark published *The working life of women in the 17th century*, in which she pointed out that historians had ignored 'the circumstances of women's lives' (Jones & Pay 1986, p. 2). What we have tried to do in this book is to focus attention on at least some of the elements of the excluded past, suggesting why they have been excluded, and why it is important to note such exclusions. The basic theme of this book is the premise that bias in interpretation and presentation exists, and that a re-evaluation of the presentation of the past within education should identify any biases, omissions, or 'distortions' (Gawe & Meli, Ch. 9), and demonstrate the relationship between these and the dominant ideologies within a society.

A number of the contributors to *The excluded past* extend and adapt this argument to contemporary multicultural societies dominated by particular groups, and argue that research, interpretation, and presentation are bound to the norms of the dominant groups concerned (Barlow, Ch. 7, Gawe & Meli, Ch. 9, Blancke & Peters, Ch. 10, Holland, Ch. 11, Devine, Ch. 16, Kehoe, Ch. 17, Garrison, Ch. 19).

These contributions describe the struggles that take place between subordinated groups who seek access to, and a re-evaluation of, their past, and those who wish to deny them this goal. Jones & Pay, for instance, have shown how women have been excluded in the past. They assert that 'it is necessary to examine, to evaluate and to discard many of the traditional analytical tools which have been used in the construction of knowledge' (Jones & Pay 1986, p. 1).

The following chapters open up discussion about the construction of knowledge about the past, extending it beyond the perspective of Jones & Pay towards a more universal focus.

What is 'the excluded past'?

We use the term 'the excluded past' in a dual sense, which encompasses both the prehistoric past, which is virtually excluded from curricula around the world, and the suppressed or denied past of many indigenous, minority, or oppressed groups.

This book demonstrates that there are vast areas of the study of the past that are almost totally ignored in school curricula. In Europe the prehistoric past is relegated to providing a starting point for what is regarded as 'proper' history (e.g. Council of Europe 1986). The past is only considered to be worth studying at the point when 'civilization' has developed. This approach assumes that society only takes on a recognizable form worth studying once literacy and so-called civilization arrive, creating an environment conducive to 'progress', and therefore true history. The real danger in such an approach from an educational point of view is that children are being encouraged to feel contempt for the prehistoric past as a period of simple technology, and therefore also contempt for so-called 'primitive' social organization and for an assumed poverty of social development associated with it. It is our contention that it is an easy step from feeling contempt for the prehistoric past to feeling contempt for any contemporary preindustrialized or nonindustrialized society. It is such contempt that allows, and sometimes encourages, exclusion of aspects of the past not directly linked to contemporary dominant groups.

This link between prehistory, 'primitive' societies, and the contemporary Third and Fourth Worlds was highlighted in a recent survey of English children's perceptions of photographs illustrating the lives of children in the Third World. After being shown the photographs, the English children

> thought that the schoolgirls in Colombo went home to sharpen their flint spears while watching black and white television. The villagers from Bangladesh rubbed sticks together to light a fire, cooked over a fire and collected water from a river. There were no shops and when asked where one woman got her sari from, one group of children claimed it came from 'inside an animal'. When asked why it could not have been bought from a shop, the children were insistent that these people wore the insides and outsides of animals that they had killed, usually with their bare hands.   (Graham & Lynn 1989, p. 23)

Why is there an 'excluded past' in education?

Elsewhere (Stone & MacKenzie 1989) we have suggested four major reasons for an 'excluded past' in education.

First, school curricula are already overcrowded, and educational decision-makers argue that time cannot be allotted to a 'new' subject when the survival of many long-established subjects is now seriously threatened by the increasing domination within curricula of job-related education and training (Mikołajczyk, Ch. 21, Planel, Ch. 23). Two contributors argue that the prehistoric past is excluded from school curricula because it is only perceived to be of any relevance at the tertiary level of education (Chakrabarti, Ch. 2, Mammini, Ch. 22).

Second, teachers have allowed important aspects of the past to be excluded through their own ignorance. The little of the 'excluded past' that is included in syllabuses is taught only with great difficulty because of the lack of suitable materials (see, for example, Nzewunwa, Ch. 3, Kehoe, Ch. 17, Mammini, Ch. 22). When suitable study materials are to be found (e.g. University of South Dakota Archaeological Laboratory 1982, Hawkins 1987, Southampton University 1986–9) they are often locally produced and difficult to obtain more widely (Blancke & Peters, Ch. 10, Devine, Ch. 16).

There are examples of school textbooks from all parts of the world that ignore contemporary understanding of the prehistoric past (Barlow, Ch. 7, Devine, Ch. 16, Planel, Ch. 23). If the little that *can* be inferred about the prehistoric past is ignored in this way – and replaced by unsupportable interpretation – then it is possible for a situation to develop in which the past can be falsely interpreted for the benefit of the dominant group (Holland, Ch. 11). Individuals who take on the responsibility of teaching, as well as archaeologists and others who have access to the most recent data, must take the lead in ensuring that this kind of misinterpretation of the past does not occur.

Third, the study of the 'excluded past' is often seen as an indulgent luxury that has no direct bearing on today's society (Chakrabarti, Ch. 2). In England, where a compulsory national curriculum is being developed (e.g. DES 1989), the Historical Association (1986) recently suggested guidelines for a curriculum that effectively cut out all but the most cursory references to prehistory. Although the document has been roundly attacked by many of those involved in teaching history (for example, Fines 1988), the guidelines stand as the Historical Association's formal position on the National Curriculum, and they epitomize the gulf identified by Planel (Ch. 23) between academic and school history. We can only conclude that academic historians in England have bowed, by and large without resistance, to the contemporary political dogma that the only real value of teaching about the past is to set the modern world into a narrow chronological framework relating solely to recent history.

We do not argue with the premise that children should be taught the recent national, regional, and world political history that has directly and most immediately shaped the world in which they live. We do argue, however, that such a limited approach ignores and excludes any wider view of humanity and that it obscures the true time-depth of human development without which there can only be a very incomplete context for more recent history. In this we agree with the argument of Alexander (1989, p. 10) that

> human history is human history and if the most important things that have happened to our species, the development of agriculture or urbanism, or the beginning of metallurgy, are known from archaeo-logical, not from literary evidence, then history must pay greater attention to that evidence and those periods.

Finally, aspects of the past may be excluded for overtly political or ideological reasons, as in South Africa and Namibia (Hinz, Ch. 6, Gawe & Meli, Ch. 9, Hall 1984).

However, even forms of political exclusion that are less overt may also be damaging to those concerned (Blancke & Peters, Ch. 10, Podgorny, Ch. 15, Garrison, Ch. 19). In another book in the *One World Archaeology* series, Condori writes that in Bolivia the past of the indigenous peoples is classified as prehistory and is therefore equated with the 'primitive' and 'uncivilized', which undermines any pride the indigenous peoples may have in their own heritage. This policy has led to the extraordinary situation of Bolivian Indians being made to pay for entrance to their own sacred sites even when visiting for religious reasons (Condori 1989, p. 48).

Platonova (Ch. 20) explains that in the USSR all humanities subjects have suffered at the expense of a concentration on science and technology. This policy has led to the bulk of teaching about archaeology and prehistory being optional and carried out in voluntary groups or 'circles'. The USSR's cancellation in 1988 of state examinations in history 'pending the writing of new history books' (*Times Educational Supplement* 11 November 1988) – an interesting consequence of academic *glasnost* – suggests that overt political manipulation of the representation of the past may now be part of history.

Archaeology and education

Several chapters in this book chronicle the development of a growing awareness of the importance and power of education about the past. They also emphasize its impact on, and relationship with, the present and future through archaeology – a discipline that has hitherto shirked its responsibili-ties in this field (Ucko 1989). This new awareness of the importance of education about the past was first brought out in an international context – and then forcefully underlined – by the events surrounding the 1986 World Archaeological Congress (Ucko 1987). We see the acceptance of responsi-bility for international education about the past as only one aspect of a more

general acceptance of responsibility by archaeologists – and others concerned with the academic and scientific study of the past – towards that past
in all its manifestations and in its relations with the present (see, for example,
Layton 1988, 1989, Cleere 1989, McIntosh *et al.* 1989, Ucko 1989, Gathercole & Lowenthal 1989).

This growing acceptance of responsibility finds a central focus in the
relationship between archaeology and education. Reynolds (1989, p. 27)
emphasizes the centrality of this relationship when he argues that 'the
primary aim of archaeology, if not education itself, is to understand man in
his landscape in time'. Education is inextricably linked to archaeology
because archaeology provides the raw data for the teaching of those subjects
concerned with the social world.

What we choose to teach, and then go on to interpret and present – and
equally what we do not choose to teach and then fail to interpret and present
– is a dilemma common to all of those empowered to communicate about
the past. Many of the following chapters show that what is seen and
understood to be a 'true' – or acceptable – picture of the past may well be
influenced by the representation of the past propagated by the dominant
group in a given society. An acceptance of general responsibility to present
an 'all-inclusive past' is of central importance in the teaching of critical
awareness and a realization of bias in source material (Vargas & Sanoja,
Ch. 5, Fawcett & Habu, Ch. 18, Planel, Ch. 23).

How the book is organized

Mention has already been made, in the Preface, of the genesis of this book,
and of the embryonic stage of debate about the teaching of the excluded
past. Several of the following chapters underline the fledgling nature of
this debate – some of them being the first serious attempts to grapple, in
print, with the concept of the excluded past and its relevance to the
countries concerned. At times the chapters overlap and in some cases
cover a wider field than that which archaeology might normally be
expected to include.

Khawajkie (Ch. 1) sets the scene with an enthusiastic whistle-stop tour of
work undertaken by the Unesco-organized Associated Schools Project. She
does not attempt a rigorous academic analysis, but rather shows how an
interdisciplinary – and often international – study of the past enhances the
experience of children. It is the enthusiasm of Khawajkie and, indeed, of all
the contributors to this book that gives encouragement and faith in the
future of the excluded past. We can despair with Podgorny when she argues
that 'the American and Argentine pre-Hispanic past is largely ignored, that
the multicultural nature of Argentine society is overlooked, and that the
vision that we have is based on stereotypes that have been put forward by
others', yet can also 'agree that all this is part of a reality that can be
modified, little by little, from the bottom up, and in its totality' (Ch. 15,

p. 187). If this book has one major goal, then it must be to encourage others to work towards such a modification.

Most of the contributors to this book take it as axiomatic that the study of the past is of relevance to contemporary society – and therefore to contemporary education – but none has thought it necessary to justify that assumption. Chakrabarti (Ch. 2) underlines the fact that in India the study of the past is *not* generally seen as relevant to contemporary society. Potter (1989) has recently begun to address some of the issues that affect our teaching of the past and our reasons for doing it. In his conclusion he argues that the reasons we have for teaching about the past – and the reasons we have for thinking that such teaching is important – must be intensely personal and, as such, vary from individual to individual. Whether or not this is true, the implications of such personal decisions may, when combined, affect the whole of society and these implications are, in effect, the subject of a number of other books in the *One World Archaeology* series (Layton 1988, 1989, Gathercole & Lowenthal 1990), and of publications elsewhere in relation to England (Corbishley 1983, Stone 1986). In this book we have only begun to examine the importance and value of 'owning' and understanding a specific past in the context of the relationship between the past and education. Much more remains to be explored.

An overview of the issues

Without exception, the chapters that refer especially to the teaching of archaeology at universities (Chakrabarti, Ch. 2, Nzewunwa, Ch. 3, Wandibba, Ch. 4) describe a picture of haphazard and restricted development, resulting in the introduction of archaeology to tertiary education within severe constraints. Around the world, archaeology has grown out of 'parent disciplines' whose theories have clearly affected the orientation and focus of the research carried out by their offspring. The situation is even worse in those cases where the nature and origin of the university discipline has already created an air of exclusion and elitism, as described by Nzewunwa (Ch. 3).

The consequences of such haphazard growth are further confused in Britain where academic and field-based archaeology, while both undergoing major growth in the 1960s and early 1970s, have developed almost entirely separately. University archaeology in Britain is, at present, undergoing a major government review that has led university-based archaeologists, for the first time and despite their varied backgrounds, to agree a common core to the single honours undergraduate degree curriculum (SCUPHA 1987). In this major review, the government has also requested that organizations responsible for the professional arms of the disciplines involved submit their comments. The Institute of Field Archaeologists has therefore made a submission supporting the university document (IFA 1987). It can only be hoped that such cooperation becomes the norm in the future.

Discussion of the nature of archaeology– including the current debate in the USA, where archaeologists are questioning the inevitability of their link with anthropology (Wiseman 1989) – should serve to strengthen our understanding of why archaeology merits study. A clearer rationale explaining why archaeology should be taught at university may itself identify some of the reasons for the inclusion of the teaching of archaeology at earlier stages of learning.

A number of contributors describe how the past of indigenous groups has been, and continues to be, excluded from national school curricula that focus almost entirely on history after the first European contact (Watson, Ch. 8, Blancke & Peters, Ch. 10, Muriuki, Ch. 14). Such emphasis often reflects the past of contemporary curricula present in the European 'mother' countries (Chakrabarti, Ch. 2).McIntosh et al. (1989, p. 76) also discuss this point:

And since those in power write histories and feature themselves prominently therein, it is not suprising to find non-Western peoples depicted in conventional Western histories as passive recipients of change inaugurated by Western culture bearers. Furthermore, the historical depiction of non-Western peoples as primitive or savage has served to justify their subjugation by the West, regardless of the human misery and suffering involved.

The continued existence of this exclusion alienates people from their own past (Blancke & Peters, Ch. 10, Holland, Ch. 11). Kehoe (Ch. 17) asserts that schooling is an instrument for transmitting establishment ideology rather than a process of education. Barlow (Ch. 7) and Watson (Ch. 8) argue from their different perspectives that the main aim of Australian education for Aborigines is still to 'civilize' Aboriginal children, a process that requires the implicit rejection of their Aboriginality (Barlow, Ch. 7). Holland (Ch. 11) presents a similar picture in his description of the activities of New Tribal Mission schools in Paraguay. Devine (Ch. 16) argues that the way the term 'civilization' is used in Canada excludes any precontact past. Not surprisingly, given such contemporary presentation of their pasts, both Australian Aborigines and Native Canadians distrust the use of archaeological evidence in teaching about the past (Barlow, Ch. 7, Devine, Ch. 16).

Despite the denial in some schools of the existence of a viable Aboriginal culture, many Aborigines still regard education as the best means of gaining their rightful position in Australian society (Barlow, Ch. 7). A similar attitude is reflected in the submission of the World Council of Indigenous Peoples to a United Nations Working Group on Indigenous Populations, which stated that

we see education as being of utmost importance to our achievement . . . of a just and rightful place in the world order . . . 'Education is the first key to the Fourth World' . . . It is the key because it focuses on our

children and grandchildren, upon whose shoulders shall fall the respon-
sibility of seeing that our dreams for self-determination of Indigenous
Peoples are realized. So we must teach them well.   (World Council of
Indigenous Peoples 1985, p. 2)

However much Aborigines and other indigenous groups see education as
the means of achieving equality, the road appears certain to be long, with
only six Aborigines from the Northern Territory matriculating from
secondary school between 1980 and 1987 (*Times Educational Supplement* 10
June 1988, and see Watson, Ch. 8).

That access to the past can be equated with access to power is not a new
contention (Mammini, Ch. 22), but it is a relationship that requires constant
monitoring. McIntosh *et al.* (1989, p. 78) argue that 'for the Hopi, the
presence of Kachinas in museums exemplifies how the world view of the
powerful has triumphed over that of the powerless'. In Australia, the New
South Wales Teachers' Federation has recently forced the state government
to include Aboriginal studies in all schools from the beginning of the 1988
academic year but they are still without appropriate teaching resources
(Saunders pers. comm. 1988). What looks good on paper may, in reality,
have little effect in practice (Ucko 1989).

Hinz (Ch. 6) and Gawe & Meli (Ch. 9) argue that education about the
past is crucial to the continued struggle for cultural and political freedom.
Indeed, much of the present 'unrest' within South Africa is centred on
schools in the townships (see, for example, *Times Educational Supplement* 13
May 1988, 24 June 1988). They suggest that the past can never truly reflect
what should be the present cultural position of indigenous groups as long as
Black people are taught history through White interpretations that both
implicitly and explicitly portray the Black past as inferior. Unfortunately, as
taught, the position of Black people and their past in South Africa and
Namibia is defined by a society that currently treats them with utter
contempt. The lack of a Black past in national textbooks (other than in
relation to colonial history) is congruent with the lack of social freedom of
Black people in South Africa and Namibia today. This White colonial
attitude in Southern Africa has parallels within the USA and Australia, and
the position of South African Black people can be compared with that of the
North American Indians as described by Blancke & Peters (Ch. 10) and
Kehoe (Ch. 17) and of Australian Aborigines as described by Barlow
(Ch. 7) and Watson (Ch. 8). It is also a matter of contemporary concern for
Black people in England in their worry that the National Curriculum for
history will be dominated by 'the unholy trinity of Vikings, Saxons and
Normans' (*Times Educational Supplement*, 17 March 1989 and see Garrison
Ch. 19).

Such manipulation and selection of the particular aspects of the past that
are taught in schools are further conditioned by the degree of control over
teacher training (Vargas & Sanoja, Ch. 5) or by the absence of any relevant
teacher training (Devine, Ch. 16, Mammini, Ch. 22, Richardson, Ch. 24).

Smardz (Ch. 25) underlines the need for training people in teaching and in archaeology jointly, since expertise in one does not necessarily imply expertise in the other.

Even the few teachers who want to teach about the excluded past, and who do have enough basic training to approach the topic with some degree of competence, are hindered by a lack of relevant textbooks (Hinz, Ch. 6, Sinclair, Ch. 12, Podgorny, Ch. 15, Planel, Ch. 23). Here the responsibility must lie with archaeologists and others who have access to the most recent data to make such information available. A few textbooks are being produced with input from archaeologists (e.g. De Freige & Saad 1987), but too many still rely on outdated information. Other groups have produced self-help newsletters for the exchange of information (e.g. the Tuniq Project newsletter and the *Teaching Anthropology* newsletter), yet the lack of good up-to-date information is still a major concern.

The lack of academic credibility accorded to the excluded past in school curricula is further reinforced by the lack of credibility given to oral history (Blacking, Ch. 13, Muriuki, Ch. 14). Exclusion of the indigenous past extends easily to a situation in which the 'true' study of the past is equated with documented history. In Africa, for example, because there was said to be no written history before European contact – a myth exposed by Muriuki in Chapter 14 – the precontact past was considered unworthy of study. Muriuki stresses that the exclusion of a cultural past is also achieved by the exclusion of indigenous languages in education, which hinders the understanding of the past of many groups – a point also made by Kehoe (Ch. 17), Gawe & Meli (Ch. 9), and Holland (Ch. 11). Khawajike (Ch. 1) argues that one of the most exciting aspects of one Associated Schools Project scheme was the recording and singing of previously undocumented Bulgarian folk songs on the point of fading from the folk memory.

Watson (Ch. 8) identifies another aspect of exclusion as being of central importance to the future. Whereas several of the above examples refer to the exclusion of indigenous groups from the White education system, Watson argues that the continued exclusion of Aboriginal teaching methods and content itself hinders the development of 'a new future, in which people and land are placed in the centre, rather than progress, technology, money, and growth in gross national product' (Ch. 8, p. 96). This point is developed by Hinz (Ch. 6) in his discussion of the concept of 'double-decolonialization'. Hinz argues that both sides of a colonial relationship have to change and develop during the birth of new nations. Not only is there the need for those who were colonized to rediscover a past that has been hitherto denied them, but so too the previous colonizers must accept the existence of this denied past and of different interpretations and views of the past. Only when such a dual development takes place can the colonial situation be fully dismantled and real progress take place.

Recent developments in Europe

The Council of Europe organized two meetings in 1985 and 1986 at which archaeologists, museum staff, educators, and politicians, came together to discuss 'Making Children Aware of the Existence, Study and Conservation of the [European] Archaeological Cultural Heritage' (PACT News 1985, 1986). The first meeting had the specific brief to look at the elementary school sector and the meeting submitted a Declaration to the European Parliament that stated that

> two attitudes are possible [towards the preservation of the threatened archaeological heritage], one based on prohibition and the other which associates preventive archaeological management with an active education policy. The second approach seems to us more likely to satisfy the cultural objective of our contemporary society. (PACT News 1985, pp. 79–80)

The Declaration went on to call for the development of appropriate teacher training, for high-quality teaching materials to be made available, and for the introduction into elementary schools throughout Europe of 'instruction in the identification and protection of the cultural heritage'.

As a result of these meetings, a 'European Centre for the "Sensibilization" of the European Cultural Heritage' was set up in Barcelona, Spain, in 1988. The Centre is developing a series of practical courses for archaeologists, teachers, and other interested groups about the teaching of the past and intends to facilitate the production of materials for use in schools across Europe.

Teaching about the past: recent developments in England

Since the Second World War a complex situation has developed in England (Corbishley 1986, Alexander 1989). Over this period a number of committed teachers have introduced children to the study of the past through archaeology. Since much of this work took place in relative isolation in individual schools, little coordinated action was possible for many years. However, in 1975, the Council for British Archaeology (CBA) set up a number of related committees to report to its Education Board, including a committee to deal with the promotion of archaeology in schools. In 1977 the CBA was able to appoint its first education officer with a wide brief to encourage the teaching of archaeology in school. Through publications (e.g. CBA 1977, Corbishley 1982a, 1982b, 1983, Croft 1982, Steane 1982), inservice courses, examination syllabuses, and advice, the CBA was able to provide the material basis for much good archaeological teaching in classrooms throughout England.

The Education Service of the Historic Buildings and Monuments Commission for England (English Heritage) – a semigovernmental organization set up in 1984 – appointed a team of four regional education officers to promote the better educational use of the historic environment (and especially those monuments in the care of English Heritage) to all sections of the education system.

Also in the mid-1980s archaeological field units and universities were at last responding to their responsibilities towards education, and a number of teams, with a specific brief to develop links with the world of education, were set up under a government scheme for the long-term unemployed. Several teams produced good materials, usually locally based, that successfully encouraged the use of the historic environment, especially by primary schools (Corbishley & Cracknell 1986).

Notwithstanding this record of endeavour, archaeology in British education is probably now undergoing its most crucial test since the Second World War. University departments of archaeology await government acceptance of the findings of an external review that may determine their development and teaching for the rest of the century. Within the school system less than 6 per cent of children aged 12 to 16 study the 'Stone Age' (sic) as opposed to over 55 per cent who study medieval Britain and over 71 per cent who study the Second World War (*Times Educational Supplement* 2 September 1988). In addition, the government is currently introducing a rigidly defined National Curriculum (Planel, Ch. 23, Richardson, Ch. 24). The report of the History Working Group (expected in December 1989) may well reflect the views put forward in a publication *History from 5 to 16* produced by Her Majesty's Inspectorate of Schools (HMI 1988). The report argues that by the age of 16 children should, as part of their historical understanding, 'know of: Early civilization: hunter-gatherer societies, the discovery of fire and the development of agriculture' (HMI 1988, p. 12). Despite this reassuring presence of parts of the 'excluded past', the report fails to refer to archaeological methods or techniques and it is not at all clear how children can be taught about these topics without some understanding of archaeology.

In an attempt to explain the value of archaeology and the excluded past to education, the CBA Education Board has produced a proposal for archaeology as a National Curriculum Foundation subject (i.e. a subject allocated a specific proportion of time in the curriculum). The Board has accepted that archaeology will never be a subject in its own right in the National Curriculum, but believes that it should be part of specific subject areas (such as history) and of the wider curriculum as a whole (Macintosh 1989, p. 17).

The future of the excluded past

By reappraising the concept of 'objectivity', and by working together with indigenous and minority groups, and with people from other disciplines such as education, archaeologists can increase the value to society of the excluded past. As a result people from different cultures will no longer view the past exclusively as a record of their own culture, or in what is considered a neutral or 'objective' way, but in a way that recognizes a plurality of pasts, each incorporating subjectivity and bias.

The contributors to this book align themselves firmly with this aim. Collectively, they open up an important debate and, whatever their differences in perspective, leave us with two inescapable conclusions. First, that archaeologists should seek to take on a role within education alongside other interpreters and mediators of the past and, for their part, educators should accept and understand the important role that archaeology alone can and should have in education. Second, if the children of the world are not taught about their own cultural pasts, then the evidence of these pasts and the cultures that exist in the present will be destroyed and lost at an ever-increasing rate, until we are all faced with a present and future without any past at all.

References

Alexander, J. 1989. Threnody for a generation. *CBA Education Bulletin*, 5–11.

Cleere, H. 1989. *Archaeological heritage management in the modern world*. London: Unwin Hyman.

Condori, C. M. 1989. History and prehistory in Bolivia: what about the Indians? In *Conflict in the archaeology of living traditions*, R. Layton (ed.), 46–59. London: Unwin Hyman.

Corbishley, M. (ed.) 1982a. *Archaeology in the classroom*. London: Council for British Archaeology.

Corbishley, M. (ed.). 1982b. *Archaeology in the town*. London: Council for British Archaeology.

Corbishley, M. (ed.) 1983. *Archaeological resources handbook for teachers*. London: Council for British Archaeology.

Corbishley, M. 1986. Archaeology for pre-university students: curricula and extra-curricula approaches and influences. In *Archaeological 'objectivity' in interpretation*. World Archaeological Congress, Vol. 3 (mimeo).

Corbishley, M. & Cracknell, S. (eds) 1986. *Presenting archaeology to young people*. CBA Research Report No. 64. London: Council for British Archaeology.

Council for British Archaeology (CBA) 1977. *Bulletin of archaeology for schools*.

Council of Europe 1986. *Against bias and prejudice: the Council of Europe's work on history teaching and history textbooks*. Strasbourg: Council for Cultural Co-operation.

Croft, R. 1982. *Archaeology and science*. London: Council for British Archaeology.

De Freige, N. & Saad, M. 1987. *Histoire Illustrée du Liban*. Paris: Larousse.

DES 1989. *The National Curriculum: from policy to practice*. London: Department of Education and Science.

Dewey, J. 1899. The School and society. In *The child and the curriculum and the school and society*, L. Carmichael (ed.), 6–150. Chicago: University of Chicago Press.

Fines, J. 1988. The search for content in a national curriculum. *Welsh Historian* Spring, 7–8.

Gathercole, P. & Lowenthal, D. (eds) 1990. *The politics of the past*. London: Unwin Hyman.

Graham, J. & Lynn, S. 1989. Altered image. *Junior Education*, January, 22–3.

Hall, M. 1984. The burden of tribalism: the social context of Southern African Iron Age studies. *American Antiquity* **49**(3), 455–67.

Hawkins, N. 1987. *Classroom archaeology. An archaeological activity guide for teachers.* Baton Rouge: Louisiana Office of Cultural Development.

HMI 1988. History from 5 to 16. *Curriculum Matters* **11**. London: HMSO.

Historical Association 1986. *History in the compulsory years of schooling.* London: Historical Association.

Institute of Field Archaeologists (IFA) 1987. Archaeology in the universities. *Field Archaeologist* **7**, 97–8.

Jones, S. & Pay, S. 1986. The legacy of Eve: towards a discussion of the interpretation of women's past experience with reference to current research practice and the presentation of the past to the public. In *Archaeological 'objectivity' in interpretation.* World Archaeological Congress, Vol. 2 (mimeo).

Keen, J. 1989. Learning through doing – a middle school explores Iron Age life. *CBA Education Bulletin*, 12–16.

Layton, R. (ed.) 1988. *Who needs the past?* London: Unwin Hyman.

Layton, R. (ed.) 1989. *Conflict in the archaeology of living traditions.* London: Unwin Hyman.

Macintosh, H. 1989. Archaeology and the curriculum – a way forward through GCSE. *CBA Education Bulletin*, 17–22.

McIntosh, R. J., S. K. McIntosh, & T. Togola, 1989. People without history. *Archaeology* **42**(1), 74–107.

Mayhew, K. & A. Edwards 1936. *The Dewey school.* New York: Atherton Press.

PACT News 1985. Papers presented to 'The First Meeting on Making Children Aware of the Existence, Study, and Conservation of the Archaeological Cultural Heritage'. *PACT News* **15 & 16**. Ravello: Council of Europe.

PACT News 1986. Papers presented to 'The Second Meeting on Making Children Aware of the Existence, Study, and Conservation of the Archaeological Cultural Heritage'. PACT News **17 & 18**. Ravello: Council of Europe.

Potter, P. 1989. Why teach archaeology? Unpublished paper presented to the Joint Archaeological Congress, Baltimore, January, 1989.

Reynolds, P. 1989. Butser ancient farm: an extraordinary classroom. *CBA Education Bulletin*, 27–32. London: Council for British Archaeology.

Richardson, W. (ed.) 1989. *CBA Education Bulletin* **6**. London: Council for British Archaeology.

Samuel, R. 1989. History's battle for a new past. *Guardian* (London) 21 January.

Southampton University 1986–9. *Archaeology and education series.* Series Co-ordinator P. Stone. Southampton University: Department of Archaeology.

Standing Committee of University Professors and Heads of Departments of Archaeology (SCUPHA) 1987. Unpublished report to the University Grants Commission.

Steane, J. 1982. *Archaeology in the countryside.* London: Council for British Archaeology.

Stone, P. G. 1986. Even older than granny? The present state of the teaching of the past to children of 8–12 years. In *Archaeological 'objectivity' in interpretation.* World Archaeological Congress, Vol. 3 (mimeo).

Stone, P. G. & R. MacKenzie 1989. Is there an excluded past? In *Heritage interpretation*, D. Uzzell (ed.), 113–20. London: Belhaven.

Ucko, P. J. 1987. *Academic freedom and apartheid: the story of the World Archaeological Congress.* London: Duckworth.

Ucko, P. J. 1989. In conclusion: some problems and questions. *Education Bulletin* **6**, 40–3. London: Council for British Archaeology.

University of South Dakota Archaeology Laboratory 1982. *Ancient peoples and places of South Dakota*. Vermillion: University of South Dakota.

Wiseman, J. 1989. Archaeology today: from the classroom to the field to elsewhere. Unpublished paper presented to the Joint Archaeological Congress, Baltimore, January.

World Council of Indigenous Peoples 1985. Submission to United Nations Economic and Social Council. Commission on Human Rights. Working Group on Indigenous Populations: fourth session. Geneva.

1 *The study of our universal cultural heritage through the Unesco Associated Schools Project*

ELIZABETH KHAWAJKIE*

Background to the Associated Schools Project

'The wealth of humanity is also in its diversity. All of its aspects should be protected: cultural, biological, philosophical, spiritual'. This statement was one of the 16 principal conclusions of the Conference of Nobel Prize winners that met in Paris in 1988.

Today's world cultural heritage is derived from those ancient and more recent civilizations that preceded it, which made discoveries and advances in all fields, for example, in science, medicine, mathematics, the arts, philosophy, literature, architecture, and music.

Learning about past discoveries and advances is an essential factor in locating the present, in comprehending the interconnections between one civilization and another, and in understanding contemporary world issues and problems. At a time when the diversity of the world heritage is threatened by a trend towards uniformity, there is a need to reinforce and preserve the cultural identities of the different peoples of the world. At the same time it is important to ensure increased contact and exchanges between cultures to foster creativity, progress and international cooperation.

Over the past three decades, one of the Unesco programmes that seeks to promote a better understanding and awareness of other countries and their cultures has been the Associated Schools Project (ASP) which includes over 2000 institutions at the preschool, primary, secondary, and teacher-training levels of education in 97 countries. Its main objectives are to promote educational activities designed to improve international understanding and peace, and to encourage and facilitate contacts and exchanges between participating institutions at national, regional, and international levels.

The ASP was launched in 1953, and has focused particularly on the development of new and effective teaching methods, techniques and materials. For example, institutions taking part in the ASP have developed a wide range of methods aimed at enhancing the promotion of education for international understanding in the classroom (Unesco 1983, 1986c). In many

---

* The ideas and opinons expressed in this chapter are those of the author and not necessarily those of Unesco.

countries the ASP has contributed to the production of new and effective teaching material on various topics related to international understanding. Recent examples include a manual on the study of world problems in the classroom (Bulgaria), a handbook for pupils and teachers on inter-dependence in the Indian Ocean (Mauritius), teaching guidelines on human rights (Chad), reference material on education and development (Costa Rica), a handbook on 'International understanding at school: methods and techniques' (Guatemala) and teaching guidelines for the observance of the International Day of Peace (Finland).

The ASP includes institutions at the preschool, primary, secondary, and teacher-training levels of education that are invited to submit annual reports for eventual inclusion in Unesco's biannual bulletin (Unesco 1986d). Schools interested in joining the ASP (for which there is no charge) can contact their own National Commission for Unesco.

The ASP gained considerable international recognition in 1974 (Unesco 1974):

> Those concerned with Associated Schools in Member States should strengthen and renew their efforts to extend the programme to other educational institutions and work towards the general application of its results.

Its important role in multi-cultural education was also recognized (Unesco 1974):

> Member States should promote, at various stages and in various types of education, the study of different cultures, their reciprocal influences, their perspectives and ways of life, in order to encourage mutual appreciation of the differences between them. Such study should, among other things, give due importance to the teaching of foreign languages, civilizations and cultural heritage as a means of promoting international and intercultural understanding.

In keeping with the guiding principles of the 1974 Recommendation, the ASP seeks innovative and effective ways and means to impart to pupils a sound knowledge of the past; not only their own cultural heritage but also those of others, all of which contribute to our universal cultural heritage. In addition, learning about other cultures enables young people to learn more about their own country and culture, their origin, history, ancient traditions and customs.

Intercultural learning at the national level

The effectiveness of the ASP was recently evaluated (Unesco 1980):

> We stand at a critical point in history. We are witnessing for the first time the emergence of a global civilization based on the diversity of

cultures and societies. But our technology has far outstripped the capacity of our social institutions to cope with it and both pose a striking challenge to those values which guide all of us in our response to the awesome global problems of conflict, injustice, disease and poverty.

The Associated Schools Project of Unesco as a voluntary world-wide network ... has achieved a remarkable record of helping teachers and students to understand better these awesome problems and the efforts of the International community to deal with them.

Such support for the ASP is based on the success of various of its projects.

Bulgaria

In Bulgaria, 2 of the 30 institutions taking part in the Project specialize in the study of other cultures – the National Secondary School of Culture L. Jivkova and the National School of Ancient Languages and Culture Constantine Cyril. The existence of these two schools is significant and reflects the importance given to the study of both ancient and modern cultures in the country.[1]

The L. Jivkova ASP school created a club called 'The Young Tourist Guide' that organizes travelling seminars to eight Bulgarian sites. Pupils study historical sources written in Greek, Latin and ancient Bulgarian during such summer work camps.

A series of archaeological and historical expeditions has been undertaken, together with the Unesco Club of the Constantine Cyril School, during which pupils traced an important part of their historical past, and documented and recorded ancient Bulgarian songs, some previously unknown outside their locality of origin. During these expeditions students also took part in excavations jointly supervised by their teachers and archaeologists. They studied the impact of folklore on church music and the continuity of folk music in different regions of Bulgaria during various historical periods. Over the last three years pupils have visited more than 520 towns, villages and monasteries and have registered 828 old folk songs, some of which are now sung by the students' choir and have become generally popular. The L. Jivkova school also maintains a close link with an experimental school attached to the University of Athens and every year an overseas school visit is organized to improve proficiency in Greek, to establish friendships with Greek students, and to visit the remains of Greek sites.

As a basis for school discussions about the need to preserve the world cultural heritage, many ASP schools in Bulgaria study Unesco conventions (for example Unesco 1954, 1970, 1972). A number of these schools also show Unesco films on international campaigns to restore and preserve some of the world's great masterpieces, in order to sensitize pupils to the need for international cooperation in this field. Films shown have included *Borobudur:*

beyond the reach of time; *Haiti: three monuments, one symbol*; *The hidden treasures of Cappadocia*; *Hue: memories for tomorrow*; and *The Saving of Venice*.

Brazil

Unesco believes that international cooperation and peace can be enhanced through a better knowledge of other cultures. An important first step in this process is for young people to learn more about their own country, its past history and its present role in world society. An ASP school in Brazil decided to compile an album of material on Brazil and its rich cultural heritage to be made available to other Associated Schools in the country. Teachers from many different subject areas, including geography, history, art, and music, took part in this interdisciplinary project. In addition to carrying out considerable bibliographical research, pupils were put in direct contact with experts who could speak authoritatively about Brazil's past and present cultural diversity. Pupils then organized debates and discussions about this information. As a result, the young people not only got to know aspects of their own country better, particularly its multiethnicity, but also Brazil's major contributions to world culture.

Cyprus

The Fifth Lyceum School in Cyprus decided to explore Unesco's global safeguard programmes to save the world's cultural heritage. Four main rescue operations were chosen for analysis: Nubia and Philae, Borobudur, the Acropolis in Athens (see Fig. 1.1), and Paphos in Cyprus. Children were divided into groups to study each site. They consulted relevant documents and reference materials, including the *Unesco courier* and *The world cultural heritage*. Once each group had completed its research, the entire project was published in the school newspaper. Thematic exhibitions of other preservation projects were also arranged in a general exhibition on 'Nature and culture: our common heritage'. This exhibition lasted three weeks and was visited by hundreds of people from outside the school. It included an explanation of Unesco's role in the movement to safeguard cultural property, as well as of the link between these activities and the aims of the ASP.

This whole approach proved to be very effective, and pupils became quite expert in their knowledge of various cultural agreements and, in particular, the world heritage list of protected monuments.

This project was linked directly to existing courses within the curriculum. Pupils were able to appreciate that history, geography, art, and literature have relevance outside the classroom, and they were able to learn much more about their own culture, since one of the chosen areas was Cyprus itself.

Figure 1.1   The Athenian Acropolis was one of the rescue sites studied by Cypriot children as part of the Associated Schools Project.

Malta

A girls' secondary school decided to study one of the old world civilizations in a project entitled 'Egypt: its past and present'. The pupils made extensive use of the library, tourist agencies and the Embassy of the Arab Republic of Egypt, which provided useful reference materials. Egyptian culture was studied in terms of history, religion, geography, politics, agriculture and architecture, both past and present. Some novel activities were undertaken, including a mathematics lesson on volume, in which a model pyramid was used to demonstrate the principle involved. The pupils enjoyed the challenge of learning about another nation and its culture in two contrasting time frames. In this way their knowledge of Egypt as an ancient civilization was complemented by studying it as a modern country in the wider world. The multidisciplinary approach permitted the children to carry out indepth studies of various features of Egyptian civilization in a way that would have been impossible in a single subject topic.

International cooperation contributes to the promotion of our universal cultural heritage

Federal Republic of Germany

The Anna Schmidt Schule invited pupils from the ASP Washington International School (USA) and the Ommen International School (Netherlands) to join them in Cyprus at an archaeological excavation at Kalavasos village near the important Bronze Age site of Aighos Dimitrios. Under the tuition of experienced archaeologists, the young people took part in the excavation, thereby gaining knowledge about the development of early Mediterranean civilization, as well as experience of making the past come alive.

During their visit the pupils were housed with local families and all were highly appreciative of the warm welcome extended to them. Thus they not only gained a valuable cross-cultural experience of modern life in Cyprus, but also established firm friendships with pupils from the other countries, and with their Cypriot hosts.

Poland

In an effort to enable ASP teachers from abroad to learn more about Polish civilization and culture, the Polish National Commission for Unesco organizes special annual summer courses in English, French and German in cooperation with the Jagellonian University in Cracow. Lectures are given by distinguished university staff on a range of topics including Polish archaeology, history, theatre, art, music and architecture. At the end of the course ASP teachers from abroad are invited to tour the country to enable them to see both the past and present of Poland.

Malaysia and Thailand

Five Malaysian ASP pupils and their teacher visited Thailand, facilitating an exchange of views and experiences with their Thai ASP student counterparts. As well as visiting a number of government and Unesco offices, the pupils gained first-hand experience of the Thai educational system when they visited two Associated Schools. After visiting Bangkok, they travelled some 500 km to the north to view the Buddhist temples. At Sukhotai Historical Park, its director explained the work that was being done to restore some of the 800-year old palaces and Buddhist temples (see Fig. 1.2). In Sisatchanalai the pupils observed some of the excavations and saw the initial cleaning, study and classification of artefacts prior to their being sent to laboratories for further analysis. Back in Bangkok the pupils continued their visits to see the city's treasures, such as the Royal Palace and the Temple of the Emerald Buddha. The pupils reported (Unesco 1986a, p. 15):

Figure 1.2 Malaysian children visited the Buddhist monuments at Sukothai and saw restoration work in progress.
(Photograph Unesco/Mireille Vautier.)

Its geography which we read about in books became real to us . . . we got to know more about its history and this has been an enriching experience for us.

The many and varied aspects of Thailand's rich culture have impressed us tremendously. We have learnt to appreciate the colourful dances, the music, the skillful handicraft and not least the food . . .

We will not easily forget the very beautiful and hospitable people of Thailand who have helped make this trip a worthwhile one.

Unesco headquarters

On the occasion of the 1986 International Year of Peace, and the 40th anniversary of Unesco, a European meeting of pupils participating in the ASP was organized by Unesco at its Paris headquarters. Some 100 young people from 27 countries, aged 16 and 17, and their teachers came together for four days to learn more about Unesco and each other. Their programme was planned in a way that would enable them to get to know each other better and to learn about each other's countries, cultures, ways of life, school systems and so on. The pupils were accommodated three or four to a room at the Unesco Club Hostel. Room-mates were from different countries, providing the opportunity for practice in foreign languages. A colourful and original 'friendship bazaar' was also set up. Pupils had previously been asked to bring with them ten small artefacts depicting their school, community or country, to trade with each other during the bazaar. The display tables contained goods such as Norwegian safety night reflectors for schoolchildren, Israeli bookmarks, Swiss pocketknives, Russian dolls and Turkish sweets.

The children described the situation as follows (Unesco 1986b, p. 9):

> We would like to point out that as a result of this meeting, we have not only become friends but we are now one international group with the same aim and now it is our task to find means for peace, disarmament, the abolition of discrimination and effective respect for human rights.

Conclusion

The Associated Schools Project is a unique organization; throughout the world and throughout the year it is actively involved in promoting the study of a world cultural heritage and the need to protect and preserve it. It aims to develop new and effective ways to enhance learning not only about the cultures of any one specific community, but also about foreign communities. Efforts are constantly being made to teach more effectively about the past and its relationship to present-day life. The Associated Schools Project fosters exchanges with schools abroad in order to stimulate understanding of the ways of life of different peoples, their customs, traditions, and values, and the way in which cultural traditions can benefit from mutual understanding and shared experiences.

The ASP will continue to attempt to foster intercultural studies, particularly during the UN's World Decade for Cultural Development (WDCD) which runs from 1988 to 1997. ASP members have already been invited to undertake appropriate activities within the framework of the Decade, which has four main objectives:

a   acknowledgement of the cultural dimensions of development,
b   affirmation and enrichment of cultural identities,
c   broadening participation in culture,
d   promotion of international cultural cooperation (Unesco 1987).

It is to be hoped that everyone will contribute to the observance of the WDCD and the fulfilment of its objectives. Schools have a particularly important role to play in this regard and their participation will achieve an improved understanding between the peoples of the world.

Note

1   Although Bulgaria occupies one of the smallest territories in the world, it takes third place in the World Heritage List with eight entries (Pirin National Park, Srebarna Nature Reserve. Madara Rider, Nesebar (Old City), Boyana church, Ivanovo rockhewn churches, Rila monastery, Kazanlak Thracian tomb), following France with 15 sites and the USA with 14.

References

Unesco 1954. *Convention for the protection of cultural property in the event of armed conflict*. Paris: Unesco.

Unesco 1970. *Convention on the means of prohibiting and preventing the illicit import, export and transfer of ownership of cultural property*. Paris: Unesco.

Unesco 1972. *Convention concerning the protection of the world cultural and natural heritage*. Paris: Unesco.

Unesco 1974. *Recommendation concerning education for international understanding, co-operation and peace and education relating to human rights and fundamental freedoms*. Paris: Unesco.

Unesco 1980. *Final statement of the international meeting of experts on the evaluation and development of the Associated Schools Project on Education for International Co-operation and Peace*. Paris: Unesco.

Unesco 1983. *Education for international co-operation and peace at the primary school level*. Paris: Unesco.

Unesco 1986a. *Why preserve the past? The challenge to our cultural heritage*. Washington, DC: Smithsonian Institution Press.

Unesco 1986b. Peace and international understanding. In *European meeting of students taking part in the Associated Schools Project – final report*. Paris: Unesco.

Unesco 1986c. Partners in promoting education for international understanding for participation in the Unesco Associated Schools Project. In *Practical manual*. Paris: Unesco.

Unesco 1986d. *International understanding at school – Special Supplement*. Nos. 48–49, 50–51. Paris: Unesco.

Unesco 1987. *A practical guide to the World Decade for Cultural Development 1988–1997*. Paris: Unesco.

2 *Archaeology in Indian universities*

DILIP K. CHAKRABARTI

Introduction: archaeological field research in India

India possesses perhaps the largest federal bureaucratic machinery concerned with archaeology in the world, the Archaeology Survey of India (established under colonial rule in 1861), which undertakes the nationwide conservation of centrally listed monuments and organizes surveys and excavations. Apart from regional administrative branches or 'circles', it has a museum branch, a chemical branch, a prehistory branch, a few excavation branches and temple surveys, and even a horticultural branch to look after gardens around the important protected monuments. It answers questions on archaeology in Parliament and is involved directly or indirectly in virtually all administrative aspects of archaeology and antiquity law in the country. Among other things, it runs the Central Advisory Board of Archaeology which includes members from the Survey, the province or states, the universities and a few 'learned bodies', and processes applications for excavation work. Administratively the Archaeological Survey of India is a part of the Department of Culture. This in turn comes under what used to be the Ministry of Education and Social Welfare, and is now the Ministry of Human Resources Development.

At the state level the situation is more diversified. Most Indian states and union territories have their own departments or directorates of archaeology and museums that are attached to various ministries, including those related to public works, information, and tourism. The status of such departments varies from state to state. In some cases they do not run to more than a cultural officer and subordinate staff, none of whom is likely to be trained in archaeology. The basic task of these units at state and union territory level is to look after monuments considered to be only regionally important, and to undertake surveys and excavations within their respective administrative borders. These organizations, which also act as the clearing agents of all applications for excavations in their jurisdiction, have been functioning only since the 1960s.

The relationship between archaeology and museums in India is very close but at the same time somewhat ambiguous. Virtually all museums of art and archaeology have archaeologists on their staff, but only in rare cases have these museums been involved in field research, although one of the earliest university excavations in India was done in 1937–41 by the Ashutosh Museum of Fine Arts of Calcutta University. None of the national museums in Delhi, Calcutta, Madras, Bombay, and Allahabad has ever been involved in archaeological field research. There are also research institutions whose academic affiliations and purposes are not quite clear, such as the Birla Archaeological and Cultural Research Institute, Hyderabad, and the Prachya Niketan Centre of Advanced Studies in Indology and Museology, Bhopal.

The third major level of archaeological operations in India is conducted by the universities. About 25 universities (out of a total of more than 100 universities and 'deemed universities') have so far been known to have undertaken field research of some kind through their history, ancient Indian history, culture and archaeology, or anthropology departments.

On the fourth level two autonomous research institutes have well-developed archaeology-related programmes – the Birbal Sahni Institute of Palaeobotany, Lucknow, and the Physical Research Laboratory, Ahmedabad. The Lucknow Institute undertakes palaeobotanical research and radiocarbon dating and palaeoenvironmental research. The radiocarbon dating laboratory in Ahmedabad was moved there from the Tata Institute of Fundamental Research, Bombay, where the radiocarbon-dating technique was first properly developed in India.

It might seem from this catalogue of organizations responsible for archaeological field research in India that very few parts of the world are archaeologically better resourced. While this is true to some extent, especially in the fields of exploration and excavation, archaeology cannot be said to have made such progress as an academic subject. The purpose of this chapter is to outline the basic situation in this regard with reference to the historical development and current status of the subject in Indian universities.

The historical development of archaeology in universities

The history of the acceptance and development of archaeology in universities is somewhat confused, at least for the pre-1947 period. Only certain landmarks can be considered here. The University of Calcutta introduced 'Ancient Indian history and culture' as a two-year MA course before the First World War. Two optional archaeology-related courses were offered in the syllabus: epigraphy and numismatics, and fine arts. The epigraphy and numismatics course also included a study of palaeography. The fine arts course dealt with the histories of sculpture, architecture, painting, and iconography. The first university professor in the subject was D. R. Bhandarkar, former 'circle superintendent' in the Archaeological Survey who had undertaken a number of excavations. Bhandarkar allowed his archaeological interests to lapse after he joined the university. In 1922–3 he supervised excavations at Paharpur, a major Buddhist site in east India. This work was funded by the Archaeological Survey and a private donation made for this purpose to the university. In the next season, however, the university inexplicably expressed regret at its inability to continue the work, although the funds were available. Calcutta University also introduced a two-year MA or MSc course in Anthropology before 1914, with special papers in prehistory. The first teacher of prehistory in this subject, P. Mitra, had published a book entitled *Prehistoric India* in 1922. Mitra had an MA in English literature, but he had written a dissertation on the history of American anthropology while at Yale University. The scheme established in the Department of Ancient Indian History and Culture and the Department of Anthropology at the University of Calcutta for a long time reflected the general status of archaeology as a purely academic subject in Indian universities.

The tradition of field archaeological investigation by Indian universities was initiated by the Ashutosh Museum of Fine Arts of Calcutta University in 1937, when it began excavations (1937–41) at the early historical site of Bangarh in east India. The work was directed by K. G. Goswami, a Sanskrit scholar who had received training in field archaeology from the Archaeological Survey of India. In the same period two anthropology teachers at the university undertook excavations at various prehistoric localities in Mayurbhanj. Both of them (N. K. Bose and D. Sen) had geology backgrounds, an unusual qualification for researchers in prehistoric archaeology in Gujarat (Chakrabarti 1988).

Little archaeology was taught in universities before India's independence in 1947. Historical archaeological data were unearthed by the Archaeological Survey of India and published in its annual reports and memoirs. Historians specializing in ancient India tried to synthesize and interpret these discoveries. This conditioned current attitudes towards archaeology in Indian universities. Archaeology was regarded simply as a set of techniques that could be learnt by working with the Archaeological Survey of India, and archaeologists were people who wore khaki-coloured shorts and pith helmets. But the entire ethos of archaeological field research was, and still is, alien to Indian universities. It was better to be an 'ancient historian' who could, after all, read epigraphic documents and interpret excavated numismatic, architectural and art-historical remains in terms of the different problems of ancient Indian studies. This general picture still applies, although the number of such source-oriented ancient historians has dwindled alarmingly since the consolidation of a 'progressive' political lobby of history in the early 1970s. Thus, for example, no history teacher at any of the three universities in Delhi is known to have edited an inscription! The study of prehistory remained in a kind of academic limbo because it had no general nationalist appeal in a country singularly rich in historical relics. Even the discovery of the Indus civilization by archaeologists in 1921–22 did not lead to a change, except that history textbooks started printing photographs of the brick-built drains of Mohenjodaro.

Table 2.1   The MA archaeology syllabus at Calcutta University.

Paper	First half	Second half
I	ethnology	ancient geography
II	history of archaeology	aims and methods of archaeology
III	prehistory	protohistory
IV	palaeogeography	epigraphy
V	numismatics	iconography
VI	sculpture, painting	architecture
VII	Mesopotamian or Egyptian history	Mesopotamian or Egyptian archaeology
VIII	conservation	viva voce

Two major archaeological investigations took place in the 1950s, namely that undertaken by Allahabad University at the site of Kausambi, one of the most important early sites of the Ganges valley, and the exploration and excavations of the neolithic–chalcolithic levels in central India and the Deccan by Deccan College of Poona University. These events probably contributed to a wind of change in 1960. In that year the Indian University Grants Commission (IUGC) gave approval for the opening of separate archaeology departments offering MA courses in archaeology at a number of universities, including Calcutta, Baroda, Madras and Poona. The Calcutta University syllabus may be considered fairly representative of the general curriculum followed in these departments. This required examinations in eight papers carrying 100 marks each. Each paper was subdivided into two halves (Table 2.1). About 10–12 weeks had to be spent in the field under university regulations and the IUGC gave grants to fund the appointment of surveyors, draughtsmen and photographers, as well as to purchase basic equipment for photography, surveying, and camping.

The universities with separate MA courses in archaeology were unable to sustain them adequately for long, and it appears that only the universities of Calcutta and Poona still run separate departments of archaeology. In all other cases archaeology departments have been merged with ancient Indian history departments, and their full title is now, subject to occasional variations, Department of Ancient Indian History, Culture and Archaeology. There is no special weighting given to fieldwork in these departments, which have generally relegated archaeology to one or two papers on prehistory, protohistory and field methods.

Reasons for the relative absence of fieldwork

There are many reasons for the relative absence of archaeological fieldwork. First, archaeology has not been considered an acceptable subject of specialization leading to job opportunities. Indeed, archaeology has been generally regarded as completely irrelevant to contemporary Indian society. The number of MA graduates in archaeology who could be absorbed into universities, museums, and official bodies was necessarily small. Even in general education, graduates with archaeology MAs found it difficult to secure employment. Archaeology had no place in BA courses and lower levels in the university-affiliated colleges. Archaeology was unheard of in the schools. No school student was expected to know anything about India's archaeology except that there had been an early civilization in the Indus valley. This meant that graduates with archaeology MAs had to compete for history-teaching jobs with others holding history MAs, and found themselves at a disadvantage. Some universities, for example Calcutta, formally debarred archaeology MAs from applying for college lectureships in history. On the other hand, recruitment for government archaeology posts in the Survey and elsewhere did not give preferential treatment to those with archaeology MAs. These had to compete on the same footing as applicants with MAs in history and various classical and medieval languages. Archaeology is not listed as a subject in the curricula of the Civil Service and other elite examinations, and this has militated against the arousal of student interest in the subject in the universities.

Another reason why fieldwork does not feature prominently is because university archaeology departments did not devise academic programmes and syllabuses that differed markedly from what was offered in the ancient Indian history departments, apart from a paper on archaeological aims and methods, and a general emphasis on fieldwork. Even the emphasis on fieldwork for archaeology students gradually weakened, mostly because of apathy on the part of university departments. The issue of compulsory fieldwork is important in India, because of the absence of the custom of employing voluntary student labour for excavations. In Indian excavations the tradition is to employ local villagers, thus depriving students of practical experience in the field. There was also a failure in most universities to create an interest in archaeology by undertaking important field programmes, and a great number of university excavations have remained unpublished. In the circumstances, there could hardly be any talk of organized expansion of archaeological studies in the universities. Exceptionally, however, purposeful leadership in the universities of Poona and Baroda in the 1960s did result in extensive field programmes, followed by substantial publications, which put archaeology in these two universities on a more solid foundation. Regrettably archaeology did not continue to flourish as an independent academic entity in Baroda.

The current status of archaeology in Indian universities

Today archaeology is an adjunct of history, Ancient Indian history, and anthropology in Indian universities. The major university centre of archaeology is Poona, because of the diversity of its field programmes and because it has a conscious multidisciplinary approach, aided by the presence of a sufficiently large number of natural scientists on the staff. The next most important is Baroda, which has had a distinguished tradition of field research and publication. In recent years it has also undertaken a number of scientific analytical studies. Allahabad also showed early signs of becoming a major centre, but things have not turned out this way. Archaeology teachers in virtually all other Indian universities operate more or less as individuals, concerned (or unconcerned, as the case may be) with their own research. The position of archaeology in the Department of History, Delhi University, which has one archaeology teacher on its staff, is fairly representative. Here there is a compulsory paper on Indian prehistory and protohistory for students who opt for ancient Indian history in the final year of their two-year MA course in history. There are also two optional papers in archaeology for such students – 'historical archaeology' (of India) and 'archaeological theories and methods'. These are 'dead' options in the sense that the students do not find them amenable to cramming for examinations, and thus do not opt for them. There is no compulsory field programme component, and the entire departmental field initiative is funded by an annual university outlay of about £250. A few MPhil and PhD dissertations have been successfully completed, but none on a directly field-related topic. Proposals to set up scientific analytical sections failed to gain even departmental support. There are three or four preliminary topics in Indian prehistory and protohistory within BA history courses. The situation is largely the same where archaeology is included in the university curriculum as an adjunct of anthropology. The Delhi University Department of Anthropology, for example, offers courses in prehistory at the BSc and MSc levels. There is only one teacher, and there is no specific field programme.

The case of the Department of Archaeology at Calcutta University raises a different issue. It has at least six full-time teachers and also draws on the help of several part-time teachers from other university departments. There are also established departmental posts, including surveyor-draughtsman, photographer, artist and museum curator. The department was established in 1960, which means that a substantial number of students have already taken its MA degrees. It has also had a tradition of compulsory field research for students, funded by the university. In 1961–2 it initiated a major excavation programme at an important Buddhist monastery site in West Bengal. Although work continued for the next 10–12 seasons, only the detailed report of the first season's work (1961–62) is available. The perfunctory reports published annually in the Archaeological Survey's *Indian archaeology – a review* have to serve as the only records available on the rest of the work. Indeed all field activities of the department after 1961–2 have remained basically unpublished. The department does not possess any scientific analytical section. So far only two PhD dissertations would appear to have been successfully completed in this department.

A systematic assessment of Indian archaeology has been made by Agrawal

& Chakrabarti (1979), and two recent reports on archaeology as an academic subject in the Indian universities would appear broadly to substantiate the views expressed earlier in this chapter.

Recently George Rapp Jr, a geoarchaeologist at the University of Minnesota, prepared a report for the Ford Foundation, Delhi (Rapp 1983). The objective was to 'assist in strengthening the natural science component in Indian archaeology through grants, primarily in universities, for equipment, personnel development and library expansion'. Some of Rapp's observations (Rapp 1983) are worth citing:

> I believe that the long-term health and vitality of Indian archaeology depend on the ability of the universities to put out high-quality PhDs ... The United States has between thirty and fifty first-rate departments of archaeology (although not all are up to par in the application of natural science to archaeological problems). I believe India must develop at least six to ten first-rate departments.

In this report the author justifiably attached importance to the work done in Poona and Baroda universities. The sentiment that 'the long-term health and vitality of Indian archaeology' depend on the development of archaeology as a vigorous academic subject in the universities echoed views expressed in the 1940s by Mortimer Wheeler (1946):

> A condition for the advancement of the study of India's great heritage is the widespread extension of archaeological research from the confines of a Government Department into the liberal activities of the universities and learned societies of India; from the monopoly of the civil servant to the free initiative of the educated public. Only then will it be possible for Indian archaeology, with its unsurpassed opportunities, to take a proper place amidst the free sciences of the world.

S. Topno, Deputy Secretary of the Indian University Grants Commission, recently came to similar conclusions (Topno 1987) about the two dozen or so universities that offer courses in archaeology, arguing that 'more creation of a few technical positions and facilities for archaeological excavations is not likely to achieve the desired goals unless teaching and research in archaeology in the University is delinked from Ancient Indian History and Culture'.

Conclusion

Such laudable sentiments and governmental measures notwithstanding, archaeology has failed to grow up as an academically dynamic subject in most Indian universities. There are several reasons for this, not the least of which is the quality of people recruited to develop the subject in universities.

But not every failure can be attributed to such personal shortcomings. The position of the subject in the general scheme of university education no doubt plays a major role. If archaeology is merely allotted one or two papers in the syllabus of a large university history department, it will remain for the most part neglected both by the students and the university authorities. In this context it is also useful to remember that the Indian university system is highly bureaucratic and status-oriented. Here everything, including research proposals submitted by university teachers, has to have official sanction. The Archaeological Survey of India will turn down a proposal to excavate if it is not routed through the university registrar. Even if an application gets past the head of the department and university registrar, its eventual sanction by the members of the Central Advisory Board (a board set up mainly to process applications for excavations) will depend not on the proposer's expertise and commitment to the subject as demonstrated by relevant publications, but on the proposer's status and, above all, acceptability. One cannot say that the Indian university departments of history are prepared to give much support to archaeological research. Moreover, in such departments there is always a fear of anything 'scientific', which historians find difficult to control.

What is perhaps more important is the notion of the Indian past. As reflected in books on Indian history in general, this is dominated by an essentially literary image. The sort of evidence of the past that only modern archaeological research can provide does not play any role in it. Again, in as large a country as India there can hardly be a coherent or strictly defined attitude towards the past. The relationship between contemporary society and archaeology has tended to become obscured as the need for being self-consciously nationalist has passed. There is no clear acceptance of the important relationship between archaeology, the past, and the present in India today.

The fact that archaeology finds no place in preuniversity education in India is rooted to some extent in the lowly position archaeology holds as an academic subject in the country. It is rumoured that in the syllabus on ancient India recently framed by the National Council of Educational Research and Training there is some emphasis on prehistory and protohistory in school textbooks. One can only hope that this seed will bear fruit.

References

Agrawal, D. P. & D. K. Chakrabarti 1979. Archaeology in India: a professional assessment. In *Essays on Indian protohistory*, D. P. Agrawal & D. K. Chakrabarti (eds), 388–92. Delhi: B.R. Publishing Corporation.
Archaeological Survey of India: Indian archaeology – a review (annually).
Chakrabarti, D. K. 1988. *A history of archaeology in India from the beginning to 1947.* Delhi: Munshiram Manoharlal.
Rapp, G., Jr 1983. *Archaeological science in India: status, potential and recommendations.* Delhi: Ford Foundation (mimeo).

Topno, S. 1987. Circular No. F.5–31/755 (HR–I), February 8. Delhi: University Grants Commission.

Wheeler, R. E. M. 1946. Editorial notes. *Ancient India* **1**, 1.

3 *Archaeology in Nigerian Education*

NWANNA NZEWUNWA

Introduction

Archaeology in education aims to teach about the prehistoric past in order to develop an awareness and appreciation of its significance for the present and the future. Knowledge of the past is acquired through learning the principles, methodology, and practice of archaeology.

Archaeology at present does not have a place as a subject of study at either the primary or secondary levels of the Nigerian education system. It is only at the tertiary level that archaeology is taught. The professional approach at this level sees it as a subject or method of research that relies on excavations to uncover objects used by humans in the past that may aid our understanding of their ways of life. In this case archaeology involves 'doing' – it is practical. A second approach sees archaeology as an aspect of history, simply as a subject that studies the past. According to this view, archaeology is seen as an end rather than a means. In contrast to the first view, it is narrative, and synonymous with prehistory. This latter view brought archaeology through the side door into the Nigerian education system, and for a long time kept it bonded to history. This chapter discusses the development of archaeology in tertiary education by reviewing the context and rationale of archaeology in education, the place of archaeology in formal and informal education, curriculum development, and the facilities available for learning about archaeology.

Context

Professional archaeology was introduced into Nigeria in the first decades of the 20th century following the visit of the German anthropologist Leo Froebenius in 1910–11. His search for objects of archaeological interest in Ife, and the publicity he gave to them in Europe, increased awareness of the place of Nigeria in the production of fine works of art. Prior to this, the 1897 British punitive expedition against Benin, which collected all the works of art it could lay its hands on before burning the city, had drawn attention to the advanced nature of wood and ivory carving, as well as copper-alloy technology, in Nigeria. With the establishment of British colonial administration in Nigeria, colonial administrators, travellers, teachers, military men and miners began to take an interest in collecting and preserving the art works of Nigeria, but their interest or enthusiasm did not seem to be for the direct benefit of Nigeria and Nigerians. This is easily demonstrated by the manner in which they carted off to Europe most of what they collected. Moreover, the received wisdom of the time was that the art of lost-wax metal casting had been taught to Nigerian groups such as the Bini by the Portuguese. Missionaries condemned masks and wood carvings as fetishes and made public bonfires of them.

The collection of Nigerian carvings became a pastime of public servants in the colonial service, none of whom had any formal education in archaeology. In the 1920s, an education officer conceived the idea of conserving Nigeria's traditional works of art, and another was appointed to consider the impact on them of European education. This ultimately led to the establishment of what was initially called the Nigerian Antiquities Service in 1943. After the Second World War, with the appointment of a trained professional archaeologist, the department began undertaking archaeological field work as well as conservation. But archaeology was not introduced into the education system as a subject of study.

Willett (1960, p. 60) records that J. D. Clark, an education officer who did much for the preservation of antiquities in Nigeria, visited Old Oyo in December 1937, and did a small amount of digging. Archaeological research in Nigeria was initially organized in areas such as Ife, Benin, and Nok, where impressive artistic objects had been discovered accidentally.

In 1945 the Elliot Commission on Higher Education in West Africa produced its blueprint for the development of higher education in the subregion. There was no specific mention in the document of archaeology as a subject for study in tertiary institutions. The nearest it came was to urge research into the past of West Africa, in order to stimulate local interest in the ancient traditions of the people. This, the Commission hoped, would help indigenous West African peoples to maintain a grip on their traditions, and keep society together in the face of the rapid changes taking place in West Africa.

By the 1950s, there was a growing awareness among government functionaries of Nigerian origin of the importance of their indigenous cultural heritage. This led to the enactment in 1953 of a cultural resource management law, the Antiquities Department Law, otherwise known as Ordinance 17 of 1953. This law not only created an institution (The Antiquities Commission) responsible for the management of Nigeria's cultural resources, but also gave sanction to prehistoric archaeological research in Nigeria. It firmly established the framework within which archaeological practice in Nigeria was permitted, but did not introduce archaeology into the Nigerian system.

Why archaeology in education?

In the 1960s archaeology was finally introduced as a taught subject into some Nigerian universities. The Nigerian historian K. O. Dike played an important role in this. He was acutely conscious of the limitations of written and oral documents relating to the Nigerian past, and appreciated the role that archaeology could play in remedying the deficiency, much along the lines suggested earlier by Thurstan Shaw (1946). In order to introduce the subject into the University of Ibadan, Dike made sure that the post of a Research Chair in Archaeology was written into the constitution of the Institute of African Studies. Shaw noted in one of the earliest surveys of Nigerian archaeology that the discipline was expanding and that for the first time archaeological appointments had been made in three Nigerian universities (Shaw 1963). A few years later, J. F. A. Ajayi (1969, p. 8) stressed the growing importance of academic archaeology, despite its recent arrival in Nigeria.

One of the earliest pronouncements on the rationale of archaeology in Nigeria was made by Shaw (1969, p. 12). He stated that it 'can very often supplement history where the historical record is inadequate and it can do something . . . in periods where history can do nothing at all i.e. in pre-history'. Until the 1970s there was no public discussion about general principles of archaeology in education. Debates in university senates on the reason for proposing the introduction of archaeology into the curriculum remained particular to each university. At this stage archaeology in Nigeria was regarded primarily as serving the purposes of history, to provide information and chronology about the remote past. During the period that archaeological fieldwork progressed, with few interruptions, until the early 1980s, archaeology in education hardly existed.

Archaeology and informal education

Archaeology in informal education is ill developed in Nigeria. Generally informal education is directed towards the majority of the populace, unlike formal education which is restricted to a small group – the younger members of society. Radio, television and the press are not regularly used for educating people about archaeology. Very few television programmes are directed towards the educated elite. Coverage of whatever is available is trivialized.

There is an absence of amateurs in Nigerian archaeology. The effect is that there are no avenues for nonprofessionals interested in participating in the task of identifying sites, assisting in excavations, writing reports, curating the finds, and protecting the cultural heritage. Popular lectures and exhibitions for a wider populace are also missing.

Adult education programmes in Nigeria are aimed primarily at teaching reading, writing and basic numeracy to the adult sector of the society, which is considered to be illiterate and innumerate. These programmes have no archaeological content. Museums and exhibitions are seen by the Nigerian public as preserves of the educated urban elite who have the time and interest to devote to such leisure activities. Informal education programmes therefore contribute insignificantly to the propagation of archaeology in Nigeria.

Archaeology in formal education

At the instigation of Shaw, who had worked in Ghana from 1937 to 1945, the first Department of Archaeology between North Africa and the Limpopo was set up at the University College of the Gold Coast, Achimota (later the University of Ghana, Legon) in 1951 (Calvocoressi & York 1970, p. 87). The present generation of scholars may not appreciate how difficult it was before the end of the Second World War to persuade colonial governments and the indigenous educated elite that there *was* any archaeology in West Africa, and that archaeological studies were a worthwhile activity. Shaw and Richard Nunoo (the first Ghanaian director of Ghana's National Museum) worked very closely together, as did Bernard Fagg and Ekpo Eyo, the first Nigerian recruit to be trained as an archaeologist (Shaw pers. comm., April 1989), but these were personal initiatives.

Archaeology in formal education was only introduced to Nigeria in the 1960s, and there are a number of likely reasons for this delay (Nzewunwa 1983, 1984, 1989). Archaeology may have been regarded primarily as a field discipline, meant to provide data for museums, and it may have been considered that it did not contribute to the enhancement of colonialism, and was therefore not encouraged by colonial governments. The need to train West African archaeologists may have been downgraded since it appeared that foreign archaeologists could satisfy the needs of archaeology in Nigeria; and in any case conventional wisdom had it that West Africans were unwilling to embrace the discipline. Whatever the case, education planners and policy makers did not consider it necessary to include archaeology in Nigerian formal education. At the University of Nigeria, Nsukka, another factor was the union of archaeology with history, which further delayed the introduction of archaeology as an item in its own right into the curriculum.

In the middle and late 1960s, following independence, archaeologists in West Africa identified three main objectives for archaeology in education in the subregion. These were:

a   to train African archaeologists to be able to carry out field research;
b   to educate policy makers and practitioners so that the government and the people would the more readily understand archaeology, and help reduce the destruction or export of the cultural heritage and;
c   to consolidate knowledge of this important historical research tool (Calvocoressi 1970).

The 1970s in Nigeria saw the expansion of tertiary education and the creation of more academic departments and new courses. For archaeology, the expansion resulted in the creation of university subdepartments of archaeology in Zaria, Nsukka and Ife, and the introduction of new archaeology courses in history departments in Calabar, Benin, Port Harcourt, Ife, Sokoto and Jos. The National Policy on Education produced in 1977 set out the rationale for Nigerian education and the ideal of citizenship that it sought to produce through the education system. It recognized the role of cultural historical studies in bringing about an enlightened populace.

In the 1980s the importance of archaeology in the education of Nigerian historians and history teachers was recognized, although Shaw had pioneered an Archaeology Workshop for history teachers a decade earlier (Shaw pers. comm., April 1989). Now fully independent university departments of archaeology at Nsukka and Ife were created. Archaeology-related courses were also increased in history departments. In two cases, Ibadan and Nsukka, postgraduate programmes in archaeology were introduced for the award of Masters' and Doctorate degrees.

Curriculum development

Nsukka

Plans were made to introduce archaeology courses in the University of Nigeria, Nsukka in 1960, but classes did not start there until the American archaeologist Donald Hartle was appointed resident archaeologist in 1963. Only three courses were offered at that time in the Department of History and Archaeology, on the 'Evolution of Man', 'Introduction to Archaeology', and 'Archaeology of Africa'.

From 1966 to 1971, the university ceased to function because of the Nigerian Civil War. By the middle of the 1970s, the archaeology staff strength had increased with the appointment of two further archaeologists. This enabled the department to introduce new courses in archaeology for a combined degree in archaeology and history, and for a single degree in archaeology. It was not until 1981 that an independent department of archaeology was created at Nsukka. Thus it took two decades to realize the dreams of the founding fathers of archaeology at Nsukka. The department today has single and combined honours degree programmes with history, religious studies, geography, geology and anthropology. It also offers a Master of Arts degree programme in archaeology.

Ibadan

The University of Ibadan introduced archaeology as a research discipline in the Institute of African Studies in 1963. From here a service course was

offered to students in the history department by the first resident archaeologist, Thurstan Shaw.

Until the 1968/69 session, archaeology was not taught formally as a
university course, although the Department of History continued to offer
lectures for undergraduates in what may now be termed Nigerian prehistory. Archaeology was later upgraded and given its own teaching department, located in the Faculty of Science.

The association of archaeology with the sciences enabled it to develop
various degree combinations with disciplines such as earth and biological
sciences and geography, as well as with the humanities such as history,
classical studies, and religious studies. These combinations made Ibadan
archaeology courses the most elaborate in Nigeria. Recently Ibadan has
expanded its scope to become a Department of Archaeology and Anthropology (Andah 1982, 1988) as distinct from the situation at Nsukka, Ife and
Zaria where departments of anthropology exist independently. This development sprang from Bassey Andah's proposal that archaeology at Ibadan
should move towards the US model, which he experienced when taking his
PhD at the University of California, Berkeley.

Ahmadu Bello University

At Ahmadu Bello University, Zaria, the Centre of Nigerian Cultural
Studies was established in the early 1970s to enable cultural and historical
studies, including archaeology, to be developed. It was, however, in the
Department of History that archaeology courses were first introduced.
Later, a subdepartment of archaeology was formed within the Department
of History. Debate about whether to grant it full independent status has
gone on for the past decade. The Zaria programme emphasizes the prehistory of Africa and the world, exposing history students to the prehistoric
links and linkages, gaps and discontinuities across regions and continents.

Ife

The recently renamed Obafemi Awolowo University at Ife first ran its
archaeological programme in the Institute of African Studies. From there, it
was moved to the History Department when the Institute of African Studies
was dismantled in the very early 1970s. There, as at Nsukka and Zaria,
history students had the option of taking one or two archaeology/prehistory
options in the course of reading for a history degree (Andah pers. comm.,
April 1989). In 1985, archaeology gained independent status as a teaching
department.

Port Harcourt

The University of Port Harcourt only offers archaeology courses in the
Department of History while practising field archaeology under the aegis of

the University Museum. Apart from an introductory course in archaeology, it teaches the archaeology of Africa, the prehistory of Nigeria, early societies in West Africa, methodology of African history, and cultural resource management. It also offers to graduate students in history a postgraduate course on issues in African archaeology. Recently a single candidate was enrolled within the Department of History to undertake a doctorate degree in Nigerian archaeology and prehistory.

Factors retarding the development of archaeology in education

The above review gives an indication of the pattern of archaeology in Nigerian university education. In other universities and colleges of education archaeology-based courses in 'narrative archaeology' or prehistory are also taught, mostly by nonarchaeologists, within history departments.

The effective development of curricula in any given place is heavily dependent on the availability of staff and facilities. The 1980s saw the departure of most expatriate archaeology staff from Nigerian universities and the appointment of more indigenous Nigerian archaeologists. Yet there is still a dearth of qualified teaching staff to service the departments of archaeology. This has affected proposals for the establishment of new departments or the introduction of archaeology courses into institutions where none currently exist. This state of affairs has adversely affected the development of the discipline as a whole.

The interdisciplinary approach to the study of Nigeria's past is reflected to some extent by the way that archaeology has borrowed theory from other disciplines. Some disciplines which are still far from being fully grasped by archaeologists include those derived from the earth and environmental sciences, such as territoriality, and the application of mathematical principles and models in the analysis of data to extrapolate about human behaviour in the past. The development of archaeology in education is also currently impaired by the nonavailability of essential literature from overseas in the local libraries and bookshops, following the slump in the national economy. The literature that is available is therefore religiously consumed and regurgitated, being regarded as dogma rather than scholarly production. This accounts for the near perpetuation of some terminologies that no longer express their original meaning, for example the 'Neolithic' (Shaw in press). In some cases theories that have become obsolete are still being taught, for example, theories about the origins of African food production.

Facilities

Archaeology in Nigerian education (as opposed to archaeological research) depends for its success on the availability of staff, literature, visual materials, structures, and accurate data and analysis. In comparison with the USA and

Europe, these facilities are grossly inadequate. Yet in comparison with most other African countries, with the possible exception of Kenya and South Africa, Nigeria may be said to be far ahead not just in the quantity but also in the quality of available facilities. In recognition of the danger posed by the shortage of middle-level personnel for cultural studies, the Nigerian government, in association with Unesco, established a School for Museum Studies at Jos to train junior to middle-level cadres to assist archaeologists and curators. There are plans now to encourage a Nigerian university to mount a postgraduate course in museology for training museum curators within the country.

It has been observed that archaeologists trained at Nigerian universities are not sufficiently prepared to enable them to undertake fieldwork independently as professional archaeologists. The National Commission for Museums and Monuments intends to establish a school of archaeology specifically to train professional archaeologists in field practice.

The infrastructure is also inadequate. Apart from the University of Ibadan, no other university has buildings designed from the drawing board to house its archaeology department. Space for stores, laboratories, work and offices is grossly inadequate. Lecture rooms are not equipped with audiovisual facilities. In such classroom situations visual demonstrations are denied to the students. This is of course a common Nigerian or indeed African phenomenon. The 'museums' in the universities are makeshift exhibition rooms that were not primarily designed for such purposes. The only museum building in a Nigerian university designed as such was commissioned early in 1989 at the University of Port Harcourt.

Conclusion

This chapter has reviewed the origin of archaeology in Nigerian education, why archaeology was introduced into the Nigerian educational curriculum, and the progress archaeology has made in universities. It has sought to review the available facilities for achieving effective education, stressing their strengths and weaknesses. As has been seen, the absence of archaeology in the informal education sphere has made it impossible to tap the popularity that archaeology could well enjoy among Nigerian people.

The absence from the primary and secondary schools of programmes in archaeology has kept archaeology away from the grassroots of Nigerian cultural education. As a result, interest in archaeology is delayed until a much later stage when students enter university. This is too late. Since only a very small percentage of the population benefits from university education, the knowledge of archaeology is further restricted to a tiny group of Nigerians. It is, therefore, an inescapable conclusion that archaeology in Nigeria is exclusive and elitist.

This is what archaeology should *not* be in Nigeria, nor indeed in any

African setting, because of its place in local Nigerian history. Since Africans view history as a continuum made up of the past, no matter how remote, the present and the future, archaeology that enhances the recovery and interpretation of this history should have an elevated status, and should be shared by a larger sector of the Nigerian society. This is what archaeology in Nigerian education should now aim to achieve. To do this requires the collective responsibility and collaboration of policy-makers in accepting archaeology into the curriculum of these lower levels of education. It also requires the recognition by Nigerian archaeologists that they must begin to popularize archaeology, make it more accessible, less mystifying, and devoid of the jargon that can only appeal to academic professionals.

There are some very practical measures which need to be implemented. These include: vigorous and active museum programmes involving schools, such as those organized by the Nigerian Museum in Lagos in the early 1970s; coverage of archaeology in newspapers, magazines, and TV and radio programmes; and production of literature for teachers and ordinary educated people (see Shaw 1975, 1977). There is no doubt that the Nigerian people are willing to 'buy' archaeology if archaeologists can only learn to advertise it properly and sell it at affordable prices. This is a major task over the next decade for Nigerian archaeologists.

References

Ajayi, J. F. A. 1969. Foreword. In: *Lectures on Nigerian prehistory and archaeology*. T. Shaw (ed.) Ibadan: Oxford University Press.
Andah, B. W. 1982. *African development in cultural perspective.* Ibadan: Ibadan University Press.
Andah, B. W. 1988. *African anthropology.* Ibadan: Shanesor.
Calvocoressi, D. S. 1970. *West African Archaeological Newsletter* **12**, 53–90.
Calvocoressi, D. S. and R. N. York 1970. The state of archaeological research in Ghana. *West African Journal of Archaeology* **1**, 87–103.
Nzewunwa, N. 1983. Uneven Development: a survey of the history of archaeology in West Africa. Paper delivered at the 9th Pan African Congress on Prehistory and Related Studies, Jos, 13–19 December.
Nzewunwa, N. 1984. Archaeology education in Nigeria. Paper delivered at the 29th Congress of the Historical Society of Nigeria, Sokoto, 19–24 March.
Nzewunwa, N. 1990. Cultural education in West Africa: the archaeological perspectives. In *The politics of the past*, P. Gathercole, & D. Lowenthal (eds), Ch. 14. London: Unwin Hyman.
Shaw, T. 1946. *The study of Africa's past.* IAI Memorandum **21**. London: International African Institute.
Shaw, T. 1963. *Archaeology and Nigeria. An inaugural lecture.* Ibadan: Ibadan University Press.
Shaw, T. 1969 (ed.). *Lectures on Nigerian prehistory and archaeology.* Ibadan: Oxford University Press.
Shaw, T. 1975 (ed.) *Discovering Nigeria's Past.* Ibadan: Ibadan University Press.
Shaw, T. 1977. *Unearthing Igbo-Ukwu.* Ibadan: Ibadan University Press.

Shaw, T. In press. The Neolithic of Africa. In *Food, metals, and towns in African history: African adaptations in subsistence and technology*, T. Shaw *et al.* (eds). London: Unwin Hyman.

Willett, F. 1960. Investigations at Old Oyo, 1956–57: an interim report. *Journal of the Historical Society of Nigeria* **2**(1), 59–77.

4 *Archaeology and education in Kenya*

SIMIYU WANDIBBA

Introduction

Systematic archaeological investigations in Kenya were begun by L. S. B. Leakey at the end of the 1920s (Leakey 1931). In line with the archaeological practice of the time, Leakey's main aim was to establish a chronocultural sequence of human activity in the country. Since then, significant archaeological work has continued in Kenya. In fact, in comparison with her East African neighbours, Kenya is far ahead in archaeological research. This is mainly due to the technical facilities that are available for comparative purposes, as well as the relatively advanced infrastructure that the country enjoys.

Despite the rich archaeological heritage and the comparatively long record of research in Kenya, the archaeological discipline remains generally neglected in the educational programmes of the country. This neglect is clearly seen not just at primary and secondary school levels but also at universities. At the time of independence, Kenya's formal educational system was very similar to that of England, both in structure and content. After eight years of primary and intermediate school, a successful student did four years of secondary school and two years of high school before going on to university. Changes in content were introduced soon after independence, and primary schooling was reduced to seven years. Most undergraduate degree programmes lasted for three years. A new system of education was introduced in 1986. According to this new system, students go through eight years of primary education, four years of secondary education and then go to university. Most of the degree programmes now take four years.

Archaeology was first introduced into the university curriculum in 1966. This is, however, something of an overstatement. Archaeology was not introduced as a subject as such. Rather it was introduced as part of history. This was perhaps to be expected in view of our European training and colonial experience.

Archaeology was considered merely as a means of extending the human historical record into the remote past, that is, beyond the realms of the written record. This is the type of training that the professors and lecturers in the Department of History of what was then the University College, Nairobi had received in Britain. It was thus natural for them to see the teaching of archaeology in Kenya through this European window. In fact, the new course was labelled 'Prehistory of the world'.

'Prehistory of the world' was made a compulsory course for all first-year history students. The course entailed a survey of the archaeological developments of the Old World. In general, however, it dealt mainly with Stone Age cultures. Having covered human evolution, the student was led through the Stone Age, the Neolithic period, a little bit of the Iron Age in Africa and the Palaeolithic Period of Asia and Europe. Although attempts were made to deal with the subject from a world perspective, this was never actually achieved. This course was in the main much more difficult than any of the history courses. Most students could hardly wait for the time when the examinations came and they were done with it. Many of them could be heard saying openly that all they wanted was to scrape through in this particular subject. There were two main factors responsible for this kind of student attitude.

First, of all the 'history' courses, archaeology was the only one to which the students were introduced for the first time at university level. I personally had never heard the term archaeology before I joined the university. To make matters worse, the subject was full of tongue-twisting scientific words. This was especially true of the lectures on human evolution. Additionally, one came across many prehistoric sites that were not only difficult to pronounce, but also to spell, especially those in Hungary and China.

The other problem emanated from the way the course was taught, and the facilities that were available. The course tended to be a mere catalogue of prehistoric sites and cultures. Consequently, it turned out to be not only difficult, but also quite dull. There was very little that could excite the students. To make matters worse, the teaching facilities were very rudimentary. For example, there was no laboratory for practical work, and the library lacked even basic texts on the subject. As we shall see later on in this chapter, these problems have continued to plague the teaching of archaeology at Kenya's oldest university, the University of Nairobi, nineteen years after it became an independent university, and twenty-three years since the course was first introduced.

After the first year, students could, and did, indeed, forget all about archaeology. Although there were many optional courses in the second year, archaeology was not one of them. It was not until the third year that the student once again met up with a little archaeology. This was, however, merely a background course to the history of Kenya, which was a compulsory course for all third-year history students. The course consisted of a few lectures on human evolution, the Stone Age, the Neolithic and the Iron Age in the country.

This structure of teaching archaeology continued until the 1972/73 academic year. It was, however, basically a history course. No wonder the programme failed to cultivate any interest or desire among the many students who passed through the department to pursue postgraduate studies in archaeology. Indeed, for the first seven years of the course's existence, only the present author, among the many hundreds of history students, was interested enough to indicate his desire to become an archaeologist, and actually went on to do so.

The 1970s

In the 1973/74 academic year, the Department of History introduced a new curriculum. Presumably one of the reasons for the introduction of the new course was to give students an opportunity to learn more about archaeology. In the first year, students were supposed to study two compulsory papers, one of which was the 'Prehistory of Africa'. In the second year, students not specializing in history had the option of studying the 'History of Kenya from the Stone Age to the present'. In this case, students could learn about the archaeology of Kenya as background to the history of the country. On the other hand, students specializing in history had to study the 'History of Kenya from the Stone Age to 1900'. They had the choice of doing so either in their second or third year.

This pattern of archaeological teaching continued until the 1975/76 academic year. In that year, the Department of History once again changed its curriculum. As a result of this change, first-year students no longer studied archaeology as a separate subject. Instead the subject was merely covered as one of the 'sources of African history'. 'The Prehistory of Africa' now became one of the 13 options available to second-year students. In general, this had the effect of reducing the importance of archaeology. Because of its technical terms, 'The Prehistory of Africa' was in many ways less attractive than any of the twelve history options.

As was the case during the pioneering period of tertiary education, the teaching of archaeology at the University of Nairobi and its constituent college, Kenyatta University College, suffered from a lack of adequate staff and facilities. For example, whereas the number of history lecturers continued to increase, there was no corresponding growth in the number of archaeology lecturers. In some cases the recruitment of the archaeology staff left much to be desired. For example, in one case recruitment was made of a person to teach African archaeology who specialized in Mesoamerican archaeology. This was done through a Kenyan friend of his who was a part-time lecturer in the department. In another instance, an Egyptologist was given one of the archaeology lectureships because his papers appear not to have been scrutinized properly. This type of recruitment was obviously not conducive to the development of archaeology as a respected university discipline.

Facilities continued to be rudimentary. For example, whereas laboratory space was acquired in the closing years of the 1970s, no attempt was made to equip the laboratory properly. In terms of books, the situation was hardly any better. Most books continued to be outdated. Books dealing with new developments in archaeology were not forthcoming. Neither did the department stock a wide range of archaeological or anthropological journals.

The 1980s

The beginning of the 1980s marked a turning point in the development of archaeological studies in this country. In 1980 a *de facto* sub-Department of Archaeology was established within the Department of History at the University of Nairobi. The idea was eventually to offer a fully fledged archaeology programme. This development was accompanied by the introduction in 1980/81 of a new curriculum that gave students their first chance to obtain a degree in archaeology. This degree structure is known as the 'BA in history (archaeology option)'.

According to this new curriculum students opting for archaeology took two papers in their first year, namely, 'Introduction to archaeology' and 'Sources in African history'. The first paper was a method and theory course that also included a cursory survey of world prehistory, whereas the second paper dealt with the various disciplines, including archaeology, and techniques available to the historian interested in African history. This did not, however, necessarily mean that such students were on their way to becoming archaeologists. They could still opt not to take archaeology courses in their second year, and could simply pursue courses in history. It was not until the second year, therefore, that those who wanted to become archaeologists would identify themselves by taking two more archaeology courses. The courses in question included the 'Prehistory of Africa' and 'Archaeology laboratory (including compulsory fieldwork)'. In addition such students took one history course, as well as a course in physical and historical geology.

In their third year, the archaeology option students took another two archaeology courses. These third-year courses included an area course and a dissertation. The area course was to be selected from a list that included Europe, the Mediterranean world, the Americas and Asia. Besides these archaeology courses, the students took a course in both geomorphology and history.

Thus to qualify for a BA in archaeology, the student took a total of ten courses. Out of these courses, however, only five were in archaeology. Of the remaining five, three were in history (see Appendix 1, p. 308). This means that archaeology students still had to do 'too many' history courses. The necessity of this is not immediately apparent. However, it might be attributed to the 'conspiracy' of historians to keep archaeology as part of history. This is probably the reason why archaeology still remains a *de facto* subdepartment. The value of the two earth science courses is, of course, clear. They were meant to give the student the necessary tools to study and interpret archaeological sites in their environmental context.

During 1983/84 the Department of History once again introduced changes in its course structure. As had always been the case, such changes also affected the archaeology programme (see Appendix 2, p. 309).

When the new system of education was launched in our public universities in 1990 a new programme of archaeology was started. The aim of this new programme is to ultimately establish a *de jure* subdepartment of archaeology. In this new programme students taking archaeology will now only take one course in history, namely, the 'History of Kenya'. However, staffing is still a problem. At the moment there are four archaeologists and one physical anthropologist. Of the four, two are on study leave while the third one is an expatriate on a one-year contract. The physical anthropologist is also an expatriate who is doing his last tour. This may mean that the new programme might lack proper implementation because of inadequate staffing.

Conclusions

One of the main points to emerge from the preceding survey is that in Kenya archaeology is still considered as part of history. Students in both primary and secondary schools normally learn bits of archaeology by way of background to their history classes. Textbooks for such courses are usually written by historians who, because they see archaeology as part of history, do not bother even to consult archaeologists. The result is disastrous in that such books end up containing information that is generally out of date and also downright inaccurate. In one official textbook for lower secondary classes, for example, the Ethiopian hominid Lucy is assigned to *Homo erectus*, when in fact it is an australopithecine. In the same book it is recorded *as a fact* that prehistoric communities hafted tools using gum and resin.

At university, archaeology continues to be taught as background to the history of Africa, or to whatever African region is being studied. Historians normally do not ask their archaeology colleagues to give such lectures, merely assuming that they know enough to give the lectures themselves. This practice has been, in my view, one of the main obstacles preventing the development of a viable archaeology programme for university education in Kenya. Other obstacles include lack of basic facilities, and the fact that jobs for archaeologists have not been created systematically. Another major problem is that the main publishing houses in Kenya are largely foreign, and their chief interest is in publishing school text books. Their main concern is making profit. Thus they are not interested in publishing more specialized books that do not sell quickly. No wonder that for a long time now no books have been published locally on the archaeology of Kenya or East Africa.

Regarding job opportunities for archaeologists, one can say that at the moment we do not know how many archaeologists we need. Many students therefore ask themselves what they would do if they were to study archaeology at university. The problem is aggravated by the fact that Kenyans generally feel that once one has studied archaeology one cannot do any job other than become an archaeologist. This, of course, is a misconception. Another problem concerns the expatriate staff who have usually been recruited on two-term tours. When they leave this creates problems of continuity. In any case, people who know they are here for just four years or so are less likely to be inclined to develop a programme they know will not benefit them in the long run. Furthermore, these expatriates find it difficult to devote all their energies to teaching, either because they are busy looking for jobs elsewhere, or are trying to improve on their curricula vitae. Lastly, none of the expatriates so far recruited has had the experience of teaching elsewhere before coming to Kenya. This has naturally deprived the programme of the benefits of experience.

This problem of staffing has mainly been caused by lack of understanding on the part of those who deal with the recruitment of staff at the University of Nairobi. Unlike in other disciplines, where prospective local candidates are hired as tutorial fellows or graduate assistants and then trained to join the staff, archaeology has generally been left out in the cold.

For a long time, the training of archaeologists has largely been facilitated through the National Museums of Kenya. The National Museums allow archaeology students free access to their collections for practical classes and they have also assisted some students with the financial support necessary to complete dissertations. Furthermore, there are students in the USA who originally obtained scholarships through bilateral arrangements between the National Museums and specific American institutions such as Bryn Mawr College and the Smithsonian Institution in Washington. The other contribution made towards the training of Kenyan archaeologists was the author's secondment to the University of Nairobi from the National Museums to teach on a part-time basis, until 1989. Finally, the National Museums were for quite some time generally the main employer of all archaeology students coming through the University of Nairobi. This availability of jobs with the museums appears to have encouraged some undergraduates to opt for the university archaeology programme.

Physical facilities are still at a rudimentary level. Archaeology books and journals are generally not available. Thus students have to rely mainly on libraries at the National Museums and the British Institute in Eastern Africa. The latter has a similar status to the British School in Athens or Rome, and undertakes archaeological and related research in Eastern Africa. The Institute has been assisting archaeology students by allowing them access to its library facilities, as well as providing scholarships to some students, or including them in its field projects. Without a good library archaeology cannot develop into a healthy and competitive university discipline. Similarly, laboratory equipment as well as excavation gear are either lacking, or in dire need of improvement. In fact, up to now the archaeology subdepartment of the Institute has no laboratory at all, and students have to come to the National Museums to do their practicals.

Finally, many people in Kenya remain ignorant of what archaeology is. This lack of archaeological awareness is in part due to the paucity of coverage that the profession receives from the mass media which only rarely report on archaeological work. Thus the National Museums have to rely on their Education Department to publicize archaeological activities. This is done through lectures to primary school children as well as to students of postprimary institutions. But this outlet is still insufficient to promote archaeology adequately in Kenya.

Appendices

Two appendices indicating the Archaeology option for a B.A. in History are shown on pp. 308–9.

Acknowledgement

I am grateful to Karega-Munene for his comments on an earlier draft of this chapter.

Reference

Leakey, L. S. B. 1931. *The Stone Age cultures of Kenya Colony*. Cambridge: Cambridge University Press.

5 Education and the political manipulation of history in Venezuela

IRAIDA VARGAS ARENAS &
MARIO SANOJA OBEDIENTE

(translated by Erif Rison)*

The subject of education has been addressed by many different authors from many different theoretical viewpoints. This chapter analyses it from a perspective of historical materialism. And although the central analysis is the political manipulation of history, it is obvious that such manipulation is only possible through education, both formal and informal.

This chapter presents some ideas on how the teaching of history in Venezuela has been the central element that sustains the process of neocolonialization of the Venezuelan people. Other authors have analysed the role of educators in this process (Bigott 1978, Solórzano 1979). Here, the focus is on the analysis of history. An underlying assumption is that any observer of the social life of a people has an obligation to educate, to project ideas about what is being researched, because that research is not merely an academic exercise but also has a social function: to know, explain, and thus assist in social change.

The Venezuelan educational system distorts and hides our past in order to prevent us from finding our historical roots. As such it constitutes the fundamental ingredient of neocolonialism (Bigott 1978). The disastrous effects of the teaching of 'official' history on the Venezuelan people has been analysed elsewhere (Quintero *et al.* 1976). From the perspective of social psychology (Montero 1984), the indigenous Venezuelan has a negative self-image, linked to the formation of the Venezuelan nation, a reflection of its condition of dependence and a result of ideological alienation. This ideological alienation has been implemented and reinforced by the ideological apparatus of the Venezuelan state, basically through the teaching of a certain type of Venezuelan history.

For Bigott (1978, p. 28), the neocolonialist exterminates the ethos of a people, their nature and their culture; we would add that the neocolonialist also strips a people of their historical memory. Learning reinforces the alienation, injects into the individual's consciousness a lack of historical

*National Association of Citizens' Advice Bureaux, London.

awareness, and converts the person into an object rather than a subject. Such learning creates a passive observer, removing the capacity to act for change by taking away the individual's capacity to recognize reality as it is. This process of incapacitation is achieved by 'wiping out' that person's historical reality, by disfiguring national history, and then by constructing 'a new panorama through false images of what his country has been' (Bigott 1978, p. 59).

Official history

Official history is the history of manipulation. History has to be politically manipulated because knowledge of real history – of the objective processes lived through by the people – constitutes the only means of explaining the present state of Venezuela – its political, economic, social and cultural dependence. Objective knowledge of history is a weapon of liberation because it shows the origin and character of the present condition of exploitation of the people and, at the same time, that this condition is transitory (Lumbreras, 1981).

The teaching of an official history achieves what traditional educational theory proclaims it should: 'to adapt the young generation to the human relations operating within a society' (Suchodolski 1966). In this way, an individual is created fit for the needs and tasks of society. But who defines these needs and social tasks? It is evident that in the case of Venezuela, and all those countries dependent on transnational centres of power, it is a definition made by the ruling class. This social class (consisting of the national and transnational bourgeoisies) needs to create a special kind of student – and thus a kind of workforce – and a special kind of political leader who will participate in society according to certain rules of behaviour, rules that do not interfere with its interests. Thus school becomes the means of reproducing the conditions of life of the capitalist system, and the conditions of exploitation.

It is useful to ask 'what is official history?' It is that which contradicts our scientific conviction that there are no discontinuities in history; it is that which denies the continuity of economic, social and political life and, thus, it is that which destroys social development. Official history tolerates explanation based on 'accidents'. Finally, it is that which nullifies daily happenings and chores, negates creativity, renovation, movement, and that which eliminates historical variables. It freezes historical factors and segments them into self-contained, self-explanatory blocks, with no projection. It creates chronological blocks of personalities, of trivialities, of contracted historical facts, which it sets within a limited timespan of depression, of momentary oddities, of banal changes which mark our lives for ever. History, when it is made official, is displaced from its function as the axis of social life. When history is weakened, ignored, and distorted, it produces a structural break that encourages dependence, i.e. colonialism.

The political manipulation of history implies the support of the machinery of power through political and social sources. What makes this power possible is the class structure, supported by economic power. The outstanding feature of this process is demonstrated by the privileges of the bourgeoisie, which needs to alienate the rest of the country in order to control it. In this way, ideology fulfils a strategic role in structuring power and in sustaining and reproducing that power. The alienation that the incomprehension and manipulation of history presupposes rests on the basis of claiming that the life of the Venezuelan nation – its history – was structured by chronologically separate periods. Each one of these periods, it is said, is identified as a group of variables whose effect extends only to the period under consideration. Thus causal factors, changes, and effects are not seen as linked.

Because of this, each period is left behind in the past, without any possibility of projecting itself into the future. For this reason, history is converted into the accumulation of experiences that may be interesting to know about but that are seen to have neither any connection with the contemporary situation nor any relevance to future change. Because of this it is not surprising that the history of Venezuela is taught segmented into periods: the pre-Hispanic, the colonial, the republican, the contemporary. Each period is taught as if unrelated to the other, except in terms of a chronological sequence.

The content of what is taught

Coupled with this situation of dysfunction is the content of what is taught. The weight given in education programmes at different levels to each period is not the same, and the selectivity of the information taught demonstrates the existence of a hierarchy of what it is felt important to teach. To this hierarchy can be added the injection of foreign values. Quintero (1970) indicates that the growth of foreign values, which in the long term results in our undervaluing ourselves, is reflected in a weakening of our potential for achievement. The negative values perpetuated by the teaching of official history proceed from the belief that the Indian is lazy, the black rude, and the Spanish an opportunist (Colmenarez in prep.). These values are fixed in the everyday consciousness of Venezuelans and are also reflex assumptions. In this way, affirmation of domination is produced as much through the transmission and acceptance of alien and negative values as through the ways in which the transmission takes place (Quintero et al. 1976).

'Informal' education

Such a situation of alienation is reinforced, stimulated, and sustained by so-called 'informal' education. Consisting of the media of mass communication (radio, cinema, television, the press, and so on), this is propped up by other educational tools such as museums. Museums should be motivators for the development of human thought, pointing out peculiarities, dissimilarities, similarities, and connections between the historical processes of different peoples. They should be didactic tools enabling people to connect facts, objects, and pictures to real life. They should provide incentives for reflection and for the private study of history. Such museums do not exist in Venezuela.

Venezuela is perhaps the only country in Latin America with the doubtful honour of having almost no museums of history (nor of anthropology), and this is no accident. Neither is the proliferation of museums of art, of automobiles, and so on, which constitute the legitimization of Western culture, 'the true culture', the one which we not only claim to preserve, but which is being imposed (Vargas & Sanoja 1988).

The absence of museums of history is consistent with the image of Venezuelan historical roots offered by formal education. Bigott (1978, p. 68) says

> the image which is transmitted today of the aboriginal people is not accidental, this is not a lamentable carelessness on the part of the Ministry of Education that they should approve the texts as being in accordance with the official education programmes; this image is not a product of the ignorance of the person who writes the texts, it is simply the logical process of devaluation which the colonialist perspective of history imposes on us.

Despite the fact that scientific research, including that of archaeology, demonstrates the importance of historical processes, information about our preconquest aboriginal peoples always reiterates negative stereotypes. It denies them any creative capacity.

A brief review of the teaching of history in Venezuela

When the history of Venezuela is discussed there is a tendency to take account of a block of time that begins at the end of the 15th century, when Columbus and his crew disembarked on the soil of the American continent and made contact with the Indian societies that inhabited the northeast of Venezuela. This leaves out the numerous groups of hunter-gatherer tribes, who for more than 15 000 years were accumulating native technological expertise. Yet despite the disruption that Indian society suffered as a result of conquest, indigenous technological skills were maintained and continued to support not only daily life but also the manufacture of consumer goods for mercantile capitalist trade between Venezuela and the Spanish empire.

It is therefore extremely important to be aware of the material and social achievements of pre-Hispanic Indian society, as well as its contribution to the consolidation of the Venezuelan nation and, subsequently, of the national state. These contributions have been obscured, partly through the isolation of the archaeological discipline, which works independently of other social sciences, and partly because of a 'folklore' approach to indigenous knowledge and techniques, which has failed to appreciate the historical dimension of this field of study. Finally, these contributions have also been obscured as a result of official documentary history, which has been concerned only with explanations of the origins of colonial institutions or with military explanations of the independence process.

Why the past is important

Examination of history should not be seen only in terms of its academic importance as a study of the past. On the contrary. It is important because it is the reason for the present. Such an approach demands a radical change to the existing concept of history as comprising exclusive blocks of chronology that can only be interpreted by similarly separate blocks of knowledge, such as anthropology or documentary history. Such a change implies a vision of history as a general process, whose main aim is the explanation of the social and material achievements of the Venezuelan people and the Indian societies which preceded them. Only by recognizing the historical unity of the Venezuelan nation, and of the cultural heritage that unites the diversity of its society and identity, can education be given a positive content.

How the past is processed

The study of the past in Venezuela is carried out in universities and official and private research centres. Nearly all the written results of these studies have a limited and specialist circulation. Officially the wider dissemination of such knowledge is entrusted to the Ministry of Education. In fact, however, the final products about national history are in the hands of private publishing businesses that market primary and secondary school textbooks.

This process has caused the impoverishment of information about national history, which has been reduced to a collection of stereotypes and sketchy formulas. As a result the general processes of history have become isolated, and students of history have become antagonistic towards the origins of their own people.

The changed status of educators

Until the 1950s, the training of educators, particularly primary school teachers, took place in teacher training institutes or National Schools. The aspiring teacher, having left school, went on to training that integrated the different fields of knowledge required for primary school teaching. This meant that the trained teacher had, in a way, a systematic understanding of the interrelatedness of the different disciplines of the social and natural sciences, which together formed the basis of the teaching material that was communicated through the education process. What was important in that training process was that the teacher could, and was expected to, develop (within the general programme of the school) the type of learning that was to be passed on to the students. Such flexibility gave teachers the chance to evaluate the subject critically, particularly history. It was not by chance that Venezuelan teachers took an avant-garde position in politics until the 1950s. It was their training in critical analysis that led them to adopt a questioning ideological position within a social environment still marked by the intolerance of the ruling class.

It was the progressive nature of teachers and the possibility of powerful education unions being formed, with teachers becoming a political resource, that led the ruling class in the 1960s to perceive a threat to the reproduction of the ideology of a system that was formally democratic, but in practice still unstable. As a consequence teachers were recruited into regimented unions and the breadth of critical training was reduced.

From the 1970s onwards training changed radically. Student teachers began to receive information and training about teaching itself, that is to say the ideology that should govern the educational process. The content of the educational process was no longer determined by the teacher, but by the ruling class. Books were prescribed for every educational level and the teachers were told what they should be communicating. This was a clear ideological line to be reproduced through the educational process.

The way in which this process has been carried out has induced confusion about learning in the students of today. In the case of history, there is a feeling of timelessness about the steps marking the process towards the creation of the Venezuelan nation. Venezuelan history is taught badly, not so much in terms of its content, but rather in the way historical facts have been ordered.

The development of basic schools

In the 1970s, work started on a new educational proposal, the basic school. The central objective of the basic school was to organize teaching into areas of critical understanding. Teachers were supposed to lead students towards an understanding of global social and historical processes, within a subject area called 'social thought and national identity', which also involved guiding students towards an understanding of their social, historical, and natural surroundings. The basic concept was of the nation as a cultural and regional plurality.

This notion of plurality met with fierce resistance from the traditional ruling class, who had always advocated a centralist vision, not only of administration and politics, but also of historical, social, and cultural ideology. The Venezuelan state, whatever its political coloration, has always tried to stimulate a uniform national culture in order to support centralism. This is perhaps a result of the secession of various provinces from the federation at the time of the first republican constitution of 1811, and the territorial uncertainty that characterized the 19th century and the beginning of the 20th century.

History teaching has always been seen by the traditional ruling classes as a strategic area, vital to guarantee the stability, not only of the system, but also of the privileges of certain power groups. For this reason the historiography of the last five centuries of our people has detracted from the historiography of the global process of the formation of the Venezuelan nation.

Writing out Indian societies

The central concept of Venezuelan historiography has been the civilizing role of Spain. Before the 16th century, it is claimed, neither history nor culture existed; Indian societies had contributed nothing to the formation of the nation. With hardly any sociohistorical developments, Indians were assimilated and swallowed up immediately by Spanish culture. Official history, therefore, says little about Indian societies, either pre-Hispanic or post-Columbian, since the origins of the nation only existed in the Spanish colonial institutions. Consistent with this posture, other disciplines like archaeology and anthropology have, generally, seen the Venezuelan Indians as objects of academic study, effectively separate from the national process. This attitude has been especially evident in Venezuelan anthropology, leading consciously or unconsciously to the creation of a division between the aboriginal past and the role of the Indians in building the Venezuelan nation and the national state. Indian groups that have survived as autonomous cultural units since the 16th century have been treated as historical forms alien to the national process. As a result there is a general educational consensus, a view also shared by the ruling class, about a pre-Hispanic past that is only capable of being evaluated in exotic terms, and not in a way equivalent to the colonial past. This pre-Hispanic past can only be appreciated aesthetically through the notion of pre-Hispanic art.

With only a few exceptions, basic research in history, archaeology, and anthropology (not to mention other social science disciplines) has contributed to the strengthening of the division of Venezuelan history into separate chronological and cultural blocks. The results of this research, when introduced into the educational system, have reinforced the stereotypes of official historiography which, together with the educational philosophy of the state, has contributed to the creation of the idea of a past with no historical time, and relativism, which virtually removes any notion of historical consciousness.

By implicitly denying the historical contemporaneity of present Indian communities and the rest of national society, ethnopopulists (Diaz Polanco 1985) have already sealed the future destiny of the Indian communities and also that of the historical past that could legitimate their existence as part of the cultural plurality of the society or the nation. They classify such people as objects for study and not as part of a cultural heritage that should be rescued and preserved as an overall process of social change. Such a cultural heritage should, in reality, be the patrimony accommodating the cumulative processes of the work and intellectual creativity of the Venezuelan peoples (Vargas & Sanoja 1988).

Today we are witnessing a process of rebirth in teaching through the basic schools. This is a laudable initiative but lacks the didactic resources necessary to encourage teachers to develop a new philosophical stance in teaching and the practice of education. The rebirth of education cannot be done by an administrative decision alone. As far as teaching history and the social sciences is concerned, it is essential to create new philosophical premises to guide strategic historical research.

The fundamental task of science is to transform society, not just to describe it. This is especially important in the context of historical enquiry. Science must provide explanations for changes within society, and eliminate value judgements, as well as stereotypes and environmental determinism. Without such elimination we will never achieve an independent historical development.

Teaching museums and history for the masses

Few countries have suffered as much neglect of the past as has Venezuela. There is a virtual absence of national or regional history museums that could be used as reference points for historical research. There is therefore no way in which teachers and students can stimulate or reinforce their historical consciousness. This is particularly unfortunate in a situation – such as that of the basic school – in which teachers and students are required to maintain a certain level of autonomy and individual participation in the historical process.

As has been seen earlier in this chapter, museums are only allowed in Venezuela when they do not challenge the validity of official versions of national history. Thus, no one objects to the creation of museums of art, where the relation between the spectator and the object is strictly personal, one of momentary aesthetic enjoyment, nor of museums of history that are merely descriptive and acontextual. Teaching museums, such as we have proposed on different occasions (Sanoja 1982, pp. 22–30, 1986, Sanoja & Vargas 1986) are a quite different matter. They aim to promote critical reflection by contextualizing the facts of history as a general process, and by emphasizing museum exhibitions relating to theories about such processes – at national or regional levels – while developing the mechanisms or strategies for critical analysis of the contents.

Such museums should be integrated into the systems of formal and informal education, although not conditioned by them. Research for teaching museums generally results in ideas and reinterpretations about historical processes that can be readily assimilated in a museum environment, but which would take years to be accepted within formal educational programmes.

In this way teaching museums would constitute one of the pillars of dialectical education: formal programme content (in school), research, and generation of critical analysis of what has been taught in school and museum. In addition, teaching museums would reassemble into an organic whole those historical keystones that are imperceptible in daily life, thus helping to raise awareness of the human experiences of work and collective efforts.

Culture, history, and education constitute a strategic area in Venezuela's national plans. This has been so before, in times of crisis when it became critical to develop processes to encourage people to identify with the cultural heritage of the nation.

Since the 1960s, with the consolidation of the democratic system and the economic stability deriving from petroleum earnings, there has been no museum development aiming to reflect the historical, social, and cultural foundations of the Venezuelan people. On the contrary, official cultural policy has given its support to elitist creative manifestations. Fine arts has been promoted to the rank of 'national culture', while the National Institute of Folklore, which deals with the literary and musical work of peasants and Indians, as well as carrying out archaeological work, has been cut back. New museums of art have been created, whereas the Museum of National Sciences, which contained exhibitions on some elements of the pre-Columbian past, has been quietly allowed to die.

Culture and education have now been officially separated as a result of the creation of the National Institute of Culture and Fine Arts, into which have been subsumed areas previously the responsibility of the National Institute of Folklore. The teaching of Venezuelan history is thus becoming dissipated into different arenas.

'Three Cultures, One Nation'

The only recent museum experiment seeking to demonstrate the component parts of the Venezuelan cultural heritage has been the exhibition entitled 'Three Cultures, One Nation', which was organized by the authors under the auspices of the Central University of Venezuela to celebrate the bicentennial of the birthday of Simon Bolivar. This exhibition became the 'Museum of Venezuelan Man', but was closed down in 1987. Prior to this, it had cooperated with schools, developing a programme of guided visits with student discussions, workshops on history teaching for school teachers, and creative workshops for children.

The 'Three Cultures, One Nation' exhibition aimed to demonstrate the confluence of the ethnic, social and cultural factors that have influenced the historical process forming the Venezuelan nation, and also sought to demonstrate the historical and active nature of Indian, peasant and urban cultures, thus creating a sense of overall value. It was undoubtedly the utilitarian concept of culture and the absence of any real consciousness of history on the part of the university authorities of the time that led to the abandonment of what could have been an extraordinary tool for taking university culture out to the community.

Conclusions: future perspectives for the teaching of history

Individual preferment in Venezuela is so intimately linked to the effective political, economic, and social system that no real change in education will be possible without a corresponding structural change in the country itself. There is, therefore, reason to be pessimistic about the future of education, and the creation of an historical sense in Venezuelan society, if present negative conditions persist.

Marx (1843, quoted in Suchodolski 1966, p. 6) has shown how education is indissolubly linked to social change:

> Educational work is understood as a social and political activity which is determinedly opposed to the concept of autonomous thought and to autonomous action on alien consciousness . . . the work of education is conceived . . . as work which leads to 'something', as opposed to retrospective concepts according to which man is formed by tradition, and not by participation in what he creates and desires.

Marx also explained that education in a class society is a tool for strengthening the power of the ruling classes because it supports and propagates ideology useful to them.

The understanding of history and the raising of the consciousness of educators to enable them to spread their message are tasks which cannot be put off. An educational system which tries to create a solid feeling of individuals belonging historically to the nation, and to their natural, social, and cultural surroundings as well as to their daily lives, is necessary to ensure either an advanced independent capitalist society or a just, democratic, and independent socialist society.

As Heller said,

> the invincibility of the substance of, and development of, values – a possibility *even in a situation of erosion of moral values* constitutes the essence of history, because *history is continuous*, despite its discrete character and precisely because that continuity is the substance of society. (1985, p. 35, our italics)

Only the creative search for historical and social knowledge will promote a critical consciousness of this historical stage of Venezuelan society and lay a foundation for the structural change that would turn Venezuelan society towards true democracy.

References

Bigott, L. 1978. *El Educador Neocolonizado*. Caracas: Editorial La Ensenanza Viva, 3rd Edn.

Colmenarez, L. in prep. *Tesis de grado sobre la historia precolonial*. Escuela la de Antropología. Universidad Central de Venezuela.

Diaz Polanco, H. 1985. *La cuestion etnico-nacional*. Mexico: Editorial Linea.

Heller, A. 1985. *Historia y vida cotidiana*. Mexico: Editorial Grijalbo.

Lumbreras, L. 1981. *La arqueología como ciencia social*. Lima: Ediciones PEISA.

Montero, M. 1984. *Ideología, alienación e identidad nacional*. Caracas: Universidad Central de Venezuela. Ediciones de la Biblioteca.

Quintero, M. 1970. *La colonización cultural a traves de la literatura infantil*. Merida: Universidad de Los Andes. Escuela de Educación.

Quintero, M. *et al*. 1976. La colonización cultural y la colonización idealogica a traves de los nuevos programas de educación primaria. *Cuadernos de Educación* **31**. Caracas: Laboratorio Educativo.

Sanoja, M. 1982. La politica cultural y la preservación del patrimonio cultural de America Latina. En: *Arquelogía de rescate*. Primera conferencia de arquelogía de rescate del Nuevo Mundo. Washington: The Preservation Press.

Sanoja, M. 1986. *El Museo Ecologico de Maturin, Estado, Venezuela. Consideraciones teoricas y metodologicas sobre su desarrollo*. Ponencia presetada en el Seminario Museos y Educación. Guadalajara: Unesco.

Sanoja, M. & I. Vargas 1986. Cultural resource management and environmental education in Venezuela: a proposal. In *Public archaeology and cultural resource management*. World Archaeological Congress (mimeo).

Solórzano, A. 1979. *Educación y lucha politica*. Caracas: Editorial Verbo Critico.

Suchodolski, B. 1966. *Teoría Marxista de la Educación*. Mexico: Editorial Grijalbo.

Vargas, I. & M. Sanoja 1988. *Patrimonio Cultural Inventario o Proceso Historico?* Ponencia presentada en el V Simposia de la Fundación de Arqueología del Caribe, dedicado al tema del Patrimonio Cultural. Rio Caribe.

6 *The right to a past: Namibian history and the struggle for national liberation*

MANFRED O. HINZ

The educational context

Access to long-term formal education within Namibia is severely limited for Black Namibians. In 1981, 93 per cent of Black children began primary school: 83 per cent of them left school before completing primary education, and only 7.5 per cent went on to secondary school. By contrast, almost 100 per cent of White children and 50 per cent of 'Coloured' (mixed race) children began secondary school. Further evidence of the discriminatory effect of official Namibian education is derived from looking at the annual expenditure on each pupil. For a White pupil, an average of Rand 1042 per annum is expended. For a Coloured pupil, the average expense is Rand 614. No precise information is available for Black pupils, but the figure is less than Rand 150 (Hinz 1988b). The teacher–pupil ratio tells a similar story. For White children it is 1:13, for Coloureds it is 1:28, while Black pupils have to be content with a ratio of 1:37. These figures become more telling if the teacher–pupil ratio is seen in conjunction with the ratio of trained and untrained or insufficiently trained teachers, which has been deteriorating. In 1971, one in three teachers had no training, or training that was insufficient. In 1983 the proportion of teachers lacking training had risen to 60 per cent. The use of Afrikaans as the only official language in school further limits the value of education for the Black majority.

The Namibia Project

In an attempt to compensate for the deficiences of this system, an alternative education system has been set up in the South West Africa People's Organization's (SWAPO) education and health centres (Hinz 1988b). As part of this nonracist education policy, the Namibia Project started in 1980 as a cooperative scheme supported by the University of Bremen and the United Nations Institute for Namibia located in Lusaka, Zambia. The Project formulates its research and practical activities as a result of consultation between the Project partners in Lusaka, Bremen and Luauda, the home of

SWAPO of Namibia. The general aim of the Project is to make a practical sociological and pedagogical contribution to prepare Namibia for the time following independence.

The Namibia Institute was founded in 1976 by the United Nations in order to counteract the deficiency in training, education and research that had arisen in Namibia as a result of South African colonialism. This had led to an almost complete exclusion of the majority Black population from the possibility of skilled work.

'To be born a nation': the right to a past

'To be born a nation' is the title of the first comprehensive portrayal of Namibian history that the majority of those living in the country can endorse. The subtitle 'The liberation struggle for Namibia' underlines the political relationship of the search for a past with contemporary society. The title is taken from a political slogan first used in the liberation struggle for Mozambique: 'to die a tribe and be born a nation'. It encapsulates the drive for unity and the bonds forged through common endeavour and sacrifice that are such vital elements of the national liberation struggle (Katjavivi 1981). This connecting up of history and the liberation struggle links past, present, and future in a continuum that relates the liberation struggle of today to the events of the precolonial and colonial past. In this respect, a past is being discussed that does not exist within the current official curriculum. What do exist are, on the one side, heroes of colonial 'pacification' (traders, missionaries and settlers), and, on the other, 'thieving', 'barbaric', 'despotic' 'tribes', all warring against one another.

The present official curriculum shows very plainly the dimension of the right to a past and the relationship between Namibian history and national liberation. An uncritical clinging to the previously largely undisputed official 'South West African' history suggests that it is an important component of the general policy of 'separate development' or apartheid. The central importance of this education policy can be seen in the way that state censorship is used to exclude alternative views of the past by banning textbooks such as *Our Namibia* and *Lehrbuch Namibia* (*Weekly Mail* 8–14 May 1987 and 15–21 May 1987). Possessing one's own past means questioning White superiority. Demanding the right to one's own past means removing White superiority.

From the right to a past to the necessity of 'double decolonialization'

It is not simply colonialism as such that stands in the way of the right to a past of one's own. The complexity of the present-day colonial consciousness is remarkable. Over a hundred years after the start of German colonial domination of Namibia, there were widespread calls for the renaming of a street (in the Federal Republic of Germany) that currently bears the name of the Bremen merchant F. A. E. Lüderitz, who pioneered the colonialization of Namibia.

These calls have been met with an array of delaying tactics – including physical violence – that continue to prevent the renaming of the street. Whoever calls what German colonialism did in Namibia in the years 1904–18 by its true name, genocide, will similarly encounter colonial consciousness structures which will designate him, according to taste, as a 'fouler of his own nest' or 'a Communist'. To talk of the actuality of the colonial relationship in this way means more than pointing to the present situation in Namibia, where the South African colonial regime oppresses the majority of the population. The fight against colonialism means fighting colonialism both in the colonized state, in this case Namibia, and in the 'mother country' – in this case West Germany.

Decolonialization demands a double change, a change both in Namibia and West Germany. Decolonialization that ends when the formal structures of colonialism have been removed has stopped halfway. Only when the colonial relationship is tackled as a whole does decolonialization achieve its aim, and this includes, in particular, accepting colonial consciousness as the subject of debate. In the preliminary considerations for the Namibia Project the question was apparently the simple one of helping to meet deficiencies in the education and health centres of Namibian refugee camps by producing teaching materials concerned with the country. However, in the attempt to organize the cooperative project, it became clear how such apparent simplicity was misleading.

On closer inspection it proved that more was necessary than the readiness to cooperate in a partnership. It became apparent that any jointly conceived work could easily result in the work affecting both the former oppressors and the currently oppressed. Both groups were faced with similar problems in the quality and content of existing teaching materials. Equally, the fact that in both Bremen and in Windhoek there was (and is) a Lüderitzstrasse reflected a common problem. Initially it was unclear whether the non-Namibian side of the Project would be in a position to cut through the 'colonial thicket' without causing divisions among themselves. It was also unclear as to whether or not the Namibian participants would recognize the extent of the changes and turnarounds necessary within their *own* society.

It soon became clear that the theoretical debate had wide-ranging practical implications. It was only possible to fuse approaches of the Third and Fourth Worlds to the dialectics of the colonial relationship once the central concept of 'double decolonialization' had been accepted. In practice this decision meant that in addition to the original aim of producing a Namibian social science textbook, a further publication was conceived of for the German-speaking public. The outline was thus created for *Our Namibia: a social studies textbook* (Melber 1986) and *Lehrbuch Namibia* (Patemann 1984). *Our Namibia* is used principally at the junior secondary level in Namibian exile schools, but is also employed for adult education. *Lehrbuch Namibia* was so conceived that individual chapters could be used as and where opportunities arose within the middle school curriculum in the individual states of the Federal Republic of Germany. In addition, the book has achieved importance as a general introduction to Namibia.

In 1984 *Our Namibia* and *Lehrbuch Namibia* were presented publicly during a symposium on 'Education for liberation' (Hinz 1988a). The education authority responsible for Bremen, where the German side of the Project is located, combined its support in principle for *Lehrbuch Namibia* with the presentation of its own small brochure on the subject, which aimed to 'continue to think more critically in those regions where light and dark, good and evil, appear all too schematically' (Kuhlmann 1984). The production of the brochure by the education authority was generally welcomed. Taken alongside the authority's support for *Lehrbuch Namibia*, the brochure was seen as an extraordinary and exemplary readiness on the part of a state institution to be open to an alternative view of history, especially given that it was an alternative view from 'below'. That the education authority actually participated in the symposium and acknowledged the existence of an alternative view of history must be seen as the most successful possible practical result of the concept of 'double decolonialization'.

The second confirmation that the Project had been right in using the concept of 'double decolonialization' came from the unequivocal approval of the Namibian partner. In view of the fact that concepts such as 'double decolonialization' can easily slide into mere theory, and too often serve only European gratification, the Namibian view that the Project had been a learning success for all those involved was a matter for considerable pride.

Since the symposium a further phase of work has been completed. Following the model of *Our Namibia*, a history book, *Namibia in History* (Mbumba & Noisser 1988) has been produced for the junior secondary level and following the model of *Lehrbuch Namibia*, another publication *Ein Land, eine Zukunft* (Mbumba, Patemann & Katjivena 1988) has been produced for the upper secondary level, and for those generally interested in Namibian questions.

The principle of 'double decolonialization'

During a workshop held in Lusaka in 1985, when the first drafts for the two publications were discussed, a debate arose about the principle of 'double decolonialization' as a method of working and a means of insight. In particular the experience gained in working with *Our Namibia* and *Lehrbuch Namibia*, which had been channelled into the preparatory work on *Namibia in History* and *Ein Land, eine Zukunft*, had made possible a clearer structuring of individual elements of the principle of 'double decolonialization'. Essentially three elements were discerned that characterized it.

The first is that of a *change of viewpoint* Kuhlmann 1984. This follows the acceptance within critical social science that there is a connection between 'recognition' and 'interest'. The recognition of a social connection, and understanding it interpretatively, is therefore distinctly different according to which side of the fence the 'recognizer' stands. For one side an event can be a rebellion (which is to be suppressed), for the other an act of resistance (which is to be regarded with the greatest respect). Only a willingness to change a viewpoint can result in further insights and permit progress towards an understanding that is fair to the situation under discussion.

The second necessary element is the readiness to enter into a particular set of interests. Those who limit themselves to attributing cynical brutality to colonialism will not be able to comprehend fully the colonial relationship. Equally, those who limit themselves to acclaiming the heroism of resistance will miss in particular those forms of resistance that are apparently insignificant, since they lack any spectacular events, but still exert a long-term influence. In this way 'double decolonialization' requires 'understanding in context', against the contextual background.

The third element is based on the materialist view of history. It emphasizes that each particular social situation has the attribute of its own inherent laws of impulse. If we assume that becoming a victim of colonial oppression does not mean losing one's own history, then the social situation involved retains its own 'impulse'. Nothing changes the existence of this 'impulse' or its effect, no matter how much oppression prevents or warps development in practical detail. It is only if we accept the existence of this 'impulse' that we can show in what way historical resistance in Namibia against German colonial rule (despite genocide over a long period) could influence what today is the struggle for national liberation. It is only through the existence of this 'impulse' that groups that only a few years ago appeared totally incapable of action are today resisting colonial oppression. An example of this is the Namibian Peace Plan Study and Contact Group (NPPSG), which consists of White Namibians active within the country for the realization of the independence plans following Security Council Resolution 435 (1978) of the United Nations (NPPSG 1987).

From 'double decolonialization' to 'creative acquirement'

In 1986 the United Nations Institute for Namibia published its report *Namibia: Perspectives for National Reconstruction and Development*. Following an historical overview and a review of the macroeconomic structures, the report presented information on trends and perspectives on all sectors of Namibian society, and discussed the possibilities and necessities that would follow independence. The report reviewed many of the existing and ongoing individual projects in Namibia and attempted to place them within a context of Namibian plans for the future. It argued that the teaching material produced by the Namibia Project needed further development in the context of creating a viable social strategy after independence. Such development implies more than acquiring knowledge in the usual sense of learning being an acquisition of knowledge. It is, in a special way, 'creative acquirement' because it includes the practical realization of a situation which until now has only existed as a political Utopia. It is 'creative', since while fitting together the existing pieces of the jigsaw, it is necessary to fill in gaps, a process that can only be undertaken, because of the lack of practical experience, by the application of political imagination. 'Creative acquirement' occurs when, as happened in a contribution to *Ein Land, eine Zukunft* (Mbumba & Patemann 1988), Namibians go in search of their traditional idea of God, and find themselves standing in some bewilderment in front of a quarry containing not only broken pieces of religious icono-graphy, preserved after the missionaries had attempted to destroy the 'heathen' gods, but also such 'pieces' of their religion as are preserved in oral tradition. In putting these different pieces together, it is clear that the picture that emerges is by no means the original. God is reconstructed in the way that they (creatively) think should be done, and in putting the pieces together they find that a lot is missing. Lost? Or never in existence? In the end they discover that they have a God who is at one and the same time old and new.

'Creative acquirement' will be fundamentally important when the curren-tly oppressed majority takes over the inheritance of colonialism in a new social form. Symbols of oppression (e.g. statues and street names) will certainly disappear or be altered, while the laws and institutions of apartheid will vanish. However, much will remain and will presumably suddenly appear alien, since it cannot simply be accepted as it was before, but must be fitted into a new social relationship. This can apply just as much to German architecture from the period of the German Empire as to other cultural 'curiosities'. In this, 'creative acquirement' is by no means a one-way street. If the White minority is prepared to contribute after independence to the construction of a new society, it will have to accept 'creative acquirement' and become conversant with the things and ways of living of the Black majority.

'Creative acquirement' will probably become an extremely important principle of survival for a new Namibian society in the same way as it did when Zimbabwe emerged from Rhodesia. How far 'creative acquirement' will proceed, whether it can lead beyond a compromise into a new culture, is a matter for hope. Only when such a new culture is created will it be possible to say that the right to a past has effectively turned into the right to the present.

References

Hinz, M. O. (ed.) 1988a. *100 Years of colonialism, neocolonialism and struggle for freedom: education for liberation*. Bremen African Studies, Vol. 1. Bremen: University Press.
Hinz, M. O. 1988b. '*Our Namibia*' and *Lehrbuch Namibia* – two results of the Project'.

In *100 Years of colonialism, neocolonialism and struggle for freedom: education for Liberation...*, M. O. Hinz (ed.), 50–8. Bremen African Studies, Vol. 1. Bremen: University Press.

Katjavivi, P. 1981. Foreword. In *To be Born a Nation*. London: Department of Information and Publicity, SWAPO of Namibia.

Kuhlmann, C. 1984. 'Namibia in Schulunterricht' in *Lehrbuch Namibia*, H. Patemann (ed.). Osnabruck: Terre des hommes.

Mbumba, N. & N. Noisser 1988. *Namibia in History*. London: Zed Books.

Mbumba, N., H. Patemann & U. Katjivena 1988. *Ein Land, eine Zukunft*, Osnabruck: Terre des hommes.

Melber, H. 1986. *Our Namibia: A social studies textbook*. London: Zed Books.

Namibia Peace Plan Study and Contact Group, 1987. *The Choice! Namibia Peace Plan 435 or Society under Siege!* Windhoek: NPPSCG.

Patemann, H. 1984. *Lehrbuch Namibia*. Osnabruck: Terre des hommes.

United Nations Institute for Namibia, 1986. Namibia: perspectives for national reconstruction and development.

7 Still civilizing? Aborigines in Australian education

ALEX BARLOW

Education as colonization

For Australia's Aborigines and Torres Strait Islanders, education remains one of the main forces still maintaining them in a colonial relationship with all other Australians. It is no exaggeration to claim that all of the eight separate state and territory education bureaucracies that control Australian education still place 'civilizing' as the primary aim of aboriginal education. 'Civilizing' in education now means overcoming or changing those traits in students that are seen to stem from their Aboriginality, and are judged to impede their gaining competence in the set of core learning that constitutes the essential curriculum.

Modern colonialism takes many forms and is variously defined. President Sukarno, at the Bandung Conference in 1955, said 'colonialism has also its modern dress, in the form of economic control, by a small but alien community within a nation'. Elsewhere we read that 'colonialism has now come to be identified with rule over peoples of different race inhabiting lands separated by salt water from the imperial centre' (Sills 1968, p. 1). Belgium proposed to the United Nations around 1950 that colonialism should be defined to include 'all ethnically distinct minorities discriminated against in their home countries' (Sills 1968, p. 1).

None of these descriptions quite fits the colonialism that Aborigines and Torres Strait Islanders experience in Australia today. There is still the economic, intellectual and physical control Sukarno talked about, and there is discrimination against them as a racially distinct minority. Above all, though, the quality that most distinguishes the Australian form of colonialism is all-pervasive paternalism (Van den Berge 1970, pp. 21–41). In federal and state legislation, in the provision of government services, in media commentary, and in general public opinion, there is always the 'but' about Aborigines. Self-determination and self-management have been basic policy at federal and most state levels for at least the past 15 years. There has been a determined effort by these governments to listen to Aborigines and Torres Strait Islanders, by setting up all-Aboriginal and Islander advisory committees, and by staffing departments that deal with their affairs with as many Aborigines and Islanders as possible. Affirmative action tactics are used to make possible such appointments. Nevertheless there is always the anticipation that Aboriginal-run organizations will need to be rescued from administrative or financial irregularity, and that they will need to be propped up by non-Aboriginal 'experts' working in key positions in the organizations. Everyone says, of course, that this is only until Aboriginal 'experts' can be trained to replace them. Maybe so, yet even this is an overt form of paternalism. It certainly smacks of 'civilizing', of training Aborigines to conform to the bureaucratic mores of public service organizations, and of overcoming or changing undesirable traits believed to stem from their 'Aboriginality'. Howard (1982, p. 159) describes these 'experts' as an Aboriginal elite 'who serve as cultural brokers for their administration patrons'. He adds:

> The existing socio-economic system, of which Aboriginal brokers are an integral part, has served primarily to block Aboriginal bids for power and drain Aboriginal society of its intellectual resources by co-opting the better educated and more articulate Aborigines and incorporating them in a structure that functions to control Aborigines. The government has thus created a rather subtle structure of indirect rule.

Hartwig (1978, p. 119) has suggested that the concept of 'internal colonialism', as elaborated by Wolpe (1975) applies 'to many of the conditions of racial discrimination that have obtained within [Australia] in respect of Aborigines'. He argues (Hartwig 1978, pp. 119–20) that the theory:

1 best helps to explain the specific terms in which ideological and political domination over Aborigines have been expressed, by relating them to specific modes of exploitation of Aboriginal societies;
2 offers an adequate theoretical framework for an analysis of the intersection of class with race and ethnicity and of the profound duality – class/nation, integration/separation – that has characterised Aboriginal aspirations;
3 provides the best theoretical perspective for locating the history of Aboriginal–White relations in the comparative history of race and ethnic relations in situations brought about by the expansion of capitalism.

In Wolpe's formulation (1975, p. 120), internal colonialism exists when a 'former colonising racial or ethnic group occupies the same territory as the colonised people', so that 'the components of the normal imperial–colonial relation are to be found within the borders of a single state to an extent which justifies the view that it constitutes an internal colonialism'. The imperial–colonial relationship is characterized, says Hartwig (1978, p. 121), by its occurring between, among others, racial and ethnic groups, and it involves 'political domination, cultural oppression and economic exploitation'.

It is obviously serious and offensive to say that Aborigines and Torres

Strait Islanders remain today in a colonial relationship with all other Australians, and to place Australian education as one of the main forces maintaining that relationship. Nevertheless I maintain the claim because:

a educational practices and policies of the past and present have served to maintain political domination over Aborigines and Torres Strait Islanders;
b the teachings of Aboriginal studies in schools, to Aborigines and Torres Strait Islanders as well as to all other Australians, has led to cultural oppression;
c the use of the curriculum, at all educational levels, to discriminate against those Aborigines and Torres Strait Islanders who resist its assimilative aims results in economic disadvantage to many and to the economic exploitation of all.

Aborigines and Islanders: an educated people

The development of this argument should be prefaced with the firm acknowledgement that the concept of education and of its basic cultural, economic, and social purposes were fully known by Aborigines and Torres Strait Islanders. Before contact with Europeans, Aborigines, in particular, expected all individuals, both male and female, to acquire not only a great deal of natural scientific and social knowledge, through informal learning, but also to master and apply a set of cultural, religious, social, artistic, and philosophical knowledge, which they had a right to receive, and which was passed on to them in formal teaching and learning modes when they had demonstrated their readiness to receive it. Biernoff (1975) gives the sequence for initiation into sacred knowledge for a man. He lists 21 separate initiations spread in sequence over approximately 30 years, and he notes that a child whose first initiation took place when he was 12 would be at least 42 years old before having completed the full set of learning available to him. That learning covers all aspects of those ceremonies and parts of ceremonies that he has responsibility for either as owner, in the case of his father's law, or as a manager, in the case of his mother's. A man who completes all the learning to which he is entitled would have the status of the most eminent of scholars in Western society. Along with his knowledge of ritual and law, he would have an immense knowledge of the history of the land to which his ceremonial knowledge relates, and he would know the power of the forces of that land. With that knowledge went the responsibility to respect that power and to release it, through ritual re-enactment, for the good of the land and its living community.

It should be noted that women also had a fund of secret ritual knowledge that placed them, through inheritance, in a particular relationship with their family's land, and gave them ritual responsibility for it. Only recently has research begun to take note of the significance of women's ritual knowledge, and of the formal processes by which women were, and are, educated in this knowledge. Two other studies help to emphasize Aborigines' awareness of appropriate learning styles and experiences in the early stages of enculturation and socialization. Harris (1984) made a detailed study of Aboriginal learning styles with Aboriginal school-aged children in Milingimbi in eastern Arnhem Land, and Hamilton (1981) studied child-rearing at Maningrida in north-central Arnhem Land. As a result, Harris (1984, p. 20) maintained that a distinction could be made between traditional Aboriginal informal education and what he calls 'traditional non-institutional formal education', the latter characterized by: (a) the conscious formal transmission of values and beliefs; (b) being separated from everyday experience; and (c) being made the responsibility of the larger social group.

Education and political domination

When, in the eighteenth century, Governor Phillip began capturing Aborigines like Colbee, Arabanoo and Bennalong with a view to resocializing them and then releasing them as ambassadors of good will, to speak well of the 'new settlers', he certainly had no perception of Aborigines as an educated people. Nor, of course, had he any understanding of the complexity of Aboriginal social organization, of the laws that directed both the economic use and the spiritual renewal of land, and of the evidence, which has since been discovered, of the long history of Aboriginal occupation of the land. Phillip's instructions (quoted in Stone 1974, p. 19) had been explicit:

> You are to endeavour by every possible means to open an intercourse with the natives, and to conciliate their affections, enjoining all our subjects to live in amity and kindness with them ... You will endeavour to procure an account of the numbers inhabiting the neighbourhood of the intended settlement, and to report your opinion to our Secretariat of State in what manner our intercourse with the people may be turned to the advantage of this colony.

It did not take Phillip long to conclude that 'intercourse' with the people could not in any way be turned to the advantage of the colony. They had nothing to trade, they were not a potential labour source, and they hindered the settlers in the establishment and spread of the settlement. More importantly, though, these initial attempts to educate captured Aborigines by trying to teach them British values, tastes and social behaviour, along with the settlers' ignorance about, or rejection of Aboriginal law and culture, established for both the settlers and Aborigines colonial patterns of relationships that have continued to the present.

Political domination by the settlers over Aborigines was achieved initially by a stroke of the pen. Australia being considered a 'terra nullius', the establishment of a settled colony there by the British put the country and all its inhabitants under British law and gave ownership of lands to the British Crown. The fact that the original owners resisted the settlers' efforts to take the land, and have continued to resist, means that political domination has had to be asserted through legal, physical and moral violence. Education has come, increasingly, to be a major means of asserting this political domination.

Missionary education

Such political domination was achieved by denying to Aborigines an understanding of what education was in settlers' terms, and of how it related to their own understanding of education. It was also achieved by shutting Aborigines out from education; both from access to education of quality, and from the opportunity to apply such education as they did manage to acquire.

Most of all domination was achieved by seeking to prevent Aborigines from getting an education in their own cultural, social, religious, scientific, and historic knowledge. The church missionaries, the very earliest educators of Aborigines and Torres Strait Islanders, were quick to discourage 'heathen practices'. Their belief, says Rowley (1972, p. 88) was that 'only by splitting the generations and interrupting the passing on of the cultural life would it be possible to civilise and Christianise'. This task was, of course, assigned to the missionaries by government. For instance, the royal instructions given to Governor John Hutt in Western Australia in 1839 were 'that you do, to the utmost of your power, promote religion and education among the native inhabitants ... and take such measures as may appear to you to be necessary for their conversion to the Christian faith, and for their advancement in civilisation' (quoted in Hasluck 1942, p. 57).

For the first sixty years of settlement in the Australian colonies, such education as Aborigines received came from the missionaries. The first school for them, established by Governor Macquarie at Parramatta in 1814, was a missionary school, with reading, writing and religious education forming the core curriculum. By 1824 this school was on the point of closure. Other mission schools operated through New South Wales, but none succeeded in educating Aborigines, and all but a few failed to survive (Bridges 1968, p. 233).

This failure lay with the schools, not with the Aborigines. Even the Reverend Samuel Marsden, who believed that Aborigines had to be civilized before they could be educated into Christianity, records some success in training and educating four Aboriginal boys he took into his home. There were many others who commented, sometimes with a tone of surprise, that Aborigines did seem to be able to learn in school (Harris 1978, pp. 24–5).

Even though some form of public education became available in New South Wales after 1848, official policy took no account of Aborigines. It neither set out to provide education for them nor to exclude them from it.

When public education became free and compulsory, policy continued to ignore them. Only when White parents at some schools complained about the presence of Aboriginal students in the schools were attempts made to set up schools on Aboriginal reserves, or to segregate Aboriginal students in separate annexes in the schools attended by White children.

In the separate Aboriginal schools, which numbered 40 by 1940, students were educated for life on the reserves, with an emphasis on manual skills and a minimum of reading, writing, and arithmetic. At the conclusion of their schooling they were expected to have reached the equivalent of the third year of primary school. Most did not even reach first-year level. Harris's summation (1978, p. 32) is that 'Aboriginal schools therefore, mostly produced barely literate people'. The hundreds of other Aboriginal children who never went to any school remained totally illiterate.

State government assimilation policies

In 1901, the separate self governing colonies of Australia were federated into the Commonwealth of Australia and each became a state with independent responsibilities within the Commonwealth. One of these responsibilities was education. Between 1901 and 1967 the states also continued to be responsible for Aborigines and Torres Strait Islanders within their territories, but there was no serious effort to educate Aborigines. That any attempt at all was made in these 70 years was only because of a major change in government policy. After 1945 there was a growing emphasis in government policy on assimilation of Aborigines into the main Australian population, as against earlier policies of protection and segregation. Dexter (quoted in Gale & Brookman 1975, p. 12) summarizes the nature of assimilation policies in this way:

> The basic assumption of the 1950s and early 1960s was that the Aboriginal minority in Australia must and should adapt to and adopt the manner of life of the majority of Australian society. Aboriginal affairs administration and programs were directed towards helping or seducing or coercing Aboriginals – the words used on the official documentation were that Aboriginals 'will choose' – to make this adaptation to the wider Australian society.

It should be noted that such assimilation was directed mainly, though not solely, at Aborigines of mixed-race descent. It was a policy that brought great hardship and sorrow to many Aboriginal families. It also created divisions between Aborigines, and raised questions of identity that continue to this day. There is a powerful racist lobby in Australia that still seeks to deny Aboriginal identity to any Aboriginal person of mixed-race descent (English 1985).

Education was the main means through which assimilation for 'part-Aborigines' was to be achieved. In many instances children were taken from their families and placed in homes as wards of states, to be educated to the compulsory school leaving age of 12 or 13, to be trained in household or field arts, and then to be assigned to work. Many of these children lost all contact with their families. They lived in isolation from their culture, and from all influences that could establish their Aboriginal identity. This was deliberate. According to its 1965 formulation (quoted in Gale & Brookman 1975, p. 72):

> The policy of assimilation seeks that all persons of Aboriginal descent will choose to attain a similar manner and standard of living to that of other Australians and live as members of a single Australian community – enjoying the same rights and privileges, accepting the same responsibilities and influenced by the same hopes and loyalties as other Australians.

Aborigines had no say about assimilation, and no choice. Dexter rightly assigns to Aboriginal affairs' programmes of that time the role of helping, seducing and coercing Aborigines to assimilate. The formulation of assimilation policy, the choice of methods used to impose it, and the bureaucratic brutality with which these methods were applied stamp assimilation as an act of political domination, and show it to be a classic form of internal colonization.

Commonwealth government educational policies

Policy, at least in its formulation, changed in the 1970s and 1980s. Responsibility for policy and funding in Aboriginal affairs was passing to the Commonwealth government which was showing itself to be willing to consult with and to listen to Aborigines. Terms like 'self-determination' and 'self-management' were freely used in Aboriginal affairs. They were variously defined according to which political party or Aboriginal action group was using them, but it was generally agreed that they required that Aborigines be heard and listened to in the formulation of all policy affecting them, and that they become increasingly responsible for delivery of services under these policies. It is instructive to note the terms used in describing this policy. The Liberal and National Country Party government of 1975 said it was 'committed to the principles that all Aborigines and Islanders should be free as other Australians to determine their own varied futures'. The price of self-determination, however, was to be an imposed policy of self-management:

> Aborigines must play a leading role in their affairs. This will include [their] playing a significant role:
> a) in setting the long term goals and objectives which the government should pursue and the programmes it should adopt in such areas as Aboriginal education, housing, health, employment and legal aid;

b)   in setting the priorities for expenditure on Aboriginal affairs within the context of overall budget allocations; and

c)   in evaluating existing programmes and formulating new ones.

As for the responsibility for self management (Australia. Department of Aboriginal Affairs 1976, p. 6):

> Aborigines not only have a significant role in these matters. They must also assume responsibility for the success of the programmes adopted. Only in this way will inefficiency, waste and disillusionment which have characterised many of the previous programmes be removed.

Put simply Aborigines *must* take the lead in setting up policy and determining programmes and they *must* take the blame if things go wrong! Again education was to have a key role. This same government policy listed nine priority programmes towards the implementation of policy. Seven of these were in areas of education and training. Significantly, Aborigines on the whole are still not receiving education comparable with that of other Australian children. There is ample evidence to support the Commonwealth Department of Education's claim (Australia. House of Representatives Select Committee on Aboriginal Education 1985, p. 21) that:

> Aboriginal education is still characterised by:
> – lower levels of access;
> – lower levels of achievement;
> – lower retention rates, particularly in secondary school; and
> – often inadequate or inappropriate curricula.

Educational success, in general Australian terms, is as important for the success of the Australian government's present Aboriginal affairs policy as it was for its previous policies of assimilation and integration. It can scarcely blame an uneducated or undereducated minority for getting its policies and programmes wrong. The ultimate policy objective remains that Aborigines, while maintaining their cultural and racial identity, should take a position of social equality with other people in Australian society. Implicit in this policy is the desire of government not to have to legislate in any special way for Aborigines any more than for any other special group of Australian citizens. The very fact that the government continues to legislate for them, and continues to formulate policies aimed at regulating their relationships with other Australians and their status within Australian society, argues that Aborigines and Islanders are still experiencing internal colonization.

In education, political domination over Aborigines is maintained through the imposition of the dominant academic curriculum in all schools, through the universal use of English as the language of academic instruction, and through the use of credentialling as the gateway to higher education. However, some independent Aboriginal schools have been unable to draw on government funding theoretically available to all independent schools because they have not satisfied state educational authorities that their curricula, facilities, timetabling and staff meet qualifying criteria.

That Aborigines and Islanders 'must' (in the terms used in the policy statements) assume responsibility for policies and programmes they are to set for themselves, means that the Australian government does not have to put them on the same footing as other Australians in determining their futures. What other Australian group is required by the government to formulate policies and programmes to meet its long-term needs, and is forced to accept responsibility for their success or failure? This, too, is evidence of political domination and of continuing internal colonization.

In sum, education now, as at the beginning of confrontation between the old and new settlers in Australia, remains a major means of asserting the political dominance of mainstream Australian society over Aborigines and Torres Strait Islanders.

Education and cultural oppression

For Aborigines and Islanders, now as in the past, gaining what other Australians have called an education has meant risking, and often experiencing, acute cultural alienation. It has meant sacrificing an education in their own culture for the sake of an education in White Australian culture. Often the result has been to produce culturally marginal people, untutored in their own culture, but equally untutored and unwanted in the culture of other Australians. This is perhaps the most extreme form of cultural oppression that Aborigines and Islanders experience today. One form of cultural oppression is 'colonial knowledge', or colonially constructed versions of Aboriginal cultures.

'Colonial knowledge' takes two forms. It is that knowledge about the cultures of indigenous populations gathered, interpreted, evaluated and used by European settlers at or near the point of contact with these cultures on the colonial frontiers. It is also the Western scientific knowledge of these cultures, based in part on early contact knowledge, but also on scientific observations and research often made with the assistance of knowledgeable Aboriginal informants. Both are outside views of the cultures they report.

'Colonial knowledge' of Australian Aboriginal and Torres Strait Island cultures has constituted the major offering in Aboriginal studies at primary and secondary school levels throughout Australia for over a hundred years. For many Aboriginal people in southern, eastern and south-western Australia it is the only knowledge of Aboriginal cultures on an Australian scale that they have.

The significant point about 'colonial knowledge' is that it identifies those elements of other cultures' behaviour that colonizers and scientists happen to be interested in – both because of preconceptions they have about indigenous populations and because of their need to use such knowledge to their advantage. Since Aborigines quickly showed themselves to be hostile to early European settlers who moved on to their lands, those settlers sought knowledge of Aboriginal techniques of warfare, bushcraft, and daily life routines in order to avoid attacks from Aborigines, and to find ways to deprive them of their sources of food, refreshment and rest. Others found a need to study the role of women in Aboriginal society and the rules of the male–female relationships. For those who had some knowledge of, and respect for, the hazards of the Australian bush, there was a positive value in learning and interpreting signs of the presence of animals, humans and reptiles in the bush. Aboriginal knowledge of bush foods and medicinal plants was also useful. For the most part settler-acquired knowledge of Aboriginal cultures was highly selective. It was also abstracted and isolated from those elements of Aboriginal culture that could have given it much greater human value and, perhaps, earned respect both for Aborigines and their cultures.

The development and application of 'colonial knowledge' about Aborigines and Torres Strait Islanders needs deeper study. By exploring its general content, and the attitudes towards Aboriginal cultures that it reveals, we can readily understand its effectiveness in culturally oppressing Aborigines. To reach that understanding it is first necessary to review the grossest form of cultural oppression that Australia's Aborigines experienced: the deliberate attempt to destroy Aboriginal societies.

Throughout the 19th century, as the Australian frontier was pushed outwards, first to the south, then to the west, and finally to the north, centre and northwest, successive Aboriginal groups came under threat of violent extinction. Usually a handful of people from each group survived, mostly women and children. With every member of a group who died, a little of that group's culture died also. Finally, all that was left were the fragments living in the minds of the survivors. Languages died. Oral traditions faded from memory. Rich ceremonial cycles, tied intimately to religious places in the land, could not be performed for lack of ceremonial leaders, songmen and other key performers. The spirits of the land were left unattended. Centuries-old technological skills were no longer used or became unusable. Almost overnight, it seemed, centuries of valued human knowledge and a whole way of life, evolved through thousands of generations of human interaction with the Australian land, almost disappeared. For most southern and eastern Australian Aboriginal cultures, one may find fragments of language, eccentrically recorded by untrained or amateur linguists. Some of these vocabularies have been collated into Aboriginal languages word lists. Oral traditions survived, much bowdlerized, in such collections as those made by Langloh-Parker (Parker 1896) in western New South Wales. Glimpses of ceremonies can be gained from accounts in the memoirs of some of the White settlers and from the paintings made by itinerant artists in the early 19th century. Some collections were made of items of material culture. Late 19th-century ethnographers, such as R. H. Mathews (1906), even managed to gather fragmentary information on social organization (including kinship), on warfare, hunting and gathering, and on rituals. All told, even when added to what Aborigines in these regions themselves managed to preserve, it amounted to very little.

Such sources provided the basis on which school-level Aboriginal studies rested until well into the 20th century. A recent series of school texts published between 1977 and 1981, for instance, draws heavily on Mathews's ethnography. Where knowledge of southern and eastern cultures is inadequate, school text writers do not hesitate to abstract general concepts of Aboriginal life and culture from the better-recorded Aboriginal cultures of central and northern Australia. This, too, perpetuates the sort of misconceptions about Aboriginal cultures that have become a part of the stock-in-trade of White cultural brokers (Howard 1982, p. 169) who are the main purveyors of 'colonial knowledge'.

Inaccurate stereotypes

A number of researchers over the last decade have identified the inaccurate stereotypes of Aboriginal cultures perpetuated in textbooks commonly used in Australian schools. Some of the research results have been discussed by Hill & Barlow (1978, 1985). The most common stereotypes deny the complex and significant differences between Aboriginal groups – differences in language, social organization, law, religious belief and ceremony, material culture, styles of art and music, and in the choice and use of foods. This is not to say there were not similarities, but they are no more than the similarities imposed by a common hunter-gatherer economy, and by the inheritance of a common ancient ancestry. Also very common is the negative description of Aboriginal cultures. The cultures are described in terms of what they are claimed to lack as compared with the cultures of the European settlers – no clothes, no religion, no houses, no law, no knowledge of mathematics and science, no farming and so on. Then there is the concentration on those aspects of Aboriginal culture that appear exotic by European standards – for example, choice of food, sexual behaviour, ritual, cannibalism, and methods of dispute settlement. Finally, there are the stereotypes about the qualities of Aborigines as people – treacherous, dishonest, cruel, dirty, childlike, intellectually limited, lazy, greedy; in every way the reverse of the honest, hard-working God-fearing Christian European gentlefolk.

The perpetuation of this kind of 'colonial knowledge' helps maintain the cultural oppression of Aboriginal and Torres Strait Islander Australians since it serves to confirm the low esteem non-Aboriginal Australians generally have for Aboriginal cultures and for Aboriginal and Islander people themselves. The esteem that Aborigines and Islanders have for their own cultures, especially the cultures of the past, is also affected. At the same time 'colonial knowledge' reduces the status of Aboriginal and Islander cultures in comparison with the mainstream Anglo-Australian cultures and of the other European, Asian, American and Middle Eastern cultures that have taken root in Australia over the last 200 years.

Scientists, who since the 1930s have attempted a more sympathetic study of Australia's indigenous peoples and their cultures, hope that their contribution to Aboriginal studies has managed to counteract the cultural oppression imposed by 'colonial knowledge'. We are talking mainly of anthropologists, sociologists, and others specializing in the study of one or other aspect of Aboriginal culture. There is no doubt that this wide-ranging and intensive research effort has produced a great amount of scientific knowledge. As a result, the scientific appreciation of historic and contemporary Aboriginal cultures has risen, along with regard for Aborigines as people (Horton 1984, p. 370). That appreciation and regard, however, has had little impact on the general public's understanding of, and attitudes towards, Aborigines and their cultures. At the same time, Aborigines and Islanders express scant gratitude for the scientific contribution to Aboriginal studies. If anything they are becoming impatient with it, and cynical about both its purpose and its usefulness. Most seem to prefer research to be problem-oriented and that it should initially produce short-term solutions, with the possibility of long-term applicability.

Archaeology and the Aboriginal heritage

The reception of archaeological research into the record of Australian Aboriginal life provides an example of the response of the general Australian public and the specific Aboriginal one. This research indicates that Aborigines here occupied Australia for at least 40 000 years, and possibly twice as long. Whatever is eventually established as the earliest occupation date, it has been demonstrated that Aborigines have as long a relationship with Australia as any other founding population has with its own land. This has established Aborigines' pre-eminent title to the name 'Australian'.

Other research has shown regional and historical variations in the way Aborigines have related to their environments and interacted with them economically, technologically, aesthetically, and intellectually. Given the scant material that Australian archaeologists have had to work with, they have achieved a great deal. The discovery of new sites for research, and the application of refined analytical techniques, should help to fill in gaps in the broad picture, and to resolve some of the present mysteries. As Horton (1984, p. 368) says, the questions archaeology poses, in Australia as elsewhere, are 'big ones'. Finding the answers to those questions should eventually force all Australians to re-evaluate Aborigines and their cultures.

Yet so far archaeological reconstruction of Aboriginal history has had little impact on the public view of Aborigines. Recent legislation aimed at preserving and protecting sites of historic, sentimental, artistic, or religious significance to Aborigines has generally met a negative response. Aborigines have been accused of 'inventing' sites in an attempt to grab choice land for themselves. Farmers and graziers have destroyed sites on their own properties to prevent Aborigines gaining access to them. Property owners have discouraged attempts to search for unknown sites on their land. At the same time, fierce opposition to the granting of land rights to Aborigines indicates that only a few people are prepared to recognize the rights to land that Aborigines can claim on the basis of thousands of years of uninterrupted occupation and their continuous and intensive interaction with the land.

It should not surprise archaeologists and other scientists working in Aboriginal studies that the accumulated results of their research have had such a small effect on public knowledge and attitudes. Archaeology and its findings in relation to Aboriginal history do not form part of the normal school curriculum in Australia. Nor do they inform the more popular accounts of Australian history. Although a few schools do include archaeology as an optional course at mid to upper secondary levels, one would expect that most schools would use the findings of Australian archaeology in Australian history or ancient history studies. Ancient history is a standard and popular course in secondary education. It has always concentrated on the history of the peoples of the Middle East, Greece, and Rome. Some Australian school syllabuses now divide ancient history into separate studies of Greek and Roman history. There is no place either in ancient history or in its subdivisions for a study of ancient Australia.

Most school history texts do make some reference to Aboriginal history. In their opening chapter, at least, they give dates for the earliest human occupation of Australia, present a theory of migration to account for that occupation, offer a generalized description of Australian hunter-gatherer lifestyles, but then hurry on to post-1788 Australian history. If Aborigines are mentioned at all after this opening chapter, it is only in a token manner, since they are generally not seen to have been contributors to post-1788 history. There are a few exceptions. McQueen (1978) includes Aborigines as one of the eight themes he pursues in sketching a social history of Australia from 1888 to 1975. Several books have been written for upper secondary Australian history studies that attempt to provide a detailed account of Aboriginal history (Broome 1982, Lippmann 1981). On the whole, though, academic findings about Aboriginal history, especially those revealed through archaeological research, have not much altered what is taught in schools about Aborigines. Nor have they had much effect on the popular view of Aborigines.

Aborigines on their past

It is clear from recent statements that Aborigines themselves are beginning to express considerable concern at the cultural oppression that scientific control over both their history and the presentation of their historic and contemporary cultures represents:

> 'The issue is control', said R. F. Langford, on behalf of the Tasmanian Aboriginal community, in 1982. 'We say that it is our past, our culture and heritage, and forms part of our present life. As such it is ours to control and it is ours to share in our terms.' (Langford 1983, p. 2)

According to Allen (1983, p. 8), the response of some archaeologists to this is to argue

> that the past only exists in the sense that it is created by people in the present, whether from historical documents, oral traditions or archaeological evidence. In this sense there can be many 'pasts' which depend ultimately upon the belief systems of the people who create these pasts, whether these are based on religion, logic or group-vested interests.

Such an argument, however, is tantamount to an admission that the past as reconstructed by archaeologists is in effect a version of cultural oppression in that it is at variance with the past as perceived by Aborigines.

Ucko (1983a, 1983b) gives ample evidence of the ways in which Aboriginal sites in Australia have been given an archaeological significance and focus that may not match that given them by the Aborigines who created them. He also points out that the significance given by sites legislation to particular places in the landscape has the effect of isolating them from the total natural and human environment that gives them significance. It was not the practice of Aborigines to isolate sites in this way. Nor are all the sites of significance to Aborigines necessarily human creations. The scientist looking for evidence that may throw further light on the past may well overlook sites that offer no evidence of human activity and occupation. As Ucko (1983b, p. 20) says: 'To Aborogines, every part of the land is of importance, as is evident from the recognition of almost every natural feature within their 'country' as the result of Dreamtime activity'. The archaeological and legislative practice of identifying and marking off places in the landscape as being 'sites of significance' in Aboriginal studies is thus clearly an unwitting act of cultural oppression (Ucko 1983a, 1983b).

Attempts to train Aborigines to accept the 'sites of significance' concept and to become active in identification and preservation of sites, are extensions of the cultural oppression model. National parks and wildlife services and their equivalents in each Australian state seek to employ and train Aborigines. Under New South Wales land rights legislation, a number of Aboriginal and land councils have been established throughout the state that have a role in identifying, recording and preserving Aboriginal sites. Some colleges of technical and further education and other postsecondary education colleges are now beginning to offer Aborigines training in site identification and recording. Archaeological techniques are not generally taught in the courses, but they do include a study of the results of Australian archaeological research. These studies include archaeological and anthropological theories on Aboriginal ritual estates and economic ranges. Through the teaching of the scientific analyses of Aboriginal and Torres Strait Islander cultures, education will continue to teach Aborigines views on their present cultures and on the past that may not be their own, and that may not accord with their own understanding of them.

Aborigines' own views on cultural oppression were stated very clearly by a group of Aboriginal historians (Atkinson *et al.* 1985, p. 40):

> It must be said that Aboriginal contributions to Australian history have fundamental cultural purposes. We are reclaiming our right to identify and define ourselves. Most of this country has been taken from our people in a little over 190 years of colonisation. In tandem with the theft of our land has been a cultural repression denying us an identity in Australian history. We, as Aboriginal people, can begin to rectify the white misconceptions about our history by writing ourselves. Colonisation was not a peaceful process, nor have we conceded defeat.

Education and economic exploitation

Aboriginal affairs in Australia is big business. In 1984/85 nearly $425 000 000 was allocated by the Commonwealth government to Special Aboriginal Advancement Programmes. Of this, 5.7 per cent went on administration, mostly in salaries to non-Aboriginal and some Aboriginal employees in government departments and other organizations that administer Aboriginal programmes. These salaries are well earned. However, almost $25 000 000 in salaries and other administrative expenses is big money. The remaining $400 000 000 does not go directly into the hands of the Aborigines. Most goes in purchasing services and materials for them: such as health and legal services, special employment support programmes, housing cooperatives, and business and housing loans. All of these programmes, while signalling the social and economic disadvantage experienced generally by Aborigines, also indicate the forms of economic exploitation open to all people involved in the business of Aboriginal affairs (Australia. Department of Aboriginal Affairs 1985, p. 95).

Aboriginal affairs is one area in which Aborigines and Torres Strait Islanders feel they should be offered particularly favourable economic opportunities. Certainly, determined efforts have been made to increase the number of Aborigines and Islanders employed in Aboriginal affairs. The Australian government and some state Labour Party governments have recently introduced equal opportunity legislation aimed at reforming employment conditions in their public service structures. Generally this legislation aims at identifying and eliminating practices that limit access to promotion and to senior administrative positions, regardless of qualification, by sex, by race and by ethnic background. The Commonwealth Government Act identifies women, Aborigines and Torres Strait Islanders, disabled people, and migrants of non-English speaking background as groups experiencing discrimination in employment.

To speed up the process of achieving equal employment opportunity for these groups, it has also become the practice of the Commonwealth and some state governments to introduce positive discrimination in employment and promotion for them, under the euphemism of 'affirmative action'.

Despite these policies, the Australian Deparment of Aboriginal Affairs only increased its Aboriginal employees by six in 1984/85, although it did appoint three Aborigines to senior management positions. The Department admits that 'difficulty has been experienced in attracting qualified Aboriginal applicants for many of the Department's advertised positions' (Australia. Department of Aboriginal Affairs 1985, p. 18). Part of the difficulty in attracting Aborigines and Islanders to the Department undoubtedly lies in the fact that there are so few qualified people available.

A recent press report (*Australia*, 9 January 1986) stated that the Australian Teachers Federation had adopted a recommendation to campaign to put 1000 Aboriginal teachers in Australian schools by 1990; at present there are about 150. The campaign will aim at open entrance to tertiary education for Aborigines, increasing the retention rate for Aboriginal students in school, and upgrading the status of Aboriginal education workers and teaching assistants.

In Australia three forms of tertiary education – universities, colleges of advanced education, and colleges of technical and further education – offer a choice of academic certification ranging from trade certificates to post-graduate degrees. Access to courses offering these forms of certification is through completion, at least at pass level, of schooling to years 10 or 12 level or their equivalent. Most tertiary institutions also have special entry provisions for adult applicants.

Aborigines and Islanders have particular difficulty meeting the requirements for entry for tertiary education. Very few of them, compared with other Australians, complete year 10, let alone at pass level. In New South Wales in 1984, 104 Aboriginal students sat for the Year 12 Higher School Certificate (HSC), which gives entry to universities and colleges of advanced education. This number represented a retention rate of 8 per cent of the Aboriginal students who began secondary education in 1979. By contrast, 30 per cent of the 1979 entry of non-Aboriginal students sat for the HSC in 1984. Of the 104 students who sat for the HSC, 90 received aggregate scores that placed them in the lower 5–0 per cent ranking. Only three were placed in the top 25 per cent ranking (Morgan 1985, pp. 7, 12). On these figures few Aborigines are finding education to be a means to economic advantage via tertiary education.

As a consequence of the failure of the schools to 'provide adequate services to Aboriginal students and communities' (Morgan 1985, p. 7), and to produce educational outcomes for them that match those of other students in the education system, Aborigines are now using a variety of alternative methods to gain access to higher levels of education and training. The colleges of technical and further education are attracting large numbers of mature Aboriginal students with their access programmes. These are courses designed to give Aborigines the literacy, numeracy and study skills they might need for tertiary entry. They also offer units that can count towards gaining a HSC or its equivalent.

Some colleges of advanced education run 'enclave' programmes that provide social and educational support for Aborigines entering degree or diploma courses. Usually these consist of an Aboriginal and Islander students' centre that provides tutorial and advisory services, child care, study facilities, and a library, and training in study techniques, assignment preparation and research. Sometimes, as part of the 'enclave' concept, courses run especially, though not necessarily exclusively, for Aboriginal students, will be credited towards the degree or diploma that is being studied for. Aboriginal studies is one such example.

Under its policy of affirmative action for groups that are disadvantaged in employment, the Commonwealth government announced in early January 1986 that it would provide 520 positions for Aborigines in higher education courses. Through its Commonwealth Tertiary Education Commission it has allocated these positions to tertiary institutions in each state. In Tasmania, for instance, six places were allocated, two at the Australian Maritime College, two at the Tasmanian State Institute of Technology and two reserved for Aborigines should they apply and meet the entry qualifications set by a tertiary institution. Whether this action is going to prove effective in increasing the number of tertiary qualified Aborigines and Islanders remains to be seen.

Can we claim, though, that education has served to maintain internal colonialism by contributing to the economic exploitation of Aborigines and Islanders? Recent research evidence indicates that those who are seen to be at a disadvantage in the schooling process may be being disadvantaged by the curriculum and by curriculum practices (Connell *et al.* 1982, pp. 189–98). Aborigines in Australia have generally expressed concern at the acculturative effects of the standard Australian school curriculum (National Aboriginal Education Committee 1985, p. 4). There is no doubt that this curriculum has been designed to meet the educational needs of White, middle-class Australians with English-speaking backgrounds. Special curriculum arrangements and curriculum practices are used for those students who are seen not to fit this curriculum. These arrangements aim to direct the student to a course of study with different and diminished outcomes to those of the standard curriculum. Practices seek to alter the student who does not fit, so as to achieve a partial fit with the standard curriculum. Both result in an education that achieves neither the outcomes nor the forms of personal development that Aborigines and other students who are disadvantaged by the system seek. Efforts by Aborigines and others to set up an alternative curriculum and practices more suited to their own educational needs are frustrated by the educational bureaucracy. Government support and approval is given to Aboriginal schools only if curriculum and practices meet core curriculum requirements.

Aborigines thus find themselves in a Catch-22 situation in education. On the one hand they are disadvantaged by the standard school curriculum and curriculum practices. On the other, the system will not allow them to 'develop an education theory and pedagogy that takes into account Aboriginal epistemology' (National Aboriginal Education Committee 1985, p. 4), and could lead to an Aboriginal curriculum with its own curriculum practices. All that the education authorities will allow the Aboriginal student is the choice of adapting to the standard curriculum and accepting its acculturative effects, or accepting a version of the standard curriculum that offers only diminished educational and opportunity outcomes.

In this sense education can be seen to be placing Aborigines in a position of economic disadvantage, and one that could lead to their economic exploitation. There are many Aborigines who believe that this is, in fact, the case. They are exposed to economic exploitation, especially in the remote areas of Australia, in that education has not equipped them with the range of skills, within their own communities, that they need to be able to manage their own affairs at every level. Consequently they have to rely on, and pay for, the expertise of non-Aboriginal people who have got from education that which has been denied to Aborigines.

Conclusion

Despite the complexity of the situation reviewed in this chapter Aborigines and Islanders nonetheless continue to regard education as a means to break from their colonial status and to gain equality with other Australians. They see, though, that this would require:

> – that Aboriginal and Torres Strait Islander education be a process that builds on [their own] cultural heritage and world view:
> – that educational programs be developed using Aboriginal learning styles accompanied by an appropriate pedagogy:
> – that Aboriginal and Torres Strait Islander education lead to personal development and the acquisition of the skills and learning needed for Australia today. (NAEC 1985, p. 5)

These are large requirements. Australian Aborigines and Torres Strait Islanders may find that breaking the nexus between education and their colonial status will continue to be a lengthy and exhausting process.

References

Allen, J. 1983. Aborigines and archaeologists in Tasmania. *Australian Archaeologist* **16**, 7–10.

Atkinson, W. *et al.* 1985. Introduction – a celebration of resistance to colonialism. *Black Australia 2*, M. Hill & A. Barlow (eds), 38–40. Canberra: Australian Institute of Aboriginal Studies.

Australia. Department of Aboriginal Affairs 1976. *Annual Report 1975–76*. Canberra: Australian Government Publishing Service.

Australia. Department of Aboriginal Affairs 1985. *Department of Aboriginal Affairs Annual Report 1984–85*. Canberra: Australian Government Publishing Service.

Australia. House of Representatives Select Committee on Aboriginal Affairs 1985. *Aboriginal education*. Canberra: Australian Government Publishing Service.

Berge, P. L. Van den 1970. *Race and ethnicity: essays in comparative sociology*. New York: Basic Books.

Biernoff, D. 1975. Land and law in eastern Arnhem Land: traditional models for social and political organisation. *University of Queensland, Anthropology Museum, Occasional papers in Anthropology* **4**, 55–92.

Bridges, B. 1968. Aboriginal education in eastern Australia (NSW) 1788–1855. *Australian Journal of Education* **12**(3), 225–43.

Broome, R. 1982. *Aboriginal Australians: black response to white dominance, 1788–1980*. Sydney: Allen & Unwin.

Connell, R. W. *et al.* 1982. *Making the difference: schools, families and social division*. Sydney: Allen & Unwin.

English P. B. 1985. *Land rights and birth rights: the great Australian hoax*. Bullsbrook, W.A.: Veritas.

Gale, G. F. & A. Brookman 1975. *Race relations in Australia – the Aborigines*. Sydney: McGraw-Hill.

Hamilton, A. 1981. *Nature and nurture: Aboriginal child-rearing in north-central Arnhem Land*. Canberra: Australian Institute of Aboriginal Studies.

Harris, J. W. 1978. The education of Aboriginal children in New South Wales public schools since 1788. *The Aboriginal Child at School* **6**(4 & 5), 35, 20–30.

Harris, S. 1984. *Culture and learning: tradition and education in north-east Arnhem Land*. Canberra: Australian Institute of Aboriginal Studies.

Hartwig, M. 1978. Capitalism and Aborigines: the theory of internal colonialism and its rivals. In *Essays in the political economy of Australian capitalism, Vol. 3*, E. Wheelwright & K. Byckley (eds), 119–41. Sydney: Australian and New Zealand Books.

Hasluck, P. 1942. *Black Australians: a survey of native policy in Western Australia, 1829–1897*. Melbourne: Melbourne University Press.

Hill, M. & A. Barlow 1978. *Black Australia: an annotated bibliography and teachers guide to resources on Aborigines and Torres Strait Islanders*. Canberra: Australian Institute of Aboriginal Studies.

Hill, M. & A. Barlow 1985. *Black Australia 2: an annotated bibliography and teacher's guide to resources on Aborigines and Torres Strait Islanders*. Canberra: Australian Institute of Aboriginal Studies.

Horton, D. 1984. Archaeology in Australia. *Hemisphere* **28**(6), 365–70.

Howard, M. C. 1982. Aboriginal brokerage and political development in south-western Australia. In *Aboriginal power in Australian society*, M. Howard (ed.), 159–83. St Lucia, Qld: University of Queensland Press.

Langford, R. F. 1983. Our heritage – your playground. *Australian Archaeology* **16**, 1–7.

Lippman, L. 1981. *Generations of resistance: the Aboriginal struggle for justice*. Melbourne: Longman Cheshire.

Mathews, R. H. 1906. Notes on some native tribes of Australia. *Journal of the Proceedings of the Royal Society (New South Wales)* **40**, 95–129.

McQueen, H. J. 1978. *Social sketches of Australia, 1888–1975*. Harmondsworth: Penguin.

Morgan, R. 1985. HSC Results. *Yakun: south coast newsletter* May–June, 7, 12.

National Aboriginal Education Committee. 1985. *Philosophy, aims and policy guidelines for Aboriginal and Torres Strait Islander education*. Canberra: Australian Government Publishing Service.

Parker, K. L. 1896. *Australian legendary tales*. London: David Nutt.

Rowley, C. 1972. *The destruction of Aboriginal society*. Harmondsworth: Penguin.

Sills, D. 1968. *International encyclopedia of the social sciences, Vol. 3*. New York: Macmillan and The Free Press.

Stone, S. 1974. *Aborigines in white Australia: a documentary history of the attitudes affecting official policy and the Australian Aborigine, 1697–1973*. South Yarra, Vic,: Heinemann Educational.

Ucko, P. J. 1983a. The politics of the indigenous minority. *Journal of Biosocial Science* Supplement 8, 25–40.

Ucko, P. J. 1983b. Australian academic archaeology: Aboriginal transformation of its aims and practices. *Australian Archaeologist* **16**, 11–26.

Wolpe, H. 1975. The theory of internal colonialism – the South African case. In *Beyond the sociology of development: economy and society in Latin America and Africa*, I. Oxaal *et al*. (eds), 228–42. London: Routledge.

8 *The affirmation of indigenous values in a colonial education system*

LILLA WATSON

Murri[1] knowledge and the processes of teaching and learning have matured in what is known today as Australia for over fifty thousand years. They began long before the last Ice Age, at a time when volcanoes were still active. They have always been based on the permanence of the land, and the cyclic rhythms of nature. Harmony with the land, knowing it, learning from it as mother and teacher, have provided a solid and permanent basis for law, and for harmony with each other.

Over countless generations, those processes have developed some distinctive characteristics (Bell 1983, Brandl 1983, King-Boyes 1977, Liberman 1985)

The process extended over the whole life-span.

They involve everyone. Each person is encouraged to develop his or her potential as a precious and important resource.

They respect the individual's maturity, and hence capacity to know, and use knowledge responsibly. Maturity is not measured in years.

While initiation ceremonies, for example, were and are times of intensive education, and ceremony, story telling, song and dance are also important, the processes include observation and involvement in everyday activities. Children especially are encouraged to investigate and experiment, and are rarely separated from adult activities. Small children are seldom punished for mistakes.

They are holistic – involving not just the intellect, but the spirit, emotions, behaviour etc. in relation to the land and to one another.

They are non-competitive, but for and by the whole community; there are few prizes or privileges to be won apart from responsibilities; there are few failures or losers.

Everyone is, to some extent, a teacher.

Above all, they have always been rooted in the land, the greatest of teachers, and our mother. The sense of belonging to the land, of responsibility for the land, of our survival depending on the health of the land, rather than the other way around, pervades the whole process.

Our history, our Laws are drawn from it, and are located in it, as a far more solid base than frail human beings. We have never allowed ourselves to be weighed down by dead heros or teachers, or the need to compare ourselves with them, or compete against them.

The effectiveness of those processes, and the dynamism inherent in the oral tradition, are plain to see. Murris in Arnhem Land today can indicate miles out to sea, ridges and sites of significance which have not been visible since the last Ice Age (Neidjie, Davis & Fox 1985, p. 13). Aboriginal names for volcanoes extinct for tens of thousands of years recall the time they belched forth ash and lava. Murris can name, describe, and identify the habitat of megafauna whose fossils are new and exciting discoveries for Europeans. Botanists, zoologists and nutritionists have been astounded by the detailed knowledge of plants and animals common among even young Aboriginal children. The ability to speak two, and often many more, languages was the norm for Murris.

Beyond these more tangible signs, of course, are value systems, law, spiritual beliefs etc. that lie at the heart of the indigenous culture, and have also been passed on from generation to generation.

Colonization

Quite recently, only 200 years ago, that process began to suffer serious disruption, with the establishment of a British penal colony in the area presently known as Sydney. As a Murri, any trip to Sydney is a sad reminder of what began here, and its consequences for us. It did not affect the people of my mother's mother's country in what is now Central Queensland until 120 years ago.

Although the processes may have been disrupted, they have not been entirely interrupted. They have even survived the policies and practices of a succession of colonialist governments. As recently as twenty five years ago, Australian governments adopted a policy of cultural extinction (Commonwealth PP 1962–3, Vol. III, p. 651), entitled assimilation, which stated that

> all Aborigines and part Aborigines will attain the same manner of living as other Australians and live as members of a single Australian community enjoying the same rights and privileges, accepting the same responsibilities, observing the same customs and influenced by the same beliefs, hopes and loyalties as other Australians.

Let us take an example of the persistence of those processes. In July 1987, the Human Rights and Equal Opportunities Commission Inquiry heard evidence from Aboriginal people of Toomelah and Boggabilla, on the New South Wales–Queensland Border. Towards the end of the first day of hearings, the president, Judge Marcus Einfeld, spoke of all living in this country as being Australians, and our inability to undo the past (HREOC

Inquiry, transcript, 27 July 1987, pp. 97–8). The next day, a respected local Aboriginal woman, Julie Whitton, took up the points in a written submission:

> for anyone to say to a Murri that 'the past is over' is just not right. We can't forget the past. White people don't forget their past. But for Murris time is different anyway. We don't divide time up into the past, present and future. This is just what the Dreaming is all about. The Dreaming is happening all the time. That's why we can't 'forget' (or put behind us) all the massacres that happened to our people here. How can we forget them and the resistance fighting of our people? For us that only happened yesterday, the other day; like our Dreaming these things are part of who we are. 'Past' is a white man's idea. We know that we can't lose anything that has happened to us. What has happened to our people is our people. It is what we are. We believe this strongly. For Murris it is what is happening that is important. That's why, for instance, when we call a meeting, the meeting starts when everyone who should be there has arrived. That's the meeting time. So to tell us to forget the past and to look to the future makes no sense at all. It's an insult to tell us to forget the past. That's the same as telling us to forget the Dreaming, to forget how the old people struggled, to forget who we are . . .
>
> Over the years there have been many times when I have gone home and said: 'that's it, no more. I'm not going to battle any more for Toomelah'. Then I have laid down and seen the faces of my Mother, my Aunties and one or two others of the old people around me. They say: 'Don't give up, Julie, you have to go on'. And I do, not for me, not for Toomelah but for them. I know we have to make things a reality for the people who've struggled before us. Those are the people who have struggled and died. I can tell you, that all you have to do is to drive down to Old Toomelah (site of the former Mission), pull up your car and you can hear it, especially at night, the sound of the old people in the bush, the old people talking still. This is what we live with, who we live for.
>
> I also want to say something about being Australian . . . It is an insult to tell us that we are Australian citizens. How can anyone tell us who we are? We know who we are. We are Murris, the indigenous people of this country. (HREOC Inquiry, Exhibit 14, 1988)

The submission of Mrs Whitton, and others, to that inquiry, show that, despite all the assimilationist pressures, three quarters of a century of living on Reserves, and being subject to white schooling, indigenous knowledge and teaching processes are alive and well, and that the dynamism of the oral tradition continues. They put paid to the myth that Aboriginality only survives in remote communities, and that elsewhere the culture has been lost or destroyed.

Now, at least, the very different teaching tradition brought to this land by the colonizers is acknowledging two things: firstly, that it is possible that they might have something to learn from Murris, and that Aboriginal studies should have a place in their curricula: and secondly, that it has failed to assimilate us. While we may have adapted some of its aspects to our use, it has failed to convince us that it has the answers to our needs.

Aboriginal studies

The interest in Aboriginal people and knowledge shown by white Australia is quite recent. There have always been a few anthropologists, amateur or professional, who saw their task as one of recording Aboriginal customs and languages before they disappeared. The efforts of some were intended to provide a basis for the control and manipulation of Aboriginal people, the exploitation of their labour (Berndt & Berndt 1987), their removal from land wanted for pastoralists or miners, and to accelerate the process of assimilation. Many others ended up being used for the same purposes, and to provide an underpinning for the process of colonization, and its accompanying brutality, and to stifle any stirrings of conscience. Some set out to find evidence to support the theories of Social Darwinism (Taylor & Jardine 1924).

So twenty five years ago, Stanner (1969), speaking of Australian perceptions of Aboriginal people was able to devote one of his Boyer Lectures to 'The Great Australian Silence'. At that time, for example, among the minority who did ask questions, it was thought that Aboriginal people had probably lived in this land for some 1200 years, and numbered some 300 000 at the time of white settlement: and that this land had either been a 'Terra nullius', or had been occupied 'peaceably'. Crowley justified the lack of attention given to black–white relations in the widely used textbook he edited (*A New History of Australia* 1974) by saying 'that the Aborigines were just not important in the early history of white settlement' (Evans 1986, p. 16).

Comparatively, the volume of research and studies published since then on various aspects of Aboriginal life, and relations with white Australia, is quite massive. From a Murri perspective, however, it is a very mixed bag. We are now recognized as having occupied this land for at least 50 000 years; the Murri population at the time of white settlement is acknowledged to have been at least 750 000. This makes the contrast with the estimated Murri population of 67 000 in 1901 even more marked, and questions about 'Terra nullius' and peaceable occupation, and the barbarism of colonization harder to ignore (see Butlin 1983, Flood 1983, Mulvaney 1969).

On the other hand, myths generated from earlier studies persist. Recently, the prestigious English newspaper *Guardian Weekly* carried a feature article claiming that Aboriginal people 'did not know that a child came from coition of a man and a woman', and quoted a contemporary historian's description of us as having had 'an almost animal-like level of life' (Coleman 1988). The silence and insensitivity linger on: in 1988, as whites celebrated 200 years of colonial occupation of this land, the eight courses offered in archaeology by the University of Sydney's Centre for Continuing Education still dealt only with Europe, Greece and Egypt (University of Sydney 1988); and only three years ago, it was discovered that the remains of some 200 Aboriginal people removed, in 1963, from a burial site near Broadbeach, on Queensland's Gold Coast, had been stored and studied in the Anatomy Department of the University of Queensland for 20 years (*The Sunday Mail, Brisbane*, 26 May 1988).

So, from a Murri perspective, while it is good to see the superficiality, paternalism and racism of earlier studies acknowledged, I suspect that much of the present output will be viewed with similar horror 25 years hence. It is still a case of white academics and writers describing us and our culture, generally using Western concepts, categories and definitions – i.e., white terms of reference. The areas of study undertaken reflect white preoccupations, perspectives and priorities.

It is refreshing to see this acknowledged explicitly in some of the better material being published. For example, Liberman (1985) acknowledges that his descriptions 'are very much the product of embeddedness in the perspectives of European sociability' (p. 105), and that a Japanese sociologist, for example, might have seen and described things differently.

Writers showing such openness and sensitivity will understand, and in no way be offended, when we say that we have had enough of being defined and described by whites, of having others determine what is relevant and important in Aboriginality. We will say who and what we are. It has taken a long time for white Australia to reach the point of being ready to hear what we say, rather than what others say about us.

This is a relatively new task for us. For the greater part of our history as people indigenous to this country, we felt no need to make any explicit definition of ourselves. As a person said to the recent Human Rights and Equal Opportunities Commission Inquiry mentioned above, 'among ourselves, we are only people; it is only when we come into contact with Europeans that we are Aboriginal' (HREOC transcript, 28 July 1988, p. 178). And as Fanon (1967) says, it is the colonizer 'who has brought the "native" into existence and who perpetuates his existence' (p. 28). In the past, it has been the colonizer who has presumed to define us.

In this context, we 'natives' in this our own country are waiting for colonial scholars to explore and appreciate the significance of the following facts:

– the borders of more than 300 autonomous areas were unchanged for thousands of years.
– there were no prisons or armies maintained in our society.
– the natural environment was not destroyed or polluted.
– our ancestors did not have any need to colonize neighbouring lands and people.

Since colonization, and especially in recent decades, we have had to clarify and confirm our identity for ourselves. Appropriate Aboriginal ways of behaving, speaking and living have been more explicitly identified and enhanced. But in recent years, for the first time in our history, we are being put in the position of having to describe ourselves to the colonizing society.

This has proved to be an especially difficult task for us. We have little difficulty in doing it, and engaging in appropriate dialogue, with people from other countries who have shared our experience of being colonized. We can do it with other peoples who have not shared that experience. Even those non-Aboriginal Australians who eschew the relationship of colonizer–colonized have difficulty in grasping the maturity and sophistication of our thought and culture. But for people who are not even aware of that relationship and its effects, the difficulty approaches impossibility.

The recognition of our right to maintain our identity and culture has involved no structural change, and has asked nothing of the white community but tolerance. It has allowed Aboriginal people and knowledge to be placed under the umbrella of 'multiculturalism', or, as a recent Australia postage stamp issue suggested, just another group of immigrants. Both these manoeuvres are, in effect, attempts to mask our status as the indigenous people of this country and belittle our unique and ancient relationship with the land, and give a facade of legitimacy to colonization.

Aboriginal people in Western education institutions

As we try to adapt Western schooling content and processes into our own terms of reference, we take our own look at them. Other indigenous people have recognized the need to do this. Some ten years ago, Julius Nyerere, until recently President of Tanzania, and formerly a schoolteacher trained in English institutions, spoke of the growth in awareness which led him to redefine education. For most of his life, he had accepted Western definitions, but had become increasingly critical of the education systems supposedly based on them, and their usefulness for the people of his country.

The system, he said, tended to turn people into a more marketable commodity – the more education they received, the more money they were worth in the job market. Rather than learning to use tools effectively, they tended to become tools. But turning people into commodities and tools did not make them more human. Africans, he declared, needed to definite and control education for themselves.

Murris have the same need. If we look at how Murri children and adults have fared in the educational institutions of colonial origin in this country, we come to the same sort of questions and conclusion. Generally, in our experience, those institutions have been, and to a large degree, still are:

a   Colonial in origin, and, for us, colonizing. They do not have roots in this land. The easy interchangeability of staff and textbooks, nationally and internationally, indicates and perpetuates that rootlessness, a detachment from this land and responsibility for it: It also points to persistence of a Western education empire.

b   Patronizing. Their desire to 'uplift' us, their commitment to helping us 'catch up', and the prevalence of the missionary mentality, wanting to bring us out of darkness and into the light, show an arrogance and insensitivity that is offensive. Before Australia was colonized, American Indians had experienced the same thing. In 1744, a treaty was negotiated with the Indians of the Six Nations at Lancaster, Pennsylvania. The Indians declined an offer in that treaty to send some of their young men to a white college, saying:

> We are convinced that you mean to do us Good by your Proposal; and we thank you heartily. But you who are wise must know that different Nations have different Conceptions of things and that you will therefore not take it amiss, if our Ideas of this kind of Education happen not to be the same as yours. We have had some experience of it. Several of our young People were formerly brought up at the Colleges of the Northern Provinces: They were instructed in all your Sciences; but, when they came back to us, they were bad Runners, ignorant of every means of living in the woods ... neither fit for Hunters, Warriors, nor Counsellors, they were totally good for nothing.
>
> We are, however, not the less oblig'd by your kind Offer, tho' we decline accepting it; and, to show our grateful Sense of it, if the Gentlemen of Virginia will send us a Dozen of their Sons, we will take Care of their Education, Instruct them in all we know, and make Men of them. (McLuhan 1971, p. 57)

c   Assimilationist. Until recent decades, and in many instances today, attempts have been made to suppress Murri values, knowledge, language and culture, and substitute the Western ones. A decade ago, it was common for Aboriginal children to be punished for conversing in their own language at school: and in many places Aboriginal English – English reflecting the syntax of a Murri language – is still suppressed.

d   Alien. Relationships, practices, structures and values (e.g., individualism, competition, direct questioning, etc.) are often quite alien and opposed to Murri ones. They serve the colonizing society, and do virtually nothing to help that society confront the arrogance, racism and barbarism which underpinned the colonization of this land, and their present day legacies.

e   Divisive. They have tended – indeed, are often intended – to alienate children from their elders, to develop an elite that will take over the pacification and control of their own people, as the Native Police were developed some 140 years ago.

f   Limiting. Where an openness to Aboriginal knowledge has been shown, its expression is limited by being contained within white terms of reference.

Of course we are told that we need the basic skills of reading, writing, arithmetic, etc., if we are to cope with the modern world. But we see that schools often fail to equip white children, especially the ones Murris tend to associate with at school, with those skills: and even where they do, we see that their chances to utilize them are often severely limited.

Is it any wonder, then, that Murri children do not readily fit into schools, or show much enthusiasm? Indeed, when I hear a Murri child say that he is enjoying school, and doing well, while I might say 'That's good!', my response varies from uneasiness to caution to suspicion. I believe this is an understandable reaction.

Of course people will point to success. For example because I'm a lecturer in a university, people will say to me that I've got on through the system. I didn't finish my primary schooling: those schooldays were the horror of my life. Big blanks hide memories too painful to recall. I got my education from my parents, who themselves had little formal schooling, and from the community. I got it despite school. I was appointed a lecturer in the University of Queensland without a degree, but on 'Aboriginal standards of intellectual excellence' (*Sunday Mail*, Brisbane, 20 November 1983). This followed extensive debate and discussion at many levels in the University community about the recognition of such standards, and of the importance of Aboriginal knowledge (*Courier Mail*, Brisbane, 13 September 1983).

This was an initiative of great significance for the Aboriginal community, and the university. It was a recognition of another intellectual tradition, indigenous to this country, entitled to a place in the university, and created a new potential for dialogue and harmony between those traditions. It opens up the vision of an enriched, more mature university, at last putting its roots down in this land, and tapping into a past measured in tens of thousands of years.

Conclusion

I hope that this chapter does not make people feel guilty: uncomfortable, perhaps, but not guilty. As the poet Bruce Dawe says, 'Guilt's a slippery thing' (Dawe 1986, p. 38). My concern has not been just to make things better for us, or better between us: but an invitation for people who have come from elsewhere to live in this country and call it 'home', to confront themselves, to own their own history in this land, and to come to grips with the colonial structures, practices and attitudes that persist today. It is an invitation to become aware of their effects on each of us, and on this land, and to work towards building a better future.

My hope is that the extent to which Western-style schooling has become subservient to the colonizing process will be recognized. In this country, such schooling perpetuates it; in the Pacific it expands it; and in some places it provides the means for pacifying, assimilating, and manipulating the colonized, justifying the colonizers and masking their economic and military interests and strategies. My hope is that together we will make schooling a process of liberation for both the colonized and colonizer, the harbinger of a new future, in which people and land are placed at the centre, rather than progress, technology, money, and growth in gross national product (GNP).

In 1988 that choice was made explicit in a special performance by traditional dancers from Cape York on the asphalt road in front of the entrance to Expo 88. And, from the Western tradition, it was recently articulated by the Canadian David Suzuki when he urged governments to aim to reduce GNP, or face ecological disaster.

My hope involves a learning process. Jean Paul Sartre (Fanon 1967, p. 12) spoke to his fellow Europeans about the colonized: 'It is enough that they show us what we have made of them for us to realize what we have made of ourselves'. The indigenous peoples know the colonizers very well, and are willing to help their growth in self-awareness – for your sake, for our sake – so that the land may be protected, made well again, for everyone. Then we might all be able to look at our history stretching as far into the future as we Murris are able to see ours stretching behind us.

It will mean that in schools, Aboriginal knowledge will not be just another optional subject – interesting, a cheap price to pay for a quiet conscience – but knowledge with a maturity so deeply rooted in this land, and concerned for its wellbeing, that its potential contribution to the building of a healthy society, and a healthy land, might be realized.

And Aboriginal students will not be seen as 'problems' requiring special methods for incorporation into the schooling system and society, but rather representatives of the challenge to that system's capacity to change, and build harmony between all people, and between people and the land.

Note

1   Europeans were happy to class all of us who lived in Australia before the whites arrived as 'Aborigines'; this term, they tell us, has something to do with those who were here first (or out of the trees?). This masked some 700 different languages and cultural groups! Nowadays, some of us 'Aboriginal' people use different terms to describe the different groups of original inhabitants of Australia – I prefer the term 'Murri' – whatever its derivation; others use the name 'Kurri'.

References

Bell, D. 1983. *Daughters of the dreaming.* Melbourne: McPhee Gribble/George Allen & Unwin.

Berndt, R. & C. 1987. *End of an era: Aboriginal labour in the Northern Territory.* Canberra: Australian Institute of Aboriginal Studies.

Brandl, M. 1983. A certain heritage: women and their children in North Australia. In *We are bosses ourselves*, F. Gale (ed.). Canberra: Australian Institute of Aboriginal Studies.

Butlin, N. 1983. *Our original agression*. Sydney: Allen & Unwin.

Coleman, T. Australia's fairy tales. *Guardian Weekly* (Manchester) 28 February 1988.

Dawe, B. 1986. Nemesis. In *Towards sunrise*. Melbourne: Longman Cheshire.

Evans, R. November, 1986. The owl and the eagle. *Social Alternatives* (Brisbane) **5**(4) 16.

Fanon, F. 1967. *The wretched of the Earth*. London: Penguin.

Flood, J. 1983. *The archaeology of the dreamtime*. Sydney: Collins.

Human Rights and Equal Opportunities Commission. 1988. Inquiry into the Social Material Needs of Residents of NSW–Queensland Border Towns.

King-Boyes, M. 1977. *Patterns of Aboriginal culture*. Sydney: McGraw-Hill.

Liberman, K. 1985. *Understanding interaction in Central Australia: an ethnomethodological study of Australian Aboriginal people*. Boston & London: Routledge & Kegan Paul.

McLuhan, T. C. (ed.) 1971. *Touch the earth*. New York: Promontory Press.

Mulvaney, D. J. 1969. *The prehistory of Australia*. London: Penguin.

Neidjie, B., S. Davis & A. Fox 1985. *Kakadu Man: Bill Neidjie*. NSW: Mybrood.

Stanner, W. E. H. 1969. *After the dreaming: the 1968 Boyer Lectures*. Sydney: The Australian Broadcasting Commission.

Taylor, G. & F. Jardine 1924. Kamilaroi and White: a study of racial mixture. *Journal of Royal Society of N.S.W.* **58**.

University of Sydney. (1988). Continuing Education Program. Supplement to *Sydney Morning Herald*, 15 January 1988.

9 *The missing past in South African history*

STEPHEN GAWE & FRANCIS MELI

> Africa is a Dark Continent . . . because its history is lost. . . . [The] roots
> . . . of Africa are buried in antiquity. They are, however, rediscover-
> able; and they will in time be rediscovered. (Paul Robeson speaking in
> 1934 [in Foner 1978, p. 88])

The colonial background

The first and second British occupations of the Cape Province, both of
which occurred at the turn of the 19th century, were followed by decades of
frenetic colonial activity in Africa by Europeans, involving 'discovery',
pioneering, prospecting, and annexing. In South Africa this climaxed, after
the Anglo–Boer War (1899–1902) in the extension of British rule to include
all four provinces of South Africa – the Cape Province, Natal, the Transvaal,
and the Orange Free State. By the Act of Union of 1909, however, the
British government gave full self-government to South Africa in a manner
that ensured continuing White domination there (Roux 1946). As a result,
there was erosion of the limited rights that some black South Africans had
had until 1909. The Act marked the transition from a situation in which the
colonizers were a dominant but foreign power to what has been called a
'colonialism of a special type' (Van Diepen 1988, p. 4). Now the White
ruling minority occupied the same territory as the oppressed people themselves. The Act of Union therefore set the conditions that made possible the
development of South Africa's peculiar and overtly racist practice, generally
known as apartheid. The term was first used in the South African Parliament
in 1944 when Dr D. F. Malan described his party's ideal: 'To ensure the
safety of the white race and of Christian civilisation by the honest maintenance of the principles of apartheid and guardianship' (Bunting 1971, p. 24).
The ideological underpinning of apartheid is Christian Nationalism, whose
pedagogic philosophy, Christian National Education, holds that the successful development of the nation depends on the young obtaining 'through
history teaching a true vision of the nation's origins, cultural tradition and
"the content of the trend in that inheritance"' (Carter 1962, p. 263).

The economic and political damage wreaked by colonialism is something
that has been well documented. There is ample recorded evidence to show
that the colonialists' search for land, cattle, raw materials, markets, and

labour power frequently resulted in genocidal wars and destruction of indigenous social systems. Although it can be argued that 'European colonial rule in Africa was more effective in destroying indigenous African structures than in destroying African culture, the tension between new imported structures and old resilient cultures is part of the post-colonial war of cultures in the African Continent' (Mazrui 1986, p. 20). A deliberate policy of attempting to influence the ideas of the colonized was practised:

> Thus we can immediately see the logic of placing the missionaries in the forefront of the colonisation process. A man who succeeds in making a group of people accept a foreign concept in which he is expert makes them perpetual students whose progress in the particular field can only be evaluated by him; the student must constantly turn to him for guidance and promotion. (Steve Biko in Stubbs 1978, p. 94)

Education played an important part in this process of subjugation, particularly in the way in which history was used to justify the systems of White domination. Biko warned that we 'would be too naive to expect our conquerors to write unbiased histories about us' (Stubbs 1978, p. 95).

Colonialism has been consistent in its use of violence to impose itself on colonized people. Such violence may take many forms. There is physical violence in various forms such as the forcible seizure of land, slavery, and indentured labour. There is also a more subtle form of violence, often in the form of authority using its political dominance to force people into an alien way of life, such as happens when missionaries insist that converts dress in European-style clothes and live in mission stations away from their unconverted relations and friends (Stubbs 1978, p. 66). But perhaps the most profound form of violence is the control of ideas. In this chapter we are concerned with the way in which history has been falsified or distorted in order to fit the presuppositions and intentions of the rulers. Such falsification of the historical record has continued ever since 1909 because of the continuing need to find moral justification for the system of apartheid much as the earlier British colonial system also needed to be justified.

Apartheid today

Prejudices that were rife in the 19th century continue in similar vein today:

> There may be those who think that a Kafir Parliament and a Kafir Governor would be very good for a Kafir country. I own that I am not one of them . . . I will not say but that in coming ages a Kafir may make as good a Prime Minister as Lord Beaconsfield. But he cannot do so now . . . nor in this age . . . nor for many ages to come . . . for the next hundred years we shall not choose to be ruled by him. (Trollope 1878, pp. 60–1)

And almost a century later:

> In many parts of the world, contact with the European civilization
> caused the disappearance of the indigenous populations. Under the
> benevolent care of the Whites, the non-Whites in South Africa not only
> survived the impact of White civilization, but began to increase at such
> a rate that they now outnumber the Whites 4:1. (*South African Yearbook*
> 1967, p. 66)

Both views are attempts to justify White domination in Southern Africa on
the grounds that it is in the interests of Black people. It is at this point that
the South African government seeks further support in spurious history,
claiming that

> South Africa has never been exclusively a Black man's country. The
> Bantu have no greater claim to it than its white population. Bantu tribes
> from Central and East Africa *invaded* South Africa at the time when
> Europeans *landed* at the Cape. (*South African Yearbook* 1967, p. 69, our
> italics)

Such distortions have in fact been discredited in reputable circles for many
years:

> To sum up, we may say that historical evidence long ago pointed to
> penetration on the east side of South Africa by Bantu-speakers, reach-
> ing as far south as the Transkei by the sixteenth century, and probably
> much earlier. (Inskeep 1969, p. 39)

Indeed, recent evidence points to the likelihood of even earlier occupation of
South Africa by Bantu-speakers:

> The Southern-Western Transvaal prehistoric Black population spoke
> Sotho-Tswana languages. The past achievements of the Sotho-Tswana
> people from circa AD 350 onwards in the Southern-Western-Central
> Transvaal, prepared these people for rapid assimilation in the local
> Transvaal economy of 1986. (Mason 1987, p. 1)

Combined with distortion, and the use of selective evidence, there is an
attempt to argue that the Blacks have always been divided, and arguments
are put forward that can be seen as an attempt to 'divide and rule':

> Some of these ancient tribal rivalries are as potent a force today as when
> they first originated, ready to erupt into violence at what, to Western-
> ers, often seems trite provocation. (*South African Yearbook* 1987/8,
> p. 176)

Some of the earlier examples of bias in the interpretation of South African history may be attributed to a tendency among professional academics to give more weight to what is written than to otherwise unsubstantiated oral evidence, provided by people who are not held to have a tradition of literacy. More recent historical works include at least some oral evidence (Boyce 1974, Keegan 1988), but continue the bias against Black history. Thus Black students studying in 1976, the year of the Soweto riots, found that they were supposed to read Boyce's (1974) history textbook which, in 123 pages devoted to South African history between 1910 and 1970, made not a single mention of the African National Congress (ANC). In general, where Black people are mentioned in history textbooks it is virtually always from a White and negative perspective. Such a negative tradition can probably be traced back to a 19th-century historian, G. M. Theal (1894, 1902), the prolific author of an 11-volume history of South Africa, of whose influence Saunders (1988, p. 37) said: 'Later [South African] historians often ignored Theal's crude and sometimes bizarre views on race and class but took over from him certain central myths, which he did more than anyone to propagate'. The Black schoolchild has therefore been presented with a view of the past that has consistently declared the role of Blacks to be negative and illegitimate, while that of the Whites is always benign and legitimate. The White account of the South African past was written. The Black account was not.

The excluded past

One form of exclusion of the past occurs, therefore, when dominant institutions are compelled by their ideology to treat as evidence only what is congenial, and to disregard what is inconvenient. Authors in Muller's *Five Hundred Years* (1981) ignored not only relevant general archaeological information, but also the specific evidence from the Broederstroom Iron Age sites (Mason 1987, p. 129).

A second mode of exclusion is peculiar to archaeological evidence. Prehistory and archaeology are not seen as 'relevant' or 'useful' subjects. In the *Oxford History of South Africa*, the first edition of which broke new ground in South African historiography, especially by its use of an archaeological perspective, the section on archaeology (Inskeep 1969) is only a small part of the book. Nevertheless this represents a beginning of the process of demythologizing South African history.

A third mode of exclusion has to do with control of the market for published material. For example, it is easier for material to be published in the West than in the Third World. In South Africa it has been particularly difficult for a Black writer to have a book published. In addition, the fact that the Department of Education, Arts and Sciences controls the selection of, and market for, school textbooks means that only 'acceptable' materials can be produced. Bias with regard to the written word in South Africa is clear in works such as *The Press as Opposition* (Potter 1975) which makes no mention of any newspapers in indigenous languages, in spite of the fact that, for example, *Imvo*, the oldest Black South African weekly newspaper in existence, has been produced since the 19th century. It consists mainly of Xhosa language articles, with some English pieces, and is read principally in Cape province. By omitting reference to *Imvo*, Potter is in line with other writers on South Africa who ignore Blacks.

The potential of archaeology in discovering the excluded past is enormous. However, this potential is dependent on certain fundamental social conditions (Hall 1984). When these are in evidence it can help to validate this past. Together with other perspectives on the past, archaeology can become a tool to throw more light on the present. In South Africa, a commitment to learning is part of the struggle for liberation because the fight for truth is not only linked with the fight for survival but is part of it (La Guma 1971, p. 229).

Another of the ways in which the past is presented in distorted forms is a result of prejudices of many kinds. Racial prejudice is a well-researched phenomenon and it has influenced a great deal of writing on South Africa. For example, Theal (quoted in Saunders 1988, p. 30) remarked, at the turn of the century, that the San were so primitive that 'one can hardly conceive of living beings entitled to be termed *men* (sic) in a lower condition than the Bushman.'

Apartheid's distortion of the past

The two principal forms of distortion that we have discussed are common to most types of colonialism as well as to the form of colonialism that is peculiar to South Africa. The ideology of apartheid needed extra props to support it. One of its main principles is a belief in White supremacy. In the Constitution of the National Party (1952) this is stated as a recognition that 'Natives and Coloureds . . . are permanent parts of the country's population, under the Christian trusteeship of the European races' (quoted in Carter 1962, p. 469). The ideology affirms that 'the Bantu in the urban areas should be regarded as migratory citizens not entitled to political or social rights equal to those of the Whites' (National Party pamphlet, 1947, quoted in La Guma 1971, p. 25). As these claims are contrary to common sense and known history it became necessary for history to be reformulated in order to give some verisimilitude to claims that the Africans have neither right nor historical justification for their demands for land and national self-determination (Bernstein in La Guma 1971, pp. 62–3).

This massive brainwashing did not end there. The Blacks had to be divided too. The Coloureds and Indians, it was said, would suffer dreadfully if Africans were to come to power because there would be chaos and a bloodbath . . . in short, racial discrimination in reverse (La Guma 1971, pp. 25–6). At the same time the same Black Africans are being exposed to propaganda that brands the liberation movement as terrorists and their enemies, in spite of the fact that it has constantly rejected terrorism. Speaking at a conference called by the World Council of Churches in 1987, Oliver Tambo, president of the African National Congress, said:

> It is perfectly clear that the source of violence throughout our region is the apartheid regime. To end that violence, we have to bring the apartheid regime to an end. We have been forced to wage armed struggle precisely to achieve this objective. To terminate that struggle would have one effect, and one effect only . . . the further perpetuation of the apartheid system . . .
>
> We would also like to make the point here that to the best of our knowledge the Christian Church has never been pacifist . . . However, it cannot be correct that the concept of a just war should be applied selectively and that the reaction of the oppressed to the violence of the apartheid state should be equated to the deliberate state terrorism of the Pretoria regime (ANC, May 1987).

Another bogey raised by some White commentators is that of the independent African states, whom South African Blacks are taught to despise because they are somehow less 'developed' than South Africa. A false patriotism that is a form of racism is thus nurtured, albeit a racism that is practised by people who are themselves victims of racism. It is a violation of the principles enshrined in the Charter of the Organisation of African Unity, which seeks to promote African unity and the harmonization of policies among African countries on the basis of nonalignment. It also overlooks the fact that South Africa has been developed through the toil and sweat of millions of Africans from Malawi, Tanzania, Botswana, Mozambique, Angola, Swaziland, Lesotho and Namibia. As migrant labourers, some of these people continue to work in the South African mines and therefore make a considerable contribution to the economic development of South Africa.

History has been mangled to justify the present land distribution in South Africa. The 1967 *South African Yearbook* argued that the process by which the present land distribution occurred was a benign one, and even the 1987/88 *Yearbook* claims, as we have already shown, that it was only the arrival of the Whites that brought peace to a land of a people mutually hostile and incapable of living together in harmony. This kind of reasoning is used nowadays to explain any fights or hostilities among Blacks. A wise man once said that when White people disagree, that is politics, when Black people disagree, that is factionalism; when White people fight, that is a misunderstanding, but when Black people fight, that is tribal lawlessness.

Religion has also been used to bolster the system. The Dutch Reformed Church has played a crucial role in adumbrating a theological basis for the policy of apartheid (Carter 1962, p. 272 ff.). Parts of the Bible, particularly the Old Testament, are used to support the ideology. Like Israel of the Old Testament, the Afrikaners have a mission, they are the chosen people. This belief is reaffirmed every year on 16 December (a day which the liberation movement has named Heroes' Day to remember the fighters for Black freedom), when Afrikaners rededicate themselves to keep South Africa White in memory of their victory in 1838 against the Zulus. In their maintenance of White supremacy, however, they use indigenous people. In South Africa itself they use Black people to fight against the democratic movement. These 'vigilantes' seem to have been given carte blanche by the South African government to wreak havoc on the liberation movement (Mzala 1988, pp. 139 ff.). The divisions thus engendered 'prove' the claims made about Blacks being historically mutally hostile. In Namibia a serious tragedy is the militarization of the !Kung San. Lee (quoted in Williams 1987) contrasts the formation of a battalion of !Kung San by the South African Defence Force with this declaration by a !Kung leader:

> SWAPO won't kill us. We're good with SWAPO and with these soldiers too . . . We're good people. We'd share the pot with SWAPO. But these soldiers are the owners of the fighting . . . I won't let my children be soldiers, the experts at anger. The soldiers will bring the killing, this I know.

The Afrikaners regard themselves as a people chosen by God for this life of privilege (Magee 1968, p. 11), for which they have chosen the !Kung San in Namibia to make sacrifices. Bestall (1986) quotes a racist statement made by the Minister of Native Affairs in 1934, after the San community (then called 'Bushmen') had demanded land rights and permission to hunt:

> It would be a biological crime if we allowed this peculiar race to die out because it is a race that looks more like a baboon than the baboon itself does. So far we have about 20 that are just about genuine. We intend letting them stay [in the park] as a tourist attraction and allow them to hunt with bows and arrows but without dogs. We regard them as part of the fauna of this country.

Even earlier, Theal had referred to these people as 'more like jackals than human beings' (quoted in Saunders 1988, p. 30). The 'chosen people' have not only changed the San from a hunting people to mercenary soldiers: they have also destroyed their ability to fend for themselves. The readiness to use the !Kung San fits awkwardly with the refusal to accord them a place in the history of the country. The denial of humanity to them is a wicked attempt to justify writing them out of South Africa's past.

Archaeology and a truer record

Archaeology has contributed to a correction of some of the myths and distortions we have mentioned. This includes the research at Broeder-stroom, to which we have already referred, which established beyond doubt the existence of complex Iron Age societies, and has helped to demolish much of the basis for the 'Stone Age' myths propagated by some White commentators. These findings cannot, however, totally eliminate distortions and prejudices, but they are invaluable tools in the right hands. Like history, the prehistoric and protohistoric sciences will always continue to be mediated by people. In South Africa most of the important archaeological and historical work so far has been done by White people, the best of whom show a high level of scholarly integrity. Nevertheless, Black people demand an educational system that will allow a far greater contribution from their own scholars.

Liberation through the past and future

The struggle surrounding the interpretation of the past is part of the struggle for liberation in South Africa. This has consequences for the conditions in which such exploration can be conducted. Like the struggle for rights, the struggle for truth is violently suppressed in South Africa. The campaign for the isolation of South Africa is therefore directly relevant in the academic context as well as in the political context. The African National Congress Freedom Charter, to which we have already referred, declares: 'The doors of learning and culture shall be opened.' (La Guma 1971, pp. 229 ff.). This demand is not for a limited freedom in the area of learning. It is an affirmation in the academic field of something that includes and transcends learning, but in which such academic research is essential. A necessary condition for such academic freedom in South Africa is the destruction of apartheid. The Arusha Conference of December 1987 called for 'the intensification of the academic/cultural boycott of the illegitimate regime while strengthening support for the academic/cultural forces of resistance' (African National Congress 1987). The Conference demanded 'urgent action by the peoples of the world to hasten the end of the apartheid system as a necessary condition and prerequisite for the transformation of South Africa into a united, democratic and non-racial country' (African National Congress 1987). Within South Africa the Congress of South African Trade Unions (COSATU) has responded positively by affirming the role of culture in the struggle. In August 1988 Chris Dlamini, COSATU's Natal president and national vice-president (quoted in *Southscan* August 1988), referred to culture as

a transformation borne out of conflict between what is emerging and what is already in existence. We need to transform, once again, the very indigenous cultural forms into an expression of what is new, what is novel and what is progressive. Culture is one of the main pillars that make people aware that they exist and that they can play a role in the broader democratic struggle.

As we have said, the struggle surrounding the interpretation of our past is part of this affirmation of our culture, and a vital aspect of the struggle for the liberation of South Africa.

Conclusion

A question arises: will this 'hidden past' feature in a future education system in South Africa? This question is all the more important if one considers that our future does not depend on some abstract hopes and wishes, but upon our actions and thinking today. In this respect there are two schools of thought, namely that of the ruling circles, and that of the people.

Within the ruling circles there are voices advocating the 'rewriting' of South African history in the light of President Botha's 'reform policy' and the 'new constitution'. As an example Bozzoli (1987, p. xv) cites Professor Floors van Jaarsveld, 'an eminent National Party school-textbook historian and author of some of the dominant versions of historical truth conveyed to countless white and black schoolchildren over several decades', who in 1985 suggested that this would be a means to persuade 'brown people' to conceive of their contribution to society as labourers and not as a 'singularly oppressed and exploited people'.

Bozzoli (1987, p. xvi) says even this new 'reformist' but still hegemonistic interpretation of history is not without problems, because old hegemonic ideas have broken down, but have not been replaced by new ones and 'it is hard for ideologues used to the language and attitude of the intellectual rapist to transfer their hard skills to the tasks of sedition'. This is not what we envisage and mean when we talk of reinterpreting the past.

Our people think differently. They are called upon – and this is more relevant now than ever before – to rediscover their past traditions, to heighten their vigilance against the national degradation that plunders and cripples their culture, to close ranks in the struggle against apartheid, and to discover and map out their place in that struggle. The development of a progressive and patriotic historical consciousness and thinking is part of the struggle for economic and social emancipation from apartheid and colonialism.

One of the forms of the political and ideological class and national struggles in our country is the growing historical consciousness. This is closely connected with the general process of polarization that is taking place in South Africa, and this process encompasses the writing of history. Apartheid theorists distort and even hide our past. But progressive historians and archaeologists in our country demand a mediated past which is free from racism and colonialism. We must expose and demolish the apologetic colonial interpretation.

Paying attention to the past is an obligation – a struggle against the forces of darkness and doom. The hidden past is part of the present, and that lays a foundation for addressing the future. Indeed the currently hidden past will feature prominently in a future education system in South Africa, especially since it will be a system designed by the very people who have suffered exclusion. In future nothing will be hidden – the people, who in any case are the makers of their past, will rediscover it.

References

African National Congress 1987. *Peoples of the world against apartheid for a democratic South Africa: programme of action*. Arusha, Tanzania 1–4 December (mimeo).

Bestall, C. 1986. A small win for the San: 200 years on. *Weekly Mail* 20 January.

Boyce, A. 1974. *Europe and South Africa: A history for Standard 10*. Cape Town: Juta.

Bozzoli, B. (ed.) 1987. *Class, community and conflict – South African Perspectives*. Johannesburg: Ravan Press.

Bunting, B. 1971. The origins of apartheid. In *Apartheid: a collection of writings on South African racism by South Africans*. A. La Guma (ed.). London: Lawrence & Wishart.

Carter, G. 1962. *The Politics of inequality: South Africa since 1948*. London: Thames & Hudson.

Dlamini, C. 1988. Speech reported in *Southscan: A Bulletin of Southern African Affairs* **2**(47). London: Southscan.

Foner, P. (ed.) 1978. *Paul Robeson speaks: writings, speeches, interviews, 1918–74*. London: Quartet Books.

Hall, M. 1984. The burden of tribalism: the social context of Southern African Iron Age studies. *American Antiquity* **49**(3), 455–67.

Inskeep, R. 1969. The archaeological background. In *Oxford History of South Africa. Vol. 1*, M. Wilson & L. Thompson (eds), 1–39. Oxford: Clarendon Press.

Keegan, T. 1988. *Facing the storm: portraits of Black lives in rural South Africa*. Cape Town: David Phillip.

La Guma, A. (ed.) 1971. *Apartheid: a collection of writings on South African racism by South Africans*. London: Lawrence & Wishart.

Magee, M. 1968. *White Christianity*. London: Sheed & Ward.

Mason, R. 1987. *Origins of Black people of Johannesburg and the southern western central Transvaal AD 350–1880*. Johannesburg: Witwatersrand University Press.

Mazrui, A. 1986. *The Africans: a triple heritage*. London: BBC Publications.

Mzala, 1988. *Gatsha Buthelezi: chief with a double agenda*. London: Zed Press.

Muller, C. 1981. *Five hundred years: a history of South Africa*. Pretoria: Academica.

Potter, E. 1975. *The Press as opposition: the political role of South African newspapers*. London: Chatto & Windus.

Roux, E. 1946. *Time longer than rope*. Madison: University of Wisconsin Press.

Saunders, D. 1988. *The making of the South African past: major historians on race and class*. Cape Town: David Philip.

South African Yearbook, 1967. *State of South Africa*. Johannesburg: Da Gama.

South African Yearbook 1987/88. Pretoria: Bureau for Information, on behalf of the Department of Foreign Affairs.

Stubbs, A. (ed.) 1978. *Steve Biko: I write what I like*. London: Bowerdean.

Tambo, O. 1987. *Speech given at the World Council of Churches Liberation Movement Dialogue at Lusaka*. Lusaka: ANC, 4–8 May (mimeo).

Theal, G. 1894 (1917). *South Africa*. London (8th edn).

Theal, G. 1902. *Progress of South Africa in the Century*. Toronto and Philadelphia: Linscott/London and Edinburgh: Chambers.

Trollope, A. 1878 (1968). *South Africa, vol. 1*. London: Dawsons.
Van Diepen, M. 1988. *The National Question in South Africa*. London: Zed Press.
Williams, G. 1987. *Namibia: writing for liberation*. (Proceedings of the Namibia 1884–1984 Conference). London: Namibia Support Committee.

10 *The teaching of the past of the Native peoples of North America in US schools*

SHIRLEY BLANCKE &
CJIGKITOONUPPA JOHN PETERS SLOW TURTLE

Introduction

The past of the Native peoples of the USA might seem to an outside observer an obvious and necessary part of historical studies in US schools. That this topic has not traditionally been a part of the curriculum therefore comes as a surprise. The general lack of knowledge of the Native past in the USA is a matter of concern to those of both Native and non-Native ancestry who see in it a mirror of racism in American society. Since the civil rights movement of the 1960s and early 1970s increasing efforts have been made to correct the situation.

The USA has generally been regarded as a Western nation whose roots are in Western European civilization, and US history has been taught to convey that view since the nation was founded (see Kehoe, Ch. 17, this volume). That Native peoples contributed anything to its development has been largely ignored, and even now to point out Native contributions to governmental principles of democracy is revolutionary.

Those teaching non-Native children about American Indian cultures quickly become aware of stereotypical views arising out of profound ignorance. Popular entertainment such as Hollywood movies reinforces the stereotype of savage primitive warriors, and many non-Indian children react with fear at the mention of the term 'Indian'. Such misconceptions are not merely a matter of academic concern. Increasingly there are Indian children in the classroom whose self-esteem and relationships with other children suffer from these attitudes.

The term 'Indian' is itself a gross oversimplification arising from Christopher Columbus's navigational mistake. It masks the complexities of a continent of 500 nations and 300 languages, but it is used in the same way that the term 'European' is used – for convenient generalization. The term 'savage' has connotations of an unlettered, childlike, and barely human being, who could not, by definition, contribute anything of significance to European 'civilization', or ultimately to a new nation built on that culture. The fact that Benjamin Franklin was able to draw on Iroquois principles of government showed his stature as a man ahead of most of his contemporaries (Johansen 1982).

To the Native peoples of North America the history of the USA is the story of the rape of their land. They know themselves to have inhabited the land since time immemorial, and consider themselves to have been created there. A Cherokee of the National Indian Youth Council wrote (Wilkinson 1981, p. 46):

> The history of Indian people is not taught as Indian history but as the history of Indian/White relations. This approach gives the impression that Indians would have no past at all if it had not been for the European invasion . . . It is difficult to see how any Indian young person could get any perspective on himself when his past is presented to him as a mere side-show in the panorama of human existence.

The organization of Indian education in the USA

In the USA there are three major categories of schools. By far the largest category is public schools financed by taxes raised in the towns where they are situated, sometimes with supplementary funds from state or federal government special programmes. A second is private or parochial (private religious) schools. The third category consists of Indian schools paid for by the federal government. The federal government plays no part in the public school system, and although it comes under the purview of the states it is made up of virtually autonomous school districts only minimally regulated by state laws.

Undoubtedly the aspect of the US school system least known to the general public is the organization of Indian education. It cannot be understood without reference to the history of the development of the USA, and the need of a young country founded by Europeans to conquer and then to control the indigenous inhabitants of the land.

For 200 years the federal government has pursued a policy of assimilation of Indians into the majority culture, a policy that followed on from early attempts by the American colonies to exterminate the Native peoples. New Amsterdam (later New York State), Connecticut, Massachusetts, Virginia, and Pennsylvania all placed bounties on Indian scalps between the mid-17th century and the mid-18th century (Waters 1977, p. 279).

Since the civil rights movement of the 1960s and early 1970s assimilationist policy has to some extent been mitigated by two education acts that greatly increased Indians' control over the education of their children, but the assimilationist trend, which has resulted in 90 per cent of Native children now being in public, private, or parochial schools (US Department of the Interior, Bureau of Indian Affairs 1987, p. 5), continues to have great momentum.

The percentage of Indian children in any particular public school may vary from 90 per cent near reservations to less than 10 per cent in big cities (Havighurst 1981, p. 329). A 1980 census recorded 1.5 million American

Indians and Alaska Natives, and in 1987 861 000 were estimated to live on or near reservations. At the present time only 10 per cent of Indian children (40 000) are in schools still operated by the Bureau of Indian Affairs (BIA), a subagency of the federal government's Department of the Interior, responsible historically for Indian education. The BIA funds 181 educational facilities, half operated by the tribes themselves who contract from the BIA (US Department of the Interior, Bureau of Indian Affairs 1987, pp. 4, 6). Most are in the western USA with the exception of three in Maine and two in Florida; eastern Indians had for the most part been integrated into non-Indian schools from an early period (Frazier 1985). Two-thirds are day schools, and one-third boarding schools.

To date 47 000 Indians have completed a college education (Swimmer 1987). In 1985 the Full Circle Consortium was formed to train and develop Indian professionals. It now comprises 17 colleges and universities across the country with American Indian programmes. Since 1970 the American Indian Program at Harvard's Graduate School of Education has been training Indian teachers, and in 1975 the BIA ranked it the most successful existing programme. The development of many Indian community colleges has also been very important for Indian higher education (Chavers 1981, p. 14).

Indian education and federal legislation

The means by which the federal government acquired responsibility for Indian education lies in the history of land transactions that also resulted in the government's removal of Indian Nations to reservations in the west. The Indians exchanged land for the federal government's promises to undertake 'trust responsibilities' to provide for their economic needs, housing, health, and education. Recently Ross Swimmer, a former Cherokee chief and now the Assistant Secretary of the BIA, has said that there are over 4000 treaties and statutes relating to Indian tribes to which the BIA is required to adhere, resulting in one federal administrator for every 19 Indians (Swimmer 1987).

Two fundamental and contradictory ideas about the legal relationship of the federal government to Indian nations emerged from the land treaties: that tribes were domestic dependent nations, which implied some measure of autonomy, and that they were as wards to a guardian (Deloria & Lytle 1983, p. 33).

Educational provisions in Indian treaties started in 1794 with an undertaking to the Iroquois Oneida and Tuscarora nations of New York State, and the Algonquian Stockbridge Indians of western Massachusetts, that some of their youth would be trained in milling and sawing (Blue Dog & Kittson 1979, p. 3). Treaty-making ended with the treaty of the Sioux Nations of Dakota in 1889 (Rosenfelt 1973, p. 492).

During the 19th century the overt reason given for educating the Indians was the need to 'civilize the savages', but even more pressing for the developing nation was the need to pacify the indigenous peoples. Indian youth who are being 'civilized' in government institutions would not have the chance to join their tribes' warriors, and Indian parents might have a healthy fear of their children being potential hostages (Rosenfelt 1973, p. 493). BIA boarding schools earned an infamous reputation for dehumanization through rigid military-like discipline and the proscription of Indian language and religion (Henninger & Esposito 1972).

By the 1920s government Indian policy had begun to change. The Merriam report of 1924 criticized lack of Indian empowerment to make educational decisions. In a few years the Commissioner of Indian Affairs, John Collier, started programmes in bilingual education and Indian culture, adult basic education and the training of Indian teachers, and also replaced many boarding schools with day schools. In 1934 the Johnson–O'Malley Act effected the transfer of many Indian children from federal to state schools, and there have been subsequent acts funding Indian education.

Developments after the Second World War

After the Second World War the federal government attempted to hasten the integration of Native peoples into the mainstream society by unilaterally starting to 'terminate' the special trust relationship of the treaties. The trusts of five nations were terminated, an act which threatened tribal culture. The BIA closed many schools, a policy opposed by some Indians who were afraid that the states would offer their children an inferior education (Rosenfelt 1973, pp. 500–2). The termination policy was reversed in 1958, but the fear it engendered continues to play a role in the present, prompting opposition to the BIA's effort to transfer responsibility for schools to the tribes (Swimmer 1987).

The first legislation that effectively empowered Native people in the education field was the Indian Education Act of 1972. This provided funds to develop special programmes for Indian students to meet their educational and cultural needs in public schools or other educational institutions, to train Indian teachers, and for adult education. Its effects were carried further by the 1975 Indian Self-Determination and Education Assistance Act. In a 1980 study of New England Native education, however, Claudette Bradley (Schaghticoke), found that Indian parents were still anxious to have more influence in the schools, and felt that non-Indians needed to be much better informed on Native history and culture (Bradley 1980, pp. 69–74).

Evaluations of government educational policies differ sharply. Robert J. Havighurst, the author of a major study of Indian education in 1971, pointed to what he regarded as elements of success. Between 1960 and 1970 the number of Indian youth attending post secondary educational institutions increased fivefold, a much better result than that attained by other 'low-income' groups (Havighurst 1981, p. 330). Dean Chavers (Lumbee) of Stanford University similarly saw great advances in Indian education, while noting Indians were still educationally behind the majority population (Chavers 1981, p. 14).

Two other Indian leaders took a different view. Gerald Wilkinson (Cherokee) of the National Indian Youth Council pointed out that a school drop-out rate two to three times higher than the national average, and a suicide rate for Indian youth four to seven times higher indicated severe alienation (Wilkinson 1981, p. 44). Vine Deloria, a Sioux lawyer and author of an Indian manifesto of the 1960s, *Custer died for your sins*, saw the increased control of Indian communities over schools as a delusion if it was thought that it implied greater self-determination. In reality, he said, what the native parents were taking over was a White educational system whose values were totally alien to Indian society. He offered a plan for training young Indians that encompassed both traditional Indian wisdom and what they needed to know to function well in White society (Deloria 1981).

Native studies in public schools

Since nearly 90 per cent of Native children are now in public schools, it is relevant to an assessment of their well-being to know if their culture and history is being taught, and if so, how well.

The teaching of history and ethnic cultures in public schools comes under the heading of social studies, a loose amalgam that may include almost any subject not considered to be science, mathematics, or language. There is, however, a dominant pattern of curriculum organization that is widely used. A report on *Social Studies in the 1980s* sponsored by the National Science Foundation, the National Institute of Education, and the ERIC (Educational Resources Information Center) Clearinghouse stated that the pattern of social studies curriculum organization is extremely similar in over 16 000 school districts throughout the USA. This pattern has been established with some guidelines from the 50 states but with no central legal or professional authority dictating the curricular organization of schools (Lengel & Superka 1982, p. 39).

Social studies curricula in elementary and secondary schools are organized around topics (places, continents, events, and subjects) that were established more than 60 years ago. The 1982 study attributed this to tradition, lack of a compelling argument for alternative patterns, and the rigidity created by the use of published textbooks that follow past patterns of success rather than innovate and risk financial failure (Lengel & Superka 1982, pp. 37–8). Ten major textbook companies out of a total of 50 control half of the textbook sales.

About 90 per cent of classroom time given to social studies involves the use of curriculum materials, and about 70 per cent of the time is spent on printed materials, mainly textbooks. As a response to studies in the 1960s that documented the inadequate treatment of ethnic and racial minorities, textbooks now contrast markedly with those of the 1950s in their depiction of the 'rich ethnic and social diversity of American people'. Yet they avoid controversial or sensitive subjects, and curriculum materials that were produced in the 1960s and 1970s by federally funded projects as alternatives to the textbooks are rarely used (Patrick & Hawke 1982, pp. 39–50).

The dominant pattern in social studies coverage may be likened to a series of concentric circles (Kehoe 1974, p. 74) or 'expanding environments' (Lengel & Superka 1982, p. 32), which start with the elementary school child's home and neighbourhood environment, and spread out to state history and geography, US history, and world cultures. In secondary school topics such as US and world history and culture are repeated with increased sophistication. Elementary education comprises seven levels, Kindergarten and Grades 1 to 6, for children aged 5 to 11. The secondary grades are 7 to 12 for children aged 12 to 17 or 18. Sometimes the lower secondary grades are referred to as Middle School.

Survey on the teaching of native studies

In an attempt to gain some direct information on the extent to which native studies are taught in the 50 states, a questionnaire was sent to state social studies representatives listed in a survey of the National Council for the Social Studies (Council of State Social Studies Specialists 1986). Questions covered the content of native studies, the grade level at which they were taught, curriculum materials, other methods of learning such as museum programmes, and the percentage of Native students in state schools.

Course content of native studies was divided into three geographic areas and four topical categories. The three areas were the state, the North American continent, and Central and South America. The four topics were archaeology (A) which refers primarily to the precontact period, i.e. the period of Native history before contact with Europeans; history (H), predominantly the postcontact period, but which includes oral history some of which could be precontact; culture (C), that body of customary beliefs, social forms, and material traits that constitutes a distinct complex of tradition of a social group; and current issues (I), matters of current concern to Native peoples that are sometimes covered in the news media, such as land cases, hunting and fishing rights, or environment problems.

Eleven of the 20 states that answered the particular question estimated that less than 1 per cent of their students were Native. Two states, Wisconsin and Wyoming, quoted figures of 1.17 per cent and 1.5 per cent respectively. States with higher Native populations were Alaska, which offered no data on children of school age, but quoted a 16 per cent figure for the total Native population, Louisiana with perhaps 5 per cent, North Dakota 4 per cent, South Dakota 9–11 per cent, and Vermont with less than 3 per cent.

All representatives except one thought that most schools included materials on Native studies, with estimates ranging from 80 per cent to 100 per cent. South Dakota quoted 10 per cent or less, and those mostly BIA schools.

Table 10.1 The state: estimated number of course units on the archaeology, history, culture, and current issues of its Native peoples in state schools

ST	Units in Elementary Grades K–6					Units in Secondary Grades Middle 7–8					High 9–12				
	A	H	C	I	(G)	A	H	C	I	(G)	A	H	C	I	(G)
AL	1	1	1		4	1	1	1			1		1		9
AK	1/2	1/2	1/2									1/2	1/4	1/4	
CA		x	x		4										
DE	1	1			2–4										
GA					5					8					
HI		M	M		K–6		M	M		7		M	M		11
IA	1	1	1												11,12
LA					K–6										
ME	+	#	#	★	4	+	★	★	★		+	★	★	★	
MD		x	x												
MS															
MO	1/2	1/2													
NE	1	1	1	1		1	1	1	1						
NJ					4	1	1	1	1						
NY					4,5					7,8					
ND					4					8					11
OH	1	2	1				2	1							
RI															
SD												25	25	1	
UT	1	1	1	1		1	1	1	1		1	1	1	1	
VT	1	1	1	1	4–6	1	1	1	1	7,8					9–11
WV					x					x					x
WI	1	1	1	30	4,5	1	1	2	5				1		
WY†															

Note. AL Alabama, AK Alaska, CA California, DE Delaware, GA Georgia, HI Hawaii, IA Iowa, LA Louisiana, ME Maine, MD Maryland, MS Mississippi, MO Missouri, NE Nebraska, NJ New Jersey, NY New York, ND North Dakota, OH Ohio, RI Rhode Island, SD South Dakota, UT Utah, VT Vermont, WV West Virginia, WI Wisconsin, WY Wyoming. ST state, A archaeology, H history, C culture, I current issues, (G) grade level. K kindergarten. x presence, M much, + little or no emphasis, ★ some emphasis, # heaviest emphasis.

† Wyoming's units were recorded as follows: Elementary Grades, A 1000, H 500, C 100, I 250; Secondary Grades 7–8, A 60, H 25, C 25, I 25. Where the Grade level only is given, no breakdown of course content was offered. Some states provided course breakdown, but no specific grade levels within the elementary or secondary grouping. Only Mississippi and Rhode Island gave no specific data in response to this question.

Table 10.2 North America: estimated number of course units on the archaeology, history, culture, and current issues of North American Native peoples in state schools.

ST	Units in Elementary Grades Grades K–6					Units in Secondary Grades Middle 7–8					High 9–12				
	A	H	C	I	(G)	A	H	C	I	(G)	A	H	C	I	(G)
AL	1	1	1		5	1	1	1		8	1	1	1		11
AK															
CA		x	x		5										
DE	1	1			2–4										
GA					5					8					11
HI					5					8					10
IA															
LA		1	1				1	1				1	1		
ME	+	#	#	★		+	#	#	★			★	★	★	
MD		1	1		4,5		+			8	+				
MS											1	1			
MO															
NE	1	1	1	1		1	1	1	1		1	1	1	1	
NJ															
NY					4,5					7,8					11
ND							1								
OH		1													
RI			1												
SD					4,6										
UT	1	1	1	1		1	1	1	1		1	1	1	1	
VT					4–6					7					11
WV		x			5							x			
WI														9	
WY								1							

Note. See Table 10.1.

Table 10.3 Central and South America: estimated number of course units on the archaeology, history, culture, and current issues of Central and South American Native peoples in state schools.

ST	Units in Elementary Grades Grades K–6					Units in Secondary Grades Middle 7–8					High 9–12				
	A	H	C	I	(G)	A	H	C	I	(G)	A	H	C	I	(G)
AL	1	1	1		6										
AK															
CA															
DE															
GA					x					x					x
HI															
IA															
LA		1	1				1	1				1	1		
ME	+	★	★	★		+	★	★	★		+	+	+	★	
MD							1	1				1	1		
MS															
MO	1/2	1/2	1			1		1			1	1	1		
NE	1	1	1			1		1							
NJ															
NY					4,5					7,8					
ND															11
OH															
RI															
SD															
UT															
VT					x					x					x
WV					x					x					x
WI	1								2				1		
WY															

Note. See Table 10.1.

The results of the question that asked for details of course content and grade levels are provided in Tables 10.1–3. A 'unit' is a four to six week period of lessons on a certain topic, and usually several units make up a course.

The answers to the survey questions lent support to the conclusions of Lengel & Superka (1982) that most school districts adhere to the 'expanding environments' model of social studies, with a topic first covered in 4th or 5th grade and again in 8th or 11th. At the same time the lack of specific grade designations by some who provided a course content breakdown suggests they may be moving towards a more flexible curriculum approach.

Most states had a unit each on their own state's Native history and culture, with only slightly less on archaeology (see Table 10.1). The exception was South Dakota, which reported 50 units in high school. However, the State social studies representative noted that those figures referred to Bureau of Indian Affairs schools, i.e. schools serving the Sioux nation. Wyoming indicated that 3 of its 49 school districts were on the Wind River Reservation (Arapaho and Shoshone nations), but despite this no high-school level courses in Native studies were recorded. Current issues fared least well, except in Wisconsin which registered an astonishing 30 units in the 4th and 5th grades. Hawaii's pattern was also exceptional, but it has had a different development from the continental states with a more centralized educational system.

With respect to studies of the Native peoples of North America as a whole the same general pattern emerged (Table 10.2), but this subject was covered somewhat less well than studies of a particular state's Native population. This conforms with the 'expanding environments' pattern. Only ten states indicated any course content on Central or South American Natives (Table 10.3). Overall, Native studies were concentrated in the elementary and lower secondary grades, which perhaps suggests they are viewed as lacking in complexity and therefore more appropriate for younger children, an enduring stereotype of the uncivilized savage.

Native studies curricular materials

Two questions on curricula tried to elicit whether state curriculum guides on native studies existed, and if not whether any curriculum on the subject was known to the state social studies representatives. The existence of such a curriculum does not necessarily imply its use however. In addition, locally developed curricula could be in use unknown to the State social studies representatives.

These questions elicited rather few detailed responses. Alaska was developing a model social studies curriculum guide that includes Alaskan studies for secondary students and a focus on Alaskan history at the elementary to 3rd grades. Hawaii's Department of Education over the period 1981 to 1986 published four large volumes of state curriculum and curriculum materials for both elementary and secondary pupils.

From the south, Louisiana cited an archaeological source, the Poverty Point, pre-historic Indian materials, written and distributed by the Office of Archaeology, Department of Culture, Tourism, and Recreation.

From the midwest, North Dakota referred to a series of 4th grade booklets called STUDY (Students Today Understanding Dakota Yesterday) which included 'The first people of North Dakota' and 'The developing Indian culture of North Dakota', and an 8th grade textbook entitled *North Dakota: a living legacy*. Utah mentioned that Indian material was included with core studies, and Wisconsin had locally developed 'Woodland Indian' units.

In the northeast, New York stated that it was greatly expanding its secondary-level coverage with the assistance of Native scholars, and had a 1975 7th grade curriculum guide entitled *Teaching a pre-Columbian culture: the Iroquois*. A major part of the Maine studies curriculum (*Dirigo*) at the 8th grade includes Native history, and Maine's representative recommended a resource book on the Wabanaki about to be published by the American Friends Service Committee. The Boston Indian Council has also developed a Wabanaki curriculum for the Boston public schools, many of whose Indian pupils come from Maine and northeast Canada.

Connecticut did not reply to the questionnaire, but in 1986 its Department of Education compiled an annotated bibliography of the Native tribes of Connecticut. The Eagle Wing Press of Naugatuck, Connecticut, a Native firm that publishes a newspaper of Indian news, produced a book on New England tribes for teachers entitled *Rooted like the ash trees* in 1987.

In Massachusetts many school systems in the Boston suburbs are developing their own Native curricula, contacting Indian people in the process. Of these Cambridge is particularly committed, with Native American culture an important focus in the lower elementary grades in a context of teaching cultural diversity. Archaeology is presented in the 6th grade. Sponsored by the Concord Museum, Barbara Robinson is developing a New England Native American Sourcebook in which she identifies nearly 30 curricula. Russell Peters, the former Wampanoag Indian Tribal Council president, was project director of a film series on Indians of the area, *People of the first light*.

To tap another source, a computer search of curricula on Native history and archaeology in the ERIC database, a listing of materials often used by teachers, produced the tally in Table 10.4.

Fifteen states were represented with materials on specific tribal groups, but the only Native nation well covered was the largest in the country, the Navajo. Some archaeology, usually pre-Contact, was included in half of the texts.

Images of native peoples in textbooks

Since those states that did not cite special materials probably use standard social studies textbooks, it might be asked what kind of picture such books convey of Native people and culture. An analysis of how Indian people

Table 10.4 ERIC database 1987: the number of history and archaeology curriculum materials by state which refer to Native peoples of that state.

State	Native Nations	Total History Texts	Texts which include Archaeology
Alaska	Aleut	2	2
Arizona	Navajo	10	2
	Pueblo	1	1
California			
Delaware	Delaware	2	2
Louisiana		1	1
Mississippi	Choctaw	2	
Montana	Blackfeet	1	
	Flathead	1	
	Winnebago	1	
Nebraska		1	
Nevada	Algonquian	1	1
New York	Iroquois	1	1
	Pawnee	5	4
Oklahoma	Ponca	2	2
	Wichita	1	
	Sisseton		
South Dakota	Wahpeton Sioux	2	
	Teton Sioux	1	
	Western Abenaki	1	1
Vermont		1	
Washington		1	
Wisconsin	Ojibway	1	

appear in 34 elementary textbooks used nationally produced the following conclusions (Ferguson & Fleming 1984).

The most important finding was that contemporary issues important to Native peoples were entirely excluded. This lends support to the question-naire results, one conclusion of which was that such material is least often taught. Generally there was little specific information on where tribes live or what resources they control. The fact that Native Americans are one of the fastest growing minority populations in the USA was ignored completely, and the only Indian contribution to American life that was given much coverage was their domestication of certain crops, particularly corn. Half the books dealt with at least some aspects of Native history after contact with Europeans, and almost all referred to the length of time Native people had been on the North American continent. But other important contri-butions to American society, such as the development of democratic prin-ciples of government, were ignored because they were generally unknown.

Curriculum development by and for Native peoples

Such a survey would present a discouraging picture if it covered the sum total of material available to schools on Native history. But a different perspective may be gained by tabulating programmes designed specifically for Indian students. Five Resource and Evaluation Centres for Native American Research were funded in 1980 to provide management and assist-ance to grantees under the 1972 Indian Education Act. Programmes in one category named Title IV, Part A, provide funds to schools to augment Indian education, and most of them include a cultural component often resulting in the local development of Native curricular materials. Center One, located in Washington, DC, serves the whole region east of the Mississippi river, and Table 10.5 quantifies its Title IV, Part A, pro-grammes in 1986.

If non-Indian teachers were to avail themselves of materials developed through this source, they might be able to overcome the shortcomings of the textbooks. Two examples of curricula developed by Native people in Massachusetts are presented below.

Native education in Mashpee

Mashpee is a town on Cape Cod that has belonged to Wampanoag Indians for most of its history. It was established as a Plantation in 1637 to reserve land for the original inhabitants of the area, the Wampanoags, as English settlers arrived in increasing numbers. The Mashpee Wampanoags adopted the English language, religion, and dress, but maintained their Indian identity. Over three and a half centuries they have struggled to retain their independence from the Massachusetts state government with varying degrees of success. They suffered white overseers and clergy who cheated

Table 10.5 The number of projects by state under Title IV, Part A, 1972 Indian Education Act, to provide tutoring and cultural programs for Native American students. Resource and Evaluation Center One, August 1986 (States east of the Mississippi river).

State	Total projects	Total students	Total projects which include culture	Total students in cultural projects
Alabama	11	7190	10	6843
Connecticut	2	123	2	123
Florida	6	659	3	357
Illinois	2	906	2	906
Indiana	1	106	1	106
Maine	4	381	3	299
Maryland	5	919	5	919
Massachusetts	3	573	2	202
Mississippi	3	98	0	0
New Jersey	3	340	3	340
New York	16	4538	11	3325
North Carolina	23	16687	20	15945
Ohio	2	285	1	200
Rhode Island	1	212	1	212
South Carolina	1	87	1	87
Vermont	1	440	1	440
Virginia	2	136	2	136

and defrauded them, but the worst threat to survival was to come in the 20th century.

In the last 20 years the Mashpees have lost control of their town and land to non-Indians who have flooded into the area in huge numbers to buy homes near the sea. In 1974 a Tribal Council was incorporated to represent the Mashpee Wampanoags in several areas of social and political concern, and the Governor of Massachusetts, Michael Dukakis, extended them state recognition as a tribe. Two years later the council fought a court case to preserve the land from unbridled development but lost it on a technicality, and the town has since been developed by non-Indians to the point of causing environmental problems (Peters 1987).

Despite an act of the Massachusetts legislature in 1789 which prohibited giving instruction in reading and writing to the Mashpee Wampanoags under penalty of death, the Mashpee built their own school nearly 50 years later. The school has been rebuilt twice, the last move occasioned by the influx of non-Indians, and is now an elementary school. High school students go to Falmouth, a nearby town.

Joan Avant Tavares, present chairman of the Tribal Council, has for eight years administered the Title IV, Part A, Indian cultural programme under the 1972 federal Indian Education Act for the Mashpee–Falmouth school district. Its purpose is to give guidance and promote cultural awareness among Indian students who are now a small minority in the area. After-school programmes are provided at the elementary school, and counselling and cultural programmes during the day at the secondary level. Tavares works with teachers to provide tutorial services in basic skills such as mathematics or reading.

Tavares has also been developing curricula on local Wampanoag culture with material on Wampanoag elders, legends, history, and values, and teachers' files on wider current issues of particular concern to Native people about which they would like the larger community to be better informed. Topics include the environment, natural resources and development issues (such as water pollution), land suits, fishing and hunting rights, and ethnic stereotyping. With the guidance of a new school superintendent, non-Indian teachers have this year shown more interest than before in using these materials.

Native high school students are particularly interested in ways of preserving their culture in today's social climate, so current issues take precedence over historical material. The fact that they are involved provides hope that the Native culture will survive.

Chabunagungamaug Nipmuck curricular development, Dudley

The Chabunagungamaug Nipmucks live mainly in the area of Dudley in south-central Massachusetts and are descendants of Nipmuck Indians converted to Christianity in the mid-17th century by the missionary John Eliot, who translated the Bible into Algonquian. Many can claim as ancestor

Eliot's Native assistant, Black James, who held office in their village or 'praying town'. This and the nearby Hassanamisco Nipmuck praying town in Grafton were described by the magistrate Daniel Gookin in 1674. An unbroken line may be traced in genealogical records because of marriage with Huguenots or adoption of their names, and also in census records.

Members of the present generation of Chabunagungamaug Nipmucks grew up attending ceremonies of the Narragansetts to the south of them in Connecticut and Rhode Island. In 1979 the Nipmucks decided to reorganize as a tribal community, forming a Chabunagungamaug Tribal Council to sponsor ceremonies and deal with community needs. Efforts were started to revive the language, since certain phrases of the Nipmuck dialect of Algonquian were still commonly used.

Over the years many members of both the Chabunagungamaug and Hassanamisco communities have given presentations to local schools and community groups on Native culture. But after the Chabunagungamaug tribal reorganization, Little Turtle, the designated tribal medicine man, and a local teacher, Christine Kwasny, worked together to provide school materials, funded by a very small state grant. Kwasny has said that she grew up in the area hearing that a long time ago Nipmuck Indians had lived there, but their way of life had long since vanished. Having discovered that they still existed she wanted to make sure non-Indian children knew about it; material in textbooks was too generalized and unspecific.

The result of the collaboration was a tape-recorded slide presentation with a teacher's guide for elementary schools called *The Nipmuck path*. It is distributed locally to many school districts within an 80 km radius. A stated primary goal is to give an accurate portrayal of New England Algonquian culture as revealed through the history, traditions, and artefacts of the Nipmuck Nation, and their contributions to American culture and society.

The tape starts with a prayer spoken in Algonquian, which is then translated; phrases of it are repeated at intervals between slides. The expressed philosophy of caring for the land and its creatures provides a novel underpinning for the slides and craft activities. It ties them together in a texture of Native spirituality through which children are helped to make personal connections with the earth through activities that teach them where natural materials come from and their uses.

The goals also express a desire to give children a better acquaintance with Native history before the European arrival, as well as contemporary Native culture. Not least are goals to promote awareness of identity and ethnic pride in children of Native ancestry, and an understanding of Native culture in children of 'assimilated tribal groups'.

Museums as teachers of Native history

The questionnaire asked state representatives if alternative methods to standard school curriculum materials were used by schools to teach Native history, such as museum programmes, Native guest speakers or teachers. Most said that all of those methods were employed where possible. For the continental states, however, the emphasis was on museum programmes and visiting archaeological or historical sites, since those were the activities for which they provided specific information, i.e. museum and site names. Only Vermont mentioned the name of an Indian group, the Abenaki Tribal Council in Swanton.

Vine Deloria spoke of invisible Indians in *Custer died for your sins* (1969, p. 94). It would of course be best if schools learned about Native people directly from them, but the social separation between Indian and non-Indian is such that they rarely do. Since so much reliance is placed on museums, the kind of picture of Native life that museums present is very important.

In the 19th century museums concentrated on increasingly sophisticated arrangements of material culture, and it was the great expositions such as the Philadelphia Centennial of 1875 and the 1893 Columbian Exposition in Chicago that introduced 'living' exhibits of Native people in their own simulated environments, rather in the manner of the modern zoo.

More recently museums have often adopted an ahistorical, 'ethnographic present' approach in their Indian exhibits that may be misleading on several grounds. If an exhibit is a mix of different periods it may foster generalized stereotypes. If it represents a past period with no reference to the present or to historical processes, it may suggest either that the people shown are extinct, or that they still live in the manner exhibited. Exhibits can convey undesirable subliminal messages that undoubtedly never occurred to their creators; for example, heads floating in space to display headdresses suggest death and extinction (Lester 1987a). Museums generally have not been sufficiently conscious of these kinds of difficulties with respect to their American Indian exhibits, although Joan Lester of the Children's Museum in Boston has been studying them for many years (1987a, 1987b).

The presentation of American Natives by museums has become politicized in recent years as Native people have become vocal about certain museum practices that disturb them. Deloria lampooned anthropologists, but his message about exploitation was deadly serious (1969, pp. 78–101). The anthropological community is only just beginning to listen and discuss those issues (Zimmerman 1985).

Undoubtedly the most important of the abuses from the Native point of view is the desecration of Indian burials, the display of their skeletons in museum exhibits, and storage of an estimated 300 000 to 600 000 bodies in museum archives, with another half million having found their way overseas (Moore 1987, Hubert 1989). No other ethnic group in the USA has been treated in this manner.

Related to the issue of the display of bones is the exhibition of grave goods and the keeping of sacred objects in museum collections. In the words of Steven Moore (1987, pp. 1, 4), a Native American Rights Fund attorney:

One might think that this impressive collection of Indian remains is nothing but an historical anachronism, and that our society had become sufficiently enlightened so as not to be so utterly, blatantly racist and disrespectful. If only that were the case! Contemporary federal law and policy, however, defines Indian gravesites and human remains as 'archaeological resources' – relics of antiquity – and elevates scientific values over religious and cultural values. As a result, the storage of Indian skeletal remains and associated grave goods continues largely unabated . . . Many traditional Indian people believe that the continuing desecration threatens the spiritual balance and harmony of the entire world . . .

Even the existence of the 1978 American Indian Religious Freedom Act, which is intended to protect sacred sites and burials, has apparently not affected federal policy. Such protection should be extended automatically to Indians, who have been citizens under the US Constitution since 1924.

In recent years Native people have been pressing more and more insistently for the reburial of Indian remains and the protection of their burials. This has brought them into direct confrontation with archaeologists and anthropologists who fear the disappearance of the data they study (Hubert 1989). A recent conference in Chicago, organized to find some compromise, aired many of the concerns of both sides. Middle ground lay in the direction of allowing a time period for study before reburial (Quick 1985).

Respect is a very important value in American Indian culture; museums have tended to show a conspicuous lack of it in their exhibits and anthropologists in their attitudes, so how could it be possible for non-Indian children to learn of its importance to Native people? The National Congress of American Indians has been confronting the Smithsonian Institution in Washington, DC about the 14 500 skeletons that are in its collections, many of which were collected on battlefields in the 19th century. These constitute over a third of its skeletal collection (*New York Times* 1987).

Many museum professionals are concerned about such problems, and are attempting to take initiatives for change. Several museums in Massachusetts, for example, are developing new Indian exhibits or programmes, and most are making an effort to ensure Native input.[1]

The experiences of three of them – the Boston Children's Museum, the Wampanoag Indian Program at Plimoth Plantation, and the Concord Museum – are presented below.

The Children's Museum, Boston

Since the 1930s the Children's Museum in Boston has had a good Native American collection, programmes, and an American Indian exhibit hall. Over the past 20 years it has pioneered the development of its programmes under the guidance of Joan Lester. In 1964, fresh from the University of

California at Los Angeles with an MA in American Indian Art, she was hired to teach and is now Senior Curator.

Lester's first project was to develop materials and activities for teachers called 'Match Boxes' funded by the US Office of Education. There were five units, one on 'The Algonquins', the others on different museum topics unrelated to American Indians. 'The Algonquins' was a generalized and largely ahistorical depiction of Eastern Woodlands Native culture. Its inadequacies are easy to see nearly 25 years after it was initiated, but at the time the kit was innovative.

Lester was typical of many museum personnel in that period in that it never occurred to her to try to contact the local Native community for information and assistance with developing her projects. In fact neither she nor most others in white Boston even knew that a local Native community existed. The conventional wisdom had it that there were no longer any Indians in New England. The story of the Children's Museum is very much one of being challenged by that 'nonexistent' community, and of being open enough to incorporate it more and more into the museum's activities.

By 1968 Lester's programmes were beginning to emphasize a temporal and spatial context, with objects placed in recreations of their original settings. Under the supervision of the director, Michael Spock, a wigwam was built, and gradually a few members of the Boston Indian community started to visit and ask questions such as: 'Why are you only teaching about the past?'.

Two years later Lester took a year's leave of absence to attend Harvard University as a special student in the Department of Anthropology. On one occasion she tried to show one of her teaching kits to a group of American Indian students there and was horrified when they silently turned their backs on her. That experience, together with attendance at multiple sections of an anthropology course taught by Native graduate students radicalized her to the Native point of view about museums, and she wrote a paper questioning the role that they had played in the stereotyping of American Indian people (Lester 1987a). In it she identified the following stereotypes unconsciously built into major museum exhibits, past and present, in the eastern USA: the Indian is extinct, mythical, assimilated, ahistorical, a-real, and a savage.

Rather than continue at Harvard, Lester chose to return to the Children's Museum to revise its exhibits because they included all the stereotypes that she had identified. Her first priority was to form an Advisory Board of Native Americans to incorporate their perspective into the museum's programme. An opportunity came in 1974 when a company wanted to publish the Algonquin Match Box kit, something which by then was out of the question as far as she was concerned. Spock encouraged her to write a proposal that included her dreams; a paid Native Board with travel allowances and real advisory power. The proposal was accepted, and together with Judy Battat, another museum teacher, and the newly formed Board, a new kit, *Indians who met the Pilgrims*, came into being. The kit contrasted life at contact with contemporary New England life, and pointed out the ongoing cultural connections between past and present.

Starting in 1974, three grants from the National Endowment for the Humanities made possible another exhibit and two years of internship programmes for Native people to train as museum personnel. The exhibit *We're still here* created by Lester and the Advisory Board focused on the past and present in local New England Indian culture, contrasting a 17th-century style wigwam with a modern house interior containing contemporary objects. The theme was 'You don't have to live in a wigwam to be Indian in 1980'. 'Study Storage', an open storage area that simultaneously protects and grants access to objects is also available to museum visitors within the exhibit area. Through a grant from Folk Arts, Lester started to add contemporary Native craft work to the collection, and has published a catalogue entitled *We're still here, art of Indian New England* (1987b).

In 1987 the Native Board, which meets periodically, continued work on the programme. In October the museum hosted two seminars, one for museum personnel from around the USA and Canada, and another for teachers called *Through Indian eyes: whose vision is it anyway?*, in which many current Native concerns were aired, particularly stereotyping and the museum display of sacred objects and Indian skeletons. An exercise in analysing Indian motifs on store-bought items identified 80 stereotypical images. In her school-outreach teaching, Lester now concentrates on the connections between the past and present Native culture of the Northeast and on combating stereotypes.

The Wampanoag Indian Program, Plimoth Plantation, Plymouth

The Wampanoag Indian Program is a department of Plimoth Plantation, a museum specializing in the reconstruction of life at the time of the Pilgrim settlement of Plymouth in the early 17th century. Great attention is paid to accurate historical detail. Guides to the reconstructed Pilgrim Village are dressed in period styles and role-play historically known individuals, even speaking in regional English accents of the time.

Near the Pilgrim Village is a 'Wampanoag Indian settlement' where the 17th-century life of the local Wampanoag Indians is demonstrated from April to November. One wigwam (or wetu) covered with mats and another covered with bark stand beside an Indian garden of corn, beans, and squash. Native interpreters in historical dress practise Indian crafts such as canoe-making and bag-weaving, and explain them as they work. Wampanoag cooking techniques are demonstrated, and explanations given of Native customs and 17th-century history. Roles are not played in the camp because of lack of biographical detail about 17th-century Wampanoags and the difficulties of reproducing the native Massachuset language, but the interpreters are therefore freer to discuss the 17th-century period in modern language. Uniformed, non-Native interpreters also participate. In winter months outreach programmes for schools are offered through the museum.

The present programme started in September 1972 when the Indian camp-site, which up to that time had been interpreted by Pilgrim guides, was enlarged. In 1970 the museum had published a seminal paper (Marten 1970) which was a detailed bibliographic search of historical sources for the Wampanoag in the 17th century, with no attempt to collect data from the local Native community.

In March 1973 a conference of local Indian leaders was hosted by Concord Academy, a private school in Concord, Massachusetts. It resolved, among other things, to meet with James Deetz, an archaeologist and Assistant Director of Plimoth Plantation on 8 April 1973 to discuss the hiring of local Indian people for the proposed new cultural displays at the museum. Helen Attaquin, a Wampanoag with a doctoral degree in education and a member of an old and respected family in Gay Head, was hired, and within a few months Ella and Eric Thomas Sekatau (Narrangansetts) had also been engaged to manage the prospective programme. Lavinia Nightsong Underwood, one of the Indian leaders at the conference, is still on the Board of Trustees of the Plantation.

Nanepashemet, an employee of the Indian Program since 1975, has been directing a scholarly and detailed reconstruction of all aspects of past Native material culture from the area, building up an expertise amongst the staff in almost forgotten Native crafts, and experimenting with ones that have been entirely lost. Information on rare Native objects and techniques, with as much photographic documentation as possible, is filed for future reference. Native material culture from the area is so scattered and so rarely preserved that many people assume it does not exist. Creation of such a file is a painstaking compilation of piecemeal data from museums, art catalogues, archaeological digs, and other chance finds.

When information on Massachusetts tribal culture is slight or missing, inferences are made from Native cultures in adjacent areas with similar ecologies, or insights may be gained from farther afield. Wampanoag turkey-feather weaving of cloaks, mentioned in 17th-century sources, is a lost art, and no cloaks survive, but Nanepashemet recently learned from the research of a friend visiting New Zealand that Maori feather-weaving used twining, a common Wampanoag weaving technique, and so is experimenting with it.

The range of objects being developed is large and they are occasionally loaned out to museums around the country for exhibit. In addition to the canoes, bags, and pottery, the staff make cattail, bulrush, and bark mats, wooden utensils such as bowls and spoons, bone awls, deer-rib mat needles, basswood twine, and ground stone tools. Knowledge gained in this way has helped in the identification of unknown archaeological artefacts; for example, a fragment of a deer-bone mat needle was recognized.

Concord Museum, Concord

In 1982 the Massachusetts Historical Commission awarded a grant to Shirley Blancke, Barbara Robinson, and Carol Dwyer, sponsored by the Concord

Museum, to develop an exhibit and curriculum materials on New England Native history and culture. Additional funding came from the GenRad Foundation of Concord. Blancke is an archaeologist trained in England and the USA, Robinson is a teacher and educator in environmental studies with an avocational interest in archaeology, and Dwyer is a land-use specialist. From the beginning their aim was to try to involve local Native people in order to create a 'living' history through contact with the present.

The exhibit was to celebrate the 350th anniversary of Concord's founding in 1635, and it was decided to compare 17th-century English culture with the Algonquian culture it encountered. Cultural contrasts and exchanges were demonstrated up to the removal of the local Algonquians 40 years after the arrival of the English, when Massachusetts erupted into war with the Indians, but the precontact Algonquian culture was also presented to provide time depth (Blancke & Robinson 1985).

Early on in the preparation of the exhibit the nearest Native people to Concord, the Chabunagungamaug Nipmucks, were contacted. Blancke and Robinson presented their project to the tribal council and asked for their comments and criticism. Their primary worry was that grave goods might be displayed. They were told great care had been taken not to select anything known to come from a grave, but as a result of the meeting, Cjigkitoonuppa, Supreme Medicine Man of the Wampanoag Nation, was invited to look at the artefacts to check whether any sacred objects had been included inadvertantly. The Chabunagungamaug Nipmucks provided the exhibit with craft items of traditional design, legends, and animal drawings by the medicine man Little Turtle, which were an important aspect of the exhibit's success.

The museum has offered programmes in local Native history in which the 4th and 7th grades of the Concord school system have participated. Part of the presentation always refers to Native Americans in the present. A particular challenge is how to treat cultural differences in the understanding of what history is, not just what version of history is offered. The dominant Euroamerican understanding is that history is an objective cause-and-effect process, verifiable by external facts. Native history is often closer to religion; a fabric of symbolic understandings that includes facts but weaves them to provide meaning in life. Native legends are increasingly being used by schools to provide authentic flavour, but the problem of their being presented as fiction, and their relationship to history has barely been addressed.

How does one present legends to children without either denigrating Indian creation stories as fiction or undermining the development of an understanding of history as a discipline? When asked about a legend, 'Is it true?' Blancke has said: 'Yes, in a sense, but it has more to do with how you live your life than how things actually happened'. This is not entirely satisfactory, but she has yet to find a better answer.

Indian cultural beliefs about origins – that they have always been on the North American continent whether through coming out of the earth or by being placed there through some other means – have brought Indians into direct conflict with archaeologists, who predominantly adhere to the theory that Indians came from Asia by way of the Bering Strait. Goodman (1981) has attempted to use creation legend as a demonstrable archaeological hypothesis, an approach that has been very popular with Native people, but for most Euroamerican archaeologists this hypothesis is unsatisfactory and does not begin to present enough factual evidence to prove its point. Yet 'objective' archaeologists are not immune to being influenced by the cultural beliefs of their own times, and have often interpreted Native people in terms of the current prejudices of their own cultures (Trigger 1980, Ucko 1988).

Summary

Teaching about the Native past in the USA is not mandated by federal or state governments. Textbooks, conservative by nature because of the publishers' profit motive, have improved somewhat in the past 15 years, but the precontact past (archaeology) and current issues of concern to Native people are still sparsely covered in contrast to postcontact history and culture. Some good curriculum materials on these subjects have been developed by both Native and non-Native people since the civil rights movement of the 1960s and early 1970s, but they are often locally developed and not easy to acquire. In the highly individualized US educational system, in which authority rests with the school district, it depends on each school district or often merely on the interest and initiative of the individual teacher whether or not the Native past is well or even adequately covered. This is serious for Native American youth, nearly 90 per cent of whom are now in public schools, but many have access to Native cultural programmes under the 1972 Indian Education Act.

With respect to precontact history, a major difficulty is largely unrecognized. Usually the viewpoint presented is that of the Euroamerican archaeologist. Rarely, if at all, is Native symbolic and ethical oral history (legend) taught as history, because the challenge that it presents to the dominant culture is substantial, and as yet most Euroamericans have not even begun to understand the problem. Yet it is encouraging that many museums have been taking initiatives to try to meet Native objections to Eurocentrism, eliminate stereotypes, and present a view of Native history that is acceptable to the Native people themselves.

Acknowledgements

Very special thanks are due to Dr Bette Haskins (Cherokee), Director of the American Indian Program of the Harvard University Graduate School of Education for providing indispensable sources and contacts. We are also indebted to Joan Lester, Little Turtle (Nipmuck), Nanepashemet (Wampanoag), and Joan Avant Tavares (Wampanoag), for letting us tell their stories, and to Dr Claudette Bradley (Schaghticoke), Dr Richard V. McCann, and Judy Battat for their assistance.

Note

1   Among those museums developing new Indian exhibits or programmes are the Berkshire Museum, Pittsfield; the Heritage Plantation of Sandwich; Children's Museum, South Dartmouth; the Springfield Science Museum; and Worcester Science Center. The Peabody Museum at Harvard University has a large new exhibit in preparation, and the Peabody Museum in Salem has specialized in Paleoindian archaeology. Elsewhere in New England, to mention only one outstanding institution, the American Indian Archaeological Institute in Washington, Connecticut, with many Native people on its staff is a leader in the field.

References

Blancke, S. & B. Robinson 1985. *From Musketaquid to Concord*. Concord, Massachusetts: Concord Antiquarian Museum.

Blue Dog, K. & D. Kittson 1979. Legal Position Paper on Indian Education. Unpublished paper, Native American Rights Fund, 10 July.

Bradley, C. E. 1980. Assessing education for Native Americans in New England. Unpublished paper, Harvard Graduate School of Education, Cambridge, Massachusetts.

Chavers, D. 1981. False promises: barriers in American Indian education. *Integrateducation* **19** (1–2), 13–18.

Council of State Social Studies Specialists 1986. *National Survey: social studies education, kindergarten – Grade 12*. Affiliate of the National Council for the Social Studies, Washington, DC.

Deloria, V. Jr. 1969. *Custer died for your sins*. New York: Macmillan.

Deloria, V. Jr. 1981. Education and imperialism. *Integrateducation* **19** (1–2), 58–63.

Deloria, V. Jr. & C. M. Lytle 1983. *American Indians, American Justice*. Austin: University of Texas Press.

Ferguson, M. J. & D. B. Fleming 1984. Native Americans in elementary school social studies textbooks. *Journal of American Indian Education* **23** (2), 10–15.

Frazier, G. W. 1985. *The American Indian index*. Denver: Arrowstar Publishing.

Goodman, J. 1981. *American genesis: the American Indian and the origins of modern man*. New York: Summit Books.

Havighurst, R. J. 1981. Indian education: accomplishments of the last decade. *Phi Delta Kappan* **62** (5), 329–31.

Henninger, D. & M. Esposito 1972. Indian boarding schools: jails. In *Voices from the Bottom*, Selection 10, E. Spargo (sr. ed.), 56–8. Providence, Rhode Island: Jamestown Publishing Company.

Hubert, J. 1989. A proper place for the dead: a critical review of the 'reburial issue'. In *Conflicts in the archaeology of living traditions* R. Layton (ed.), 131–66. London: Unwin Hyman.

Johansen, B. E. 1982. *Forgotten founders*. Ipswich, Massachusetts: Gambit Publishers.

Kehoe, A. B. 1974. The Inquiry method: catalyst in the reaction between anthropology museums and school social studies in the western nations. In *The role of anthropological museums in national and international education*. Multinational Seminar, Moesgaard Museum, Denmark, 3–5 June, 73–9.

Kehoe, A. B. 1990. In fourteen hundred and ninety-two, Columbus sailed . . . In

The excluded past: archaeology in education P. Stone and R. MacKenzie (eds), Ch. 17. London: Unwin Hyman.

Lengel, J. G. & D. P. Superka 1982. Curriculum patterns. In *Social studies in the 1980s*, I. Morrissett (ed.), 32–38. Alexandria, Virginia: Association for Supervision and Curriculum Development.

Lester, J. A. 1987a. Lowering curatorial blinders. Paper presented at the American Association of Museums Annual Meeting, June, San Francisco. Tape cassette, Vanguard Systems Inc., Shawnee Mission, Kansas.

Lester, J. A. 1987b. *We're still here*. Boston: The Children's Museum.

Marten, C. 1970. *The Wampanoags in the 17th century: an ethnohistorical study*. Plymouth: The Wampanoags Indian Program, Plimouth Plantation.

Moore, S. 1987. Federal Indian burial policy – historical anachronism or contemporary reality? *Native American Rights Fund Legal Review* **12** (2), 1–7.

New York Times 1987. Indians seek burial of Smithsonian skeletons. 8 December, C13.

Patrick, J. J. & S. D. Hawke 1982. Curriculum materials. In *Social studies in the 1980s*, I. Morrissett (ed.), 39–50. Alexandria, Virginia: Association for Supervision and Curriculum Development.

Peters, R. M. 1987. *The Wampanoags of Mashpee*. Boston: Nimrod Press.

Quick, P. McW. (ed.) 1985. *Conference on Reburial Issues*. Proceedings of 14–15 June 1985 conference, Society for American Archaeology and Society of Professional Archaeologists, Newberry Library, Chicago.

Rosenfelt, D. M. 1973. Indian schools and community control. *Stanford Law Review* **25**, 489–550.

Swimmer, R. 1987. Statement of the Assistant Secretary, Indian Affairs, before the Subcommittee on Interior and Related Agencies, Committee on Appropriations, United States House of Representatives. In *Department of the Interior news release*, 27 October, Washington, DC.

Trigger, B. 1980. Archaeology and the image of the American Indian. *American Antiquity* **45** (4), 662–75.

Ucko, P. J. 1988. Foreword. In *Who needs the past?* R. Layton (ed.), ix–xv. London: Unwin Hyman.

US Department of the Interior, Bureau of Indian Affairs 1987. *American Indians Today*. US Government Printing Office no. 0–179–782, Washington, DC.

Waters, F. 1977, *Book of the Hopi*. New York: Penguin.

Wilkinson, G. 1981. Educational problems in the Indian community, a comment on learning as colonialism. *Integrateducation* **19** (1–2), 42–50.

Zimmerman, L. J. 1985. A perspective on the reburial issue from South Dakota. In *Conference on Reburial Issues*, P. McW. Quick (ed.), Proceedings of 14–15 June conference, Society for American Archaeology and Society of Professional Archaeologists, document 2, 1–4. Newberry Library, Chicago.

11 Whispers from the forest: the excluded past of the Aché Indians of Paraguay

LUKE HOLLAND

Introduction

During one of my visits to an Aché group, which had emerged from the forest only a few years previously, I learnt that it had taken the Indians a year to acquire the confidence to speak normally again. For some 20 years prior to their emergence, a period of constant fear and flight, they had tried to avoid detection by speaking only in whispers.

The Aché Indians are one of Paraguay's last tribes of hunter-gatherers. During the past three decades the Aché have been forced into violent contact with the dominant Paraguayan society. Hundreds of Indians have been killed by Paraguayans or have died as a result of introduced diseases, enslavement, and despair. The German anthropologist Mark Munzel (1973, p. 4) estimates that in the four-year period 1968–72, as many as 600 Aché Indians may have been 'either killed or kidnapped on private or official manhunts'. This chapter considers the recent history of the Aché and some of the attitudes that underpin relations between the Paraguayan state and the country's surviving Indian peoples.[1] It examines ways in which Paraguayan historians and self-styled archaeologists have attempted to rewrite the history of the Aché in terms that are palatable to the military establishment of former Paraguayan dictator General Alfredo Stroessner. The work of a fundamentalist mission from the USA, which acts as mediator between the two societies, is also considered.

The feudal estate

Paraguay is small by South American standards. Isolated and landlocked, it lies at the heart of the southern cone. Little news emanates from within its borders. This is no accident. From May 1954 until his removal in a military coup on 3 February 1989, the country was ruled rather like a feudal estate by General Alfredo Stroessner. His military regime had much to hide and preferred to operate untrammelled by the constraints that a free press would impose. Thousands of Paraguayans have been imprisoned, and 1500 have died in the name of 'national security'. As Augusto Roa Bastos, an exiled novelist, has observed, Paraguay has slipped from the world map. A veil of silence masked the activities of one of the last in a long line of Latin American dictators.

If little is heard of Paraguay outside its borders, the situation of the country's 17 surviving Indian tribes is even more poorly reported. In a total population of over 3 million, they represent, at just 38 000, according to official statistics, a little over 1 per cent. The majority of the population are of mixed European (principally Spanish) and Indian descent. A massive recent influx of almost 500 000 impoverished Brazilian settlers into eastern Paraguay and the arrival of tens of thousands of South Korean immigrants has meant a further marginalization of Paraguay's original inhabitants. During the course of this century there has been a fairly constant stream of new arrivals, with Germans and Japanese prominent among them.

The Paraguayan government's estimates of the Indian population are considered unreliable. The true figure may be twice as high. As elsewhere in Latin America, Indian numbers are played down, to minimize their import- ance and justify the correspondingly low levels of state support they receive. This manipulation of data, perhaps the least serious in the catalogue of injustices committed against the Indians, has been described to me by an Indian acquaintance as 'administrative genocide'.

That the Guarani indigenous Indian language is still so widely spoken is not only a consequence of Paraguay's colonial past but also one of the paradoxes of the country. Lacking the mineral wealth that attracted vast numbers of Spanish colonists to the Andean countries of Bolivia, Peru, and Ecuador, Paraguay and its riverside capital at Asunción (founded in 1573) was little more than a military outpost on the overland trade route between Peru and Argentina during the first period of the Spanish conquest. The soldiers who formed the Spanish garrison found wives among the Indian tribes that had offered hospitality to the new arrivals, or, as frequently, had been conquered by them. The Indian language, the mother tongue, sur- vived, in part as a legacy of this liaison.

Guarani is just one of at least five Indian languages spoken in Paraguay. Its dominance today is evidence of an alliance forged in the early years of the conquest between the Spanish Conquistadores and the Guarani Indians to crush their common enemies, the nomadic tribes of the Paraguayan Chaco. Like the Portuguese among the Indians of Brazil, Spain's military victories in South America were due, in no small measure, to their success in pitting one Indian tribe against another.

Paraguay also played host to a remarkable Jesuit experiment. From 1607 to their expulsion one and a half centuries later, Paraguay was the heart of the Jesuit empire in Spanish South America. At one point the 'Jesuit Republic' extended to some 30 mission settlements or *reducciones*. The Jesuits were expelled and their missions disbanded when they became too powerful for their ecclesiastical masters in Rome and an inconvenience to the courts of Spain and Portugal. Their *reducciones* have been variously praised as unique examples of 'Christian communism' and vilified as little better than 'concentration camps' for their Indian converts. However, even the detractors concede that the Jesuit regime was a key factor in forging Paraguay's peculiarly Indian identity, especially with regard to the survival of the main Indian language, Guarani. The spectacular remains of their cathedrals and other mission buildings are today the focus of tourist pilgrimages in southeastern Paraguay and northeastern Argentina. The missions' archaeological remains have also been invoked, as we shall see below, to lend credence to a singularly bizarre and implausible theory regarding the origins of the Aché Indians.

Indian exclusion from contemporary Paraguayan society

Today, and in striking contrast to the status of their languages within the country at large, the Indians of Paraguay are divided, exploited and dispirited. They live at the margins of settler society, struggling to retain what remains of their traditional culture and of their formerly extensive lands. Land is the key to Indian survival and in Paraguay land is monopolized, perhaps more than in any other South American country, by a powerful few. The bulk of the Paraguayan population are impoverished peasants living in rural areas. Despite having one of the world's highest per capita ratios of cultivable land, the absence of any comprehensive land reform programme has meant that 70 per cent of the population subsist on tiny unproductive plots. In 1978 the average per capita income in rural areas was just US $137. Land speculation has resulted in frequent expulsions of peasants and Indians and the land thus cleared has been sold to members of the economic elite, the military, or foreign companies.

Traditionally the Paraguayan economy has been dominated by agricultural production, with cotton, soya beans, beef, and timber products prominent. During the 1970s the construction of major hydropower projects, principally the joint venture with Brazil to create the world's largest hydroelectric scheme at Itaipu, led to a massive but poorly managed expansion of the national economy. This has resulted in few long-term benefits and today much of the Paraguayan economy is fuelled by contraband. International agencies such as the World Bank estimate that imports are 45 per cent and exports 60 per cent higher than the officially declared figures (Latin America Bureau 1980). Paraguay has for decades been the regional centre of an illicit drugs trade in which the senior military establishment is centrally involved.

Among the more successful tribes (and 'success' should here be regarded as a very relative concept) are the 5000 Pai Tavytera. Their strong sense of community, the improbable patronage they enjoyed from a sympathetic general, and the support they received from a team of aid-funded anthropologists (the Proyecto Pai Tavytera, run under the auspices of Paraguay's Misión de Amistad), has ensured their survival and legal entitlement to at least a portion of their traditional forest lands. They live in eastern Paraguay, in an area that has been virtually logged out, and they are now coming under the most intense pressure as government officials of the National Indian Agency, INDI, join commercial loggers in an attempt to 'persuade' them into selling off their valuable timber.

Following a series of recent meetings, the Indians anounced a complete halt to all logging operations on their land. They are now engaged in an unequal struggle to enforce that decision as government officers dispense alcohol and offer bribes to undermine their resolution and unity (Holland n.d.). Recently their lands have been invaded by a detachment of armed soldiers, supervising a team of illegal loggers who cleared the timber, advancing through the Indians' forest like a great caterpillar. According to Pai Tavytera tradition (Melia *et al.*, 1976, p. 204),

> the land and the human body are one and the same thing . . . In the same way that the body has hair, the land has trees. If the land is not to become sick, the ecological balance must be maintained. The Pai Tavytera therefore consider large scale forest clearance as something irrational. They regard problems of wind and water erosion as evidence of the imminent destruction of the world.

Among the tribes in the Chaco region of western Paraguay – which is often referred to colourfully but not particularly accurately as a 'green hell' – the Chulupi or Nivacle Indians are perhaps the most secure. This security is, once again, relative and decidedly precarious. In any event, with some 7000 individuals, they are easily the largest of the Chaco tribes. In common with other Indian tribes in the region, the Chulupi have been forced to abandon their traditional way of life as their lands are taken over by white cattle ranchers. They now depend on seasonal work, on the farms and in the factories of the Mennonites, European settlers who first arrived in Paraguay in the 1920s and have now established a powerful economic presence in the heart of what was formerly Indian territory.

The Aché

Until recently, the Aché were the last group of forest Indians living the traditional life of hunter-gatherers in eastern Paraguay. All that, however, has changed. Today 500 or so survivors have been forced to live in four isolated settlements. Indian leaders and their supporters claim that a further 100 Aché are living with Paraguayan families in conditions akin to slavery. The manhunts and enslavement of the Aché during the past two decades, in which the Paraguayan military, government employees, settlers, and even fundamentalist missionaries were implicated, caused a storm of international protest. They provoked charges of genocide against the Paraguayan government, international press coverage, and formal complaints to the UN and other human rights agencies.

Figure 11.1 Aché children have suffered from the negligence and persecution of a Paraguayan government that has brought their people close to extinction.

The Aché were finally forced to abandon their nomadic existence just ten years ago, following decades of persecution and flight. During the past 20 years the Aché have been pushed to the very brink of extinction. In 1975, the Jesuit priest and Guarani linguist Bartomeu Melia and the North American anthropologist Robert Smith carried out a genealogical survey among a group of Aché survivors. Their results were published by Survival International and reveal, in dispassionate yet harrowing detail, the causes of Aché deaths during the preceding 60 years. In their study of a total of 579 people (267 living and 312 dead), 20 per cent of all Aché deaths recorded by the study were at the hands of Paraguayans. With the exception of illness, this was easily the largest category. Combined with kidnappings, this total rises to 28 per cent and in one of the three generations represents no less than 56 per cent – more than the cause of all other deaths combined. While Smith & Melia (1978, p. 12) state that 'intention here is probably impossible to establish', they add that 'two of the acts listed, killing members of the group and forcibly transferring children of the group to another group [see Fig. 11.1], have been committed and with such intensity that the Aché may soon cease to exist', and conclude that 'de facto genocide has occurred. The Paraguayan Government is responsible for it in terms of its failure to protect its citizens'.

A report by Munzel (1973), first alerted the international community to the Aché tragedy. It was followed by a number of others (e.g. Arens 1976).

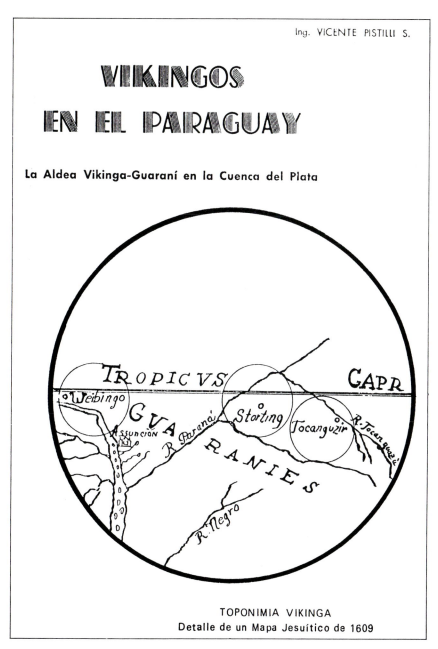

Figure 11.2 The front cover of Vicente Pistilli's book *Vikingos en el Paraguay*.

The Aché Indians have been denied their past as part of a wider move to deny them their very existence. Efforts to bring about their physical extinction have been matched by bizarre attempts to deny their truly indigenous status and, as the following account shows, improbable archaeological evidence has been invoked as part of this distortion.

'Vikings' in Paraguay

Known by most Paraguayans as 'Guayaki', the surviving Aché are regarded with pity, contempt, loathing, and indifference. Their unusually light skins, distinctive features, and facial hair have given rise to several theories about their origins. Perhaps the most improbable of these is one that led to the publication of *Vikingos en el Paraguay* (Vikings in Paraguay) (Pistilli 1978) and merits special attention. Written by a lecturer at the National University, and published by the Paraguayan branch of the pseudoscientific, Buenos Aires-based Instituto de la Ciencia del Hombre (Institute of the Science of Man), the book argues that the Aché Indians of Paraguay are 'degenerate' descendants of the Vikings, who, it is claimed, established their villages among the Guarani in the first quarter of the 14th century, before heading on to establish Tihuanaco on the Bolivian Altiplano and other centres of pre-Columbian civilization elsewhere in South and Central America. The map that illustrates the cover of Pistilli's book (Fig. 11.2) purports to lend credence to this theory. This notion, promoted by the self-styled professor and archaeologist Jacques de Mahieu, is utterly lacking in scientific credibility. Its promulgation in Paraguay only begins to make sense when one looks more closely at the racial and political make-up of Paraguayan society and examines national attitudes to the country's Indian past.

As already stated, the Paraguayan people owe their origins to the intermarriage of Indians and Europeans, predominantly Spanish. Paraguay is a country of paradoxes. Not least among these is the fact that despite the low esteem in which the surviving Indians are held, Guarani is the preferred language of over 85 per cent of the population. Over half of Paraguayans, especially in the countryside, are monolingual and speak only Guarani. Spanish is of course the other lingua franca, and while Guarani shares, at least nominally, its official status, Spanish is the language of official discourse. Most Paraguayans seem genuinely proud of their Indian, especially Guarani, heritage, yet seem strangely incapable of relating their impoverished Indian neighbours to the warrior race whose ancestry they are so anxious to claim.

Vikingos en el Paraguay is the kind of publication one might, in other circumstances, dismiss as a ridiculous, albeit harmless, fantasy. However, in the context of prevailing official attitudes to the Indians of Paraguay, and the fact that the book enjoys the seal of approval, quite literally, of the Paraguayan Minister of Defence, it cannot so easily be cast aside. It is introduced

Figure 11.3 Photograph of the 'runic inscriptions' from eastern Paraguay that Vicente Pistilli attributes to the Vikings. Note the so-called swastika in the centre.

by an effusive letter to the author written by General Marcial Samaniego. It invokes the name of former President Alfredo Stroessner and thanks Pistilli, for his 'elevated spirit of patriotism' in establishing a branch of the 'Institute for the Science of Man' in Asunción, with the purpose of 'studying man in all his many and varied manifestations'. There follows a further letter from 'Prof. Dr.' Jacques de Mahieu congratulating Pistilli on his initiative in setting up the Asunción branch of his Institute and adding that the archaeological studies they will jointly pursue will 'throw light on a glorious past of which our supporters will be justifiably proud'.

The book retails a series of claims to illustrate its central thesis of a Viking presence in Paraguay. It includes photographs of 'runic inscriptions' (Fig. 11.3) which Mahieu claims to have identified in the traditional forest territory of the Aché, in a remote area of eastern Paraguay. Among the indistinct etchings picked out in a blurred photograph is what appears to be a rather poorly defined 'Hakenkreuz' or swastika at the centre of the image. Pistilli presents a singularly unpersuasive linguistic analysis of Viking place names and attempts to draw comparisons with Guarani terms. Plans of Viking settlements are compared with those of traditional Indian villages and the case is strained further by a comparison of Viking and Indian tools. The book includes a photograph of Mahieu posing, with just the right amount of gravitas, on top of the very substantial and well-constructed foundations of a partially excavated stone building. The caption claims the ruin as 'an ancient temple left by the Vikings'. The much more plausible explanation, confirmed to me by someone who knows the site, is that it is the remains of one of Paraguay's many Jesuit mission buildings.

Paraguay and the 'Indian problem'

Indian affairs in Paraguay are under the centralized control of the Ministry of Defence. Paraguay is a military dictatorship and it is clear that resolving the 'Indian problem' is regarded as a military objective. The Indians represent a threat to political hegemony and military control. They are the only social group not formally incorporated into the centralized and highly controlled political machine of the Colorado Party – the party of former President Stroessner. The relationship between the surviving Indian tribes and national society is mediated by a range of factors, including their numerical strength, their success in securing title to what remains of their lands, their proximity to centres of population, the support they enjoy from national agencies, their history of contact with the wider Paraguayan society, and the resilience of their own political and economic institutions.

The elite's denial of their Indian past

The prevailing attitudes towards particular tribes are also significant. A chart (Fig. 11.4) was prepared by General Ramón César Bejarano, formerly

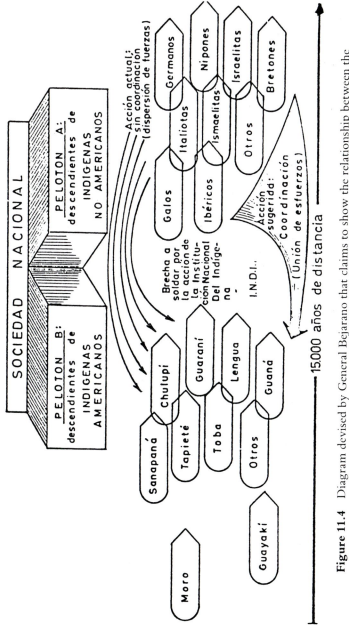

Figure 11.4 Diagram devised by General Bejarano that claims to show the relationship between the descendants of American and non-American indigenes in Paraguay over the last 15 000 years.

an advisor to ex-President Stroessner on Indian issues and, in his own way, among the most enlightened of the senior government figures working in this field during the past two decades. It lacks any scientific credibility, but like the Viking theory is highly instructive of official attitudes. According to Bejarano, Paraguayan society divides naturally into two groups, descendants of indigenous people who are non-American and descendants of those who are American. His chart features a 15 000 year time-scale in which the 'Nipones' (Japanese), closely followed by the Germans, lead the non-American field. Other categories – there is even the obligatory 'other' to lend a spurious kind of legitimacy to the exercise – include 'Iberians' and 'Italians' before we reach the approximately 3000-year gulf separating the two major categories. Among the nine Indian tribes, arbitrarily represented, the Guarani lead the field. The Aché, referred to by their perjorative title 'Guayaki', come a poor sixth and tail the 'Nipones' by no less than 13 000 years.

What is disconcerting about all this is the fact that these officially endorsed views, dressed up as objective scientific facts, are used to inform and justify official policy towards the Indian peoples of Paraguay. Bejarano is a former president of the quasi-official Asociación Indigenista del Paraguay and played a key role in setting up the National Indian Institute in 1976, in part as a response to international criticism of Paraguay's Indian policies. Given the levels of official ignorance and prejudice, the results of a national survey of attitudes to Paraguay's Indian peoples will come as no surprise. Carried out in 1971 by the Centro de Estudios Antropologicos, today part of the Catholic University, the study sought the opinions of a representative sample of 500 Paraguayan adults. In response to the question, 'What is the difference between Indians and us?', 77 per cent opted for the response: 'They are like animals – unbaptized'. Less than 1 per cent answered: 'Different cultures'. Asked for their opinions of the Indians, no less than 86 per cent replied that they were inferior beings.

Further anecdotal evidence of Paraguayan attitudes to the Indians emerged during my meeting with Padre José Dotto, a former Salesian missionary who spent many years in the Paraguayan Chaco. He repeated to me his earlier claim; that as recently as 1955 a soldier serving in the Chaco could secure a reduction in his compulsory military service if he produced the severed head of an Ayoreo Indian.

All this may provide some clues as to why a book like *Vikingos en el Paraguay* should enjoy official blessing. The leaders of Paraguayan society, among them ex-President Stroessner, who is part German, prefer to rationalize their Indian heritage in terms of an exclusively European ancestry. Who better than the Aryan Vikings to fulfil this dubious role? It is indicative that on 3 May 1986 the leading Asunción daily *Hoy* (edited by Stroessner's former son-in-law) advertised a city-centre mass to commemorate the 41st anniversary of the death of Adolf Hitler.

The Aché before contact

The Aché are forest nomads. Traditionally they lived in small bands of perhaps 50 individuals bound by kinship. They moved frequently and knew with absolute certainty where the boundaries of their territory met those of another Aché band. They lived on forest game, deer, tapir, coati, wild fowl, heart of palm, and wild oranges. According to Aché myth, hunting is the crucial link that binds the Indians to their forest world. The animals and the trees are regarded, in a very real sense, as their ancestors, and on the death of an Aché the soul will reintegrate with the natural world, but only if the Aché continue to hunt. The Aché gathered wild honey in large quantities and used their stone axes to fell trees, returning months later to eat the grubs that flourished in the rotting trunks. They collected the leaves and twigs of yerba mate (*Ilex paraguayensis*) which they roasted and used to make their indigenous tea, now widely adopted as the national drink of Paraguay.

Even before the arrival of the White settlers the Aché were regarded with a mixture of hostility and fear by their more settled Guarani neighbours, who lived in large and well-established agricultural communities. However, the principal danger they faced came not from other humans but from the jaguar. Even today, when all the Aché have become sedentary, many of them bear the scars of their fights with jaguars. The older hunters frequently describe encounters with the main forest predator, which was feared and respected in equal measure.

Evil creatures of the forest

As with virtually every South American tribe, there are today at least two terms to describe the Aché Indians. Aché is the name the Indians use to describe themselves – it translates simply as 'people'. The other term, and the one by which most Paraguayans know them, is Guayaki. One of the Aché translated this for me as 'evil creature of the forest which is never seen', while Munzel (1973) has come up with 'rabid rats'. Either way, the term is clearly one of contempt and effectively sums up the popular view of these particular Indians.

The arrival of European settlers, the Spanish adventurers and Catholic priests, opened a new and terrifying chapter for the Aché. Their well-regulated forest existence, with its seasonal patterns of migration to one or other area of their well-defined territory, their centuries-old rituals and their celebrations of birth, initiation and death, were rudely shattered. Their nomadism acquired a new and desperate urgency. Now it was motivated by fear and flight. In the very first references to the Aché, which appear in the chronicles of the Jesuit historian Nicolas del Techo (1651), the Aché are already cast in a mould that would determine their fate for the next five centuries:

They are physically deformed, to the point of being virtual monsters, looking more like monkeys than humans, especially their noses. . . .

There is absolutely no difference between their behaviour and that of the forest animals. They pounce down from overhanging branches, especially at night and kill travellers who, unwisely, have slept in their territory. This is less likely to be for revenge, nor to acquire outside goods, but rather as the result of an innate ferocity. They have learned from the jaguars with which they are engaged in an unending struggle. (del Techo (1651) quoted in Melia *et al.* 1973, p. 7)

The hunters and bowmen, uniquely adapted to their rich forest environment, with a deep knowledge of the plant and animal world, were suddenly transformed into 'evil creatures of the forest', mythical beasts that served as a perfect foil to the European's sense of vaunting racial superiority. Only after protracted debate among the pioneer Jesuit missionaries was the vexed question of whether the Aché actually had the 'intellectual capacity' to understand the Christian message finally resolved in their favour, and only then by invoking the notion of 'divine misericordia', which embraces 'men and brutes' equally.

'Manhunts'

This question resolved, the work of evangelization commenced. One of the earliest recorded 'manhunts', the first of many, led to the capture of a band of Aché. They were promptly tied up to prevent their escape. Nicolas del Techo (1651) takes up the story: 'they were biting the bonds with their teeth, though the bonds were of iron, like rabid animals. . . . If they were left tied up for a certain length of time, they refused food.' Their missionary captor responded with appropriate haste: 'he asked each one if he believed in the mysteries of Christ: upon their saying 'yes', he set about baptising those who wanted it. A short while later they all died, without exception' (Smith & Melia 1978, p. 8). A pattern of 'manhunts' had been established that was to continue to the present day.

'The silent war'

Pressure on the Indians intensified dramatically with the completion in 1965 and 1968 of two highways that sliced through the heart of their traditional lands. This opened up their area to the settlers, loggers and cattle ranchers – their principal enemies. The rate of deforestation showed an immediate and marked increase. One particularly well-documented 'manhunt' occurred at the end of August 1971. It led, according to the Paraguayan bishops' conference, to the massacre of 'twelve to twenty persons' (Münzel 1973, p. 17).

The Indians of Paraguay are under few illusions about official attitudes towards them. On more than one occasion during my visits to their communities they said, 'ellos quieren terminar con los Indígenas'. This translates ambiguously either as 'they want to be rid of us' or, more sinisterly, as 'they want to finish us off'. Further confirmation came in the moving statement made to me in 1986 by an Indian leader. He described the sustained pressure his community was suffering to abandon its lands and said:

> As far as I can see, this is happening all over the world. This is why I call it a silent war, a peaceful war against all Indian peoples. They don't even need sticks or bullets. They just steal our land and refuse to give us work. This is how they are trying to wipe us, the Indians, out. (Holland n.d.)

These officially endorsed efforts to deny the Indians of Paraguay their ancestral status and their lands have been matched by an assault on their belief systems and traditional values. A US-based mission organization, working with official backing, has had a particularly disruptive impact on the Aché, where a determined effort has been made to replace traditional beliefs with a system of values more acceptable to the status quo.

The New Tribes Mission: an approach to cultural ethnocide

Cerro Moroti is the National Colony, and one of the largest centres of Aché population. It was events here in the early 1970s that provoked so much controversy and fuelled charges of genocide against the Paraguayan government. Over the years, the National Colony had received a succession of visitors. It was here that the Munzels conducted their anthropological fieldwork and gathered the data that formed the substance of two reports on genocide against the Aché (Munzel 1973, 1974).

Arens (1978) and Lewis (1985) concluded that the Paraguayan government was practising genocide against the Aché, while Howe & Maybury-Lewis (1980) played down such allegations. The controversy provoked by the competing claims of the investigators has had widespread repercussions, not least in its divisive effect on the worldwide pro-Indian movement.

Aché culture is also under threat from religious influences. Responding to my charges that the New Tribes Mission (NTM) was imposing its religion on the Aché (Holland n.d.), Paul Heckert, one of the missionaries, replied, 'There are no rice Christians here'. His wife added, 'If the whole village understands that Christ died for them and then rejects that, that's fine by us. We will leave and consider our job done.' I asked about the frequent Church services at the National Colony. Heckert replied, 'Going to church is traditional. We're living in the 20th century. Everybody works five or six days a week and then there is a day of rest. All the civilized world considers Sunday the day of rest. I'm not shooting down the Aché culture. I'm just introducing something new.' His wife added, 'We see our job as training them to be responsible members of the Paraguayan society'. The Heckerts claimed that over 100 of the Aché, including children as young as six, had 'come to Christ'.

I asked the Heckerts how they regarded the Aché, who incidentally are not allowed into the missionaries' homes. Heckert replied, 'I believe the Aché are born with a sinful nature'. The missionaries have clearly conveyed this notion to the Indians under their tutelage, as I was to discover the following day when I asked a young Aché man about the traditional Aché songs and why they are no longer heard on the mission. Without hesitation he told me, 'The singing is bad. When the Aché sing it is all foolishness. The way the Paraguayans sing, that is good. The way we sing is bad. Once we had the *takuara* [flutes]. Now there are none. Now there are no old people here – just young people. That is why we no longer have the old customs and the music.' I was reminded of the contrast with the Aché settlements I had visited previously, where traditional Aché music was regularly heard, and where the older Aché were not the only singers and musicians (Holland n.d.).

The NTM booklet *Jungle methods* was written by one of their missionaries, Sophie Muller. It contains instructions on how to organize a ten-day introductory crusade in 'unreached' tribal villages. Early on the first day the Indians are presented with a new pencil and lined paper: 'This is the bait'. At the end of the evening Gospel meeting, 'When there is a pause in the praying, sing the Doxology and tell them to go to sleep so they will be ready to study the next day. Otherwise they might start their dances, which ruins them spiritually as well as intellectually.' On the fifth day intending missionaries are instructed to teach the Ten Commandments and are encouraged to 'add one or two more: "Thou shalt not drink liquor or do witchcraft"'. The concept of original sin is also drummed into potential converts, whose baptism is conditional on their acceptance of a comprehensive list of prohibitions and their ability to complete a questionnaire. Muller's questions include the following: 'Where should men go to swim that don't wear trousers? They should go swimming far from women; also women should go swimming far from men.'

Towering over the low, wooden school building at the centre of the mission was an immense flagpole, with the national flag of Paraguay fluttering at its head. At its base were two rows of neatly uniformed children reciting the national anthem and saluting the flag. It looked an incongruous and improbable scene and simply served to reinforce my conviction that the NTM's educational work was essentially ethnocidal. The destruction of Aché culture and identity was accompanied by the imposition of a totally new set of values and rituals. The daily school parades and anthems were only the most visible expressions of this process.

I was struck by the fact that the school bore the name Escuela Nacional Aché – Guayaki No. 12506. The name Guayaki is a term of abuse. It is a term widely used by Paraguayans and sums up their contemptuous attitude to the Indians. To see it incorporated in the title of the mission school simply confirmed that the Paraguayan government and the missionaries regarded the Aché in a similar light. One of the Indians with whom I discussed this shared my view but saw little prospect of any change. 'It would be better to have just the name Aché', he said, 'but the government says it must be Aché/Guayaki and the missionaries do what they are told.' This was confirmed when I took the matter up with one of the missionaries, who stated blandly, 'This is government property, so they decide on the name' (Holland n.d.).

Among the mission Indians, the use of Spanish names, something openly encouraged by the NTM missionaries, takes place at the expense of the Aché's traditional names. One young Aché, Tykuarangi, said that he had received his Spanish name, Jaime Mendoza, from the Paraguayan 'who stole me from Pereira' (a notorious Paraguayan slave-owner who organized many of the expeditions against the Aché and was finally removed from his post of National Colony administrator following a concerted international campaign). The Indians' Aché identity is further eroded by this process, since for the Aché names are an expression of their vital link to the animals of the forest and represent much more than a convenient label. The missionaries with whom I took up this issue seemed unimpressed by my argument and replied that Spanish names would help the Aché 'to integrate in national society' (Holland n.d.).

Miguel Chase-Sardi, one of the Paraguayan critics of the NTM's work, has said that

> the religious fanaticism of these missionaries, who regard the Indians as degenerate and given to dealings with the devil, made them systematically oppose the few remaining tribal customs and ceremonies which they regard as pagan. They confuse the essential principles of Christianity with the particular values of Western culture, and teach the latter as though they were the former. (Chase-Sardi 1972, p. 207)

Little effort had been made by the missionaries, some of whom were accomplished linguists, to make nonreligious material available to the Aché in their own language. For example, none of the Aché at the NTM mission was familiar with a single clause of the important legislation regarding their land rights (Law 904/81) yet they could all recite by heart lengthy passages from the Gospels. Land is the key to Indian survival and despite the NTM's professed concern for the future security of the Indians, no steps had been taken to ensure that they were aware of their rights in Paraguayan law and therefore better able to defend themselves. Worse still, the NTM, who had been installed at the National Colony in a fanfare of self-righteous publicity by the Paraguayan government in 1972, had presided over the Colony during a period in which its 5000 ha of forest lands – which one of my missionary informants told me actually extended to 10 000 ha – had been progressively reduced, by a series of invasions, to a little over 1000 ha at the time of my visit in 1986 (Holland n.d.).

An official US view of relations between Indians and the state in Paraguay

The plight of the Aché has provoked a great deal of controversy, claims and counter-claims. Among the more interesting reports to address this issue, was one commissioned in 1978 by the US Embassy in Asunción (US Embassy in Paraguay 1978) to answer charges made by Arens and others. It was obtained under the Freedom of Information Act and, given the crucial role of successive US governments in propping up the Stroessner regime over a period of three decades, provides some fascinating insights into the official US view of relations between Indians and the state in Paraguay.

Among other things the report considers education programmes for the Indians and the inappropriateness of much of the content of literacy programmes. It describes the conflict in 'value systems' and the disorientation that many Indians suffer, and states that 'learning that traditional religious practices are evil and unnatural can produce alienation and the ensuing fragmentation of the individual's personality can be devastating to whole peoples' (US Embassy in Paraguay 1978). It gives several examples and refers to a visit to the New Tribes Mission's Chaco base at El Faro Moro where, 'one of the missionaries pointed out the schoolhouse and listened proudly while aborigine children recited passages of the New Testament aloud in their native dialect' (US Embassy in Paraguay 1978, Appendix O).

In discussing the merits of encouraging the use of Indian languages in their schools or, as is widespread, restricting them to Spanish, the US Embassy's report (1978) states that 'while from the standpoint of national integration one could say this homogenization is desirable, it lends credence to the argument that ethnocide is being perpetrated in Paraguay'. Since education in Paraguay is based on a government-controlled national curriculum, this conclusion contrasts oddly with the claim made elsewhere in this report's summary (US Embassy in Paraguay 1978, p. 2) that 'charges of government direction of a campaign of "ethnocide" are without foundation'.

A bridge to the excluded past

Despite the forces ranged against them, some Aché have survived. The manhunts and the massacres have stopped. There are no longer any 'uncontacted' Aché in the forests, which in any case are themselves disappearing. Their situation remains critical. However, the scenario is not entirely bleak. Despite the entrenched and institutional racism within Paraguay (of which the Viking story is a particularly graphic example and one characterized for me by a Paraguayan acquaintance as *auto-racismo*), there is a growing awareness of the value of tribal society.

A muzzled press has failed to stifle the increasingly vocal opposition to the former Stroessner dictatorship and its policies. The 'Indian issue' is becoming a focus of concern for people who see government policies towards the surviving Indians, in education and other spheres, as a symptom of their contempt for justice and human rights for the wider Paraguayan society. The oppression and exploitation of the Indians can be perceived as a cynical device to undermine rural solidarity and drive a wedge between the Indians and their natural allies, the landless peasants. I am reminded of a conversation in Washington with an exiled peasant leader from Paraguay who said: 'We must learn to respect the Indian. He is our brother. We share the same grandfather.' His statement is part of an increasingly widespread and welcome view, that the Indians of Paraguay represent a crucial bridge to the country's excluded past and perhaps the key to a more just and equitable future for all Paraguayans.

Note

1 All unreferenced quotes are extracts from the author's unpublished field notes.

References

Arens, R. (ed.) 1976, *Genocide in Paraguay*. Philadelphia: Temple University Press.

Arens, R. 1978. *The Forest Indians in Stroessner's Paraguay*. London: Survival International.

Bejarano, R. C. 1977, *Solucionemos nuestro problema indigena con el INDI*. Asuncion: INDI.

Chase-Sardi, M. 1972. The present situation of the Indians in Paraguay, in *The situation of the Indian in South America*, W. Dostal (ed.). Geneva: World Council of Churches.

Holland, L. n.d. Unpublished field notes.

Howe, J. & D. Maybury-Lewis 1980. *The Indian peoples of Paraguay: their plight and their prospects*. Boston: Cultural Survival.

Latin America Bureau 1980. *Paraguay power game*. London.

Lewis, N. Manhunt. 1985. *Sunday Times Magazine*, 26 January.

Meliá, B., L. Miraglia, M. Münzel & C. Münzel 1973. *La Agonia de los Aché-Guaki: Historia y Cantos*. Centro de Estudios Antropológicos Universidad Católica, Asunción: 'Nuestra Señora de la Asunción'.

Melia, B., G. Gruenberg & F. Gruenberg 1976. *Los Pai Tavytera*. Asuncion.

Muller, S. 1960. *Jungle methods*. Wisconsin: New Tribes Mission.

Munzel, M. 1973. *The Aché Indians: genocide in Paraguay*. Copenhagen: *IWGIA* Document 11.

Munzel, M. 1974. *The Aché: genocide continues in Paraguay*. Copenhagen: IWGIA.

Pistilli, V. 1978. *Vikingos en al Paraguay*. Asuncion.

Smith, R. & B. Melia 1978. *Genocide of the Aché-Guayaki?* London: Survival International Review.

del Techo, N. 1651. Quoted in Meliá *et al.* 1973.

US Embassy in Paraguay 1978. *Status of the indigenous peoples in Paraguay*. File P780 170–1592, 'Unclassified'. Asunción.

12 *The earth is our history book: archaeology in Mozambique*

PAUL J. J. SINCLAIR

Introduction

For many years Mozambique has been considered one of the blanks in African archaeology. Notwithstanding the early reports of rock paintings to the Portuguese Royal Academy in 1721, very little notice was taken of Mozambican prehistory before the beginning of the 20th century. From then on, despite sporadic, but in some cases excellent treatment of Stone Age sequences (e.g. Diás 1947, Barradas 1965), and a series of descriptive papers by D'Oliveira (e.g. 1960, 1963) and Barradas (1967), colonial archaeology can fairly be said to have almost completely neglected the excavation of sites from the more recent periods of the past. This did not apply to the same extent to the study of early Portuguese colonial relics, which became the central focus of the activities of the Historical Monuments Commission, the findings of which were published in the journal *Monumenta*. The main contributions to the archaeology of the later periods came from visiting scholars, notably Smolla (1976) and Dickinson (e.g. 1975).

Museum displays in so far as they existed were very small and reflected similar biases. In fact in Lourenço Marques (now Maputo), non–Portuguese Mozambican prehistory was relegated to a section of the natural history museum. In Beira, however, pioneers such as D'Oliveira did manage to display some examples of material culture from the farming community, and these efforts were paralleled by displays in the Nampula Museum of Ethnography in northern Mozambique. It was only at the end of the colonial period that the University of Lourenço Marques started to teach courses in prehistory and ethnohistory.

At independence, Mozambique was faced with a catastrophic lack of educated personnel. Less than 1 per cent of the population of almost 12 000 000 had attended any secondary school, and there were fewer than 60 resident Mozambicans with university degrees (Johnson 1984). When Mozambicans had managed to obtain schooling, it had been almost entirely related to the Portuguese metropolitan frame of reference. Accordingly, very little was known about Mozambican as opposed to Portuguese history, and precolonial Mozambique was a completely neglected field of secondary level teaching.

Post-independence shifts of emphasis about the past

Since independence there has been a concerted effort to increase public awareness of the cultural value of the archaeological heritage. This has been expressed through the emphasis at different educational levels on such subjects as hominid evolution, the history of Africa, and precolonial Mozambique. In terms of research this has involved a reorientation of priorities to the later periods of the archaeological record and an increased awareness of the potential contribution of oral tradition to archaeological and historical work. Public involvement has been an integral part of this process, and students from primary and secondary schools, and people living in the rural areas have contributed fundamentally to the success of the research efforts.

In May 1976 the University of Lourenço Marques became Eduardo Mondlane University. During the ceremony, President Samora Machel spoke of the need to reorient the work of the university towards the needs of the country, and to proceed systematically to investigate areas of sciences and humanities relevant to the needs of the people of Mozambique. This marked a fundamental break with a tradition of esoteric scholarship that had previously characterized the colonial university.

Different institutional frameworks have been organized to carry out the objectives of a national programme to preserve and stimulate interest in the archaeological heritage. The Department of Museums and Antiquities has been collating information on historical monuments, while the National Historical Archive has completed a highly successful campaign to retrieve colonial documents. This was implemented as part of an annual campaign to involve as many university student and staff members to work in rural areas. At the university, an archaeology section was created in the Institute of Scientific Research in 1975, and this was responsible for carrying out primary archaeological research throughout the country. In 1980, in response to the development of research and extension activities described below, the archaeology section was upgraded to the present Department of Archaeology and Anthropology of the Eduardo Mondlane University to make their work more relevant to the public.

A more relevant past

The work of the Department has continued to establish the basic chrono-stratigraphic framework of four areas of the country, the Nampula and the Cabo Delgado Coast regions of the north, the Vilanculos district of south-central Mozambique, and the southern Maputo region. This work has been described in detail elsewhere (Duarte et al. 1976, Adamowicz 1983, 1985, Morais 1984, Sinclair 1987), and the present concern is to illustrate some of the public extension efforts that were undertaken as part of the research programme. First it should be emphasized that the archaeological team operating in Mozambique after independence seldom numbered more than three professionally trained archaeologists. War conditions prevailed, and for the most part scientists were faced with serious logistical difficulties. These problems were however to a great extent alleviated by the great lengths to which ordinary Mozambicans as well as government officials were willing to go in order to help our work, especially after we had realized the importance of directing the primary focus of our work to meeting the real needs of the Mozambican public.

We found that as soon as the historical consciousness of the public was made the central priority a number of changes affected the research process. No longer were academic papers in foreign journals taken as the yardstick of achievement.

At Manyikeni in south central Mozambique (Garlake 1976) local residents had been assisting the Eduardo Mondlane University and British Institute in Eastern Africa teams in implementing an excavation programme. In 1977, after two seasons of unpaid work on the site, the residents of the Manyikeni locality decided that it was necessary for some visible local return for their efforts to be forthcoming. A series of public meetings was held and the issues were discussed over a number of days. The researchers from the university suggested the building of a site museum and cultural centre, together with research excavation, as the two main foci of activity. It was collectively decided that residents from a radius of about 40 km would voluntarily participate in rotation for a single working day on the site. The time on site would be split between education and assisting in the excavation work. One local resident was chosen by general agreement to act as guide and curator of the site. This role had been ceremonially passed on by the traditional custodian of the site, an office that had apparently been filled since the abandonment of the site, perhaps as long ago as 300 years.

The result of this series of meetings was that more than 450 people participated in morning lecture tours around the site, and afterwards helped the university specialist team with the excavation work (Fig. 12.1). Many more participants were involved through the efforts of the media (Morais & Sinclair 1980, Sinclair 1987). Seven onsite displays were complemented with a display centre in which paintings by Jeremias Libombo, a 17-year-old museum trainee, illustrated the contexts of selected archaeological finds from the site. The primary aim of the display centre and the archaeological site museum was to demonstrate physically and visually the existence of precolonial Mozambique, knowledge of which, given the educational situation, could not be taken for granted.

The Manyikeni site museum became a nationally recognized cultural contribution that asserted the value of the archaeological heritage in the midst of the Zimbabwean liberation war. The national significance of the work was reflected in the issue of postage stamps (Fig. 12.2) and the change of the locality name to the name of the archaeological site. Work at Manyikeni provided a unique opportunity to balance the research and museological aspects of archaeology, while addressing at the same time the

Figure 12.1   Volunteers sort through finds from an archaeological excavation.

needs of the local residents and the broader issues that should be faced in a
postcolonial context.

Human evolution

> In Soweto the police often called us monkeys and now you are doing
> the same. If this is true then where have our tails gone?

As archaeologists, we were often called on during research work, to
explain in evening lectures, the process of human evolution, and the above
quote comes from one encounter with young South African refugees. A
balanced view on human evolution had long been recognized as important
in the Frelimo education programme, and a number of booklets on evolution had been produced. As part of a move to modernize the adult education
programmes, members of the archaeology department were invited to
produce a new course structure reflecting the latest research positions.

A number of collective discussions were held at the university, and we
produced together a much simplified version of 'Human origins' distilled

Figure 12.2 Archaeological finds from the Manyikeni site feature on a series of Mozambican stamps.

from university lecture notes and widely distributed European and American popular accounts of human evolution. After considerable effort over some weeks, we were proud of being able to produce a 'clear straight-forward outline' in 12 sides with some simple line drawings. We decided to test our work at a secondary-level adult training centre close to Maputo.

After only five days of intensive work we were left in no doubt that most of our efforts had been in vain. Our texts were too complex, the examples either uninteresting or irrelevant for the students and, perhaps more significant, the concepts not clearly comprehensible for the teachers, many of whom had graduated from the same school only a few years previously. Particular problems were encountered in dealing with the time spans outside normal experience, and in explaining morphological changes. Faced with this rather chastening experience, we sat down and completely rewrote the texts. We discussed various examples with the students and selected those that were most easily understood. We then designed complete additional source books for the teachers.

We found that the most useful examples were those taken from the immediate experience of the students. The number of grains in a handful of sand or a bag of rice gives a much more immediate perception of quantity when dealing with the millions of years required for morphological change than does any widely suggested clock analogy. Similarly we found that the concept of change can be more easily dealt with by reference to the differing composition of immediate family members over time, and the conditions which prevailed in their lifetimes, than by reference to the admittedly excellent *Time-Life* illustrations of different geological epochs. After considerable experimentation and follow-up visits, we found that it was quite possible to put across ideas of morphological change and human evolution when these were presented in a suitable way for both students and teachers and when focused on temporal change and the basics of archaeological research procedures.

It would be gratifying to be able to report that the process of integrating the new versions of the texts and the handbook for teachers into the education system had proceeded smoothly but, once again, a series of obstacles presented themselves. These included the fact that the Ministry had different subject priorities and also, interestingly enough, that Frelimo trainees – educated in a European tradition – resisted the use of African examples such as *Australopithecus* and *Homo habilis*, instead of the more restricted focus on Steinheim and *Homo neanderthalensis* that had characterized the earlier pamphlets on human evolution. We were faced with a situation (which seems to occur widely) where the producer of even relevant scientific knowledge does not control the ambits within which such information is to be used.

Nampula province in the northern sector of the country was to prove the most successful focus of public extension work by the department. Archaeological work in northern Mozambique had been initiated by Duarte in 1976 and continued by Cruz e Silva and the present author from 1977.

Since 1980 Adamowicz (1983, 1985) has been carrying out detailed studies of late Stone Age and early farming community settlement patterns in the region. Often working in complete isolation because of the war Adamowicz has combined with the provincial authorities for education and culture to generate a network of archaeological extension services that use, and considerably elaborate upon, our previous work. The services include adult and student education courses and an archaeology-by-correspondence facility that aim to answer the many questions that readers and radio listeners put about precolonial Mozambique. This correspondence course, which currently involves more than 250 participants, has also led to reports of some important sites.

All of the material that we had previously worked on was incorporated by Adamowicz into these courses. In addition, together with co-workers from the university and the television and radio media, he has used a much wider range of illustrative source material in a very successful series of radio and television programmes on the origin of the Earth, human evolution, and sociocultural differences. The public response to this work has proved once again both the widespread popularity of archaeology and the importance of its role in providing a postcolonial cultural identity.

Subsequently, information on Mozambican precolonial archaeology provided by the Department of Archaeology and Anthropology has been used at a national level in recently published primary and 5th-grade textbooks. As yet the coverage of the population that this represents is limited, as only some 40 000 children a year reach 5th grade. In addition, agreements between Mozambique and international banking agencies have led to the introduction of fees for education and for the purchase of school books. Accordingly, even though the textbooks now exist, many families cannot afford to buy them (Johnson et al. 1987).

Acknowledgements

The work reported on here was done as part of a collective effort. I owe particular thanks to Joas Morais, Ricardo Duarte, Jeremias Libombo, Ana Loforte, Teresa Cruz e Silva, Benta Bingam, Tika Rodrigues and Leonard Adamowicz, as well as students and staff at the Adult Education Centre in Macubulane, who, in different ways, have contributed to this chapter. A. Johnson has also discussed the issues with me raised in this chapter.

References

Adamowicz, L. 1983. *An investigation of residential patterns in Nampula province viewed from an archaeological perspective: a progress report.* Textos para debate 3. Maputo: Departmento de Arqueologia e Antropologia, Universidade Eduardo Mondlane.
Adamowicz, L. 1985. *Report and comments on the progress of 'Cipriana 81/85' research project, Nampula Province.* Textos para Debate 6. Maputo, Departmento de Arqueologia e Antropologia, Universidade Eduardo Mondlane.

Barradas, L. A. 1965. Age of the last transgression on the South Mozambican coast. In *Proceedings of the V Congresso pan African Congress of Prehistory, Tenerife.*

Barradas, L. A. 1967. Primativa Mambone e Suas imediaçôes. *Monumenta* **8**, 41–54. Lourenço Marques.

Diás, M. B. 1947. The chronology of the quaternary in the "Sul do Save" province. In *Proceedings of the I Pan-African Congress of Prehistory*, Nairobi.

Dickinson, R. W. 1975. The archaeology of the Sofala Coast. *South African Archaeological Bulletin* **30**, (3–4), 84–104.

D'Oliveira, O. R. 1960. Breves noticias sobre a arqueologia de manica e Sofala. *Bol S.G.L.* **78**. Lourenço Marques.

D'Oliveira, O. R. 1963. *Amuralodos da Cultura Zimbaué-Monomotapa de manica e Sofala.* Bol. U.N. da Beira (Servicos Culturais), Artes Graficas. Lourenço Marques.

Duarte, M. L. T., da Cruz e silva, T., de Senna Martinez, J. C. Morais, J. M. and Duarte, R. T. 1976. Iron age research in Mozambique. Collected preliminary reports. Maputo, IICM, CEA, *Secçâo de prehistória*, Universidade Eduardo Mondlane.

Garlake, P. S. 1976. An investigation of Manekweni, Mozambique. *Azania* IX: 25–47.

Johnson, A. M. 1984. *Education in Mozambique 1975–1984: A review.* Stockholm SIDA Education Division Documents No. 15 March 1984.

Johnson, A. M., Kaluba, H. Karlsson, M., Nyström, K. 1987. *Education and economic crisis: the cases of Mozambique and Zambia*, Stockholm SIDA Education Division Documents No. 32 November 1987.

Morais, J. M. 1984. Mozambican Archaeology: past and present. *The African Archaeological Review* **2**, 113–28.

Morais, J. M. and Sinclair, P. J. J. 1980. Manyikeni, a Zimbabwe in southern Mozambique. In *Proceedings, VIII Panafrican Congress of Prehistory and Quaternary Studies*, R. E. Leakey & B. A. Ogot (eds). Nairobi, TILLMIAP: 351–4.

Sinclair, P. J. J. 1987. *Space, time and social formation – a territorial approach to the archaeology and anthropology of Zimbabwe and south central Mozambique c 0–1700 AD.* 9 August, Department of Archaeology, Uppsala University. Uppsala: Almquist and Wiksell.

Smolla, G. 1976. Archaeological research in the coastal area of Mozambique. *Proceedings of the VIIth Pan-African Congress of Prehistory*, 265–70, Addis Ababa.

13   Culture houses in Papua New Guinea

JOHN BLACKING

This chapter is about the living past in Papua New Guinea, a rapidly developing, future-oriented country, and about problems of reconciling a rich variety of preindustrial cultural heritages with the need for some degree of uniformity in a modern state. I call it the 'living past' because tens of thousands of the country's citizens are actively pursuing ancient ways of life that have been implicitly declared out of date by modern developments. What makes Papua New Guinea particularly interesting as a case study are its extraordinary social diversity, with over 700 languages spoken by a little over three million people; the dynamism and adaptability of the people of the Highlands, especially since they entered the modern labour market less than 40 years ago; and the determination of many young, educated people that traditional arts should be integrated into modern life, and not become merely tourist curiosities. Perhaps the most evocative of these attitudes is the new National Parliament Building in Waigani (Fig. 13.1) near Port Moresby: it is shaped like a large traditional house, and its woodwork and basic structure have been adorned by master carvers, painters, and sculptors who were brought in from many parts of the country.

Differing attitudes to traditional cultures

Zambia

Attitudes to cultural development in Papua New Guinea contrasted quite sharply with those of politically committed students whom I encountered in Zambia in 1981. There, they were convinced that traditional music and dance in particular, and traditional cultures in general, must be an excluded past, and could not be used in socialist development programmes because they were products of obsolete means and modes of production. They argued that music and the performing arts must reflect the patterns and values of social and economic life, and therefore regarded Zambian urban music as being more 'in tune' with the needs of a modern socialist nation, even though its sounds and means of production were obviously associated with European and American capitalism. They seemed to equate developments in technology, whose aim is to produce material goods quickly and

Figure 13.1 Modern materials and techniques are combined with traditional forms in the new Parliament Building at Port Moresby. (a & b) Architect's drawings showing how the *haus tambaran* and the village round house were unified into a single structure; (c) the finished building.

efficiently, with developments in music and the arts, whose aim is to enhance human experience and communication.

In Zambia regional variety in the arts was considered incompatible with the goal of national political and economic unity, because it seemed to reinforce precolonial 'ethnic' divisions in much the same way as South Africa's policy of 'compulsory folklife', or apartheid. Many were therefore critical of the Zambian national dance company, because it performed traditional 'ethnic' dances. But there was, in fact, an important difference between the Zambian company and some other national companies in Africa, Europe, Asia, and elsewhere, which encourage and present perform- ances of dances associated with particular culture areas by people who come from those regions. Members of the Zambian company were indeed recruited from different regions, but they performed dances from all parts of Zambia, learning them from other members of the company. Thus the performers were not so much members of different traditional 'ethnic' groups, as modern Zambian citizens, performing an amalgam of regional dances and also developing new movements and styles.

Jamaica

In Jamaica, by contrast, the past was revived in a different way by their national dance company, founded and developed by Rex Nettleford, whose work is personally known to me. Beginning as a company with its roots in ballet and contemporary dance theatre, it incorporated movements and dance genres from Jamaican folk and urban life. It portrayed aspects of the cultures of the different social groups that have contributed in various ways to Jamaica's history, and, in the same way that some planters' 'great houses' have been refurbished as museums and cultural centres, it also acknowl- edged that slave-owners produced part of Jamaica's cultural heritage. The past of the majority of Jamaica's citizens has been excluded for much longer than that of Papua New Guinea and Zambia, partly because of the length and nature of contact with Europeans, and partly because many felt that an effective escape from slavery required a complete break with the past. It is only in the past ten years or so that a national Memory Bank has been set up to record as systematically as possible all aspects of Jamaican oral tradition. But again, as in Zambia, the future of such an enterprise has been viewed with scepticism by those who see modernization and industrialization as tasks of revolutionary proportions that cannot be achieved without exclu- sion of the past.

Thus attitudes to the past, as well as definitions of what is or is not past, vary from one country and one social class to another. The past is not determined by an objective chronology or by its state of animation. That is why many contemporary Papua New Guinean lifestyles can be included in an assessment of the past in education, although they are not archaeological in the strict sense of the word: they are the past in the present, the living past and their exclusion would inevitably involve the exclusion of living people.

The Unesco report on cultural development, 1983

In 1983, sponsored by Unesco, I undertook a four-week mission to Papua New Guinea to evaluate the work of the National Cultural Council and the provincial centres and the relationships between them, and to advise on the development of cultural centres with special regard to their structures, functions and programmes, as well as their coordination.[1]

Provincial cultural centres had developed differently in line with the ideas of different organizers and the characteristics of the local cultures. All had small museums but one was an art school, another included the public library, and another promoted a drama group. In the course of the study, the role of the arts in formal education emerged as a crucial factor, because the work of cultural centres could be negated by diminishing attention to the expressive arts in schools. A comparison and synthesis of the centres suggested that they should move in the direction of catering for all sections of the community and combining traditional (e.g. dance) with modern (e.g. public library), so that different classes of people should not become estranged from each other.

In my report to Unesco I suggested that the National Cultural Council's role could be primarily one of liaison in relation to the provincial centres: organizing inservice training, especially for curatorial roles, seminars and workshops, and circulating information about the centres. I argued that decentralization and autonomy of the provincial institutions should be coupled with greater coordination between the national institutions, which could be brought closer together, and so function as a national cultural centre, providing leadership for the provincial centre by force of example rather than decree. Training and performance in drama, and work in the visual and graphic arts were well developed, but music and dance lagged far behind. Interesting developments were taking place in film-making. Some cultural centres had been quite successful in relating their work to tourism, and the National Cultural Council was urged to consider ways in which progress in the expressive arts could be stimulated through attracting tourists to cultural centres.

This chapter does not seek to cover events since 1983 (Groube 1985), but is concerned with the principles of the structure and role of culture houses in education in a multicultural society such as that of Papua New Guinea, and how they might best come to incorporate the past in the present and yet look forward to the future. Since my study, the Government's Cultural Development Act of 1986 has replaced the Cultural Development Act No. 35 of 1982, and the National Museum and Art Gallery Act No. 28 of 1983, and many changes have no doubt followed.

The organization of education in Papua New Guinea

There is an excellent formal education system in Papua New Guinea which was developed by Australian and British civil servants and teachers, as well as by different missionary enterprises. Since independence, this has been expanded by the government with the help of a considerable number of expatriates on fixed-term contracts. Primary schools have been set up in every part of the country, but pupils may have to travel some distance to attend secondary school.

There are two main university campuses, in Port Moresby and in Lae, at the foot of the road to the Highlands. There is a campus for teacher training at Goroka and a training college in Mt Hagen. Since contact with central and provincial governments has come to these areas only in the past 40 years, there are striking contrasts between the ways of life of many older people and of their children and grandchildren.

Cultural policy in Papua New Guinea

The National Cultural Council (NCC) of Papua New Guinea was vested with full statutory powers in 1975, under the aegis of the Ministry of Culture (later the Ministry of Culture and Tourism), to advise the government on policies that would best promote cultural development. An important objective of the Council was 'to help the emergence of a Papua New Guinean identity' and to create 'an awareness of cultural heritage'.

This does not mean that the NCC advocated a wholly conservative policy of preserving and promoting every different cultural system that had been invented in the country. Prime Minister Michael Somare, who underwent traditional initiation in 1973, stressed the value of being 'exposed to two different cultures in one's childhood', but he also wrote in his autobiography that 'one of our greatest and most urgent tasks in Papua New Guinea today is to forge a new national unity out of the multiplicity of cultures' (Somare 1975, p. 1).

The first publication of the National Cultural Council (Crawford 1977) recalled an extract from the Constitution of the Independent State of Papua New Guinea:

> We the people of Papua New Guinea,
> – united in one nation
> – pay homage to the memory of our ancestors – the source of our strength and origin of our combined heritage
> – acknowledge the worthy customs and traditional values of our people, which have come down to us from generation to generation
> – pledge ourselves to guard and pass on to those who come after us, our noble traditions . . .

However, the Director of Cultural Affairs and first Director of the NCC, wrote (Haugie 1977, p. 11):

> Culture is a continuing process of change. Culture is not changed. It is, in itself, change. The word 'Culture' has many meanings in Papua New

Guinea. People often think of old carvings, traditional dancing and the customs of the past. These elements are a part of our culture. But culture is not a thing of the past. It is an on-going thing. Other cultures are now invading our ways and bringing about change. We have now recognised this and since culture is a part of every part of life, we also recognise that this invasion cannot be stopped. We do not seek to put a stop to these influences but we seek to place emphasis on our own unique culture, so that the new ways blend with ours. We must not lose our own identity in the pace of modernisation. We cannot hope to preserve our ways in museums, or at institutes of the arts because culture is inseparable from everyday aspects of our life. It is a part of our village, city, home and community life.

That our culture remains a meaningful part of our life in Papua New Guinea is the main responsibility of the National Cultural Council.

Others elaborated on the crucial role of artistic activity in reinforcing communal values and generating 'a spiritual movement of all our people towards a better future' (Narokobi 1977, p. 15), so that:

With the foundations of our past and the hindsights of other civilizations, we can look into future green pastures. We can plan for a better future where cultural creativity is a desirable value to promote. We can build political, economic, legal, social and other institutions based on values we cherish . . . If we have to use a steel wheel or a steel needle, let us not be afraid to do so. But let us shape our pot and weave our basket. Let us not accept the steel pot made for us in Germany or an aluminium pot made for us in Japan.

In this vein, examples of traditional customs could be adapted usefully: employment conditions might be reshaped so that working mothers could take their babies to work, and no one should be unemployed in a city suburb that was run on a communalistic basis. Similarly, much training could be done 'on-the-job', instead of in separate institutions: 'in our traditions, the whole world was the classroom for education' (Narokobi 1977, p. 16).

Government policy and the statements of influential people involved in cultural affairs, therefore, went beyond the notion that cultural development is merely a part of national development, which can be attended to when the economic and political infrastructure has been satisfactorily organized. They suggested not only that cultural organization is a vital part of the infrastructure of any society, but also that cultural development is the first, and crucial, step in national development, especially when most political and economic decisions are subject to external pressures. Just as the concept of an independent nation generated the energy and inspiration that made Papua New Guinea possible, so it is undeniable that political organization of people's imaginations and affective culture can stimulate the construction of new social formations, and in turn can help to raise levels of political consciousness and economic well-being.

Key cultural institutions

The National Cultural Council was based in the capital Port Moresby, and was responsible for the allocation of funds to five national institutions, to the provincial theatre groups and local cultural centres, and to Village Arts, which organized the production and marketing of arts and crafts.

The national institutions were:

a   The National Museum and Art Gallery, together with the J. K. McCarthy Museum in Goroka, the latter being primarily concerned with Highlands cultures.

b   The Institute of Papua New Guinea Studies, which was responsible for research and publication on all aspects of traditional cultures.

c   The National Arts School, which provided training in visual and graphic arts, and also music (especially rock music). Its original aim was for *unschooled* artists to practise in freedom and without academic constraints. Although artists had been coming in from all over the country to work there, especially on the new parliament building, the majority of students were, in fact, schooled, and found jobs in industry, commerce and education. The original aim of the National Arts School was perhaps most effectively fulfilled in some provincial cultural centres. At Wabag, for instance, the Enga cultural centre had promoted new kinds of art in copper and different coloured local sands. Many of those who were involved with the cultural centre were 'community school dropouts', but they found a new interest and source of income in their art work.

The music department of the National Arts School was intended primarily to train music teachers and professional musicians. But although its work was not duplicated by the music department at Goroka Teachers' Training College, it was threatened with closure. Some people felt that it had no effective output, and was producing only rock music and concerts. This was accentuated by the great commercial success of a group of talented students who formed themselves into a group called Sanguma and produced some very successful new music, based on traditional models. This contrasted significantly with the South Sea-type music which was played in tourist centres like Madang and Port Moresby, and with imported rock and pop, which were imported in large quantities. Sanguma could perhaps be described as more authentically Papua New Guinean.

d   The National Theatre Company, which aimed at encouraging and developing dance and drama as art forms. Villagers were invited from all over Papua New Guinea to live with the company and to teach their dances and songs: in turn the company regularly toured the provinces.

e   The Raun-Raun Travelling Theatre based in Goroka, which was rather more directly involved in development. It provided local entertainment in a specially built theatre complex, and it offered cultural education for local town-dwellers no less than for visiting tourists, who wanted to see the famous 'Mudmen'. The theatre had toured widely and had also been used by various organizations to communicate information and advice about such things as coffee production, family planning, and water resources. Perhaps its most famous and successful production, which also toured abroad, was *Sail the Midnight Sun*, based on a poem written in English by John Kasaipwalova, who, in turn, had based his poem on the story of a Trobriand *Kesawaga*, or dance-drama.

f   The success and influence of Raun-Raun stimulated the formation of provincial theatre groups and local cultural centres in Wewak (Raun Isi), Madang (Mabarasa), Lae (Dua dua), and Bougainville (Theatre Toro), as well as several little theatre groups in villages. The fortunes of provincial cultural centres varied considerably, and often depended on the skills and initiative of the cultural officer or a volunteer enthusiast, and sometimes on the support of organizations like Rotary International, members of which helped to build the Museum of the Enga Cultural Centre. On the other hand, although the World Bank supported the Enga development programme, it did not support the cultural centre, which contained a museum, but which paid little attention to the developmental significance of nonverbal communication (Brennan 1982), which was and is of great importance in traditional Enga communities.

Problems in implementing cultural policy

One of the major problems in developing cultural centres and executing Papua New Guinea's official cultural policy was the inequality of opportunities between regions. This was caused partly by the location of necessary raw materials and natural resources, and partly by the externally oriented interests of industrial entrepreneurs. This was epitomized by contrasts of lifestyle in Port Moresby, and by the current predicament of the Trobriand Islanders.

Port Moresby is potentially a very attractive city, but the contrast between the living conditions of rich expatriates and poor Papua New Guinean workers is too great to generate a vibrant, modern community. The Trobriand Islands, which Malinowski made famous as an island paradise, seem not to have changed greatly in 70 years. True, there is a small airport, whose traditional-style departure lounge has been replaced by a modern terminal building, and young men are still producing beautiful carvings for tourists. But there are no chances for young Trobriand boys or girls to develop their potential in the place where they were reared. People have to get out of Kiriwina to continue their education and they do not return to live there.

Port Moresby is a victim of exploitation, the Trobriand Islands of the country's problems of communication. For a start, the capital is in the wrong place. Most parts of Papua New Guinea cannot be reached from Port Moresby except by air or sea, and in particular the whole heavily populated, rapidly developing region of the Highlands is cut off from the capital. This makes it essential that cultural centres should have a great deal of autonomy, but it also deprives them of contact with the central institutions through which their staff, whether local or university trained, can keep up or acquire skills and exchange ideas. The background and training of the staff of the cultural centres vary considerably. Although they generally work in areas where they were born, they had been away in Port Moresby and elsewhere to receive training as teachers, artists, or, in one case, as a social anthropologist. Few, it seems, have any formal training as museum curators or development officers.

If poor communication has been a disadvantage both to the Highlanders and the Trobriand islanders, distances do not deter Highlanders from coming together from great distances, for example, to share in a *sing-sing* and football match at Mendi, organized by the enterprising cultural officer, and director of the Southern Highlands Cultural Centre and Museum. This museum was sited in the school grounds in an attempt to overcome the growing barrier between those with formal education and those with informal traditional skills. Similarly, at the West New Britain Cultural Centre, in Kimbe, the gap between the two has been further closed by placing the public library in the same complex as the museum and traditional craft shop.

Similar reconciliations of past and future, traditional and modern, old and young, have been achieved at a number of other cultural centres, and most notably in some secondary schools, like Sogeri High School in Central Province, and the Mt Hagen Technical College. For some weeks before the annual independence celebrations, students learn dances and songs from their elders: and when they perform them in full costume people from home are there to help them dress and paint up, adjust costumes, and check dance steps during performance.

Problems of cultural development

In considering Papua New Guinea's problems of development and the creation of culture complexes and culture houses, there remains the task of criticizing and evaluating cultural systems and institutions. The Papua New Guinean writers quoted earlier were rather more progressive than some of the Unesco documents and pronouncements on the subject. For example, in 1982, Unesco resolved that 'the equal dignity of all cultures . . . must be recognized as an inviolable principle' (Unesco 1982, p. 183), but at the same time delegates condemned apartheid and the Zionist regime of Israel. To condemn particular regimes, which are ways of life or cultures, it is necessary to accept that no culture is inherently or automatically good, and that whole cultures or parts of a culture can be dangerously deviant, as was Nazi culture.

In my view, in planning cultural development in a multicultural society such as Papua New Guinea, and especially in trying to forge a national identity out of scores of smaller regional identities, · the components of culture must be assessed critically, and if necessary be changed. For example, although anthropologists predicted that the dignity and cultural identity of the Dani of Irian Jaya would be disastrously undermined if warfare were outlawed, in fact, the Dani adopted a peaceful style of life without culture shock and decay. In extreme cases, an emphasis on cultural identity, as distinct from individual identity and self-actualization, can run the risk of becoming pathological: racism is but an extreme form of the policy of asserting cultural identity. Culture is not some fixed commodity but can be seen as a sort of floating resource that is available for use, or not, as part of the process by which individuals develop their human capabilities through social interaction, sharing ideas and learning skills. Cultures are the crutches that human communities have devised at different times and at different places not only to derive a material living, but above all to provide a framework for making sense of profound emotions, institutionalizing love and the joy of association, and finding new ways of extending the body. Culture does not determine individual personality: the differences amongst individual Irishmen and Englishmen, for example, are much greater than differences that might exist between Irishmen *as* Irishmen and Englishmen *as* Englishmen. People are not 'cultural dopes': from the cradle to the grave they use, adapt, and change cultural identities and corresponding behaviours according to the requirements of different situations. There can only be true human development when people live beyond culture and not *for* culture; for cultural systems provide people not so much with lifestyles as life chances, with the means of realizing their full human potential.

In the process of making and changing the cultural systems that people use to order their experience, the arts have played a crucial role. The exercise of artistic capabilities is one of the chief means by which human consciousness is roused, and by which human imagination and inventiveness can be stimulated and harnessed. Practice of the arts is not an optional luxury that can be afforded only when more basic needs have been satisfied. The arts are not merely part of the cultural superstructure which reflect the patterns and values of social and economic life, they are expressions of the most fundamental and distinctively human of all capabilities, the artistic process, or the exercise of artistic cognition, and the application of aesthetic energy. Other forms of cultural invention are derived from this generalized 'artistic' process.

To claim that 'artistic cognition' is the basis of all culture is not just a pious dogma. It is a scientific hypothesis about human development that is being increasingly borne out by studies of the anthropology of the performing arts, of the affective and cognitive development of infants and children (and especially their nonverbal and prelinguistic behaviour), and of the workings of the left and right hemispheres of the brain (Blacking 1982, pp. 41–2). 'Artistic' cognition is not just a mode of thought, a way of knowing: it is the most fundamentel extension of the body as human being, from which other modes of action and thought, such as scientific thought, are derived. The work of the National Cultural Council and its associated bodies, and indeed the whole problem of cultural policies and cultural development in Papua New Guinea, cannot be considered apart from the role of the expressive arts in education. Cultural development is not simply about festivals and *sing-sings* and traditional dance in community schools, it is about arts education.

It is not just about the maintenance of free expression and creativity (cf. Brash 1983, p. 143), which are the natural inheritance of all healthy children, but about social and intellectual discipline and the 'subliminal' acquisition of values. Although primary education follows a national syllabus, the influence of the culture(s) of the region in which schools are located is often very strong, especially in the expressive arts, where local resources are tapped. Even so, education in the expressive arts still has to be treated with the same respect as 'core subjects' such as English, mathematics, science, and history if the purposes of the government's cultural policies are to be achieved: otherwise students will lose respect of the expressive arts because there is no progress in the curriculum, as there is with the core subjects. Furthermore, they will come to think that they have learnt all they need to know about the arts by the time they reach the end of their primary education, because they will consider that they know about the arts of their own ethnic group, and that is sufficient. Thus there is always a danger that they will come to see artistic expression as little more than a statement of group solidarity, and possibly a pleasant emotional experience, and the educational developmental functions of artistic practice will pass them by.

Cultural centres as spiritual powerhouses

In Papua New Guinea, the *wantok* system (one talk, one language) helped to hold societies together during the years of rapid economic and political change. But its effectiveness will not last unless it is supported by new cultural developments that can bridge the gaps between places, generations of people, lifestyles, and ideologies. When high school and university students rehearse and perform traditional dances, there is a partial closing of a gap. But when their own children are at school and university, will they be able to want to attend and monitor the rehearsals, as parents and elders do at present? Technical development in the expressive arts must be experienced and understood if the old is to be related to the new and to be an effective force in people's lives, rather than a curiosity. Without education which reveals the links between *sing-sing*, *Sanguma*, Shostakovich, *samba* and *shamanism* as human expression, and between those artistic creations and the societies from which they emerged, traditional music and dance will become for young Papua New Guineans merely museum objects, rather than sources of self-awareness and national pride, totemic emblems of ancient divisions rather than signs of the richness of human cultural invention and symbols of important values. If they are to play a significant role in Papua

New Guinea's overall development, cultural centres must be more than static museums that preserve and recall the provincial heritage, shops that sell craft goods, and venues for entertainment. They must be dynamic places for continuing education about the present and future, as well as the past, and spiritual centres whose work ensures that members of the community can participate in the processes of achieving modernization without losing the richness of regional diversity.

In outlining a model of the kind of cultural centres that could best serve the spiritual and intellectual needs of communities in a rapidly changing society I envisaged (Blacking 1984) lively, convivial places that could be used with equal joy by men and women, young and old, university graduates and unschooled gardeners, visitors and local people, tourists and citizens of Papua New Guinea. Ideally a cultural centre should be a complex of buildings and open spaces, which ought to include a museum and public library; a shop and/or a cultural village where craftsmen and women could work; a place or places for practising music, dance, and drama, and for painting and carving; some kind of restaurant or refreshment kiosk; and an arena or amphitheatre for public performances. Sooner or later, all cultural centres would have to consider opening at weekends, as they do at Madang, and running regular evening classes, as well as sponsoring occasional lectures, films and dramatic performances. It was suggested in the course of discussions with officials that this kind of centre would be far too expensive for the limited budget of any province, and beyond the scope of the NCC's budget. My response to this objection was that traditional societies allocated a considerable amount of resources for their 'culture houses'. In the report of the NCC Working Party in a section on the National Museum and Arts Gallery, for instance, Avei (1980, p. 135) had written that:

In Papua New Guinean societies we have spiritual houses which serve as a centre for the community's spirit. In a village where the spirit house is still built, the community is responsible for its maintenance.

In traditional Papua New Guinean societies, culture houses were important centres for reflections on, and assimilation of, the good things of the past, and adaptive education for the future. The idea of the culture house, appropriately changed in size and scope, is no less suitable for modernization and national development in contemporary Papua New Guinea.

It was very good of the Australian Rotarians to build the museum at Wabag. But why were the people of Wabag not inspired to build their own 'spirit house', using the building talents of the local community to lay the foundations of their own centre? Some buildings and some parts of buildings may need trained workers, but the nucleus of any centre could be made by members of the community for members of the community. Moreover, the investment of time and effort in building cultural centres would ensure that, as in the past, people are more likely to take an interest in their activities, and help to maintain them. By doing so, new generations will be encouraged to accept the educational potential of the past in the framing of the future.

Note

1 After 10 days spent in Port Moresby visiting the Department of Education and the University and studying the national institutions, the National Theatre and Arts School, the National Museum, and the Institute of Papua New Guinea Studies, and the activities of Sogeri National High School, three provincial cultural centres were visited in the Highlands, at Mt Hagen, Wabag and Mendi. Then in Goroka, Eastern Highlands, I visited the Raun Raun Theatre and the J. K. McCarthy Museum, which are national institutions; the Skul Bilong Wokim Piksa, which is a training centre for film and video-making; and the Goroka Teachers' college. This was followed by visits to cultural centres in West New Britain (Kimbe), North Solomons (Kieta), to the Madang Museum and Cultural Centre, and to Rabaul, North New Britain, and to Kriwina, Trobriand Islands.

References

Avei, M. 1980. *National Cultural Council: report and five year plan*. Cyclostyled report.

Blacking, J. 1982. A case for higher education in the arts. In *The arts and higher education*, K. Robinson (ed.), Research into Higher Education monographs No. 48. Surrey University: The Society for Research into Higher Education.

Blacking, J. 1984. *Promotion of cultural policies: Papua New Guinea Cultural Development*. Assignment Report, Serial No. FMR/CLT/CD/84/155. Paris: Unesco.

Brash, E. 1983. In *Arts education seminar*, R. Frost & M. Walker (eds). Papua New Guinea Department of Education. Port Moresby: National Institutions Division.

Brennan, P. 1982. Communication. In *Enga: foundations for development*, B. Carrad, D. Lea & K. Talyaga (eds), 198–216. Enga Provincial Government Publication.

Carrad, B., D. Lea, & K. Talyaga (eds) 1982. *Enga: foundations for development*. Enga Provincial Government Publication.

Crawford, A. L. 1977. *The National Cultural Council: its aims and functions: with guidelines for establishing and operating cultural centres within Papua New Guinea*. Boroko: National Cultural Council.

Groube, L. 1985. The ownership of diversity: The problem of establishing a national history in a land of nine hundred ethnic groups. In *Who owns the past?*, I. McBryde (ed.). Melbourne: Oxford University Press.

Haugie, J. 1977. A message from the director. In *The National Cultural Council: its aims and functions; with guidelines for establishing and operating cultural centres within Papua New Guinea*, 11–12. Boroko: National Cultural Council.

Narokobi, B. 1977. Foreword. In *The National Cultural Council: its aims and functions; with guidelines for establishing and operating cultural centres within Papua New Guinea*, 14–16. Boroko: National Cultural Council.

Somare, M. 1975. *Sana: an autobiography*. Port Moresby: Niugini Press.

Unesco 1982. *Final Report of the World Conference on Cultural Policies*. Paris: Unesco.

14 *The reconstruction of African history through historical, ethnographic and oral sources*

GODFREY MURIUKI

Introduction

Until the 1950s hardly any university in the world taught African history. Such interest as existed in the subject was confined to colonial and imperial history or, more usually, a study of European activities in Africa. Colonial history, however, attracted few followers and was always regarded as a poor relation of mainstream history (Coupland 1939a, 1939b, Boxer 1961, 1965). Invariably, African historiography became the domain of amateurs who largely consisted of explorers, traders, missionaries, and administrators.

The reasons for this hiatus are not hard to find. To begin with, the development of history as a distinct academic discipline had placed the written word on a pedestal. Historians became so obsessed with the written word that it became the only acceptable form of historical evidence. Unfortunately for Africa, such records only existed for isolated parts of the continent, such as Ethiopia, Muslim Africa, and a few coastal areas. Consequently, it was generally assumed that Africa did not have a history worthy of study. Many certainly agreed with Newton when he said that Africa had 'no history before the coming of the Europeans. History only begins when men take to writing' (Newton 1922–3, p. 267). This Eurocentric view had a profound effect on African historical studies. Put simply, there was a general consensus that no African history existed before the arrival of foreigners, such as the Arabs and Europeans. These are the people, so the argument went, who had stimulated whatever minor developments were discernible in Africa. To Seligman (1966, p. 61), for example, 'the civilizations of Africa are the civilizations of the Hamites, its history the record of these peoples and of their interaction with two other African stocks, the Negro and the Bushman'. This view dominated imperial history and, to a large extent, buttressed the case for the conquest and partition of Africa between the various colonial powers. It was self-righteously argued that benighted Africa required the assistance of Europe if it were ever to enjoy the benefits of modern civilization. That is, white people had a moral obligation to spread their particular brand of civilization to Africa for the sake of the African peoples. Hence the epithet 'white man's burden'.

The upshot of all this was that it was firmly believed that colonial rule was necessary in Africa. Inevitably, therefore, the focus of historical studies was on the activities of Europeans or sometimes Arabs in Africa in their capacity as major initiators of historical developments and processes. In this scheme of things, the indigenous people of Africa had no place.

Post-1945 developments: the search for national histories

The situation described above lasted for most of the colonial period. However, such placid historical waters were increasingly being muddied by nationalist stirrings that gained a significant momentum after the Second World War. The birth of the new nations brought history to the foreground. These newly created, self-conscious, fledgling nations required the consciousness of a common historical experience in order to weld together the disparate groups that had been haphazardly lumped together by the colonial governments. Consequently, one of their vital and urgent initiation rites was the search for common historical roots. It was argued that history is so vital to the maintenance and continuity of human societies that no society could possibly exist without it in some form. The new nations therefore called upon history to discover their origins, as well as to provide a knowledge of their development through the ages. In short, history was given the tall order of providing the historical basis for the national identity of a diverse range of new nations. The matter was urgent because at independence national identity was a commodity in desperately short supply, because colonial boundaries had ridden roughshod over ethnic diversity. Indeed the commonest social and political glue in these newly independent nations appeared to be their short colonial experience. And that could not be relied upon to hold them together for long.

Political imperatives apart, the second impetus for a national history emerged from academic circles. The process of decolonization accelerated the development of African universities. For example, the late 1940s and 1950s witnessed the birth of universities in the Gold Coast (now Ghana), Nigeria, Sudan, Senegal, Uganda and Belgian Congo (now Zaire). In these institutions of higher learning African students cautiously demanded to be taught African history alongside European history. These initial timid demands bore fruit, and by the close of the decade most of these universities had revised their history curricula to include African history. For instance, Makerere College (Uganda) introduced a course on the History of Tropical Africa in 1951; and Ibadan, Nigeria, appointed K. O. Dike, a Nigerian, to be Director of African history in 1956 (Curtin 1981). These developments were mirrored across the continent.

Elsewhere, European intellectuals of a liberal persuasion vigorously fought to demonstrate the legitimacy of African history as a respectable academic subject. It is partly because of these pressures that the University of London appointed the first lecturer in African history at the School of

Oriental and African Studies in 1948. At about the same time, the Paris-based journal *Présence Africaine* began encouraging a proper study of African history. These measures were followed by a flurry of seminars and conferences that eventually culminated in the birth of the *Journal of African History* in 1960. This journal, not coincidentally, appeared at the dawn of the era of African political independence. Quite clearly, nationalist demands had reinforced the call for the introduction of African history into the mainstream of academic studies, both in Africa and elsewhere. In short, this also signalled the beginning of the long road towards academic self-reliance. At long last African history was finally accepted as a respectable and full member of the historical discipline, rather than tolerated as a poor kinsman (Fyfe 1976, Fage 1981, Ray *et al.* 1981).

A brief review of the written sources

Contrary to the argument reviewed above that Africa had had no history because there were no written records to demonstrate such a history, it is clear that the African continent possesses some of the oldest written sources in the world. Quite apart from the considerable body of written material from Egypt that dates back to the fourth millennium BC, Africa has been in contact with Mediterranean Europe and the Middle East since that time. At the beginning of the Christian era Egypt had become a centre of Hellenistic culture, as well as part and parcel of the Roman and Byzantine Empire. The result was that between the 4th century BC and the 7th century AD there is a considerable body of Greek and Latin literature that comments on events in Africa, particularly North Africa, Nubia and East Africa. The main classical historians of Africa are Polybius, Pliny, Strabo, Ptolemy and Herodotus, while the major sources are Ptolemy's *Geography* (*c.* AD 140), *The Periplus of the Erythraen Sea* (*c.* AD 230) and *Topographica Christiana* (*c.* AD 535), amongst others (Freeman-Grenville 1962, Snowden 1970, Thompson & Ferguson 1969, Djait 1981).

In the 7th century, Islam spread to North Africa, which subsequently became part of the Islamic world. It did not take long before Muslims spread their religion to the 'infidels' of the Sudanic belt, and as far as East Africa. Muslims were largely interested in trade, but a minority of them settled among the indigenous peoples, with whom they intermarried.

Muslims were extremely conscious of the historical role of Islam. As a consequence they were anxious to leave a record of their religious activities. They also trained the local people, who acquired literacy in the Arabic script. Both groups wrote *tarikhs* (histories) and chronicles, which have proved to be valuable sources for African history. Centres of learning were also established, such as the ones in Timbuktu and Sokoto in West Africa in the 16th and 17th centuries. From the 9th century onwards, therefore, Muslims left a valuable body of source material (Hunwick 1962, Lewicki 1969, Hopkins & Levtzion 1981). Among the many authors are al-Bakri

(11th century), al-Idrisi (12th century), Ibn Battuta (14th century) and Ibn Khaldun (14th century). It should also be noted that Muslim African historians from the Sudanic belt and East Africa used Arabic script to write down oral traditions, such as those relating to ancient Ghana, Mali and Songhay. The history of the three ancient West African empires, for example, has been largely pieced together from such sources. Indigenous scholars also wrote in local languages, using Arabic script. For example, such materials exist in Kiswahili, Hausa, and Kanembu.

Written sources about Africa became more plentiful after the European Renaissance. This phenomenon was no doubt given impetus by the invention of the printing press, which made books cheaper and more freely available. The thirst for knowledge and the concomitant dawn of the Age of Discovery spurred on many adventurers to produce travelogues that were avidly read in Europe. The most notable of these early travelogues are Mandeville's *Travels*, written about 1360, and Hakluyt's *Principles of navigation*, published in 1589, which incorporated travel accounts of Thomas Windham to the Gulf of Guinea in 1553 and John Lok to the Gold Coast between 1554 and 1555 (International Council on Archives, Pearson 1970).

The coastal regions of Africa were well documented by Portuguese, Dutch, British and French sources. But these sources rarely extend to the interior of Africa, except in a few regions such as Senegal, Gambia, the Niger delta, Benin, Kongo and along the Zambezi. South Africa also features in early accounts by shipwrecked sailors. But the material only becomes significant after the establishment of the Dutch Colony at the Cape in 1652. Besides official documents, there are 19th-century narrative accounts by travellers, missionaries and traders.

Ethiopia is particularly well-endowed as far as written sources are concerned. Written in Ge'ez, a local language, Ethiopian records go back for nearly one thousand years. Ethiopian scholars also wrote royal chronicles, probably from the 13th century on, recording the major events of each reign (Blundell 1923, Gabre-Selassie 1930–2, Beckingham & Huntingford 1954, Hable-Selassie 1967). At the same time, since Ethiopia was the fabled home of the legendary Christian king Prester John, it attracted travellers from Portugal, France, Italy and Britain. This resulted in rich archival sources in many languages, some unexpected, such as Russian, Czech, Swedish and Turkish.

European sources became particularly abundant in the 19th century. Attempts to explore the interior of Africa, the campaign to end the slave trade, and the colonial partition increased the tempo of production of written material on Africa, both official and public, published and unpublished (Freeman-Grenville 1962, da Silva Rego & Baxter 1962–7, Hrbek, 1981). Inevitably, these documents are scattered in state and private archives or libraries in Africa and the metropoles.

A variant of this genre of historical documentary evidence has been produced by educated Africans. Among the Fante of Ghana, for example, work was produced in the 18th century by Jacobus Capitein, A. William Amo and Philip Quaque. And liberated African slaves – such as Ignatius

Sancho (1781), Ottobah Cugoano (1787) and Olaudah Equiano (1789) – tell about the slave trade and the conditions under which Africans toiled in Africa, the Americas and Europe. During the nineteenth century Africans and people of African origin, for example, Samuel Ajayi Crowther (a Nigerian) in Nigeria and Thomas Birch Freeman (a black Englishman) in Ghana travelled widely, and recorded their experiences at a critical period in the history of these countries.

Towards the end of the 19th century, a number of African rulers from Central and Southern Africa, including Lobengula, Moshesh and Cetshwayo, corresponded with colonial authorities. A small, but important, group of African scholars wrote specifically about the history of their own peoples (e.g. Reindorf 1895, Johnson 1921). In the second half of the 19th century, newspapers written in local languages started to appear, and are a mine of historical information.

While Arabic texts declined from the 15th century as European ones increased in number, they remain an important source, particularly for Muslim Africa. The 16th-century nautical works of Ahmad bin Majid, Abu Makhrama's *Chronicle of the Fortress of Aden* (16th-century) and Sali ibn Raziq's *Imams and Sayyids of Oman* (19th-century) are all cases in point. Above all, Jenne and Timbuktu in West Africa remained centres of learning, and the art of chronicle writing spread to other areas in the Western Sudan.

Several observations can be made from this survey of written sources. Their most serious drawback is that they are unevenly distributed in time and space. Until the 15th century, for example, coverage is restricted to North Africa, the Sudanic belt and the coast of East Africa. Even then, the authors were not particularly interested in Africa as such – Muslim chronicles concentrate on the spread of Islam, and usually little is said about what was happening to the indigenous peoples. European sources focused mainly on what was supposedly a strange African world, with emphasis being placed on the unfamiliar and exotic. The authors had no real interest in Africans; they were chiefly preoccupied with geographical problems, such as the sources of the Nile and Niger rivers, or with their own activities on the continent. More problematic is that nearly all of the accounts were ahistorical, since Africa was assumed to have no history of its own. In short, very little effort was made to try and understand African societies. Much of this European material is superficial and frequently inaccurate.

Nonwritten source materials

For large areas of Africa and for long periods historians have had no written material to guide them. Consequently historians interested in the history of Africa have been forced to discard the notion that only written material deserves to be recognized as historical evidence. Of necessity, historians in Africa have had to seek the assistance of other disciplines, such as archaeology, linguistics, and anthropology, and to combine the use of oral traditions, social science methodology and an interdisciplinary approach. For example, historical linguists have provided valuable data on the peopling of Africa over the last thousand years. Archaeologists have not only contributed to an understanding of African prehistory, but have also complemented historical evidence obtained from other disciplines. It is such a multidisciplinary approach, for example, that has enabled scholars to trace the expansion of the Bantu-speaking peoples, who now occupy two-thirds of the African continent south of the Sahara. In short, the previously unwritten excluded past is increasingly being incorporated within historical studies.

Oral traditions

Oral traditions have been defined as 'oral testimonies concerning the past that have been transmitted by word of mouth from generation to generation' (Vansina 1965, see also 1985). By their very nature, oral traditions pose serious problems for the investigator. First, they take cognizance of personal interests, cultural values and political environment. Second, oral testimonies are also influenced by the concept of history prevailing in the given society. Third, oral traditions are selective, and normally emphasize what is acceptable to a particular social milieu. This point is highlighted in tales of origin that are widespread throughout Africa. In virtually every society, the need for social stability and continuity dictates that all the inhabitants of a community must share a putative common ancestor. It is for this reason that anthropologists argue that oral traditions are coded statements about past epochs that are difficult, if not impossible, to understand or decode. Anthropologists note, for example, the use of archaic language and esoteric imagery that are difficult for the contemporary generation to decipher. As such, origin myths are symbols and myths which, though valuable as social charters, are of dubious value as historical evidence.

Oral traditions depend on human memory. This quite often leads to omission and confusion. In this regard, the situation is aggravated by the fact that the narrator's personality has an important bearing on the testimony transmitted. Experts in oral traditions are artists. They may add their own interpretation to the testimony, and pass this on as part of the original tradition or even include information that was not there originally. Frequently, content is subtly adjusted to suit the audience.

Studies carried out in Africa and elsewhere have shown that oral traditions appear only to be capable of recalling about 500 years of a group's past (Muriuki 1974). Some societies even appear to suffer from historical amnesia (Jacobs 1968). Many oral traditions lack any time scale, and events are telescoped in such a way that, in some cases, they appear to have taken place only yesterday (Henige 1971, 1974a).

Oral traditions have suffered greatly due to the spread of literacy. The introduction of formal Western-style education witnessed a gradual decline of more traditional systems of education, in which oral traditions had played a prominent part. Consequently, in some areas, oral traditions have suffered. In some parts of Africa, including Karagwe (Tanzania), Zambia, Bornu (Nigeria) and Elmina in Ghana, revival of interest in oral traditions has led to a situation whereby written material has been incorporated into oral traditions. This phenononen is not peculiar to Africa, and has been reported from Iceland, Norway and Oceania (Henige 1974b).

Oral traditions that have recorded are also defective in two respects. During the colonial period, African colonial functionaries were sometimes appointed on their claim to traditional leadership. It was not surprising, therefore, to witness the manufacture of dubious genealogies and other historical evidence in order to lay claim to colonial recognition. In other cases, particularly in Nigeria and Tanzania, colonial governments, in the process of introducing indirect rule, were anxious to establish local authorities. This required that traditional systems of government be identified and re-established.

The study of African history was discouraged in the 1930s and 1940s by synchronic functionalist approaches to the study of African societies by social anthropologists. The collection of oral traditions became sporadic, since they were not of paramount academic interest at the time.

In spite of these obvious drawbacks, it is important to recognize that oral traditions have a vital role to play in attempts to reconstruct the history of Africa. To begin with, in many parts of Africa literacy was introduced quite recently. Even today, a large proportion of the African population do not read or write. The significance of this is that oral traditions remain an important element in the traditional educational system. Unlike in the Western world, for example, oral traditions are alive not dead. In short, they form the core of living history. Nonliterate societies have a large capacity for memory, and in many cases great care is taken to ensure that oral traditions are transmitted correctly.

In parts of West Africa a special category of experts – called *griots* – were the custodians of oral traditions. Their responsibility was so great that punishment for carelessly transmitting oral traditions might include death. Prior to the intrusion of Western influence, a similar situation existed in Rwanda where *bairu*, experts in traditional lore, played the same role. But even where no specific group was entrusted with the correct transmission of oral traditions, youth were instructed in traditional lore during initiation ceremonies. On such occasions the initiates were segregated from the rest of the population and temporarily housed in makeshift barracks which were transformed into formal schools. While there, they were taught by experts who were chosen to perform this task because of their acknowledged role as custodians of the cultural heritage (Kenyatta 1938, Nyamiti 1969, Langley 1979, Fadiman 1982). Initiations are therefore the occasion for instruction in oral traditions. They mark an individual's transition from childhood to adulthood, and mastery of oral traditions is regarded as one of their essential elements.

The days of haphazard and amateur collection of oral traditions are long gone (Hoopes 1979). Indeed, efforts to consolidate oral traditions as a methodological approach to the study of the past have culminated in the publication of specialist journals such as *History in Africa: A Journal of Method* and *Oral History Review*.

Chronology, however, still remains a problem. The genealogical generation – which is defined as the period between the birth of a man and that of his first child – has been widely used as a measure in the absence of absolute chronology. Studies carried out in East Africa have estimated that a genealogical generation is about 27 years. This is little different from dynastic genealogies in Europe and Asia, which have been calculated at between 26 and 32 years. Some societies kept a record of their past with reference to age sets. Among the Maasai and Kikuyu, for example, initiation of the male took place over five years, followed by a closed period of nine years. Those initiated during the open period formed a regiment which acquired its name from the most important event that had taken place during the initiation. Age-set names, therefore, provide a useful summary of the major historical events that occurred at a particular moment in time (Jacobs 1968, Muriuki 1974). Age-set names also offer a chronological referent since it took 14 years to form each regiment.

Conclusion

Studying oral traditions as an important source of history is nothing new. Indeed, they constitute the oldest way of preserving knowledge about the human past. Homer, Herodotus, and Thucydides are a part of this tradition. There is considerable evidence to show that in Europe written sources did not begin to acquire their final commanding heights until the 14th and 15th centuries, and oral sources continued to be widely used for another two centuries. Oral sources appear to have been discredited only in the 19th century, as a consequence of the development of modern academic historiography (Henige 1982, Thompson 1984, Tosh 1984).

Since the 1960s there has been a renewed interest in oral sources in Africa. This resurgence of interest has had a significant influence on the study of history. Oral traditions have yielded information regarding population movements, material culture, state formation, economic development, demography, social structure, and religion. Indeed, a comparison of oral traditions and written sources, where both genres do exist, attests to the value of the former and demonstrates that its supposed defects – such as bias, selectivity, omissions, and so on – are not peculiar to this genre of historical evidence. They are as common in written sources.

There has now been a definite shift in the study of history. The values and assumptions of traditional historiography have been challenged, with the result that methods and topics hitherto frowned upon have gained grudging acceptance. Social science, for example, has developed a close link with history, leading to an interdisciplinary approach to historical studies. Even more important, interest in the social history of everyday life has also increased in the Western world. The study of peasants, the oppressed, women, and political radicals has increased. This trend has demonstrated the inadequacies of written sources, and indicated the need for 'unconventional' approaches. In this regard, personal reminiscences have proved useful in the study of rural communities, by providing authentic testimony of human life as actually experienced by the silent majority. Thus ordinary people have a chance to take part in the production of historical knowledge, hitherto the monopoly of the academic elite (Triulzi 1981). Consequently, oral history has finally gained academic respectability (Tosh 1984). As part of the excluded past, it has proved that it can enrich our understanding of historical processes throughout the world.

References

Beckingham, C. F. & G. W. B. Huntingford (eds) 1954. *Some records of Ethiopia, 1593–1646*. London: Hakluyt Society.

Blundell, H. W. 1923. *The royal chronicle of Abyssinia, 1769–1840*. Cambridge: Cambridge University Press.

Boxer, C. R. 1961. *Four centuries of Portuguese expansion, 1415–1825*. Johannesburg: Witwatersrand University Press.

Boxer, C. R. 1965, *The Dutch seaborne empire, 1600–1800*. London: Hutchinson.

Coupland, R. 1939a. *East Africa and its invaders*. Oxford: Clarendon Press.

Coupland, R. 1939b. *The exploitation of East Africa, 1856–1890*. London: Faber.

Cugoano, O. 1787. *Thoughts and sentiments on the evil and wicked traffic of slavery*. London.

Curtin, P. D. 1981. Recent trends in African historiography and their contribution to history in general. In *General history of Africa, Volume 1: methodology and African prehistory*, J.Ki-Zerbo (ed.), 54–71. London: Heinemann for Unesco.

da Silva Rego, A. & T. W. Baxter (eds) 1962–7. *Documents on the Portuguese in Mozambique and Central Africa, 1497–1840*, 7 volumes. Lisbon: Centro de Estudos Historios Utramarinos.

Djait, H. 1981. Written sources before the fifteenth century. In *General history of Africa* Vol. 1, J. Ki-Zerbo (ed.) 87–113. London: Heinemann for Unesco.

Equiano, O. 1789. *The interesting narrative of the life of Olaudah Equiano, or Gustavus Vassa the African, written by himself*. London.

Fadiman, J. A. 1982. *An oral history of tribal warfare: the Meru of Mount Kenya*. Athens, Ohio: Ohio University Press.

Fage, J. D. 1981. The development of African historiography. In *General History of Africa* Vol. 1, J. Ki-Zerbo (ed.), 25–42. London: Heinemann for Unesco.

Freeman-Grenville, G. S. P. 1962. *The East African coast: select documents from the first to the earlier nineteenth century*. Oxford: Clarendon Press

Fyfe, C. (ed.) 1976. *African studies since 1945: a tribute to Basil Davidson*. London: Longman.

Hable-Selassie, S. 1967. *Source material for the ancient and medieval history of Ethiopia*. Communication to the International Congress of Africanists. Dakar.

Henige, D. 1971. Oral tradition and chronology. *Journal of African History* **12** (3), 371–89.

Henige, D. 1974a. *The chronology of oral tradition: quest for a chimera*. Oxford: Clarendon Press.

Henige, D. 1974b. The problem of feedback in oral tradition: four examples from the Fante coastlands. *Journal of African History* **14** (2), 223–35.

Henige, D. 1982. *Oral historiography*. London: Longman.

Hooper, J. 1979. *Oral history: an introduction for students*. Chapel Hill.

Hopkins, J. F. P. & N. Levtzion (eds) 1981. *Corpus of early Arabic sources for West African history*. Cambridge: Cambridge University Press.

Hrbek, I. 1981. Written sources from the fifteenth century onwards. In *General History of Africa* Vol. 1, J. Ki-Zerbo (ed.), 114–41. London: Heinemann for Unesco.

Hunwick, J. D. 1962. Arabic manuscript material bearing on the history of western Sudan. *Bulletin of News of the Historical Society of Nigeria* **7** (2), 1–9.

International Council on Archives 1970. *Guide to the sources on African history outside of Africa*. Lug.

Jacobs, A. H. 1968. A chronology of the pastoral Maasai. In *Hadithi*, B. A. Ogot (ed.), 10–31. Nairobi: East African Publishing House.

Johnson, S. 1921 *History of the Yorubas*. London: Routledge.

Kenyatta, J. 1938. *Facing Mount Kenya*. London: Secker & Warburg.

Langley, M. S. 1979. *The Nandi of Kenya*. London: C. Hurst.

Lewicki, T. 1969. *Arabic external sources for the history of Africa south of the Sahara*. Wroclaw-Warsaw-Krakow.

Muriuki, G. 1974. *A history of the Kikuyu, 1500–1900*. Nairobi: Oxford University Press.

Newton, A. P. 1922–3. Africa and historical research. *Journal of the African Society* **22**, 266–77.

Nyamiti, C. 1969. Christian and tribal initiation rituals: a comparative study of Maasai, Kikuyu and Bemba rites in view of liturgical adaptation. D. Theol. thesis. Catholic University, Louvain.

Pearson, J. D. (ed.) 1970. *A guide to documents and manuscripts in the British Isles relating to Africa*. London: Athlone Press.

Ray, D. I. *et al.*, 1981. *Into the 80s: the proceedings of the eleventh annual conference of the Canadian Association of African Studies*. Vancouver.

Reindorf, C. C. 1895. *The history of the Gold Coast and Asante*. Basel: Basel Mission.

Sancho, I. 1781. *Letters of the late I. Sancho, an African . . . to which are prefixed memories of his life*. 2 Vols. London.

Sellassié, G. 1930–2. *Chronique du règne de Ménélik II, roi des rois d'Ethiopie*. Paris: Maisonneuve.

Seligman, C. G. 1966. *Races of Africa*. London: Oxford University Press.

Snowden, F. 1970. *Blacks in antiquity: Ethiopians in the Greco-Roman experience*. Cambridge, Mass.: Harvard University Press.

Theal, G. M. 1898–1903. *Records of South-Eastern Africa*. 9 Vols. London: Swan, Sonnenschien.

Thompson, L. A. & J. Ferguson (eds) 1969. *Africa in classical antiquity*. Ibadan: Ibadan University Press.

Thompson, P. 1984. *The voice of the past: oral history*. Oxford.

Tosh, J. 1984. *The pursuit of history: aims, methods and new directions in the study of northern history*. London: Longman.

Triulzi, A. 1981. Decolonising African history. In *People's history and socialist theory*, R. Samuel (ed.). London: Routledge & Kegan Paul.

Vansina, J. 1965. *Oral tradition*. Harmondsworth: Penguin

Vansina, J. 1985 *Oral tradition as history*. London: James Currey.

15 *The excluded present: archaeology and education in Argentina*

IRINA PODGORNY

Introduction: the educational context

In his analysis of the educational system of Latin America Tedesco (1986) defines two central parameters: 'disequilibrium and unsolved problems of the past', and 'the challenges of a world that is increasingly "knowledge intensive"'. These he sets in a climate of regional economic crisis.

Problems identified by Tedesco include an increasing internal differentiation in the educational system in relation to the social sectors that it serves: a limited ability to define curricular and organizational models appropriate to the special characteristics of each country; an increasing dissociation between academic culture and social culture; and administrative inefficiency and rigidity.

In Argentina problems inherited from the past have been exacerbated by the policies of recent governments. Thus we find the 'technocratic' response (military government, 1966–73); 'social modernization' (constitutional government, 1973–6); 'political freeze' (military government, 1976–83); and the contemporary 'modern–democratic' (constitutional government, 1983 to date) (Tedesco *et al.* 1987).

The most influential of these legacies is the 'authoritarian educational programme of 1976–83' (Tedesco *et al.* 1987) of the last military dictatorship, the most blatant phase of which involved the expulsion and prosecution of teachers, the control of curricular content, and the regulation of visible behaviour (e.g. haircuts, discipline). This period was marked by increased privatization as well as increased authoritarianism within the family, and the greater influence of the Roman Catholic Church.

The military government continued to fund both religious and secular private education while at the same time allowing central contributions to state education to fall to the lowest levels of the decade. In 1976 such contributions amounted to almost half of the financial support for education, the remainder deriving from provincial governments. In 1978 the central military government decided, without consulting the provinces and without the approval of the civilian population, to transfer responsibility for primary education to the provincial authorities, including total responsibility for financing it. As a result, teachers' salaries in primary and secondary schools varied from province to province depending on the provincial authority concerned.

By 1983, the Argentine educational system had developed a number of characteristics including:

a a high degree of bureaucratic complexity that was matched by a low level of formal and informal participation in organizational matters by teachers, parents, and students;

b a poorly equipped, and deteriorating set of buildings – despite the raising of international loans specifically aimed at improving such premises;

c a teaching body in much disarray, with little clear organizational structure or uniformity.

Archaeology in Argentina

Archaeology is studied as part of anthropology, which is sometimes integrated with the Faculty of Philosophy (Buenos Aires) or with the Faculty of Natural Science (La Plata). Recently, a School of Archaeology has been established in Catamarca (northwest Argentina).

Under the last military government, anthropology departments were accused of subversive teaching and such courses were gradually wound down in the majority of universities. In La Plata anthropology managed to survive with a 'tamed' syllabus. Since 1983 there have been attempts to return anthropology to its previous position. Pressure groups, formed by students, young graduates and professionals, discriminated against during the last dictatorship on ideological grounds, are demanding new syllabuses, new appointments and the re-establishment of degree courses. However, although some changes have taken place, the inheritance of the military government is still very much in evidence.

The position of anthropology has to be understood within the wider framework of contemporary university education, which suffers from a general lack of resources, reflected especially in university libraries that are deficient and outdated.

There have been Argentine archaeological conferences since 1970 but the proceedings of many recent ones have not been published. This is in part due to the general problem of resources and in part to the decline in the national publishing industry. The few books that do exist on Argentine archaeology are frequently out of print or are priced beyond most people's pockets, and are luxury editions that focus on archaeology as art history. One of the few exceptions to this, and a book with the highest circulation and consulted most often outside university circles, is *Argentina indígena, vísperas de la conquista* (Native Argentina on the eve of the conquest) (González & Pérez 1976). It is the first volume in a series on Argentine history.

University archaeology in Argentina is characterized by a positivist style, an absence of theoretical debate, and isolation from professional field archaeologists. It also has little contact with the rest of Latin American archaeology (Bonnin & Laguens 1984–5). Very few grants are available for research, and those that do exist originate from the state, through the National Council for Scientific and Technical Research (CONICET – Consejo Nacional de Investigaciones Científicas y Técnicas) and through provincial research councils.

There is no national organization to which all archaeologists in Argentina belong. There are about 100 archaeologists based in universities, and most are female. One possible explanation for this gender bias may be the low salaries that university teachers and researchers receive. The response of many parents – and much of society in general – is to ask their sons: 'Archaeologist? How will you support your family?' Given the social and economic values of the middle class this problem is not so acute for women.

Argentina has no central register of archaeological projects. However, on the basis of information obtained from CONICET (Alvarez et al. 1986), it is possible to say that archaeological research concentrates on Tierra del Fuego, Patagonia and the northwest. In the first and second of these regions work is focused on hunter-gatherers and in the third on agricultural-ceramic societies. Historical archaeology is rare.

Archaeological research tends to be carried out in an academically inward-looking context and, in this sense, archaeologists can be said to be contributing to the lack of attention given to the pre-Hispanic past in the wider context of Argentine education. In fact, there exists more than a century of research findings demonstrating an Argentine history going back much further than the 16th century. There is no public awareness of this pre-Hispanic past. Part of the process of conquest and subordination to which indigenous peoples have been subjected has included the neglect of their past and history.

Archaeology in primary and secondary education

In schools archaeology and related subjects form part of the social sciences and history syllabuses, the latter being characterized by its emphasis on events, the highlighting of battles, heroic characters, and the glory of patriotic and military deeds. The accepted view is that history begins in 1492. Anything that is earlier than this is 'native' and belongs to something that is alien to the Western world view. It is part of this view that the nature of 'native' has been either denied or overstated, but always excluded from the 'real' world.

The denial of an indigenous past, or the distinction between such a past and what is called 'civilization', accompanies concepts such as 'desert' to describe the lands that are inhabited by natives and which are therefore taken to be 'uninhabited' by human beings, the epithet 'barbarian', and the gross underestimation of the length of time that the American continent has been inhabited.

D. F. Sarmiento, President of the Republic between 1868 and 1874, fully supported this view of the native past and was also one of the founding fathers of the Argentine education system. His writings on 'indigenous races and their moral attitudes' have to be seen in the historical context of colonial expansion over the Indian territories:

> The Indians have a skin which is thicker and less sensitive than that found in other parts of the world. Having examined the skulls that were excavated from ancient tombs, they have been found to be thicker than average: they are coarser . . . From the intellectual point of view the savages are basically stupid, while civilised peoples comprise individuals who are like the savages, others of mediocre capacity, others who are intelligent and others who are superior. (Sarmiento 1883, p. 87)

An opposite trend can also be detected. Overstatement created the image of the Heroic Indian, of just and peaceful societies and regret for a lost paradise. Depending on the period and on the government in power, official history in Argentina emphasized one or other of these two extremes. We could call the first one Europeanist, and the second one Revisionist.

Archaeology is dealt with in schools in two or three classes every year, under the title, 'Native Cultures of Argentina and Latin America'. The nature of the teaching is influenced by the lack of regional histories as well as a number of stereotypical attitudes such as:

a   admiration for the Inca, Maya and Aztec civilizations, their great monuments and their similarities to elements of the 'Old World';
b   a feeling of resignation because of the absence of remains comparable to those left behind by the Central American and Andean cultures;
c   surprise and pride at the ruins of 'cities' in the northwest of Argentina that are just as impressive as Inca ones;
d   the lumping together of all the rest of archaeological remains in the northwest of the country under the term *diaguita* (the name of the group of natives occupying the region at the time of the arrival of the Spanish);
e   sympathy for the rude nature of the savages of the Argentine plains and Patagonia who did not even have stone houses.

It is important to realize how little views had changed until very recently; the image had remained the vision of conquerors. School maps that showed the distribution of native Argentine cultures combined, as if they were all contemporary, those who were murdered 400 years ago, those who were murdered 100 years ago, as well as the living. To represent those still living in this manner, was clearly the best way of silencing them.

In 1984 a new educational policy was introduced. As part of the new curriculum the national Ministry of Education for the first time included in secondary school syllabuses subjects such as human rights and aboriginal groups in contemporary Argentine society.

The draft syllabus for 'American aboriginal communities' for children in grade 7 and first year in the province of Buenos Aires includes archaeological subjects such as the importance of material remains for the reconstruction of the past and the study of American and Argentine archaeological remains. The aim of this syllabus is to 'apply spatial, temporal, and causal concepts and widen the knowledge of the natural and cultural environment' (Dirección General de Escuelas 1985). However, the textbooks that are being used for this new syllabus have been written by the same authors who wrote those in use under the military government.

While educational administrators explain how enough curriculum time has been found for these changes, the problem remains that teachers and teacher training colleges lack the necessary knowledge to teach them. The response 'I have never taught this subject' sums up the situation.

In conversation with archaeologists, teachers and headmasters, no one denies the importance of the inclusion of archaeology in the school syllabus (Podgorny n.d.). Everyone agrees with the responses 'To know what is ours'; 'our roots', 'our identity', 'to rescue the values of our cultural heritage' when the question is asked, 'Why do it?', and yet these responses appear to have no real meaning. Who defines the values? How can we talk about what is 'ours' if we have not established who 'we' are?

The new educational changes are said to be aimed at producing a democratic community that is in harmony with nature and with its neighbours. However, at present this is, in fact, no more than an ideal in the minds of those in government.

Given the above situation, the value of continuing to talk about archaeology and education, as two areas working together, can be questioned. However, we must continue to do so.

We must accept the following points: that the past is part of our identity, that the American and Argentine pre-Hispanic past is largely ignored, that the multicultural nature of Argentine society is overlooked, and that the vision that we have is based on stereotypes that have been put forward by others. We must also accept the view that all this is part of a reality that can be modified, little by little, from the bottom up, and in its totality.

Archaeology, and archaeologists, have a number of skills to offer in any such modifications:

a   a subject that demonstrates the interrelatedness of subjects that are normally separated in today's educational system – for example, human societies, environment, art, scientific thought, and politics;
b   a subject that deals with concepts of change and time;
c   a methodology to discover the remains of the past around us, and which, through that past, allows us to analyse the contemporary world.

The problem is to know how far such aims can be achieved within an unsympathetic educational environment? A characteristic of Argentine education is the constant contradiction between what is said and what is done.

This contradiction is so evident that no one can any longer believe the rhetoric of educational theory. Radical changes in the curriculum do not ensure the transformation of society. At the same time, however, the effective maintenance of a previous curriculum does not necessarily imply the exact reproduction of the system that generated it.

Education multiplies messages. At present the educational message appears to be: to repeat without questioning and to pretend that what has been repeated is important. In contemporary Argentina there is an ambivalent attitude towards education: nobody trusts it nor the certificates and other pieces of paper that it produces, yet everyone needs to be part of the formal education system as the means of climbing the social ladder.

An 'Archaeology and Education' project

After numerous administrative problems an 'Archaeology and Education' community project has been introduced into schools with the assistance of the Directorates of Culture (Dirección de Cultura) of two municipalities of Gran Buenos Aires, Quilmes, and Berazategui. Both are relatively recent municipalities with no previous contact with archaeologists.

Several research projects have now been under way for some eight months and include:

a   A workshop in a primary school for the fourth, fifth, sixth and seventh grades (children from 10 to 12 years), to introduce the children to a part of the pre-Hispanic past and to the current problems of the native population. The work was divided into four modules: archaeology and the first Americans; early American ceramic cultures; Argentine rock art; and contemporary native peoples. Educational approaches used included classroom discussions, experimentation, play, and the use of audiovisual media. The modules were introduced by the author and by teachers of music, ceramics and the plastic arts. We attempted to identify the relevant images that children have accepted about the indigenous past. We asked the children to draw an Indian. The image that appeared was that of a lone individual, immobile, and dressed as a 'redskin', like a television or cartoon character. At the end of the project the children were asked to repeat the drawing. This time they placed the Indian within domestic contexts.
b   A series of talks for the first year of a technical school, and a visit to the Museum of Natural Sciences of La Plata, with the objective of complementing work previously done in class. The series began with a talk on the origins of the universe, the origins of the human species, and discussion of American and Argentine cultures.
c   An afternoon workshop with a group from the third year of a school of commerce, to introduce them to some of the practical techniques used by archaeologists.

From this initial work we have identified a willingness on the part of some teachers to use archaeology in the curriculum in an exciting way. As a result, the educational project has now received the support of the University of La Plata which allows it to be extended to cover the whole question of the insertion of archaeology into the education system.

The success of this initial project so far has also revealed an important additional factor that needs to be considered. For archaeology to flourish within the school system requires archaeologists to modify their current position and to recognize archaeology in school as an important educative subject in its own right rather than just a youthful pastime when it is undertaken by schoolchildren.

Acknowledgements

I should like to thank María Rosa Neufeld, Gustavo Politis, Stella García, Muñeca Zago, Gloria Masan for all their help and comments with regard to this chapter, all the children and teachers who have worked with us and especially Eduardo for everything he has done. All errors and mistakes are mine alone.

References

Alvarez, M. *et al.* 1986. Sobre qué aspectos de la realidad social trabajan los antropólogos argentinos hoy. Informe elaborado por los jefes de Trabajos Prácticos de Antropología. *Ciclo Básico Común para el ingreso a la Universidad de Buenos Aires*. Buenos Aires.

Bonnin, M. & A. Laguens 1984–5. Acerca de la Arqueología Argentina de los últimos 20 años a través de las citas bibliográficas en las revistas Relaciones y Anales de Arqueología y Etnología. *Relaciones de la Sociedad Argentina de Antropología*, 16. Buenos Aires.

Dirección General de Escuelas. 1985. *Lineamientos curriculares de educación básica.* Provincia de Buenos Aires.

González, A. R. and Pérez, J. 1976. *Argentina indígena, vísperas de la conquista.*Historia Argentina vol. 1. Buenos Aires: Paidos.

Podgorny, I. n.d. Data from unpublished research carried out at Quilmes and Berazategui in preparation for a thesis.

Tedesco, J. C. 1986. Crisis económica, educación y futuro en América Latina. *Nueva Sociedad* **84**.

Tedesco, J. C. Braslavsky, C. & Carciofi R. 1987. *El proyecto educativo autoritario. Argentina 1976–1982*, Miño & Dávila (eds). Buenos Aires.

Sarmiento, D. F. 1883 (1946). *Conflicto y armonías de las razas en América*. Buenos Aires: Intermundo.

16 *Archaeology in the Alberta curriculum: an overview*

HEATHER DEVINE

Introduction

Formal education in Canada is administered regionally, and had its beginnings in the activities of missionaries and fur traders who established schools in the far-flung settlements of the frontier. As different regions became more heavily populated and provincial governments were established, the administration of schooling became a provincial, rather than a federal, responsibility. Today, each of Canada's ten provinces and two territories develops and implements its own school curricula. Federal involvement in education is restricted to the administration of education at military bases and on Indian reserves. However, many Indian bands across the country are now in the process of establishing and administering schools that fall under their own, rather than provincial or federal, control.

The result of this decentralization of school administration across Canada is curricula that reflect the multicultural heritage of the country. In areas with large francophone populations, for example, the medium of instruction is French. Education in the Yukon and Northwest Territories is geared towards serving its large constituency of Dene and Inuit (northern Athabascan Indian and Eskimo) students.

Despite the regional administration of education, there is a reasonably consistent pattern of grade levels and curriculum composition throughout the country. In Canada, the length of most precollege school programmes is 12 years. Children generally start school at age 6 (Grade 1) and finish school at age 18 (Grade 12). The minimum legal age for leaving school is 16 years. School programming tends to consist of a mandatory core content in mathematics, the sciences, and the humanities. Elective programming consists of specialized courses that complement the core curriculum. Some elective courses are developed by the provincial departments of education. Others may be special programmes devised and implemented within the regional or local school jurisdiction. Elective programming offers teachers and students the opportunity to explore topic areas that may receive little or no emphasis in the core programme (Katz 1974, pp. 11–70).

Because of the perceived esoteric nature of archaeology, it is within the context of elective programming that most curriculum content pertaining to it is to be found. In Alberta, most of this content is tied to curriculum content in the social studies programme. Social studies, although treated as a discrete subject within the Alberta curriculum, is in fact, comprised of course content from a number of different disciplines: geography, history, economics, world affairs, and anthropology.

A rationale for research

Since its inception, the Archaeological Survey of Alberta has been primarily a regulatory agency. To carry out this function successfully many of its activities have traditionally revolved around research and resource management. Resource management includes initial evaluation of the potential for damage to heritage resources by proposed development projects, monitoring these developments and subsequently assessing their impact on the archaeological resource base. Archaeological research is the other main activity of the agency.

In recent years, however, the Archaeological Survey has recognized the importance of the need to educate and inform the public. To this end, a public education officer (the author), was appointed to coordinate the development and dissemination of instructional and informational materials for schools and the public.

It is not enough, however, merely to hire an educator to develop materials dealing with archaeology. Such materials are not likely to be perceived as credible instructional classroom aids without evidence of a great deal of preliminary investigation on the part of the developer. An investigation was therefore undertaken by the author to determine instructional needs of those studying archaeology and native prehistory in Alberta schools.[1]

The following questions (Devine 1985) were addressed:

a   What is the current status of archaeology/prehistory as a topic in schools in general, and Alberta schools in particular?
b   What is the nature (i.e. content and methodology) of educational material relating to archaeology and prehistory employed in Alberta schools?
c   What are the weaknesses and strengths of archaeology/prehistory curricula as perceived by classroom teachers, curriculum specialists and archaeologists?
d   What role does the Historical Resource Division (specifically the Archaeological Survey of Alberta) play at present in education about archaeology/prehistory and how can it make a greater contribution?

Answers to these questions provided the information necessary to understand instructional needs and the subsequent design of useful instructional materials. The completed study was submitted to the Curriculum Branch of Alberta Education in June of 1985 for review and comment. It was hoped that some of the recommendations arising from the study would be incorporated within the curriculum revisions that were then taking place.

Archaeological content in the Alberta curriculum

In the 1985 Alberta school curriculum there are three areas where archaeology is formally included; (a) at Grade 6 in Social Studies Topic 6(A) – 'How people in earlier times met their needs'; (b) in an elective unit developed to complement Topic 6(A) entitled 'Archaeology' (Alberta Education 1981); (c) as part of the Physical and Cultural Anthropology 30 elective offered at the high-school level (Alberta Education 1976).

In Topic 6(A), ancient civilizations are discussed in relation to the means by which early peoples satisfied physical, psychological and social needs. As part of the investigation, students are required to be familiar with the roles of archaeologists and historians in providing information about the past through the use of 'artifacts, fossil remains, pictorial data, oral traditions, and written records' (Alberta Education 1981, p. 46). However, the topic description specifically states that content 'is to be selected from ancient Mediterranean civilizations (e.g. Greek, Roman, Egyptian) or pre-Columbian America (e.g. Mayan, Inca, Aztec)' (*ibid.*).

A culture is defined as a civilization when it features the following integral elements:

a the establishment of cities characterized by permanent structures and monumental architecture;
b the systematic production and distribution of surplus foodstuffs and goods;
c a formal written language;
d the use of arithmetic and geometry in making scientific calculations; and
e a hierarchical class system (Hoebel 1972, pp. 219–20).

Alberta was not home to 'civilization', as defined anthropologically, until the arrival of EuroCanadians, a little over 200 years ago. By implication, content pertaining to prehistoric native culture is excluded, as the nomadic lifestyle characteristic of Alberta's earliest inhabitants does not include all of the elements integral to 'civilization', despite a cultural heritage that has survived many thousands of years. Yet, because the decision was made to study ancient civilization, rather than culture, the present curriculum ignores this lengthy period of Alberta's history, despite the wealth of archaeological information available.

Archaeological content in electives

Native prehistory is explored in an archaeological context in one suggested elective unit entitled 'Archaeology' developed to coincide with Topic 6(A) (Alberta Education 1981). The learning activity in this elective unit revolves around the use of the simulation game *Dig* (Lipetzky 1969). In the simulation, students are divided into two competing teams. Each team creates the culture for a hypothetical civilization, stressing the interrelationships of cultural patterns, economics, government, family, language, religion, and recreation. The teams construct artefacts that reflect the cultural patterns, and then bury them in the ground. Each team then scientifically excavates, restores, and analyses the other team's artefacts, learning about culture patterns in the process. These learned skills can then be applied to the analysis of contemporary culture. In addition to the simulation, students are directed to read the archaeology content in *Exploring civilizations* (Linder 1979) and *Alberta's prehistoric past* (Chevraux 1980). Activity cards, charts, and exercises based on the texts are provided at a learning station, where students individually select and pursue learning activities based on Alberta archaeology. Students then compose a 'synthesis of life in earlier times' based on archaeological finds. A field trip to Drumheller, Alberta – the site of some of the most extensive dinosaur bone deposits in the world (Alberta Culture and Multiculturalism 1988a) – is suggested as a suitable concluding activity.

There are aspects of this elective activity that may be problematic, as the outline provided in the Alberta Education electives monograph does not provide sufficient information to utilize the game successfully.

First, merely obtaining the game may be difficult. Second, the references suggested for use contain misleading material, specifically *Exploring civilizations* (Linder 1979) and *Alberta's prehistoric past* (Chevraux 1980). *Exploring civilizations* presents a rather fanciful description of an archaeological dig in Egypt complete with singing diggers and supervising archaeologists who scold the workers and 'do little actual digging' (Linder 1979, p. 18). The stated purpose for, and methodology of, the described dig are so vague and simplistic that they would provide little guidance to students wishing to learn more about the 'archaeological processes of enquiry'. The photographs accompanying the chapter may cause even more confusion, as they obviously illustrate non-Egyptian archaeological activity. Subsequent chapters present a 'first person'(?) account of the discovery of Troy by Schliemann, and a sketchy, simplistic summary of events in ancient Egypt.

Other inaccuracies in content and presentation scattered throughout the text have been highlighted elsewhere at length (Decore *et al.* 1981). This publication is due to be withdrawn by June 1991 as a basic resource at Grade 6 (Alberta Education 1987–8, 1989–90). *Alberta's prehistoric past* (Chevraux 1980) provides an overview of Alberta archaeology, but is written in a way that could lead to misinterpretation. The fictionalized account of the life of Small Eagle, a Plains Indian boy, has a number of inaccuracies (Decore *et al.* 1981, p. 100).

The culminating activity for this unit, a visit to Drumheller, Alberta, is inappropriate from an archaeological standpoint. Despite the importance of Drumheller as the home of the Tyrrell Museum of Palaeontology and the significance of the surrounding area as a Unesco World Heritage Site (Alberta Culture and Multiculturalism 1988a), a visit to Drumheller serves to reinforce the misconceptions people have concerning the relationship between archaeology and palaeontology. There are many more suitable archaeological sites for school students, such as the Strathcona Archaeological Centre outside Edmonton, the Head-Smashed-In Buffalo Jump outside Fort McLeod, and certain provincial parks (Alberta Culture and Multiculturalism 1987). Unfortunately this elective unit is not likely to be revised, and it is no longer listed in current curriculum publications.

Possible areas for curriculum enhancement

There are a number of social studies topic areas other than Topic 6(A) where material dealing with Alberta archaeology would enhance the content. Inclusion of content dealing with Alberta archaeology could be featured wherever native prehistory is discussed. The province has a wealth of prehistoric archaeological features, including buffalo kill sites, tipi rings and cairns, tool-making and campsites, and rock carvings and paintings. All are of cultural significance and a study of the importance of any one of these features in telling us more about native lifeways would be of benefit.

The natural resources of Alberta are also studied in Grade 4. Alberta was the location of much industrial activity early in its history. Some of this activity is being brought to light through archaeological research at sites such as the abandoned townsite of Lille where coal was once mined and processed into coke. If we want to understand the evolution of Alberta's resource-based economy thoroughly, the consideration of now-extinct industrial activity through archaeology is necessary.

In Grade 5, the exploration and settlement of Canada is discussed. Alberta was home to a number of fur trading posts, Northwest Mounted Police posts, missions, and pioneer settlements, many of which have been or are currently being excavated. The information obtained from these excavations tells us a great deal about the daily activities of such settlements not dealt with in currently available historical records.

In the Grade 7 social studies programme, the field of anthropology is discussed in the context of an introduction to culture. Supplementary material dealing with the role of the archaeologist in anthropological research could be developed, as could resources dealing with career opportunities and training in archaeology.

Archaeology in language arts

A basic text for Grade 6 Language Arts entitled *Starting points in reading* (Level C – First Book) (Cross & Hulland 1974) contains a reading unit dealing with archaeology entitled *I Dig*. An autobiographical tale called 'Being a spare-time archaeologist' describes how archaeologist Jim Ingram acquired his interest in archaeology as a child. Although the story may be factual, from an archaeological standpoint it promotes some destructive practices. Not only does the young Ingram dig rather dangerous pits in his search for arrowheads to add to his collection, but at one point in the story he digs up an Indian skeleton with his bare hands, removes the skull and arrowheads, and races off to the local newspaper with his find, where, in a later issue, he is lauded as a 'young archaeologist'. In actual fact he destroyed at least one archaeological site, disturbed a burial, and stole artefacts. What the young protagonist did in the story is illegal (in most, if not all, Canadian provinces) and morally wrong, but nowhere is this indicated in the story.

The publishers are currently phasing out this particular textbook series, and distribution of it to Alberta schools will cease from June 1989 (Alberta Education, *Buyers Guide* 1987).

Ironically, 'Being a spare-time archaeologist' was the only poor story in an otherwise good unit, which also contained 'Four boys and a dog', an account of the discovery of the cave paintings of Lascaux, and 'Taking care of old things', a discussion of how archaeologists carefully preserve what they find. Both stories present situations where archaeological finds are dealt with responsibly. (One can only hope that the teacher will make distinctions between the irresponsible 'archaeological activities' in 'Being a spare-time archaeologist' and the more careful handling of archaeological finds in the stories that follow.)

High-school anthropology

The final curriculum examined was the (physical and cultural) *Anthropology 30* programme (Alberta Education 1976) which is offered as a social sciences elective at high-school (Grades 10–12) level. The two basic course references were a textbook (Cover 1971), and a pamphlet from Alberta Culture (1976). Cover provides a good overview of anthropology, but the archaeology content is confined to approximately four pages of text. The pamphlet is no longer available, although other publications subsequently produced by Alberta Culture and Multiculturalism would be more suitable.

The main problem that exists with the programme is the overall lack of direction provided to teachers in the presentation of material. Topics are listed and supplementary references are suggested but that is all. If the teacher did not have access to the supplementary references, it would be difficult to teach the course, as the primary references do not contain enough to facilitate the discussion of certain topics in depth, particularly archaeology. Suggested student activities also suffer from this lack of material and subsequent lack of concept development. One suggested activity that pertains to archaeology requires groups of students to 'bury artifacts', excavate 'sites' and hypothesize as to the nature of civilization (Alberta Education 1976, p. 10). A simulated dig is a complex undertaking requiring a great deal of preparation of both materials and procedures. If the simulation is not planned and executed correctly, it will degenerate into a 'treasure hunt' where the main objective is to uncover artefacts, rather than to interpret the nature of the artefacts in the contexts within which they were found. The curriculum provides no references to assist the teacher in planning such an activity other than the film entitled *Five foot square* (Trent

University 1970), from which it is assumed that teachers will be expected to acquire the information needed to undertake a simulated dig.

Too much of the Anthropology 30 programme relies upon the resources and imagination of the teacher to successfully 'carry it off'. Although it is not unreasonable to expect a competent teacher to be able to plan and teach a programme in anthropology, it should be remembered that the resources that are readily at hand in school libraries and resource centres may be somewhat limited due to the perceived 'esoteric' nature of the subject. It should also be noted that there are few teachers who possess a sufficiently strong background in anthropology to enable them to teach a programme without some support materials and, in some cases, inservice training.

Anthropology is presently classed as a low enrolment course (approximately 400 students province-wide in 1988). This low enrolment, and the removal of the two primary resources from the 1989–90 *Alberta Education Buyers Guide*, does not bode well for anthropology's continued inclusion in the curriculum.

The treatment of archaeology: some observations

Certain aspects of the Alberta curriculum detract from a comprehensive understanding of archaeology. As noted earlier most of the content relating to archaeology revolves around the study of Mediterranean and MesoAmerican archaeology, which usually involves the examination of ancient civilization. This effectively excludes any concentrated study of Alberta archaeology, which is concerned primarily with precontact native remains and a few historic sites. The concentration on ancient civilization may also indirectly reinforce the notion that archaeology is 'treasure hunting', and that archaeology implies the unearthing of stone monuments, gold and jewels, and other exotica. Although the study of MesoAmerican aboriginal civilization is included, study of the barbaric aspects of certain societies (e.g. the Aztecs), coupled with the notion that all of these native cultures crumpled in the face of European technology, may unwittingly reinforce the notion that European culture is superior to, rather than different from, native culture. The study of Greek and Roman civilization to the exclusion of Alberta-based native culture further reinforces this stereotype.

Methods used to teach archaeology do not always help. In almost every instance where archaeology content is presented, little guidance is provided to the teacher to facilitate the preparation, gathering, and utilization of resource materials dealing with archaeology. Most instructional settings do not lend themselves to the kinds of activities (e.g. simulated excavation and experimental archaeology) that are most appropriate for the development of archaeology concepts. The result is a heavy reliance on verbal, print, and film transmission of this information, and a neglect of hands-on activity.

The bulk of the archaeology content is delivered at the elementary school level, where teachers are expected to be subject generalists, rather than specialists. Course content in university elementary education programmes tends to be highly structured, with few opportunities to take elective courses. As a consequence, student teachers are unlikely to take courses in archaeology or anthropology, unless it is a subject of personal interest, since there is no emphasis on archaeology in teacher training. Teachers who wish to pursue archaeology topics with their social studies classes must be prepared to gather information and develop units independently.

Native education and archaeology

Since 1985 a series of textbooks dealing with native history and culture has been produced under the auspices of the Native Learning Resources Project, Alberta Education. To accommodate this cultural content, the Alberta social studies curriculum has been revised to include content dealing with native lifeways before the arrival of Europeans, in Grade 4, Topic B – 'Alberta: its people in history'. A native community and a fur trade settlement *must* be covered in this topic, which is an improvement over the previous programme which, as indicated above, largely excluded Indian prehistory. Topic 5(B) – 'Early Canada: exploration and settlement' also offers opportunities for inclusion of historic archaeology and what it reveals about European–Indian interaction in the early historic period.

Despite the presence of prehistory content in a number of available books relating to native education (Rempel & Anderson 1987, Cardinal & Ripley 1987, Pard 1985), archaeology content is still dealt with in a very superficial way. Because the Native Learning Resources Project was initiated in response to the generally poor quality of textbooks dealing with Native people, the participants were given the mandate to develop learning resources that reflected Native culture and history from the Native point of view. Despite the involvement of the writer as a resource person, the Native steering committees, largely responsible for determining the content of the textbooks, have chosen to present Native culture and history from an ethnohistorical, rather than archaeological perspective. Unfortunately, this emphasis is not only indicative of curriculum requirements that emphasize prehistory rather than archaeology, but also of the deep-seated ambivalence that many Native people have regarding archaeological research.

Some Native people take issue with archaeological theories that may contradict traditional beliefs (e.g. the Bering land bridge migration). Others object to the preoccupation of archaeologists with lifeways of the past, feeling that it serves to entrench stereotypical images of Native people as primitive hunters and gatherers whose culture is now extinct (Devine 1988). Numerous additional concerns – for example, the disposition of Indian artefacts, and the lack of meaningful Native participation in and control over archaeological research – combine to discourage Native people from endorsing archaeology as a means of exploring their distant past (Greene 1984).

Although these concerns are being voiced by North American Native people, they are nonetheless relevant to the practice of archaeology in any country where the bulk of the archaeological record is that of indigenous people. In Canada, there is an increasing trend towards placing power and control over the schooling of Native children back in the hands of Native people. This is epitomized by the Native Education Branch of the Alberta Department of Education, whose broad mandate ensures that Native people will not only have meaningful input into the education provided to their own children, but will also influence how content dealing with Native history and culture is presented in all mandatory learning resources used in Alberta classrooms. As there tends to be considerable diffusion of educational method and theory from country to country, it is only a matter of time before nations with similar aboriginal minority populations implement curriculum development policies of this nature. Keeping this in mind, archaeologists in these countries should consider the steps needed to ensure that Native people develop an understanding of, and subsequent support for, the goals of archaeological research.

The future of archaeology in Alberta schools

Although the inclusion of Native prehistory in the Alberta curriculum is a welcome development, archaeological research in Alberta continues to receive minimal emphasis in the Alberta Social Studies Programme. Despite considerable lobbying by the Archaeological Survey of Alberta to have archaeological content germane to the study of Alberta and western Canadian history included in the curriculum, it is disappointing and frustrating that the potential for more archaeology content is not only reduced, but also that what *is* there continues to be introduced in the context of ancient civilization. An initial review of the newly developed scope and sequence for the proposed elementary Social Studies Programme (Alberta Education, October 1987) indicates that ancient Greek civilization will be the topic through which archaeology is introduced to students.

There are ample materials presently available for those teachers wishing to teach ancient civilization. There is also a teaching unit available on the Aztecs, produced at considerable effort and expense by Alberta Education (1979). At the present time there are few materials dealing with Alberta archaeology that would be suitable for use as basic resources.

Why does this situation exist? First, commercial publishers will not risk time and money on materials development unless a market exists. Publishers who were willing to take a gamble on Alberta archaeology a few years ago are less inclined to do so now, particularly given the new curriculum emphasis. Regulatory agencies like the Archaeological Survey of Alberta have limited funds for programme development, and are therefore compelled to develop public education materials that will serve a number of audiences rather than one target group.

The Alberta Department of Education has strict evaluation criteria for assessing instructional materials for classroom use. Resources that do not exhibit the correct curriculum 'fit' may be rejected. Unless there is a clear indication that instructional materials will be available to suit a topic area, the topic may be given minimal attention or be excluded altogether. The result of this vicious circle is that archaeology in Alberta schools and the instructional materials that go with it will continue to receive minimal emphasis without commitment from, and cooperation between, publishers, professional archaeologists, and educators.

Nonetheless, there continues to be increased interest among teachers and students in Alberta's archaeological past. The activity of staff from the Historical Resources Division continues to raise the profile of Alberta archaeology at teachers' conventions, native education conferences, and inservice training sessions for teachers. Hands-on activities in archaeology continue to be an integral, and popular, part of on-site interpretive programming at those Alberta historic sites that have archaeological features.

Recently Alberta Education began the development of a new elective curriculum dealing with Outdoor and Environmental Education for Junior High School (ages 12–15). Archaeology has been mentioned as possible course content. Perhaps there is light at the end of the tunnel after all.

Note

1 The investigation took place in 1985 and based its findings on a curriculum immediately prior to its revision. Following that revision, a revised programme is now being implemented in Alberta schools.

References

Alberta Culture. 1976. *Archaeological Survey of Alberta.* Edmonton, Alberta.

Alberta Culture and Multiculturalism. 1988a. *Lost reality at the Tyrrell Museum of palaeontology.* Edmonton, Alberta.

Alberta Culture and Multiculturalism. 1988b. *Experience the past.* Edmonton, Alberta

Alberta Department of Education 1984. Committee on Tolerance and Understanding: *Final report.* Edmonton, Alberta.

Alberta Education, Curriculum Branch. 1976. *Curriculum guide for anthropology 30.* Edmonton, Alberta.

Alberta Education, Curriculum Branch. 1979. *How should people meet their basic needs? Teaching unit 6A.* Edmonton, Alberta.

Alberta Education, Curriculum Branch. 1981. *1981 Alberta Social Studies curriculum.* Edmonton, Alberta.

Alberta Education, Curriculum Branch. 1981. *Teaching the elective portion of the Social Studies programme.* Edmonton, Alberta.

Alberta Education, Curriculum Branch. 1984, 1985. *Review of Secondary Programmes.* Edmonton, Alberta.

Alberta Education, Learning Resources Distributing Centre. 1987. *Buyer's guide, 1987–88*. Edmonton, Alberta.

Alberta Education, Learning Resources Distributing Centre. 1989. *Buyer' guide 1989–90*. Edmonton, Alberta.

Alberta Education. 1987. *Social Studies e.c.s. to grade six: Proposed programme of studies* (draft). Edmonton, Alberta.

Alberta Education. 1987. *Summary of developmental activities in Social Studies* (draft). Edmonton, Alberta.

Cardinal, P. & D. Ripley 1987. *Canada's people: the Metis*. Edmonton, Alberta: Plains Publishing.

Chevraux, S. 1980. *Alberta's prehistoric past*. From the Alberta Heritage Learning Resources Project – Books for Young Readers series. Edmonton, Alberta: Department of Education.

Cover, L. B. 1971. *Anthropology for our times*. Agincourt, Ontario: Gage Publishing.

Cross, M. & J. Hulland 1974. *Starting points in reading – c: First book*. Scarborough, Ontario: Ginn.

Cross, M. & J. Hulland 1984. *Starting points in reading – c–1. Teacher's guidebook*. Scarborough, Ontario: Ginn.

Decore, A. M., R. Carney, C. Urion, D. Alexander & R. Runte 1981. *Native people in the curriculum*. Edmonton, Alberta: Alberta Education, Curriculum Branch.

Devine, H. 1985. *Curriculum development in archaeology and prehistory: A needs assessment in Social Studies education*. Unpublished report on file at the Archaeological Survey of Alberta, Edmonton.

Devine, H. 1988. Archaeology, prehistory, and the Native Learning Resources Project. A paper (unpublished) presented at the *Annual Conference* of the Canadian Archaeological Association, Whistler, B. C. 11–14 May.

Greene, E. (ed.) 1984. *Ethics and values in archaeology*. New York: The Free Press, Collier-Macmillan.

Hoebel, W. A. 1972. *Anthropology: The study of man* (4th edition). New York: McGraw-Hill.

Ives, J. W. (ed.). 1986. *Archaeology in Alberta 1985*. Archaeological Survey of Alberta Occasional paper 29. Edmonton: Alberta Culture.

Katz, J. 1974. *Education in Canada*. Vancouver: Douglas, David & Charles.

Linder, B. L. *et al.* 1979. *Exploring civilizations: A discovery approach*. New York: Globe/Modern Press.

Lipetsky, J. 1969. *Dig*. Lakeside, California: Interact Publishers.

Lipetsky, J. 1982. *Dig 2*. Lakeside, California: Interact Publishers.

Pard, B. 1985. *The Peigan: A nation in transition*. Edmonton: Plains Publishing.

Rempel, D. C. & L. Anderson. 1987. *Annette's people: the Metis*. Edmonton: Plains Publishing.

Trent University. 1970. *Five foot square*. 16 mm film, 29 minutes. Peterborough: Trent University.

17 'In fourteen hundred and ninety-two, Columbus sailed . . .': the primacy of the national myth in US schools

ALICE B. KEHOE

'Historians are the theologians of the state.' (Boulding 1987)

American archaeology and US schools

According to US schools, American history began when Christopher Columbus landed on San Salvador on 12 October 1492. Twelve millennia or more of human habitation of North America are dismissed in a few introductory pages – ranging from 8 to 21, out of totals of 726 to 842 pages, in a sample of six high-school texts (Glazer & Ueda 1984, pp. 4, 18). This allocation of textbook space makes a powerful statement: America hardly existed before European colonization. That assertion is the framework moulding discussion of the American past in US public schools.

This chapter deals with formal education in US public schools, an instrument of the state's compelling interest (to use legal terminology) in the formation of its citizenry. Compulsory public education, particularly its social studies component, is expected to instil the qualities of a good citizen (e.g. Todd 1962, p. 290, Gross & Dynneson 1980, p. 372, Hartoonian & Laughlin 1986). Inevitably, the state's interest engenders tension between free inquiry and patriotism. The USA's colonial history must be reconciled with the hallowed Jeffersonian rhetoric of an inalienable human right to liberty and the pursuit of happiness. Placing the USA's indigenous nations out of reach of the curriculum nullifies the disturbing testimony they have to offer of US policies that betray that ideal. It also negates any role for archaeology, the primary producer of data about the precolonial American past.

In theory each of the 50 states controls formal education within its borders and further decentralizes control through municipal school districts. In practice, national standards and practices prevail because of the influence of national professional organizations and the implementation of regulations governing federal funding, which is essential to state and local systems. A national culture is also promoted through commercially produced media, including textbooks. The publishers of these have as compelling an interest as the state in reaching every American (Fitzgerald 1979, Lengel & Superka 1982, p. 37, Patrick & Hawke 1982, pp. 48–50). The prevailing public and private need to create a national culture that will facilitate a national market, a national labour pool, and related economies of scale productive of profits (monetary or political), reinforce an image of the American past supporting contemporary institutions.

Countering the prevailing national myth are groups with relatively little outlet for their views that are struggling to claim a more equitable share of the national wealth and a greater political franchise. Such groups include the traditionally unenfranchised – especially women, Blacks, and American Indians – and the traditionally unrecognized, including people living in colonies that were swallowed by the USA (Cajuns, New Mexican Hispanics), immigrants, and labour unions. All of these are constructing pasts that legitimize their claims. The same international revolution that discomfited overt political imperialism stimulated these groups to form and voice their claims at the beginning of the 1960s. These claims have been given token representation in formal education in the USA, but real successes in shifting the balance of power have awakened backlash movements that attempt to negate the recognition of the rights of the traditionally powerless. In 1987, for example, the voters of California passed a law naming English as the state's official language, an act widely perceived as a means of hindering Spanish-speaking and Asian residents' inroads into political power. A salient characteristic of discussions of US education in the latter third of the twentieth century is this equivocation between reproducing or revolutionizing the status quo.

America's past: the national myth

Trigger (1980, p. 662) argues that 'the most important single factor that has shaped the long-term development of American archaeology has been the traditional Euroamerican stereotype which portrayed America's native peoples as being inherently unprogressive'. This stereotype comes from the foundational national myth of Manifest Destiny: European Christians covenanted to fulfil God's mandate to 'replenish the earth, and subdue it; and have dominion over every living thing' (Genesis 1: 28). So long as these chosen peoples carry out God's mandate, they are destined to overcome the pagans and apostates. The Puritans based their claim to American territory on this principle, and it was articulated as the foundation for much official British imperialism by John Locke when he organized the Board of Trade in 1689. To apply the principle, it was necessary to show that peoples to be conquered had failed to 'replenish and subdue' their land; that it lay as *vacuum domicilium* – 'waste'. Failure was forfeiture; Locke argued that wars of conquest for such land were just wars (Wood 1984, Ch. 4).

On the basis of these 17th-century propositions legitimatizing colonization, 18th-century philosophers created the universal histories. These were armchair constructions fitting observations from the Bible, classical authors, and contemporary travellers into an overarching framework of evolutionary development (Meek 1976). Human existence was ordered into four stages, savagery, barbarism, agriculture, and the age of commerce, the last manifested only by the 'polished nations' (Febvre 1973) of Western Europe. Exemplifications of all four stages were presented from a variety of published accounts. Savants debated whether the contemporary savages and barbarians had degenerated from an agricultural stage (thus meriting subordination to those peoples who had not degenerated), had stagnated, or had failed to evolve as rapidly as the 'polished nations'. What mattered was that, as David Hume (Hume 1753, quoted in Bracken 1984, p. 62; see also Popkin 1980, pp. 251–66 on Locke and Hume) insisted:

> There never was a civilized nation of any other complexion than white, nor even any individual eminent either in action or speculation. No ingenious manufactures amongst them, no arts, no sciences.

Textbooks to teach American students what they should know of their history appeared as early as 1787, immediately after the formal establishment of the USA under its Constitution. One such textbook published in 1797 was entitled *A plain political catechism intended for the use of schools in the United States of America, wherein the great principles of liberty and of the federal constitution are laid down and explained by way of question and answer, made level to the lowest capacities* (Rumpf 1974, pp. 13–14). By the early 19th century, history, 'civics', and (physical) geography were generally included in American precollegiate education, and although not plainly labelled 'a political catechism' they were designed to inculcate the conviction that the USA is the Redeemer Nation (Van Zandt 1959, O'Gorman 1961, Tuveson 1968). To this end, the material was selected to provide students with the concept of God's New World vouchsafed to the English bearers of Western culture, and then the tools of knowledge of government structure and of geography, the natural sciences, and the mathematics necessary for surveying (Dupree 1972).

Towards the end of the 19th century, impelled by a perceived need to protect American national culture (Nasaw 1979, p. 115), a flurry of committees were formed to examine and improve American education. In 1892, the National Education Association (NEA) set up a Committee of Ten chaired by Harvard's president, Charles W. Eliot. A conference on 'History, civil government, and political economy' was held under the auspices of the Committee of Ten in Madison, Wisconsin (in the centre of the Progressive movement in both politics and education). Woodrow Wilson, later US President, was one of the scholars participating in this conference. The report of this prestigious group (quoted in Rumpf 1974, p. 18) read:

1   *Resolved.* That history and kindred subjects ought to be a substantial study in the schools in each of at least eight years . . .

2 *Resolved.* That American history be included in the program . . .
3 *Resolved.* That English history be included in the program . . .
4 *Resolved.* That Greek and Roman history, with their Oriental connections, be included in the program . . .
5 *Resolved.* That French history be included in the program . . .
6 *Resolved.* That one year of the course be devoted to the intensive study of history . . .
7 *Resolved.* That the year of intensive study be devoted to the careful study of some special period, as for example the struggle of France and England for North America, the Renaissance, etc.

The Committee continued on through another two dozen recommendations. Cumulatively, they reinforced the customary exclusive focus in formal education on European culture and history. Eliot's leadership ensured acceptance of a hidden premise, that Herbert Spencer's Law of Progress underlay American history (Cremin 1964, p. 93).

Although traditional, Eurocentric history would seem to have been well served by the NEA, the American Historical Association (AHA) moved to consolidate its discipline's dominance (Robinson & Kirman 1986) in the schools by appointing a Committee of Seven (six professional historians and one educator) in 1896. Published in 1899 after two years of consultations, the AHA's report recommended four years of history in secondary schools:

1 Ancient History, with special reference to Greek and Roman history, but including also a short introductory study of the more ancient nations. This period should also embrace the early Middle Ages, and should close with the establishment of the Holy Roman Empire (800), or with the death of Charlemagne (814), or with the Treaty of Verdun (843).
2 Medieval and Modern European History, from the close of the first period to the present time.
3 English History.
4 American History and Civil Goverment.

(quoted in Rumpf 1974, p. 22)

In 1911, after examination of the reception of the 1899 report by a new AHA Committee of Five, appointed in 1907, the AHA modified its earlier recommendations. It now advised that English history should be included in the second year of European history, and that more time should be devoted to modern history. Five years later, an NEA committee on secondary education published recommendations largely endorsing the AHA's revisions, but reflecting the influence of the Progressive movement by suggesting the final year be given to 'Problems of democracy – social, economic and political' (Rumpf 1974, p. 27).

Meanwhile the AHA had turned its attention to elementary education. Its 1905 Committee of Eight spent three years researching English, French, and

German curricula as well as American practices. It recommended that children in the first two years of school study Indian life, George Washington, the two national secular holidays of Thanksgiving Day and Memorial Day, and local events. In third grade, children should study the Fourth of July and Columbus Day. The last five years of presecondary education should present US history and 'civics' (government, emphasizing citizen responsibilities) (Rumpf 1974, p. 23). Most children in the USA at this time left school after Grade Eight (aged 13 to 14 years) (Nasaw 1979, p. 117).

In 1921, the National Council for the Social Studies was founded as an independent organization although it met jointly with the AHA until 1935. Impetus for this professionalization of an emerging field grew out of a 1915 Committee on the Social Studies that was part of an NEA Commission on the Reorganization of Secondary Education established in 1913.

A member of the Committee on the Social Studies was Arthur William Dunn, who in 1907 had published a textbook, *The Community and the Citizen*, exemplifying the pragmatic 'fusion' (of disciplines) concept for precollegiate education advocated by John Dewey and others (especially Harold and Earle Rugg and George S. Counts) in the Progressive movement. The NEA Committee on the Social Studies' first report was issued in 1915 as *The teaching of community civics*. Its major report, in 1916, urged a 'cycle' of courses: a sequence of geography, European history, American history, and civics for grades 7–9 (four subjects in three years), and European history, American history, and problems of democracy for grades 10–12. The first cycle would prepare working-class youth for citizenship; the second would teach the subjects in greater detail for the middle class who would be expected to assume managerial tasks in politics as well as in commerce.

This paramount goal of producing US citizens induced the creation of the National Council for the Social Studies to bring together and build pedagogical methods and curricula fusing, as the NCSS continue to phrase it, the academic disciplines. Social studies have been framed in a 'scope and sequence' conceived as parallel to the maturing child's expanding world (cf. Ravitch 1987):

Kindergarten – the school, home, self
Grade 1 – families and neighborhoods
Grade 2 – neighborhoods and communities
Grade 3 – communities and cities
Grade 4 – state history (including native Indians) and world geography
Grade 5 – US history
Grade 6 – world cultures (cultural geography)
Grade 7 – world cultures including eastern hemisphere; state history
Grade 8 – US history
Grade 9 – world cultures, state history
Grade 10 – world history
Grade 11 – American history, American studies

Grade 12 – sociology, government, psychology, economics, anthropology, geography. (These are 'electives' for students to choose among. In contrast in grades K–11 all students take the same subject, with no options, as a rule, allowed.) (Wisconsin Department of Public Instruction 1982, p. 32; similar lists in Wisconsin Department of Public Instruction 1986 and *Social Education* 1986.)

These subjects are taught primarily by lecture from textbooks, often a single text. Elementary-level teachers supplement lecturing from the text with discussion, assigned reports, library reading, role play, simulations, and 'hands on' materials; secondary school teachers lecture to a greater extent (Fancett & Hawke 1982, pp. 69–70). Congruent with the principles of the Progressive movement, the assertion 'We teach the child – not the subject' has been common in US education rhetoric since the 1920s but in actuality most teachers feel compelled to 'get through the book' within the school year. Given the repetition of subjects in the sequence – justified by the belief that younger children cannot learn material in depth, so must be presented with ever-increasing detail as they become capable of understanding more – the 13 years of public schooling endured by nearly all American children constitute a relatively narrow and inflexible curriculum that is, furthermore, national rather than locally diverse because most schools use textbooks from major national publishers.

Throughout the history of US public education, schools have openly cultivated above all the qualities desired of the citizen. The earliest compulsory education laws were enacted by the Massachusetts Bay Colony in 1642, directing persons responsible for children to instruct them 'in learning and labour and other employments profitable to the commonwealth' including the capacity 'to read and understand the principles of religion and the capital laws of the country'. Five years later, Colony communities were compelled to maintain public schools for these purposes (Swift 1971, p. 60). It cannot be sufficiently stressed that learning, knowledge for its own sake, has never been even rhetorically highly valued by Americans engaged in public education. Schools were in business to turn out law-abiding citizens (Nasaw 1979), and as 'efficiently' (economically) as might be (Swift 1971, pp. 84–97). Citizens in a participatory democracy should love their country as themselves, they being themselves the fabric of the nation, and love of country, 'America the Beautiful . . . from sea to shining sea', was what the public schools taught.

Public precollegiate education in the USA had no concern with America's past before European colonization except where the activities of American Indians set the conditions for European settlement. American Indians are described as the background, the passive 'virgin land', as if they and their constructions are part of the physical geography of the New World (Josephy 1985, p. 22). American Indians were not citizens of the USA until 1924; they were more or less intractable obstacles to the citizens, obstacles to be discussed, of the same kind as forests to be cleared for fields, rough landscape to be cut and paved for roads. Invoking Spencerian evolution permitted the demotion of American Indians to a less than fully human status, and therefore considered neither to possess histories (Wolf 1982, Council on Interracial Books for Children 1977, p. 68) nor to be a proper subject for study in schools maintained by taxpayers to produce good citizens.

The national myth of the American past begins with a fertile 'country that hath yet her maidenhead' as Walter Raleigh said (quoted in Kolodny 1984, p. 3), ornamented with rivers, meadows, rich forests, ores, and a bountiful harvest of native plants, but also swarming with rugged mountains, foaming Niagaras, and fierce savages. The virgin land was penetrated by the thrusts of bold European men beginning in 1492. Eventually, men – the Puritans – brought over women to begin true colonization. This Plymouth colony in 1620, was the real start of American history. That is why children in the first year of school study, and re-enact, 'the Pilgrims' First Thanksgiving' but virtually no other 'history'.

Order, and its creation, is a pervasive theme in US public schools (Wisconsin Department of Public Instruction 1970, p. 45, Nasaw 1979, Cusick 1983, Goodlad 1984, p. 241). Vane (1975, p. 5) noted that in textbooks, 'environments generally are pictured as arranged with many straight lines'. America before European colonization is described as wild and its Indians as disorderly, 'roaming' and 'wandering' (Vane 1975, p. 6, Council on Interracial Books for Children 1977, p. 67). America's history is a recapitulation of God's creation of the world recounted in Genesis, the bringing of order out of chaos. America is the New World vouchsafed to Englishmen who would reorder the Magna Carta into the Constitution of the continent. The national myth begins in the dark hold of the aptly named *Mayflower*. From this womb, the Pilgrims stepped onto the firm Rock of America, and with their axes cut down the wilderness and built their neat rectangular cabins. George Washington worked as a young man as a surveyor, extending order (Dupree 1972). Then he begat the USA.

The national myth claimed that the USA has been a melting pot, God's Crucible (Zangwill, quoted in Cremin 1964, p. 68). During the 19th century, the hot fire under the crucible overran the South: Henry Adams recalled that the Civil War was fought 'to enforce unity and uniformity on people who objected to it' (quoted in Hofstadter 1945, p. 3). Raw ores of immigrants were smelted into Americans. With the building of great factories, order dominated at last. The fast-food chain McDonald's is the epitome of America, its golden arches spanning sea to sea over neat assembly lines of measured portions doled out in square nondegradable boxes (Kottak 1981).

Archaeology and precollegiate education

The national myth promoting the production of citizens in US public schools has little use for archaeology. Because the myth constructs the precolonial past as a primeval, virgin wilderness, it cannot recognize, much less seek, evidence of purposeful human activities in that past. Because the past it describes is a heroic narrative of destiny fulfilled, it needs no evidence from material culture to support its story (cf. White 1973, Gossman 1978). In the context of the public schools, Americanist archaeology, working with data from that primeval wilderness upon which the colonists acted, fits most comfortably with physical geography. Archaeology in the USA has been assigned to the natural sciences. As a discipline, it appears in the social studies only as a minor technique for extracting data, as a component of geography, or as a subfield of anthropology (Owen 1986).

Precollegiate education in the USA most often utilizes archaeology as a pedagogical technique to teach 'inquiry skills'. Sputnik, the USSR's 1957 extraterrestrial satellite, shocked Americans. Nurtured on Manifest Destiny, they were unprepared for a technological breakthrough by a nation that was not even in Western Europe. The shock of an event at odds with national ideology was compounded by the real threat posed by the clear Soviet capability to develop intercontinental offensive missiles. Responding to the signal sent by Sputnik, the USA passed the National Defense Education Act.

Originally designed to support science and mathematics education to overcome the apparent gap between Soviet and American scientific achievements, the National Defense Education Act was extended to allow funding of social studies curricular projects and graduate education for social studies teachers. A National Commission on the Social Studies, appointed in 1958, had identified obsolescence in social studies curricula, recommending cooperation between social scientists and education specialists to remedy this. In 1963, the federal Department of Health, Education and Welfare created 'Project Social Studies' to support twelve major proposals to improve social studies, and in 1967 the National Science Foundation added its resources to the pool social studies projects might tap. As the first NDEA projects had spawned 'new maths', this influx of Federal money gave the nation the 'new social studies'.

In the new social studies, history, geography, and civics were no longer to be taught as such; 'inquiry skills', 'concepts', and 'value clarification' (or, in an unfortunate shorthand, 'values') were to be taught by 'discovery methods'. Children were to be stimulated and assisted in learning through exercise of an essentially scientific method of observation, formulating hypotheses, and testing these through discussion with the teacher. Trained to think in this manner, American children might be more likely to become productive scientists. Sputnik subtly shifted social studies from a postwar general focus on 'concepts and values' (NCSS in 1955 convened a Committee on Concepts and Values in the Social Studies) to more pragmatically pedagogical projects. Conflating a process of analysis appropriate to the sciences with the goal of training citizens found ready acceptance among professional educators, for it was part of John Dewey's programme (Longstreet 1985, p. 358).

Rhetoric on 'creative thinking' abounded in the late 1960s, yet the mission of the public schools did not change. In 1960, the President's Commission on National Goals had declared:

A higher proportion of gross national product must be devoted to education purposes. This is at once an investment in the individual, in the democratic process, in the growth of the economy and in the stature of the United States. (Quoted in Wisconsin Department of Public Instruction 1970, p. iv)

Wisconsin's Department of Public Instruction published a handsome curriculum planning guide for 'the new social studies' in which the nature of 'facts', 'concepts', and 'generalizations' are illustrated in its opening pages by figures charting 'price determination theory in a competitive market' (Wisconsin Department of Public Instruction 1970, pp. 3–4). The discussion in the opening chapter, 'Knowledge in the new social studies', concludes with this example of a generalization:

Changes in the British colonies between settlement and the American Revolution are positive cases of the generalization that cultures always change. Had there been no inventions and no borrowing of cultural traits from Indians, French, or Spanish in the colonies, this relationship between culture and change would be a negative case of the principle of constant cultural evolution. (Wisconsin Department of Public Instruction 1970, p. 9)

Far from being new, the new social studies was the final triumph of that Progressive education that began with John Dewey in the 1890s (Rumpf 1974, p. 64). Far from constructing a new social studies, most of the projects – over 90 supported through Federal funding by the end of 1967 – developed curriculum units. The projects in anthropology (Dynneson 1975, 1986) included the K–7 (kindergarten to Grade 7) series, 'Anthropology curriculum project', from the University of Georgia; the one-semester high school course 'Patterns of human history' and two independent units, on Iroquois and Kiowa, prepared by the Anthropology Curriculum Study Project under American Anthropological Association sponsorship; and the four-unit 'Man: a course of study', from the Education Development Centre. The last, referred to by its acronym MACOS, particularly exemplified Progressive tenets and became highly controversial. It was attacked in Congress as Communist-influenced because it presented communal economic enterprises as good (shown in films of traditional Netsilik Inuit); attacked as godless because it implied evolutionary relationships between humans and other animals; and attacked as too frank and brutal for children because its films showed baboon dominance fights and Netsilik killing and butchering game (Dynneson 1975, p. 44). The more the curricula taught anthropology, the more they conflicted with the mission of public schooling in the USA.

All the anthropology curricula emphasize the unity of the human species and cultural relativism, none glorify the USA. None have been widely adopted.

Most commentators (e.g. Rumpf 1974, pp. 61–2) attribute neglect of the new social studies in general, and anthropology curricula in particular, to 'the reading problem' (but see also Patrick & Hawke (1982, p. 47), whose research cites 'loss of a major advocate, unrealistic expectations … and problems resulting from misapplication'). The new texts used a relatively sophisticated vocabulary (deliberately in Georgia's 'Anthropology curriculum project'), at a time when increasing concern over school drop-outs targeted illiteracy as the cause of pupil dissatisfaction with school. Illiteracy was assumed to stem from teachers' ineptitude, which could be corrected by refinement of techniques for teaching reading. Schools were called upon to teach reading more effectively to enhance students' 'feelings of self-worth', to use a popular cliché, in the expectation that self-confident youths would stay in school to graduation and then enter gainful employment. Texts that challenged students to increase their vocabulary and stylistic finesse were criticized as unrealistic and elitist.

Allegedly related to 'the reading problem' was the lack of 'role models' in textbooks for Black, Latin American ('Hispanic'), American Indian, and Asian children, and for girls. If textbooks portrayed people from these populations in skilled and professional roles, children from these populations prone to drop out would be persuaded to remain in school and gain skills required by employers. Individuals' motivation, not societal structure and economics, was targeted for change. Consistent with American cultural premises, the crisis of unemployment tied to an increasingly large underclass was to be solved with a simple technology fix: teach the mechanics of reading and change pictures in school textbooks.

The ambitious curriculum projects fell, during the 1970s, along with the national economy, and teachers heard a 'call for more stress on basic education (reading, grammatical writing, arithmetic), fewer electives, … more homework, more discipline, more patriotism' (Sanders 1987). The new social studies has nevertheless left a mark (Patrick & Hawke 1982, p. 47, Dynneson 1986, p. 162), or perhaps it is that Progressive education continues to be adaptive to American public schools (Swift 1971, pp. 197–8). Culture as the term is understood by anthropologists has become one of the basic concepts to be taught in social studies (Wisconsin Department of Public Instruction 1982, pp. 36, 65, Downey 1986 [note that he is a professional historian], Hartoonian & Laughlin 1986). 'Inquiry' remains an accepted technique, labelled as 'approach', 'method', or 'skills'. No longer heralded as *the* technique, 'inquiry' – the scientific method of observation, comparison, and generalization – becomes a means of enlivening the classroom, a change of pace from textbook-set lecturing and discussion. Archaeology can be seen as a *resource* for teachers, a source for 'inquiry' projects, though not as a subject to be taught.

Examples of classroom-based archaeology

Two examples of the use of archaeology in social studies were offered by high-school teachers at the 1987 annual convention of the Wisconsin Council for the Social Studies. One, 'Anthropology – early man' deals with the physical and cultural evolution of early hominoids and hominids from prehistoric times up to the advent of agriculture. The teacher does not employ a text, but rather relies on recent articles from periodicals and newspapers. These sources are used to emphasize an inquiry approach towards the subject matter, particularly the formation and testing of hypotheses (Scamfer & Kaliebe 1987). The other presentation, 'Archaeology as an integrating discipline in the study of history', included a model of the kinds of archaeology (prehistoric, classical, historical and nautical) that can be directly applicable to the study of US history, world history, area studies, and anthropology. The multimedia nature of archaeology when used in the classroom will be demonstrated (LaLeike & O'Flyng 1987).

A third type of utilization of archaeology as resource rather than subject is the construction and excavation of a site, usually in a sandbox within the classroom, sometimes in the schoolyard. A unit called *Dig* was made commercially available in 1969, complete with detailed instructions, lesson plans, and worksheets for two teams of children to create a 'culture' with artefacts, bury them, and dig up and interpret the other team's data (Dynneson 1975, p. 58). *Dig* is now listed generically as a recommended exercise in curriculum guides, without reference to its originator, Jerry Lipetzky (Wisconsin Department of Public Instruction 1986, p. 102; see also Devine, Ch. 16, this volume, with regard to *Dig*).

Archaeology as a resource for enlivening the classroom with 'hands-on' material for teaching what is really the scientific method, 'inquiry', can be extended to studying American prehistory, still without challenging the national myth. One extension is field trips to actual sites. The Foundation for Illinois Archaeology in Kampsville (the centre for the ambitious Lower Illinois Valley project [Struever 1971, p. 18]) has been hosting classes of high-school students for week-long participation in excavation and observation of laboratory analyses. Because most excavation necessarily takes place during the summer when public schools are not in session, participation in real field projects is seldom practical for school classes. Ancient monuments could be visited by school classes but, congruent with the national myth, there is relatively little public knowledge of prehistoric monuments and few teachers are aware even of reasonably nearby sites with visible remains. Only the abandoned Anasazi pueblos in the desert southwest are well publicized; they lie in a region of little economic potential other than tourist and retirees' entertainment, and their emptiness is popularly understood to testify to the 'vanished' status of the American indigenes.

Material support for classroom-based archaeology

Another extension of the inquiry approach has been through kits of reproductions of artefacts, with or without accompanying text. A number of
museums, such as the Boston Children's Museum, lend out packages of
artefacts, text, and pedagogical suggestions. In the early 1970s, the NASCO
biological supply house (Fort Atkinson, Wisconsin) contracted with archaeologist Janet Spector to prepare a kit containing dozens of accurate plastic
reproductions of Middle Woodland artefacts, a set of slides of Middle
Woodland site excavations, a cassette tape narrating the slides, transpar-
encies of site maps and diagrams, a pair of children's workbooks and two
texts for teachers, a handbook and a teaching guide. This exemplary curriculum unit was of course expensive (the argument that it was indefinitely
reusable did not seem to persuade school budget directors) and NASCO
reluctantly retired what had been planned as a series of similar kits.

What is now available in the Midwest is *Indians: an activity book*, one of a
set of *Good apple activity books for grades 4–8*. Page 52 of this book is entitled
'Finding and collecting Indian artifacts', and on the next page (Artman n.d.,
p. 53) we read:

> If any of your students or their fathers have collections of Indian
> objects, ask them if they will bring these to your class and discuss how
> they found or obtained the objects and what collecting Indian articles
> means to them. (Before anyone presents such a collection, tell your
> class that everyone must be very careful when viewing/handling any
> object because of the rarity and value of such an historical article.)

Another company, The Learning Works, Inc., has an activity book
Mythology, archaeology, and architecture which, on page 45, under the title
'What is archaeology?' presents a simplified drawing of an excavation unit,
two brief paragraphs describing archaeology, and three activities for
students, of which the third is to 'Draw a small poster symbolizing your
values'. These activity books may represent Gresham's Law at work, to
borrow a 'generalization' from a new social studies curriculum guide
(Wisconsin Department of Public Instruction 1970, p. 9). They surely
indicate that American public school systems are unlikely to demand, or
invest in effective means of teaching children the complexity and achievements of precolonial American societies.

Conclusion

Public schools in the USA are meant to fulfil a basic tenet of Jeffersonian
democracy, the production of an enlightened citizenry. Except for a brief
flurry of calls around 1970 for a 'noncurriculum' to obvent 'establishment
propaganda' (Hartoonian 1987a, p. 7), Americans agree that 'the institution

of education is responsible for the maintenance of the cultural heritage and the improvement of self and society' (Wisconsin Department of Public Instruction 1986, p. 1; see also Task Force on Scope and Sequence 1984). This loaded statement in a well-received up-to-date social studies curriculum guide bears close attention. It states that education is an 'institution' rather than a process; that this 'institution' has the mission of 'maintaining' – keeping as well as transmitting or reproducing – the cultural heritage; that 'the cultural heritage' is a single entity; that a second duty of the institution is to 'improve' two contrasting entities, the individual and the society. The last charge reflects American espousal of 'progress', strongly linked with Manifest Destiny, and the basic American premiss that the part is dichotomous from the whole.

It must be stressed that archaeology as the study of human occupation of the American continent is incompatible with the mission of the schools in the USA. English culture is the basis of 'the Cultural Heritage' of the USA (Jennings 1985, p. 37), and it is the schools' obligation to maintain it by teaching in the national language, English, the national myth that democracy was born in England with the Magna Carta, carried to America by the Pilgrims, institutionalized through the Declaration of Independence and the Constitution, and most perfectly realized in the contemporary USA, with acknowledgment of civil rights actions in the 1960s to imply that 'improvement' is still to be valued. Material evidence of a non-English, precolonial past can be permitted only insofar as it appears simple, crude, and a component of nature on the American continent.

Textbooks now refer to the USA as a pluralistic society and teachers more than ever put on shows of 'ethnic' material culture, but the overall message is that these 'individual' cultures, the 'selves' of native Indians and immigrants are subordinated within the frame of the national cultural heritage. The fundamental problem from an anthropologist's perspective remains unaddressed: that teaching in the students' native language when it is not English and inclusion of cultural materials other than standard American ones in curricula are said to be ways of building the 'self-worth' of individuals, who in the fundamental dichotomous premise are by definition not the society. Thus 'improvement of self' does not affect 'society'. The social studies can discharge its primary obligation of maintaining *the* cultural heritage, singular and national and, at the same time, not only accommodate demands for recognition of non-English heritages, but by designating such accommodation critical to the *individual's* 'self', distance these disparate heritages from 'the society'.

Since the 1960s revisionist histories have opened up many heretofore unadmitted pasts (Van Tassel 1986). American Indian ethnohistory is now a substantial subfield of history, and a college textbook (Kehoe 1981, revised edn 1992) on North American Indians using a stream-of-history approach from late-Pleistocene to the 1980s has been widely adopted in preference to the conventional ethnographic-present vignettes text. The first survey textbook for college history courses incorporating revisionist social and cultural studies was published in 1982, according to one of its authors (Tuttle 1985, p. 64), and established a type that will be increasingly used. Already in 1983, conservatives sounded the alarm against such 'overzealous and unsteady' recognition of a pluralist society (Glazer & Ueda 1983). Opposing such conservatism, a leader in social studies education urges that teachers and students alike must 'become a loving critic of society and self . . . with the right to have full and creative access to the cultural heritage . . . the knowledge and wisdom of the human family' (Hartoonian 1987b, pp. 2–3).

When the college students of the 1980s become leaders in American social studies, will they teach an American history that begins at least a dozen millennia before Isabella's adventurer sailed the ocean blue? Will the national myth be transformed? Tune in tomorrow . . .

References

Artman, J. n.d. *Indians: an activity book*. Carthage, Ill.: Good Apple.

Boulding, K. W. 1987. Workshop presentation, COPRED annual meeting, Milwaukee, Wisconsin, 14 November 1987.

Bracken, H. M. 1984. *Mind and language*. Dordrecht: Foris.

Council on Interracial Books for Children 1977. *Stereotypes, distortions and omissions in U.S. history textbooks*. New York: Council on Interracial Books for Children.

Cremin, L. A. 1964. *The transformation of the school*. New York: Vintage (first published 1961, Random House).

Cusick, P. A. 1983. *The egalitarian ideal and the American high school*. New York: Longman.

Downey, M. T. 1986. Time, space and culture. *Social Education* **50**(7), 490–501.

Dynneson, T. L. 1975. *Pre-collegiate anthropology*. Anthropology Curriculum Project. Athens, Ga: University of Georgia.

Dynneson, T. L. 1986. Trends in precollegiate anthropology. In *Social studies and social sciences: a fifty-year perspective*, S. P. Wronski and D. H. Bragaw (eds), 153–64. National Council for the Social Studies Bulletin No. 78. Washington, DC: National Council for the Social Studies.

Dupree, A. H. 1972. The measuring behavior of Americans. In *Nineteenth-century American science*, G. Daniels (ed.), 22–37. Evanston, Ill.: Northwestern University Press.

Fancett, V. S. & S. D. Hawke 1982. Instructional practices. In *Social studies in the 1980s*. I. Morrissett (ed.), 61–78. Alexandria, Va: Association for Supervision and Curriculum Development.

Febvre, L. 1973. Civilisation, trans. K. Folca. In *A new kind of history*. P. Burke (ed.), Ch. 10. London: Routledge & Kegan Paul.

FitzGerald, F. 1979. *America revised: history textbooks in the twentieth century*. Boston: Little, Brown.

Glazer, N. & R. Ueda 1983. *Ethnic groups in history textbooks*. Washington, DC: Ethics and Public Policy Center.

Goodlad, J. I. 1984. *A place called school*. New York: McGraw-Hill.

Gossman, L. 1978. History and literature. In *The writing of history*. R. H. Canary & H. Kozicki (eds), 3–39. Madison: University of Wisconsin Press.

Gross, R. E. & T. L. Dynneson 1980. Regenerating the social studies: from old dirges to new directions. *Social Education* **44**(5), 370–4.

Hartoonian, H. M. 1987a. Traditions of the social studies: Discussion paper for the State Social Studies Curriculum Committee. Unpublished. Madison: Wisconsin Department of Public Instruction.

Hartoonian, H. M. 1987b. When reason sleeps: the illusion of knowledge. Unpublished paper distributed by Wisconsin Department of Public Instruction, Madison.

Hartoonian, H. M. & M. A. Laughlin 1986. Designing a scope and sequence. *Social Education* **50**(7), 502–12.

Hofstadter, R. 1945. *Social Darwinism in American thought*. Philadelphia: University of Pennsylvania Press.

Jennings, F. 1985. Some implications of human status. In *The impact of Indian history on the teaching of United States history*. Occasional Papers in Curriculum Series no. 2, 31–38. Chicago: Newberry Library.

Josephy, A. M., Jr. 1985. The impacts of recent American Indian history. In *The impact of Indian history on the teaching of United States history*. Occasional Papers in Curriculum Series No. 3, 1–37. Chicago: Newberry Library.

Kehoe, A. B. 1981 (revised edn 1992). *North American Indians: a comprehensive account*. Englewood Cliffs NJ: Prentice-Hall.

Kolodny, A. 1984. *The land before her*. Chapel Hill: University of North Carolina Press.

Kottak, C. P. 1981. Rituals at McDonald's. In *The American dimension*, 2nd edn, S. P. Montague & W. Arens (eds), 129–36. Sherman Oaks, Calif.: Alfred.

LaLeike, L. D. & D. O'Flyng 1987. Archaeology as an integrating discipline in the study of history. Sectional presented at 1987 annual convention, Wisconsin Council for the Social Studies, Oconomowoc.

Lengel, J. G. & D. P. Superka 1982. Curriculum patterns. In *Social Studies in the 1980s*. I. Morrissett (ed.), 32–38. Washington, DC: Association for Supervision and Curriculum Development.

Longstreet, W. S. 1985. Social science and the social studies: origins of the debate. *Social Education* **49**(5), 356–9.

Meek, R. L. 1976. *Social science and the ignoble savage*. Cambridge: Cambridge University Press.

Nasaw, D. 1979. *Schooled to order*. New York: Oxford University Press.

O'Gorman, E. 1961. *The invention of America*. Bloomington: Indiana University Press.

Owen, R. C. 1986. Coming of age in anthropology. In *Social studies and social sciences: a fifty-year perspective*, S. P. Wronski & D. H. Bragaw (eds), 139–52. National Council for the Social Studies Bulletin No. 78. Washington, DC: National Council for the Social Studies.

Patrick, J. J. & S. D. Hawke 1982. Curriculum materials. In *Social studies in the 1980s*. I. Morrissett (ed.), 39–50. Alexandria, Va: Association for Supervision and Curriculum Development.

Popkin, R. H. 1980. *The high road to pyrrhonism*. San Diego: Austin Hill Press.

Ravitch, D. 1987. Tot sociology. *American Scholar* **56**(3), 343–54.

Robinson, P. & J. M. Kirman 1986. From monopoly to dominance. In *Social studies and social sciences: a fifty-year perspective*. S. P. Wronski & D. H. Bragaw (eds), 15–27. National Council for the Social Studies Bulletin No. 78. Washington, DC: National Council for the Social Studies.

Rumpf, A. H. 1974. The development and assessment of a new social studies program for seventh grade pupils in the Milwaukee public schools. Unpublished EdD dissertation, Graduate School, Marquette University, Milwaukee, Wisconsin.

Sanders, N. 1987. Chart of social studies trends in national context. Presented at the State Social Studies Advisory Committee meeting, 4 October 1987, Waunakee, Wisconsin.

Scamfer, R. & J. Kaliebe 1987. Anthropology – early man. Sectional presented at the 1987 annual convention, Wisconsin Council for the Social Studies, Oconomowoc.

Social Education 1986. Social Education 50(7), special issue on 'Scope and sequence: alternatives for social studies'. Washington, DC: National Council for the Social Studies.

Struever, S. 1971. Comments on archaeological data requirements and research strategy. American Antiquity 36, 9–19.

Swift, D. W. 1971. Ideology and change in the public schools. Columbus, Ohio: Charles H. Merrill.

Task force on scope and sequence, National Council for the Social Studies 1984. Report. Social Education 48(4), 250–62.

Todd, L. P. 1962. Afterword: revising the social studies. In The social studies and the social sciences. American Council of Learned Societies and the National Council for the Social Studies. New York: Harcourt, Brace & World. Oy.

Trigger, B. G. 1980. Archaeology and the image of the American Indian. American Antiquity 45, 662–76.

Tuttle, W. H., Jr. 1985. The impact of Indian history on the teaching of United States history: a textbook author's perspective on the recent period. In The Impact of Indian History on the Teaching of United States History. Occasional Papers in Curriculum Series no. 3, 55–66. Chicago: Newberry Library.

Tuveson, E. L. 1968. Redeemer nation. Chicago: University of Chicago Press.

Van Tassel, D. D. 1986. Trials of Clio. In Social studies and social sciences: a fifty-year perspective, S. P. Wronski & D. H. Bragaw (eds), 1–14. National Council for the Social Studies Bulletin no. 78. Washington, DC: National Council for the Social Studies.

Van Zandt, R. 1959. The metaphysical foundations of American history. The Hague: Mouton.

Vane, S. B. 1975. The need for anthropologists to play a role in high school curriculum materials evaluation. Unpublished paper presented to 74th annual meeting. American Anthropological Association.

White, H. 1973. Metahistory. Baltimore: Johns Hopkins University Press.

Wisconsin Department of Public Instruction 1970. Knowledge, processes and values in the new social studies. Bulletin 185. Madison: Wisconsin Department of Public Instruction.

Wisconsin Department of Public Instruction 1982. Program Improvement for Social Studies Education in Wisconsin. Bulletin 3211. Madison: Wisconsin Department of Public Instruction.

Wisconsin Department of Public Instruction. 1986. A Guide to Curriculum Planning in Social Studies. Bulletin 6251. Madison: Wisconsin Department of Public Instruction.

Wolf, E. 1982. Europe and the people without history. Berkeley: University of California Press.

Wood, N. 1984. John Locke and agrarian capitalism. Berkeley: University of California Press.

18 Education and archaeology in Japan

CLARE FAWCETT & JUNKO HABU

Introduction

When a group is large – a nation, for example – its origins will often be described in terms of formal, standardized history. Usually this history is government-controlled. But even when not explicitly upholding government policy, history is still strongly influenced by the opinions and ideologies of politically and economically dominant groups.

Japan is a country where history, especially official history, has been an important means of defining the Japanese national identity since a centralized school system began authorizing textbooks in 1883 (Duke 1978, p. 250). Interpretations of Japanese ancient history have changed drastically over these hundred years. The most dramatic and rapid transformation came in 1945 after Japan's defeat in the Pacific War. Before the Second World War, mythological texts were used to describe the origins of the Japanese people and the Japanese state to schoolchildren. Since 1945, archaeology has become the primary means of understanding the prehistoric and protohistoric past of Japan. The question that has continued to preoccupy archaeologists and educators since the war is whether historical education, as manifested in textbooks, has really been purged of ideology. It is true that the distortions of emperor worship ideology have been eliminated, but the purpose of formal historical education in Japan, as in many other countries, continues to be teaching young citizens patriotic nationalism, civic pride, and acceptance of mainstream political and social values. With such goals history inevitably justifies and maintains a status quo advantageous for certain politically dominant groups in Japanese society but perhaps disadvantageous to other weaker groups and individuals. Furthermore, archaeologists, educators, and others interested in educational policy are constantly wary of a return to nationalist values in Japan. Under these circumstances can Japanese historical education be considered neutral and free of ideology? In this chapter we examine this question with reference to past and present history textbooks used in Japanese middle schools.

The past in Japanese education

In contemporary Japan, education, especially formal education, is seen as crucially important by children and adults alike. From the Meiji Period (1868–1912) until today, education has been the key to social advancement in Japan. In addition, schools have been primary centres of national socialization. It is in school that students learn about their place in Japanese society and Japan's place in the world.

The structure of Japan's contemporary educational system was established during the years immediately following the Second World War. Because Japan was occupied by the USA, the American educational system was the model for the new Japanese system. Consequently, Japanes: students now attend nine years of compulsory education; six years in primary school followed by three years in middle school. Although the subsequent three years of upper secondary school are not compulsory, in 1976 92 per cent of students completing middle school continued their studies for at least three more years. Many then went on to acquire post-secondary qualifications in two-year college or four-year university courses. All these students had studied history during their second year of middle school when they were approximately 14 years old. All of them had used textbooks authorized by the Mombushō (Ministry of Education), a national government agency (Beauchamp 1982, p. 7).

One of the goals of formal education in Japan is to prepare students for adult life by preparing them to pass examinations that are crucial entry points into higher education and most careers. Preparations for school and university entrance examinations form core parts of all school curricula in Japan. Students spend the greater part of their academic careers preparing to write examinations in mathematics, English, Japanese, social studies (including history) and the natural and biological sciences. Since examinations test standardized knowledge, which textbooks provide, the latter have become important foundations of the Japanese educational system. Even teachers who prefer not to teach from textbooks owe it to their students to provide them with information broadly defined by the scope of the textbooks so that the students can compete with others who have followed these closely. History textbooks, then, are the main way in which Japanese children and adults acquire a base for understanding the past. This foundation can later be built on using other media such as television, popular books and magazines, museums, and newspapers.

The passages we have chosen to analyse are taken from the ancient history sections of middle-school textbooks published by the Tokyo Shoseki company. We have selected this particular series for two reasons. It includes texts used in schools from the early 1950s, when the authorization of texts by the central government became standard procedure and, second, because Tokyo Shoseki texts were used in 31 per cent of middle schools in 1983, making them the most widely read history texts at this level (Shuppan Roren Kyōkasho Taisaku Iinkai 1984). The discussion of contemporary textbooks is based on an analysis of the 1984 edition of Tokyo Shoseki's history textbook, entitled *Revised new society: history* (*Kaitei Atarashi Shakai: Rekishi*) (Ukai *et al.* 1984).

Education about the past: some comparisons with other countries

In an analysis of worldwide historical education, Ferro (1981, p. vii) points out that the images we hold of ourselves and of other peoples reflect the history we are taught as children (see also Parker 1975, Fitzgerald 1979, Vincent & Arcand 1979). In his opinion, the control of knowledge of the past is a prerequisite of effective social control in the present. For this reason, the dominant interest groups in any society, be they the state, political parties, churches or private individuals will try to control history. They will do this through control of the media and through schools, both important means of teaching individuals about their own and their society's past.

Vincent & Arcand (1979), in a study of dominant history in Québec, have also discussed this issue. They show how the image of the North American Indian in textbooks authorized by the Québec Ministry of Education is simplified and distorted to fit the White society's stereotyped image of native peoples and conclude that any history will reflect specific interests. The best we can do is to make explicit our ideological orientation and, in this way, try to control the propagation of stereotypes and other prejudices. This is best done through a historical education which is both thoughtful and self-critical.

Nationalism and ideology in Japan

The teaching of history in Japan has long been regarded as a crucial means of creating and maintaining nationalism, and this nationalist ideology remains at the centre of debate about policy on teaching prehistory and history. In Japan 'nationalism' and 'ideology' have specific meanings. The term ideology refers only to explicitly stated political ideologies. Communism and nationalism are both considered ideologies in Japan. If an idea, statement, or book is declared ideological, it is, by implication, biased. Ideologies are not necessarily linked to the viewpoint of the dominant groups of a society. Nor are they simply generalized world-views shared by a number of people. Rather, they are believed to be distortions of knowledge and as such are diametrically opposed to idea systems derived from 'science', a body of knowledge considered to be neutral, value-free and, therefore, nonideological. Nationalism in Japan today is a complex topic. Suffice it to say here that nationalism refers to those viewpoints and government policies that echo prewar values. Policies of the conservative Liberal Democratic Party (LDP) government, in power since 1948, are often described as nationalist, since they tend to stress the need for a militarily and economically strong Japan and emphasize the notion of the Japanese as an exclusive group of people within the world community. The status of the emperor and the state also continue to be hotly debated issues when the government is accused of nationalist leanings. The death in January 1989 of Hirohito, the Showa Emperor, has prompted vigorous discussion about the role of the emperor in contemporary Japan.

The trend toward nationalist education began during the Meiji Period when Japanese leaders, anxious to bring their country out of almost 300 years of self-imposed isolation, tried to establish Japan as a technical, military and economic equal to nation-states such as the USA, the UK, France, and Germany. These pragmatic considerations were paralleled by efforts to create a strong feeling of national pride at all levels of Japanese society.

The focus of prewar and wartime Japanese nationalism – an ideology that encompassed militarism, imperialism and notions of Japanese superiority – was the nation (kuni).[1] Great emphasis was placed on the need to protect the nation militarily. Distinctive of Japanese nationalism, furthermore, was the melding of the concept of the nation with that of race or ethnicity (minzoku);[2] the Japanese nation was thought to consist, by definition, only of Japanese people. The imperial house was a centre of nationalist attention. By the end of the 1930s, veneration of the emperor as a descendant of the gods – an aspect of the Shinto religion[3] – and the leader of the Japanese national family was firmly established as government policy. Emperor worship, as an ideology, stressed the sanctity of the imperial line. It was developed in policy statements and documents such as the Meiji Constitution (1889),[4] the Rescript on Education (1890),[5] and the Cardinal Principles of the National Entity (Kokutai no Hongi) (1937).[6]

Extreme nationalism and veneration of the emperor affected historical education directly. By the late 1930s and early 1940s history courses in schools and universities taught a view of history exclusively centred on the emperor and the imperial family. The origins of the Japanese nation and the imperial line were explained by the mythological and quasi-historical tales of the Nihon Shoki[7] and the Kojiki[8] texts. Those archaeologists and historians who continued to use material remains from sites to interpret prehistory were removed from their research and teaching posts, and some were jailed. As a consequence, most research from this period was devoted to the relatively innocuous typological study of artefacts. Historical education focused entirely on imperial history.

The past in postwar Japan

In August 1945 the Japanese government surrendered to the Allied forces; the Second World War was over and the occupation of Japan by US troops began. The goal of the Supreme Commander for the Allied Powers

(SCAP)[9] was to change the political philosophy of Japan. SCAP's administration aimed to instil the principles of democracy in Japanese youth as an antidote to prewar nationalism. With the onset of the occupation, the Japanese were forced, as a society and as individuals, to question their entire official world-view.

The reforms were carried out in myriad ways at formal and informal levels. Drastic changes in the economic and political organization of Japan ran parallel with attempts to change the fundamental belief systems and ethics of individual Japanese by reforms in religious and educational institutions. Textbooks came under immediate scrutiny by SCAP. Officials found ultranationalist doctrines to be so central to textbooks in history, geography, and ethics that from the end of 1945 they suspended these courses.

The first history books used after the war were prepared under the direction of SCAP by a committee of scholars from Tokyo Imperial University, as the soon renamed Tokyo University was then still called. The resultant history book, *Footsteps of the nation* (*Kuni no Ayumi*), was issued in 1946 as a national textbook (*Kokutai Kyōkasho*). This book was severely criticized by some members of the Democratic Scientists' Association (*Minshu Shuqi Kaqakusha Kyōkai*). They argued that the text, while seemingly neutral and scientific, was actually written from a perspective that emphasized the importance of imperial history and supported militaristic ideals. Whatever faults the book may have had, however, it did derive its interpretation of the ancient past from the results of archaeological and anthropological research. The mythological tales that had been central to prewar history were set aside (Duke 1978, p. 253) and replaced by interpretations derived from empirical evidence of past lifeways.

This change in direction had profound effects on young Japanese and on the discipline of archaeology. An entire generation of children, then in their early to middle teens, felt betrayed by teachers and other leaders who had taught them imperial history, an interpretation of history that they were told to forget virtually overnight. Archaeologists, on the other hand, promised to use concrete, empirical data to understand the historical development of Japanese culture and society. Archaeology became a popular field of study for professionals and amateurs alike. The empiricist and positivist orientation of contemporary Japanese history stems partly from this time. After the war, archaeologists were painfully aware of the potential for the political manipulation of prehistory. Some tried to side-step this problem by avoiding theoretical discussions and focusing on the typology and description of artefacts, features and sites. Others wrote papers with an explicitly Marxist slant to counteract any revival of nationalist thought.

By 1948, a Textbook Authorization Committee had been organized by the Ministry of Education under the direction of SCAP. The committee's job was to authorize textbooks written and published by individual authors and private publishing companies for use in schools. This gave the Ministry of Education, and hence the national government, far less power over textbooks than they had had prior to the war.

Controversies over texts

After 1953, Ministry of Education control over textbooks suddenly tightened after a series of administrative and bureaucratic manoeuvres that led to
curriculum committees becoming appointive rather than elective and Textbook Selection Districts being made larger and therefore more difficult to
control from the local level. These changes reflected a shift in Japanese
educational philosophy towards a more conservative and, some would say,
nationalist position. As Ministry of Education control over textbooks
strengthened, those written from a socialist perspective (let alone a his-
torical-materialist angle) were often refused authorization. Those socialist
texts that were authorized were rarely selected for classroom use by the
curriculum committees.

The controversy over texts came to a head in 1965 when the first of three
lawsuits (a second was made in 1967 and a third in 1984) was brought against
the Ministry of Education by a Tokyo Education University professor,
Ienaga Saburō. One of the original authors of the textbook *Footsteps of the
Nation*, Ienaga had been submitting versions of his history text to the
Ministry of Education since 1947. He was not in 1947, nor is he today,
considered a scholar of left-wing or socialist persuasion. Nevertheless his
book was rejected in 1963. In 1964 he rewrote and resubmitted it. The text
was accepted on condition that Ienaga made substantial amendments.
These, Ministry of Education officials felt, were necessary because the book
was according to them incorrect and inadequate. The reasons put forward at
the trial to support this claim were that the book failed to recognize the
achievements of Japanese ancestors in creating Japanese civilization, it gave
the students no sense of being Japanese, and it did not foster affection toward
Japan (Duke 1978, p. 241). The Ministry of Education was particularly
critical of Ienaga's stress on the mythological nature of the *Nihon Shoki* and
the *Kojiki*. Ienaga's rebuttal argued that the authorization procedures were a
form of censorship that contradicted the Fundamental Law of Education and
were consequently illegal.

Ienaga's second lawsuit was heard in the Tokyo District Court, which
found in his favour in 1970. In 1975 the Tokyo High Court heard Ienaga's
case and affirmed Ienaga's position. The Japanese government appealed the
case to the Japanese Supreme Court but, in 1982, the Supreme Court sent
the case back to the Tokyo High Court. This court decided, in 1989, that
there was no merit to Ienaga's case because the textbook authorization
procedures had been changed since Ienaga's textbook had originally been
rejected by the Ministry of Education. Consequently, the case was dismissed at the level of the Tokyo High Court.

Ienaga's third lawsuit was initiated in response to the tightening of the
textbook authorization procedures after 1979. These changes were made after
1979 by the LDP and nationalist factions who alleged that Ienaga's texts had a
leftist bias (Yoshida 1984). One of Ienaga's major points in this lawsuit was that
the Ministry of Education had no right to authorize texts. He also argued that
the eight corrections the Ministry of Education made to his textbook in 1980
and 1983 were inadequate. In 1989, the Tokyo District Court decided that the

Ministry of Education had a legal right to authorize textbooks and that only one of the corrections the Ministry had made to Ienaga's textbook was inadequate. Ienaga appealed the matter and it is still pending.

The textbook controversy has continued for over 20 years. During that time, the nationalist leaning of the texts has changed as criticism by nationalists, toned down after 1965, was vigorously revived around 1980. Observers see Ienaga's defeat in 1986 as representative of this change in governmental policy.

The early 1980s saw an international incident involving Japan and several Asian nations when the government of the People's Republic of China and the Republic of Korea (South Korea) formally protested to the Japanese government about suggestions made by the Ministry of Education since the 1960s that the wording of the texts be changed to downplay Japanese aggression during the Second World War. Although the proposed changes mainly involved modern history, with a few revisions to medieval history but none to ancient history, the issue demonstrates the significance of historical education in Japan; the teaching of both contemporary and ancient history continue to be contentious issues in Japanese educational policy.[10]

Changes in content

In Japan today there are seven companies publishing middle-school textbooks. Selections are made on the basis of recommendations from a District Selection Committee (one of 497 throughout Japan) which selects appropriate texts for individual schools administered by each local Board of Education (Shuppan Roren Kyōkasho Taisuku Iinkai 1984, pp. 77–85). If the contents, or even the wording, of a textbook deviate from these strictly defined norms the book can be rejected by Ministry of Education officials.

The guidelines have changed five times since 1946 when they were originally implemented. These revisions took place in 1951, 1955, 1958, 1969, and 1977. The texts themselves are generally rewritten every three years. According to the 1977 guidelines, history texts should examine Japanese history in relation to Asian and world history; detail the characteristics of each historical period and show how contemporary Japan is a result of accumulated experiences; explain how certain individuals and groups have contributed to the development of the Japanese state, society and culture; teach students appreciation of the historical interaction between Japan and other cultures and traditions; and nurture a historical awareness by training students to judge and evaluate the significance of historical events (Mombushō 1977). Given guidelines such as these and the fact that texts are controlled by the national government, it is not surprising that they focus on the contrast between Japanese and non-Japanese history, take an evolutionary and progressive view of the past, discuss the development of Japan in the international context paying attention to the diffusion of people and culture from other Asian countries, and emphasize the methodology of historical study.

The Tokyo Shoseki's *Revised New Society: History* (1984) textbook is an example of the implementation of these guidelines. The introductory paragraph explains to students that the study of history is important because knowing about the past will help them understand life in the present. Studying history shows how our ancestors lived and how today's lifestyle developed over years of hard work and human effort. In the first chapter this theme is amplified in a discussion of four subtopics: 'The beginning of the human way of life', 'The beginning of civilization in the ancient world', 'The beginning of Japan', and 'The birth of the ancient Japanese state'. The first two of these subtopics outline human physical and cultural development using evolutionary theory. The emergence of prehominid primates, palaeolithic hunters, neolithic farmers and civilizations (the latter in the four great centres of Egypt, the Tigris–Euphrates and Indus river valleys and central China) are discussed, as are Greece, Rome and early Christianity.

'The beginning of Japan' sketches Japanese prehistory, starting with a description of the early palaeolithic hunters who migrated from continental Asia to Japan during the Ice Age. The subsections on the Jomon Period (*c.* 10000–300 BC)[11] and the Yayoi Period (300 BC–AD 300)[12] stress the prehistoric lifestyle and subsistence of these people, illustrating how indigenous cultural development and imported cultural traits were both important in the formation of early Japanese culture and society. Foreign influence is especially emphasized in the discussion of the Yayoi Period since this was the time when the diffusion of ideas and material culture (and possibly the immigration of people) from the continent brought rice agriculture and iron and bronze technology to Japan.

The final subsection of Chapter 1, 'The birth of the ancient Japanese state', outlines in one paragraph the archaeological evidence of state formation during the Kofun Period (AD 300–600).[13] The rest of the subsection is devoted to a description of political and cultural interactions between Japan, Korea, and China. Japanese culture is portrayed as stemming from a combination of native belief systems and sophisticated techniques of pottery manufacture, sericulture, a writing system, and Buddhist worship imported from China.

The *Revised New Society: History* text presents students with a summary of their country's early history. Indigenous cultural developments are stressed in discussions of Japanese history to the end of the Jomon Period. After the summary of the Yayoi Period, Japan's connections with Asia are emphasized in discussions of the cultural, social, technological, and political development of the emerging Japanese state. The question of the relative importance of internal origins versus imports from mainland Asia in the development of the culture and social institutions of Japan has been a major problem of archaeological study for decades. Although many of the 'simpler' features of Japanese domestic culture are seen as native to the islands, the ruling elites have, for centuries, borrowed and transformed continental institutions such as writing, an efficient bureaucracy, and the Buddhist religion, all of which are stressed in the *Revised New Society: History* text.

Looking at how changes were made in the Tokyo Shoseki's middle-school history series between 1952 and 1984, we found that the number of pages devoted to the Palaeolithic, Jomon and Yayoi periods has gradually decreased. The contents of these sections, furthermore, have become less interpretive and more descriptive. Subsections such as 'Life in a village' and 'Religion', which were featured for one and a half pages in the 1954 version of the book, had by 1956 been merged together and shortened to half a page. This subsection had been eradicated by 1962 (Nishioka *et al.* 1953; Atarashii Shakai Henshu Iinkai 1955, Nishioka *et al.* 1962).

Most of these changes occurred in response to shifts in the orientation of Japanese educational policy and the resultant guideline revisions although some were due to increased knowledge about the archaeology of Japan, the result of postwar field research. After 1953 the texts were criticized by conservative politicians, including Nakasone Yasuhiro, later LDP Prime Minister of Japan. As a result, authorization procedures were suddenly tightened. In addition, the 1958 guidelines specifically warned authors against delving too far into archaeology. Consequently, beginning with the 1962 edition of *New Society: History* (which for the first time included a section on the Japanese Palaeolithic, discovered in 1949[14]), there has been a drastic reduction in the number of pages allocated to discussion of the Palaeolithic, Jomon and Yayoi periods.

It is clear from our analysis of changes in textbook contents that since 1952 emphasis has shifted away from discussions of the prehistoric and protohistoric past; the relative number of pages covering these periods has decreased and what is left is less interpretive and less interesting. Early history has been reduced to a discussion of prehistoric periods. This makes it difficult for students to feel an affinity with the people who inhabited Japan in the past. The reason for these trends is covertly rather than overtly political. The best way to teach prehistory and protohistory is not the question debated by politicians, bureaucrats, and educators. Much of the textbook controversy focuses on modern not ancient history. Those with strong nationalist leanings cannot reasonably argue that the myths of the *Kojiki* and *Nihon Shoki* are true; there is too much archaeological evidence that clearly refutes this. Nevertheless some archaeological results indicate more clearly than others that the early emperors were mythical. By reducing the number of pages devoted to prehistory and protohistory, potential conflicts between renewed nationalism and archaeological interpretations of ancient history can be avoided.

A second reason why prehistory and protohistory have been de-emphasized in the later versions of the texts is that in Japan, as in many other countries, history usually refers to political history – the history of powerful elites – rather than social history – the history of the common people. History known primarily through archaeology is not political history and is considered relatively unimportant by the politicians and bureaucrats who push for strong national state control of Japanese society.

Nationalist influence on texts

When discussing education and archaeology in Japan it is important to remember that all history texts are government controlled and that since 1948 the party forming the government has been the conservative and increasingly nationalistic LDP. Although they are written by historians and archaeologists, texts are always authorized by government officials. Textbooks are political. Revisions of the guidelines for authors over the past twenty years have made them more nationalistic (Ritsumeikan Daigaku Kodaishi Kenyūkai 1955, Matsushima 1958, Naai *et al.* 1959, Nishikawa 1961, Sato 1970, Miyahara 1973, Amakasu 1982).

What does this nationalism mean? The ideological orientation of Japanese archaeology has changed over the past 50 years. Before and during the Second World War, Japanese history texts reflected the imperial ideology of the ultranationalist government. During this period, archaeological research focused on uncontroversial and apolitical problems of pottery chronology in order to avoid confrontation with the ideology of emperor worship. After the war there was a rush to make a direct connection between the contemporary Japanese people and their ancestors, the prehistoric people who made the artefacts found at the excavated sites. Archaeologists acknowledged the potential political importance of their work and used studies of prehistoric people to counteract the effects of prewar ideology. They provided proof that neither the emperor nor the Japanese people were descended from the gods. Much of this research continued in the highly empiricist tradition of prewar prehistoric studies, focusing on the description and classification of artefacts rather than examining the relationship between archaeology and society. In the immediate postwar period, however, historical materialist interpretations of prehistory and history were in vogue. Consequently some archaeologists concentrated on trying to reconstruct ancient lifestyles and determine relationships between the prehistoric subsistence base and the social structure. With this work they hoped to incorporate Japanese history into the broader framework of world history interpreted using historical materialist concepts. This was a clear move away from the inward-looking prewar nationalism which saw prehistory only in terms of the *Kojiki* and *Nihon Shoki*. It was an attempt to examine the everyday life of the common people of early Japan in an international framework. The earliest textbooks echoes this trend in prehistoric study. As mentioned above, the 1952 version of Tokyo Shoseki's text included a page and a half about the life and beliefs of the common people.

Despite this boom in theoretical prehistory, the highly empirical studies of the prewar era continued to affect prehistoric research. The new ideological orientation of historical materialism soon lost its place in Japanese archaeology. One reason for this was that the methodological difficulties of reconstructing past lifeways, social organization, and belief systems from only the material remains soon became apparent. Furthermore, young archaeologists, tired of ideological manipulation, decided to 'get back to the facts' to interpret prehistory. Finally, as Japanese society and politics swung to the right and the nation turned to technology as a guide to the future, 'science' became a keyword for archaeologists. Research efforts were once again concentrated on producing verifiable, empirical data to understand the past.

The new conservatism in Japanese society and archaeology is not blatantly nationalistic or ideological. It is, rather, a position of detached neutrality. Archaeologists today merely deny the political role of their work and concentrate on discovering what they believe is the factual 'truth' of the prehistoric record. Most Japanese archaeologists, furthermore, are not seriously interested in discussing archaeological education and the textbook problem. They see these issues as ideological and nonscientific and therefore having nothing to do with their studies.

Conclusion: a false neutrality?

The problem with supposedly neutral attitudes towards archaeology is that they deny the contextual nature of archaeological research. Archaeology is not done in a vacuum. Archaeological data, although they may be unadulterated and neutral when they come out of the ground, must be interpreted. When archaeologists take an apolitical stand the interpretation falls on the shoulders of politically dominant groups, for example, government bureaucrats who write textbook guidelines or politicians who dictate educational policy. It is in this sense that the teaching of archaeology in schools is becoming increasingly nationalistic.

Historical education is not taken lightly in Japan. For decades, educators and archaeologists have been considering the implications of prehistory for understanding past and present Japanese society. In this chapter we have touched on several issues involved in Japan's ongoing debate about historical education. Inevitably we have raised and left unanswered many questions. What, for instance, is the role of implicit ideology or world-view in the teaching of the Japanese past? In Japan discussions about archaeology and ideology revolve around debates over the effects of specific ideologies, such as nationalist ideology, on archaeology and on historical education. Another sort of analysis might show how basic assumptions about what it means to be Japanese or about Japan's place in relation to other nations have influenced and, in turn, been affected by the teaching of history and prehistory. These are the sorts of questions that will guide future research into archaeology and education in Japan.

Notes

1   Before 1945 Japanese people were taught that the Japanese nation was founded in 660 BC by Jimmu Tenno, the first emperor of Japan. Today debate continues among prehistorians over the origins of the Japanese state.

2   In Japanese, *minzoku* means ethnicity but on occasion may also mean race. Before 1945, the concepts of race, ethnicity and nationality were not clearly differentiated.

3   Shinto, directly translated as the 'Way of the Gods', is Japan's native religion. Through the Meiji Period (1868–1912), Taisho Period (1912–26) and during the prewar and war years (1926–45) of the Showa Period (1925–89) Shinto was used by the nationalist Japanese state as a means of binding the Japanese people together under absolute imperial rule. The Japanese were told that – through Jimmu Tenno, the first emperor and founder of Japan – the emperor was a direct descendant of the gods and was therefore 'sacred and inviolable'. During the Occupation (1945–52), religion and the state were legally separated. Shinto still plays a role in the lives of many Japanese people but the religion is not part of an all-encompassing, nationalist ideology as it was before 1945.

4   Promulgated in 1889 as a gift to the Japanese people by the Meiji Emperor, the Meiji Constitution formalized the idea of the emperor as 'sacred and inviolable' and as the leader of the country. The constitution was rewritten in 1947 by Japanese politicians guided by Supreme Commander for the Allied Powers administrators. Today the emperor is the symbolic leader of Japan. He has no political power.

5   The Rescript on Education is a document issued by the Japanese government in 1890 that outlines the cardinal principles of the imperial ideology. Using Confucian concepts, the Meiji Period leaders presented the idea of Japan as a large family with the emperor as a symbolic father to his subjects. They also stressed the need for all Japanese citizens to obey the law and work for the good of the nation rather than for their own personal gain. The Rescript on Education became one of the bases of the prewar educational system and was an important means of teaching nationalism to the people.

6   The Cardinal Principles of the National Entity was a document issued by the government in 1937. It stressed the concept of *kokutai* or 'national body' and the need for the Japanese people to sacrifice themselves for the sake of the emperor and the nation.

7   The *Nihon Shoki* is a historical chronicle completed in 720 and written in the Chinese style. It describes the ancient history of Japan, including the founding of the Japanese nation and the exploits of the various early emperors.

8   The compilation of the *Kojiki* was completed in AD 712. The book, often called Japan's native history, discusses the preliterate history of Japan and was probably derived from early geneaological records passed down by word of mouth, and from oral mythology and legends. The *Kojiki* describes the formation of the Japanese islands, the gods and the Japanese people as well as the foundation of the Japanese state. It became a central feature of prewar nationalism.

9   The occupation of Japan by SCAP lasted from 1945 until 1952. Throughout this time the country was run almost exclusively by the US military under the command of General Douglas MacArthur. SCAP implemented reforms in the Japanese political and economic systems as well as in education.

10 According to a recent newspaper article (*Asahi Shimbun*, 15 March 1989, p. 1), Ministry of Education officials have announced the drastic revision of guidelines for primary, middle and high school textbooks. The new guidelines, which will be enforced after 1992, mean that primary school students will soon be exposed to the *Kojiki* and *Nihon Shoki*. These texts explain Japanese history in terms of

myths, legends and traditional Japanese religion. Previously students studied the ancient myths but did not necessarily study the *Kojiki* or *Nihon Shoki*. The reason for this change is that the Japanese government wants to interest young Japanese in the formation of the Japanese state. Many historians and archaeologists are worried that the new regulations might result in the merging of myth and history when teaching about the ancient Japanese past, a situation that occurred before 1945.

11   The Jomon Period is distinguished by distinctive pottery types and by a subsistence base generally relying on hunting, fishing and gathering.
12   The Yayoi Period saw the establishment of wet-rice agriculture and iron and bronze metallurgy in Japan.
13   The Kofun Period is distinguished by its enormous 'key-hole-shaped' tombs. It was at this time that the early Japanese state was formed.
14   The Japanese Palaeolithic dates from between either 100000 BC or 30000 BC to 10000 BC. Thousands of Palaeolithic sites with lithic remains have been found throughout the Japanese archipelago.

References

Amakasu, T. 1982. Kyōkasho mondai no ichisokumen. *Kōkōqaku Kenkyū* **29**(2), 1–2.
Atarashii Shakai Henshū Iinkai. 1955. *Shinpen Atarashii Shakai*. Tokyo: Tokyo Shoseki.
Beauchamp, E. R. 1982. *Education in contemporary Japan*. Bloomington, Indiana: Phi Delta Kappa Educational Foundation.
Duke, B. C. 1978. The textbook controversy. In *Learning to be Japanese*, E. R. Beauchamp (ed.), 240–63. Hamden, Connecticut: Linnet Books.
Ferro, M. 1981. *The Use and abuse of history: or how the past is taught*. London: Routledge, Kegan Paul.
Fitzgerald, F. 1979. *America revisited: history schoolbooks in the twentieth century*. Boston: Little, Brown.
Matsushima, T. 1958. Shakaika ni okeru kōkogakuteki bunya no toriatsukai. *Kōkōqaku Techō* **4**(1).
Miyahara, T. 1973. Mombushō kyōkasho chōsakan no kodaishi zō – Chisai san bu no Murao Jirō shōgen o kiite. *Kōkōqaku Kenkyū* **19**(4), 1–4.
Monbushō. 1977. *Chūgakkō Gakushū Shidō Yōryō* Tokyo: Mombushō (Ministry of Education of Japan).
N. Teruki, S. Sumita, K. Nakada and H. Nishimura. 1959. Keitai gakushū shido yōryō (chūgakkō rekishi) o yonde – Genshi, kodaishi o tadashiku shidō suru ni wa koreda yoi no ka. –. *Kōkōqaku Kenkyū* **5**(3), 22–4.
Nishikawa, H. 1961. Kiro ni tatsu kōkōqaku – Kōkō gakushū shidō yōryō no kaitei o megutte –. *Kōkōqaku Kenkyū* **7**(3), 1–3.
Nishioka, T. *et al.* 1953. *Atarashii Nihonshi*. Tokyo: Tokyo Shoseki.
Nishioka, T. *et al.* 1962. *Atarashii shakai 2*. Tokyo: Tokyo Shoseki.
Parker, F. 1975. *The battle of the books: Kanawha county*. Bloomington, Indiana. Phi Delta Kappa Educational Foundation.
Ritsumeikan Daigaku Kodaishi Kenkyūkai. 1955. Kodaishi wa dō kakarete iru ka? – shin kyōkasho no hihan no naka kara –. *Watashitachi no Kōkōqaku* **4**, 19–21.
Sato, N. 1970. Shinwa to rekishi kyoiku. *Kōkōqaku Kenkyū* **17**(3), 1–3.
Shuppan Roren Kyōkasho Taisuke Iinkai. 1984. *Kyōkasho Report 1984*.
Ukai, N. *et al.* 1984. *Kaitei Atarashii Shakai: Rekishi* Tokyo: Tokyo Shoseki.

Vincent, S. and B. Arcand. 1979. *L'Image de l'Amerindien dans les manuels scholaires du Québec*. Ville La Salle, Québec: Hurtubise HMH, Limitee.

Yoshida, T. 1984. Mittsu no Kyōkasho soshō no gendaikai. *Rekishiqaku Kenkyū* **531**, 36–42.

19 *The Black historical past in British education*

LEN GARRISON

We Africans have a beautiful history and tradition as teachers of mankind, creators of world civilization and true custodians and preservers of human values. (Makgabuka 1987, p. 2)

Introduction

Despite the long history of a Black presence in Britain, there is still not a single national institution that has accepted responsibility for preserving and documenting that experience. Over the past nine years there has been a move to establish a Black Cultural Archives Museum to house documents, artefacts and other memorabilia relating to the Black presence in Britain, and its connections with the Caribbean and Africa. This chapter explains the historical circumstances relating to British Black people of African descent that now make it imperative for a Black Cultural Archives Museum to be established in Britain in the 1990s. It argues that such a museum would enable British Black people to reclaim an African-Caribbean historical past while acknowledging their historical British connections. By giving access to personal and organizational records, collections of primary sources, and documentation of oral histories, and by preserving such records for present and future generations, British Black people would be in a position to evolve a synthesis of their 'Triple Heritage' (Mazrui 1986).

The forgotten Black people in British history

One element of Black's 'Triple Heritage' is the fact that a sizeable number of British people are Black. Black people of African descent have lived in Britain for well over a thousand years, and yet their existence has been forgotten and their presence ignored or dismissed in the annals of British history and the school syllabus. If anyone wishes to find out what Black people's accomplishments and contributions have been in Britian, they would be hard put to find any information in current textbooks. This indicates that Black people have not been seen in mainstream British history as active makers of that history, or worthy subjects for documentation and

study. Yet there is, for example, historical evidence that a sizeable proportion of the Roman army stationed in Britain originated from North Africa.
Emperor Septimus Severus who ruled Britain from his seat in York in AD
208 until his death in AD 211 was a North African Negro, and among the
earliest recorded forerunners of African persons to have a significant impact
in Britain (Fryer 1984, p. 2, Birley 1988). Yet British school textbooks
seldom give recognition to his African origin.

The image of Black people prevalent in Western historiography is one of
poor benighted slaves and destitutes (Braidwood 1982, p. 211). These
stereotypes have been exposed by Devisse (1979) who has reproduced large
numbers of artistic representations of Black people at all levels of European
societies for over a thousand years. Images abound of Blacks as knights in
armour, noblemen, saints, priests, prophets and in a host of other important
roles in the medieval societies of Britain and Western Europe. Unfortunately, most of these paintings and manuscripts are not easily accessible as
reference materials for historical research or as proof of the forgotten Black
presence.

There are few accurate records as to the number of Black people who
settled in Britain before the eighteenth century. By the 1780s the number of
Blacks has been estimated at around 15 000 across the country (Braidwood
1982, p. 212). They had arrived through a range of circumstances; some had
returned with the loyalist refugees from the American War of Independence;
some had served with the British army or with the Royal Navy. Many had
served as slaves, and in this period the employment of Black servants was
highly fashionable in aristocratic circles. By the 1780s the majority of Blacks
were no longer slaves or servants in wealthy households, but freemen and
independent householders or tenants. William Hogarth, the prolific painter
and engraver, often depicted Blacks of his day, recognizing them as integral
to contemporary society (Dabydeen 1985).

What is not generally appreciated is the wide distribution of Black settlement throughout Britain; not only in London or the other major cities.
According to Shyllon (1977, p. 21):

> They were dispersed in every nook and corner of the country. London,
> Liverpool and Bristol, as slaving ports, were naturally the centres of
> Black settlement, but they also lived in Manchester, Bedfordshire,
> Nottinghamshire, Carlisle, Plymouth and the Isle of Wight. They were
> also in Kent, Essex, Sussex, Barnstable, Kidderminster, various parts
> of Scotland and other places.

Two recent publications (Fryer 1984, Greater London Council Ethnic
Minorities Unit 1986) have given us invaluable references and information
about the lives of numerous Black persons who lived in London and
elsewhere in Britain, thus enabling a revaluation of their previously ignored
involvement in, and contribution to, British history. Notable were George
Bridgetower, a professional violinist, who was a close friend of Beethoven;

Figure 19.1   Mary Seacole: neglected Jamaican heroine of the Crimean War.
(Artist Ossie Murray.)

Ira Aldridge, the famous actor whose performances of Othello are said to have been unsurpassed on the English stage; Francis Barber, assistant to Samuel Johnson, and many others.

A typical case of the serious omission and neglect of the Black past in British documentary history and education is the contribution made by Mary Seacole (Fig. 19.1) in the 1854 Crimean War. A Black Jamaican born in 1805 (Alexander and Dewgee 1984), she learned as a young woman to tend the sick, and practised the use of traditional remedies. Until recently her bravery and sacrifice on the battlefield of Balaclava in 1855 has gone unrecognized (Fryer 1984, p. 250, Alexander & Dewgee 1984, pp. 3, 27), yet Florence Nightingale is cast today in many history books as the only heroine in that war.

Mary Seacole was the first woman to enter Sebastopol, after the withdrawal of the enemy, to treat wounded British troops left there. She nevertheless returned to England in poverty. As a tribute, some of the veterans whom she had tended in the war held a four-day festival to raise money for her in Surrey Gardens, Kennington, South East London.

Mary Seacole died in relative obscurity and poverty in London in May 1881 and was buried in Kensal Green Cemetery in West London. It was not until 1981 that a group of Black women in the community, who sought to remember her name, established the Mary Seacole Society which now honours and commemorates her death each May. Recently a group of Black nurses also campaigned for a blue plaque to be put up by the late Greater London Council in George Street, West London, where she lived.

A clear example of omission occurs in the Jackdaw for history students pack No. 11, *The Crimean War* in relation to the source materials it contains. This pack consists of a number of reproductions of documentary evidence relating to the Crimean War, including a report about Florence Nightingale and a full page contemporary report to *The Times* by William Russell from the battlefield. There is no reference to Mary Seacole in any of the extracts from Russell's reports, although he had praised her work fulsomely (Fryer 1984, p. 250; Alexander & Dewgee 1984, p. 27).

Such omissions point to the way in which historical evidence has been presented from a selective Eurocentric standpoint.[1] The Black presence has been all but forgotten. To remedy this situation requires that all the evidence about the Black contribution to the British past be brought together in accessible form. As we shall see later, there was a major influx of Black people to Britain in the 20th century, especially after the Second World War, which gave further impetus to the need to establish a Black Cultural Archives Museum to ensure that Black's 'Triple Heritage' is not forgotten.

Colonialism and the denial of the Black past

A second element of the 'Triple Heritage' is the African connections of many Black people in Britain, however distant in time these may have been. Hence, how Africa and Africans have been treated in Western historiography has a direct bearing upon how British Black people regard themselves, and how they are regarded by other British people.

For African people everywhere, the experience of slavery, colonial domination and assimilation resulted in tragedy and nightmare, so far as their traditional values, culture and historical continuity were concerned. For the new European masters it was indigenous cultural systems that were the priority targets, as their destruction would, they believed, facilitate the process of Western domination (Dubois 1969, p. 39).

By minimizing the importance of evidence from archaeological sources such as the Great Zimbabwe stone city ruins, historians and archaeologists of the Western tradition denied African people a claim to their own pre-historic and historic monuments. They found it necessary to attempt to disprove claims of Great Zimbabwe's African origin (Garlake 1973, p. 66). Instead they constructed theories to suggest that its builders were either Persians, Phoenicians, Portuguese, Arabs or Chinese. As well as denying the African origin of Great Zimbabwe, ownership of its treasures was also denied to the African people. According to Van Sertima (1984, p. 16), 'when the great city was found, Europeans not only began to steal the treasures but refused even the right of the native Africans to lay claim to their own civilization' (Van Sertima 1984, p. 16). They stole everything. It has been argued that such plunder was a systematic and deliberate attempt to denude Africa of its land and resources, its traditions and its people, thus creating the conditions for underdevelopment (Rodney 1972, p. 32).

Africa rediscovered

Van Sertima (1984, p. 5) notes that his work is the first of its kind in the English-speaking world that gives credence to a lost African science. It is important because it begins to reassess and revalue Africa's scientific achievements before the coming of the Europeans. Another major contributor to the reconstruction, and thus the understanding, of the African past has been Davidson (1978, 1984), who has, over the past three decades, tried to show how Africa's past has been shrouded in unnecessary mystery. He has also shown the richness of Africa's contribution to world history (*Africa*, Channel 4 TV, 1984). Another recent television series about the African past, *The Africans: The Triple Heritage* (BBC TV, 1987), presented by Ali Mazrui, made a further important contribution to the understanding of Africa's past for 'outsiders' (Mazrui 1986, p. 25).

Such reassessments are beginning to affect not only the way in which the study of Africa is treated in academic circles, but also the popular notions held about African peoples in and outside Africa. Ultimately they must also affect the perception and images of Black people as presented in British educational textbooks and in the classroom. The Black Cultural Archives Museum could be an essential part of such a process of challenge and change.

The Caribbean experience

Unlike most other migrant groups to Britain, West Indians did not bring with them a distinctly West Indian identity and culture. The

West Indian immigrant has none of these stabilising institutions and sanctuaries within which to hide and seek solace from a hostile host community. (House of Commons Select Committee Report 1976/7, p. 130)

The third element of the 'Triple Heritage' is the more recent Caribbean connections of many Black people in Britain. These connections evoke powerful memories of a colonial experience for older generations, but many younger Black people who were born in Britain may never have visited the birthplace of their parents.

Afro-Caribbean people have a unique historical and cultural experience, much of which has been submerged beneath the colonial history of the Caribbean. Peoples of African descent whose historical ties were severed from their roots, found a new history, derived from resistance against slavery – an involuntary existence. Wynter (Carew 1969, p. vii) writes of this period of survival:

Africans cut off from Africa and from a continued tradition of any single and persistent African language, were compelled to invent, create and fuse a language in which to express themselves. As with religion and culture, so with language; the African element in the New World cut off from contact with home became of necessity the most boldly inventive.

The official colonial history of the Caribbean denied people access to the historical process and traditions on which to build a folk culture and history. The new oral framework, which mixed languages such as Akan (Twi and Fante), Ga, Ewe, Yoruba, and Igbo, deprived them of a common language, and thereby lessened the incidence of slave revolts by making it more difficult for Black inhabitants to organize and communicate. At the same time, the absence of the traditional African village oral historian, the *griot*, ensured loss of historical continuity. Although there were creative and pioneering initiatives in the Black communities, these were not seen as meriting documentation and recording in history books. Until after their countries' independence in the 1960s and 1970s, Caribbean school pupils were not taught about local histories or national heroes and Black pioneering figures. In Jamaica, such omissions included people like Paul Bogle and William Gordon; Nanny, the great woman leader of the Maroons; and Marcus Garvey, the Jamaican Negro patriot leader of the 1920s and 1930s. Indeed the wider aspect of African cultural history was omitted, although 75 per cent of the population were of African descent.

Generations of West Indians were taught the history of Britain and the British Empire; they were schooled to consider England as the Motherland, and the Monarch in England as their ruler. Within this frame of reference, the notion of a West Indian status and identity was meaningless, and attempts to set up a Federation of West Indian states in 1958 failed after a few years.

The 20th-century Black British experience

The Black contribution to Britain and Western Europe in the 19th and 20th centuries has still to be comprehensively reassessed and revalued. There is a void to be filled in Black history in Britain. Thousands of Black men gave their lives in two world wars, and, together with Black women, made valuable contributions through volunteering their services for war duties. Unfortunately, these have regularly been forgotten in the annual tributes and remembrance of those who bravely served King and Country.

Samuel Coleridge Taylor, the Black musician who composed over 250 pieces of music before his death in 1912 at the age of 37, is still to be given his due recognition as an Anglo-African who was proud of his African heritage. His famous choral work, *Hiawatha's wedding feast*, has often been performed during the last 60 years without appreciation that he was a Black person. In 1984 workers for the establishment of the Black Cultural Archives Museum staged a concert based on his music in which for the first time Coleridge Taylor was given full recognition as a Black person.

Apart from individuals like Samuel Coleridge Taylor, very little is yet known about Black persons who lived in London around the turn of the century. According to Green (1986, p. 107), by 1919 London's Blacks were numerous enough to publish a journal, to be the victims of racial riots and to organize a group called the African Progress Union. An orchestra and choir from the USA visited them and London Blacks boasted a sports club, several merchants and businessmen, three medical practitioners and enough soldiers and sailors to have their own meeting place in Drury Lane.

Black settlement after the Second World War

The arrival in Britain of thousands of West Indian migrants in the post-Second World War period (1947 onwards) from the many islands of the Caribbean, created the notion of a West Indian identity and community in Britain where Federation and a unified identity had failed in the West Indies itself. Many Blacks, however, became disillusioned with the concept of Britain as the Motherland, where they would be welcomed home. For some it was to have been a temporary sojourn; for others it was intended as a permanent home. The period since the Second World War has seen the establishment of probably the largest settlement of Blacks in Britain in the long history of their presence there. During this epoch we have seen the shift from temporary migration to permanent Black settlement.

The Black identity in Britain and the Triple Heritage

Most adversely affected are the young West Indians born in this country. They are divorced from the West Indies, without the comfort of the nostalgic memories their parents have. (House of Commons Select Committee 1976/7, p. 153)

The sense of alienation and the feeling of not belonging nor of being a whole person among Black people in Britain stems from the racism and disillusionment felt at being rejected even after ostensible assimilation. The assimilationist solution advocated by many liberal activists in the 1960s and 1970s in effect expected Black people to see themselves through other people's eyes as object rather than subject of history, as perpetually in the shadow of their White counterparts, handicapped and maintaining a negative self-image. Black British people at that time were denied access to accurate information about the Black historical tradition in Britain and Western Europe.

In this state of racial and cultural rejection by other British people and institutions, despite the fact that Britain is the country of their birth, it is of little comfort to Black youth to hear their Rastafari and Reggae idols, such as the late Bob Marley, talk of home in Africa, while their parents talk of home in a Caribbean island. It is difficult to identify with either place of origin. For many, the sense of alienation and rejection leaves them in a void with questions such as 'How can I reconcile home on three points of the compass?' and 'How can I recover and combine the triple parts of my heritage from Africa, the Caribbean, and Britain?'.

For years some young Black people have faced the forces of racism and its contradictions and have been ashamed to identify their Blackness as a positive attribute. Victims of the assimilation process, their lack of a recognized history has rendered them invisible, thereby disinheriting and undermining their sense of a Black British heritage. The Black Cultural Archives Museum would hope to play a part in improving the image and self-image of people of African and African-Caribbean descent by seeking to establish continuity and a positive reference point. Advancing this scheme within an educational context, outside a university setting, is a development that would bring primary sources of archaeological, historical and contemporary materials within reach of both Black and White communities. It would also provide a basis for recording the social and cultural history of Africa and Afro-Caribbean people in Britain. In the wake of the 1960s protest movement for change in North America, the development in Harlem, New York, of the Schomburg Research Library has led to the collection of over 100 000 archival and museum items and documents relating to the Black presence in America (Schomburg Collection Brochure 1984). What comparable evidence have we assembled of over 1000 years of the Black presence in Britain, in particular, and in Western Europe in general?

The Black presence in Britain and antiracist education

Racism is neither a natural nor a permanent feature of society. It is an artificial creation devised to facilitate and perpetuate inequalities. (Ali 1985, p. 2)

Discussion about implementing antiracist and multiethnic education in some British schools has still not confronted issues to do with correcting the distortions and omissions relating to the Black historical past.

Black youth of African or Afro-Caribbean descent born in Britain, or who have grown up there, have a major identity crisis. This is caused by their having a fractured historical past, as well as their exposure to a heritage based on myths and distortions of African and Caribbean societies. The second and third generations are being deprived, through serious omissions and lack of acknowledgement, of a sense of continuity and confidence about the contributions that Black people have made to British history.

The Black person of African or Afro-Caribbean descent born in Britain needs cultural and historical reference points. People who have not sustained the tragic dislocation and discontinuity suffered during or as a result of slavery may regard this issue as an unnecessary luxury. For the Black person in a state of non-belonging and rejection it is a crucial necessity.

We do not assume that historical data and artefacts by themselves are going instantly to change a child's self-image. They will, however, provide the environment and structure within which the Afro-Caribbean child can extend and build positive frames of reference, and a basis for White children to understand the Black presence in an antiracist context.

Multicultural approaches to education about the past

To tackle this major question within the mainstream of British education is to challenge the core principles on which that education based. We have to accept that the basis of plurality, of cultures coexisting, must allow the Black person the right to maintain a positive notion of his or her history, identity and self-image, and have that reflected in the wider society. Cultural and racial differences can be an asset rather than a handicap, contrary to the view held within the assimilationist approach of the 1960s.

It is also recognized that children's capacity to learn is affected by their confidence in themselves. The continuous scholastic underachievement and low performance of many Black British schoolchildren can be attributed partly to the prevailing social conditions, which have continued to undermine their confidence and sap their self-esteem. It is now recognized and presented in Inner London Education Authority (ILEA) discussion documents that the subject of self-image and identity is vitally important to every individual, and that it is influenced both at home and at school.

A child's sense of who she or he is as an individual is shaped by many factors. These include: the sense of belonging to a particular ethnic or cultural group. This is an attachment which is linked to physical characteristics like skin colour; is deeply rooted in family tradition; language and dialect; religious belief and personal values. These all help individuals to define who they are and the group or groups to which they belong. It can also be shaped by the child's perception of how his or her ethnic group is regarded and treated by others, and by the way other people express the opinion and expectation they have of the child as an individual (ILEA Discussion Document 1984, p. 15)

This recognition and acknowledgement that children are children, and that the identity of a Black child is shaped by his or her physical colour, as well as by historical and cultural reference points, is at the centre of multicultural praxis. Without this realization, the Afro-Caribbean child exists in a vacuum. The function of an antiracist educational strategy is to ensure that the right climate and conditions prevail to enable all children – including Black children – to realize their fullest potential.

Antiracism: implications for archaeology, history, and education

It is widely acknowledged that the forces of racism, seen and unseen, have been the hidden mechanism that have operated against the Black person in British society (Rampton Interim Report 1981). To understand racism and its manifestations in personal and institutional forms, and how it is derived, will clear the way for the introduction of a less divisive educational format which militates against ethnic or racial groups in British schools and in the wider educational arena.

It requires strong commitment and action to tackle institutional forms of racism that underpin common associated patterns of behaviour and practice that have operated against Blacks and other people. The Swann Report's conclusion in 1985 on the functions of racism pointed to a range of:

long established systems, practices and procedures within both education and the wider society. Functions which were originally devised to meet the needs and aspirations of a relatively homogeneous society, can now be seen not only to fail to take account of the multi-racial nature of British society but also to ignore or even actively work against the interests of ethnic minority people and communities.

The report argued that 'such practices may not be racist in intent, but may be and often are racist in effect in depriving Black people of the equality . . . which the White community takes for granted' (Swann Report 1985, p. 28 para.5.7).

Antiracism in practice

Replacing the myths, ignorance and denigration of the African people's past, is the primary task of the Black Cultural Archives Museum initiative.

It relates to the work undertaken over the past 12 years by the Afro-Caribbean Education Resource Centre (ACER), based in London.

ACER materials and teaching strategies represent an example of the new practice in which the Black child's perspective is more fully integrated and represented in mainstream education. As an independent educational initiative, ACER points the way for the wide-ranging educational input that is currently missing in White British educational perspectives. Its remit is to produce learning materials that give a better representation of the Afro-Caribbean image and perspective, for inclusion in the school curriculum aimed at Black and White pupils. A Black Cultural Archives Museum would greatly enhance this work by enabling the Black historic past and accomplishments to be appreciated better in British thought and practice.

An antiracist strategy as part of a multicultural framework must allow the plurality of cultural, racial or ethnic groups to develop within the majority unitary state. This new formulation will have far-reaching consequences for the treatment of 'the Black Historical Past in British Education'. It will also, for example, concern the following altered perspectives in learning about the past; content; concepts of Africa and African people; research and resources; attitude change; sharing power over resources. The curriculum development process will also include recovering, reuniting, preserving and restoring Africa's and Black people's past and present contributions, and the re-education and retraining of teachers for teaching in a multicultural Britain of the 1990s.

Creating a Black Cultural Archives Museum

As stated in the Introduction, Britain desperately needs an institution charged with preserving and documenting the Black experience. Collecting and structuring the pieces of evidence from fragmented African history, as well as the more recent history of Black people of African descent who now live in Europe and elsewhere, is a mammoth task.

A mental reorientation will be necessary in approaching the subject. Africa can no longer be seen as a dark, passive continent. Its peoples are actively engaged in determining their own futures and are beginning to recognize their contributions to European development throughout the course of Western European history.

The site earmarked for the Black Cultural Archives Museum Centre in Brixton, South London (Fig. 19.2) is an ideal location because of the area's association with the post-war migrant settlement from the West Indian islands. Application was made to obtain the site on a lease of 125 years, in the first instance, for the Black Cultural Archives Museum building. After sustained campaigns and petitions containing nearly 10 000 signatures, Lambeth Council has reserved the site for the Black Cultural Archives Museum, while the Executive Committee of the African Peoples, Historical Monuments Foundation is actively seeking funds for its construction.

Figure 19.2　The proposed site of the Black Cultural Archives Museum at Brixton.

Figure 19.3　An artist's impression of the Black Cultural Archives Museum.

Application for funding through the government's Inner City Partnership Scheme has been made over the past five years to start the first phase of the building programme, but the scheme has been unsuccessful in attracting finance due to the low priority and lack of commitment on the part of the government to this kind of development in the community.

A Black Cultural Archives Museum (Fig. 19.3), built on a site with such important associations for Black people in Britain, would ensure that present and future generations accord the Black presence its proper place in British historical studies. Support for the establishment of the Black Cultural Archives Museum initiative in Lambeth has grown over the past seven years. Celebrations across London during 1988 to mark the 40th anniversary of the *Empire Windrush*, the ship that brought the first postwar migrants from the West Indies to help rebuild Britain, showed the increasing interest in recognizing the Black communities' accomplishments and history. The development of a new Black British identity involves synthesis and challenge for those concerned with this personal, private, and public reconstruction. We have to know who we are before we can talk about race, class or gender equality in Britain. The task of piecing together the strands of the Black British historical tradition should be the priority of social historians into the first years of the 21st century, aided by a securely established Black Cultural Archives Museum.

Note

1   Recently Michael Bath has written a play *Black nightingale* about the life of Mary Seacole, which is now in repertory with Dual Control Productions.

References

Alexander, Z. & A. Dewgee 1984. *Wonderful adventures of Mrs Seacole in many lands.* Bristol: Falling Wall Press.

Ali, M. 1985. *White lies: racism and underdevelopment.* London: Third World First, Link Series.

Birley, A. 1988. *The African emperor: Septimus Severus.* London: Batsford.

Braidwood, S. 1982. Initiatives & Organisation of the Black Poor 1786–1787. *Slavery and Abolition* **13**(7), 211–27.

Carew, J. 1969. *Black Midas.* London: Longman.

Dabydeen, D. 1985. *Hogarth's Blacks: images of Blacks in 18th century English art.* London: Dangaroo Press.

Davidson, B. 1978. *Discovering Africa's past.* London: Longman.

Davidson, B. 1984. *The Story of Africa.* London: Mitchell Beazley.

Davies, J. 1964. *The Crimean War.* Jackdaw Pack No. 11. London: Jackdaw Publications.

Debrunner, H. 1979. *Presence and prestige: Africans in Europe.* Basel: Basel Afrika Bibliographien.

Devisse, J. 1979. *The image of the Black in Western art*, Vols. 1 & 2. New York: William Morrow.

Dubois, F. 1969. *Timbuctoo the mysterious.* New York: Negro Universities Press (first published 1897).

Fryer, P. 1984. *Staying power: The history of Black people in Britain*. London: Pluto Press.

Garlake, P. S. 1973. *Great Zimbabwe*. London: Thames & Hudson.

Greater London Council Ethnic Minorities Unit 1986. *A history of the Black presence in London*. London: GLC.

Green, J. P. 1986. Black community – London 1919. *Immigrants & Minorities* **5**(1), 107–16.

House of Commons Select Committee Report on Race Relations and Immigration sessions 1976/7. Vol. 1 *The West Indian community*. London: HMSO, HC 180–1.

Hume, D. 1977. In *Great treasury of Western thought*, J. Mortimer, A. & C. van Doren (eds). New York: R. R. Bowker.

Inner London Education Authority 1984. *Multi ethnic education for primary school*. ILEA Discussion Document. London: ILEA.

Makgabuka, K. 1987. Pan Africanism: an African perspective – unpublished paper presented at the Marcus Mosiah Garvey Convention, 14–17 August. Manchester: West Indian Centre.

Mazrui, A. 1986. *The Africans: a triple heritage*. London: BBC Publications.

Rampton Interim Report. 1981. *West Indian children in our schools*. London: HMSO. Cmnd 8273.

Rodney, W. 1972. *How Europe underdeveloped Africa*. London: Bogle L'Ouverture.

Schomburg Research Library 1984. *Schomburg collection brochure*. New York.

Shyllon, F. 1977. *Black people in Britain 1555–1833*. London: Oxford University Press.

Swann Report 1985. *Education for all. The Report of the Committee of Inquiry into the Education of Children from Ethnic Minority groups*. London: HMSO Cmnd 9453.

Van Sertima, I. 1984. *Blacks in science*. New Brunswick: Transaction Books.

20 *Popularizing archaeology among schoolchildren in the USSR*

NADEZHDA PLATONOVA

(translated by Katharine Judelson* &
Genevieve Wheatley)**

Soviet children receive compulsory education between the ages of 7 and 17. While the centralized curriculum is fairly broad and varied, the overall trend of the last ten years has been to concentrate on science and technology at the expense of the humanities. As a result, history – and therefore archaeology – has had to fight to retain its curriculum position and has concentrated on the national past. Because of this the study of local history, aspects of which are the study of local architectural and archaeological monuments, is not a compulsory subject in Soviet schools. This means that study sessions or projects in this field are not subject to any special regulations laid down by any of the authorities responsible for school education. As a result the teachers concerned have considerable scope when it comes to creatively tackling this task. Before the mid-1950s the dissemination of archaeological knowledge among schoolchildren in the USSR was carried out mainly by individual enthusiasts – museum personnel and teachers who organized voluntary study circles for the investigation of local history and environment. This work was on an entirely voluntary basis without remuneration. More recently, study circles and special sections for the study of children's home localities (under the auspices of Centres and Clubs for Young Pioneers and Schoolchildren, DPS) have taken over the main responsibility for this work. Institutions of this kind, which are specially concerned with provision for leisure-time activities for children aged between 7 and 16, are to be found in any large centre of population. Large towns usually have one or two Centres for Young Pioneers in each urban district and also a Club for Young Pioneers and Schoolchildren, catering for children from all over the town, which children from any urban district can join.

Study groups and clubs in the DPS cater for a very wide range of interests (creative writing, biology, geology, craft design and technology, drama and ballet, art, music and so on). From the 1950s onwards hiking and camping

* Modern Languages Department, Totton Sixth Form College, Hampshire.
** 123 Adelaide Road, St Denys, Southampton, SO2 1HY.

trips for children began to be organized on a large scale, and right from the outset, this was closely linked to the study of local history. In view of this link a large number of DPS set up special sections for local history plus hiking and camping which involved a number of different study circles. Teachers or group leaders in these sections can be members of the permanent DPS staff, or highly qualified experts, who combine such activity with their main work in research institutes, museums, or institutions of higher education. Their work is paid according to specially laid-down fees. Academic qualifications held by those involved do not affect the size of the fees they earn. The study sessions in these sections are free to all children and there is no limit on the number of children who can put their names down at the beginning of the academic year. In the course of the year some children, who turn out not to be sufficiently interested in the subject, abandon the group.

An example from Leningrad

Children's organizations of this kind in the city of Leningrad provide an interesting example of the way in which study circles for young archaeologists have developed. In the 1950s and 1960s archaeology study circles played only a rather modest part in the work of the DPS local history plus hiking and camping sections. The main focus was on hiking and camping activities, sports, expeditions linked in with the study of flora and fauna, and trips to places associated with the history of the revolutionary movement and the Great Patriotic War (1941–5). Nevertheless, as early as the late 1950s a survey of several dozen archaeological monuments in the Leningrad and Pskov regions had been conducted by the children enrolled at Leningrad's Central DPS. This work was undertaken under the auspices of the so-called 'multi-disciplinary expedition' organized to find the site of the Battle on the Ice (1242) (in which Prince Alexander Nevsky defeated the Teutonic Knights). The descriptons of the archaeological monuments discovered by the young people who went on a canoeing expedition along the rivers of the Leningrad and Pskov regions were later published. In addition, members of the expedition carried out excavations of ancient Russian graves dating from the 12th to the 14th centuries under the supervision of archaeologists from Pskov. The 'full scientific' expedition lasted for a number of years. The scientific materials it collected and the administrative correspondence it carried on were later entrusted to the depository for ancient finds of the Pskov Museum (G. Karaev's archive).

When the work of this 'full scientific' expedition was finished in the early 1960s, there was a decline in the dissemination of archaeological knowledge among young people. In the 1970s, however, the first permanent archaeological study circle was set up in Leningrad's Central DPS, under the leadership of A. V. Vinogradov (who at that time was a student of Leningrad University, but who since 1980 has been a lecturer in the archaeology department of the University). His fruitful ten years' work attached to the DPS laid the foundations for the well-developed network of study circles for young archaeologists in the city of Leningrad that exists today.

It was actually in the 1970s that the Central DPS archaeology section developed into a rather special centre for the training of young archaeologists for the future, since by then a good number of Vinogradov's pupils had taken up archaeology as their profession. At the same time it should be stressed that the main aim behind the setting up of these study circles for young archaeologists was not so much to train future specialists as to spread the fundamentals of archaeological knowledge among young people and to give them a careful and caring attitude to the monuments of the ancient past.

At present there are more than ten groups of young archaeologists being run by Leningrad's Central DPS, each of which has on average twenty members. In addition, similar groups have been set up in a number of the DPS covering individual districts of the city and also at the city's Base for Young Hikers (BYH). This last organization differs from the DPS in that there are no archaeology groups there that are not also tied in with hiking and camping activities.

Teaching methodology

The teaching methodology used in the archaeological study circles organized by the DPS and the BYH gradually took shape as their work developed during the 1970s and 1980s.

A theoretical course in the foundations of archaeology (first and foremost relating to fieldwork) is covered by young people at sessions organized throughout the academic year. The composition of this course allows for considerable flexibility. Those teaching these courses in Leningrad study circles are usually young archaeologists or students from the archaeology department of Leningrad State University (LGU). Specialists in many different branches of archaeology are invited to conduct one-off sessions with the children. They always provide their services free of charge. As a rule young people who have been members of the study circles and later gone on to study archaeology in institutions providing higher or specialized secondary education play a very large part in running these study circles. Many of them keep in touch with the study circles and visit their sessions from time to time or help to organize fieldwork trips and other activities.

Apart from their interest in history, the children who attend these study circles are often attracted by their atmosphere, which is very different from what they are used to in school. Sessions involving lectures alternate with practical work (sorting and processing materials, deciphering, and restoration work) and sometimes the sessions take the form of discussions among members of a study circle or club. Day trips to look at archaeological or architectural monuments are frequently organized. During school holidays (in the autumn, winter, and spring) trips to other towns, lasting between three and five days, are organized. During the summer holidays the children take part in month-long expeditions.

Archaeological expeditions organized by the DPS are financed as follows. Children's fares are paid for only when the trips are within the confines of the Leningrad region. Fares for trips farther afield are paid for by parents, who also pay a third of the price required for the children's food during the expeditions. The DPS pay the remaining two-thirds and also provide some money for small-scale equipment. Each group (of no more than 20 children) is accompanied by a group leader and a helper, who are both paid a salary and have their fares and food provided during the expedition. Everyone taking part in the expedition is issued with tents and sleeping bags. The group leader chooses the subject of the group's investigations. If the group leader is a graduate archaeologist, who has the right to carry out independent excavations, the work of the 'young archaeologists' can be organized without reference to any other institutions. However, more often than not, the 'young archaeologists' work in the field in close contact with large-scale expeditions organized by either the USSR Academy of Sciences' Institute of Archaeology, other university departments, or museums. While being independent from an organizational point of view, they carry out a research programme drawn up by experts.

In the 1970s members of the Vinogradov study circle worked in the Leningrad region and in Central Asia in the context of a large-scale expedition organized by the Leningrad department of the USSR Academy of Sciences' Institute of Archaeology. In 1973–9 they joined in the search for, and subsequent excavation of, sites relating to the early Scythian period in Tuva. At the 1978 USSR Exhibition of the People's Economic Achievement the stand exhibiting their finds from burial mounds in Siberia was awarded a silver medal.

In the 1980s a number of new scientific trends developed in the work of the archaeology study circles run by Leningrad's DPS and BYH. At present members of these study circles travel regularly to the Kuban, where they are taking part in the excavation of Bronze Age burial mounds; to the Ukraine in order to excavate monuments relating to the Chernyakov culture; and to parts of northwestern Russia, where they are investigating the Slavonic and Russian heritage and neolithic peat-cutting settlements.

Other organizations

A rather special role in the archaeological study circles in Leningrad is that assumed by the circle of young archaeologists at the State Hermitage Museum. The method of teaching used there is fundamentally different from that which has gradually evolved within the DPS and BYH circles. Here leading specialists on the Hermitage staff lead the work sessions free of charge and most of the sessions consist of lectures. Archaeological expeditions sponsored by the USSR Academy of Sciences' Institute of Archaeology, museums, including the Hermitage Museum itself, and other institutions of higher education may not employ anyone under 16. Consequently, the atmosphere found in the study circle organized at the Hermitage is like that to be encountered in a public lecture hall rather than at a club for children.

A number of special features also set apart the kind of instruction available at the so-called 'little history faculty' (LHF) in Leningrad State University. As a rule these sessions are attended by young men and women who are preparing to take their university entrance exams. It has become the accepted practice that teachers and postgraduates from the History Faculty lead these work sessions and each of the nine academic staff in charge of the various departments always give one general lecture. At these lectures the overall trend of the work going on in that particular department is described as well as the specific features that distinguish it from that of other departments. In addition, the staff of each department run lectures and seminars twice a week for those attending the LHF. These provide an overall view of important contemporary issues in historical science. The course on the foundations of archaeology is given by the director of the Leningrad University Museum. Other experts invited by the director give one-off lectures and seminars. At the end of the course students write long essays and are awarded certificates. If they complete this course successfully they can then obtain recommendations that will go towards their qualifications for acceptance for a university place. Similar recommendations can also be issued to able pupils by those running the study circles organized by the DPS and BYH and the Hermitage Museum.

There are no special expeditions for those attending the LHF. However, those who attend its lectures maintain close contacts with students who have in the past been members of the archaeological study circles run by the DPS and BYH and this often results in their also attending those study circles which enables them to take part in the summer expeditions.

All Leningrad schoolchildren can take part in the annual 'Olympiad' history competition. Essays and original pieces of investigative work in archaeology are assessed by a special committee, which consists of representatives from the Department of Local History and Geography and Tourism from the Central DPS and also of experts from the Leningrad Department of the USSR Academy of Sciences' Institute of Archaeology and Leningrad State University. The best entries are awarded special certificates.

It is worth noting that attendance at the sessions organized by the study circles proves very helpful to young people who are anxious to take up this branch of science seriously. If the narrow specialism of the leader of a study circle at a DPS or BYH coincides with the range of questions that the pupils want to learn about, that person can become one of the academic supervisors of the group. The children acquire practical skills in working with archaeological materials as they process artefacts and ceramic collections unearthed during summer excavations. In those cases where a subject chosen by the pupils has little in common with the interests of the teacher, then the latter can offer it to an expert from the appropriate field from another institution. As a rule, in such cases, no one turns down school-children's requests for one or several consultations on questions that are of interest to them. Thanks to the recommendations made by the leaders of the study circles the most able schoolchildren can be granted access to archive materials and museum collections of, for example, the Leningrad Depart-ment of the Institute of Archaeology or the Hermitage. As a result of the experience of archaeological study circles run by DPS, supervised by a number of archaeologists including A. V. Vinogradov, T. A. Zheglova and the present author, there have been a number of cases when essays for the 'Olympiad' competitions have been almost of university standard. Apart from city 'Olympiads', members of the study circles run by the Central DPS are able to give talks to the scientific and technological conference for senior school pupils that is held in Leningrad every year.

Fairly close contacts exist between the 'young archaeologist' groups in Leningrad and those in the towns of the Ukraine, in particular those in Kiev and Chernigov. Again, most archaeology teaching for children is provided by the DPS. However, a special feature of the archaeological study circles in Kiev, Chernigov, Kharkov and other such towns, is that these are rarely supervised by students or permanent staff members of the DPS. Instead, the work is undertaken for the most part by research staff working for the Ukrainian Academy of Sciences' Institute of Archaeology and museums. The network of study circles for 'young archaeologists' in the DPS of the Ukraine are known as 'school academies'. Using these units as a grass-roots organization, conferences for young people interested in archaeology are organized in republics, at which schoolchildren deliver reports or describe original pieces of investigative work that they have carried out.

The growing interest shown by children in archaeology over the last 20 years, and the enhanced role of the DPS and BYH study circles that have been outlined above with reference to Leningrad, clearly reflect the situation that has been developing over most of the USSR. Of course, such develop-ment applies primarily to towns where there are major research centres or historical-archaeological museums (Leningrad, Moscow, Smolensk, Novo-sibirsk, Chita, Vorkuta, Riga, Kiev, Chernigov, Kharkov, Tbilisi and so on). Experience over the past 20 years shows that work with schoolchildren within the network of archaeological study circles is not only fruitful from an educational point of view, but that it also encourages young people who will later be embarking on archaeological studies in the history faculties of Soviet universities. The study circles run by the DPS and BYH are now acquiring more and more importance as an independent branch in the programme of scientific expeditions. The rare degree of enthusiasm and commitment on the part of the children who take part in the fieldwork on their own initiative, without any coercion from adults, is maintained thanks to the atmosphere of comradeship and the sense of responsibility with regard to the work they are carrying out. The present author has had the opportunity at first hand to discover how effective the work of the members of the study circles can be and I have been impressed by their keenness to achieve good results and by how much their membership of 'young archaeologists' clubs has meant to them. Their contribution to real archaeological work has been considerable. In particular, those working under the auspices of Leningrad's Central DPS in the period 1978–9 made an enormous contribution to initial survey work in parts of the Leningrad and Pskov regions. They also took part in the excavation of a number of monuments in northwestern Russia which belong to the period between the second half of the first millennium and the first half of the second millennium BC (excavations undertaken by Y. M. Lesman, V. Y. Konetsky, E. N. Nosov, and this author among others).

It should be noted that the archaeological study circles in various towns, which came into being spontaneously and independently of each other, are now tending to favour coming together within the framework of a single organization. Contacts for the purpose of exchanging experiences are becoming increasingly close. Visits to other towns and summer expeditions are also frequently organized on a joint basis. It is possible that subsequent expansion of this work and improved methods for conducting study sessions with children will lead to the organization of 'young archaeologists' becoming an important factor in the campaign to protect monuments of the ancient past in the USSR. In January 1988, for the first time, an All-Russian Conference for leaders of archaeological study circles was convened at the Leningrad Department of the USSR Academy of Sciences' Institute of Archaeology. The holding of this conference testifies to the continuing consolidation and growing importance of these organizations in the life of our society and in the protection of the past.

21 Children and the past in Poland: archaeology and prehistory in primary schools and museums

ANDRZEJ MIKOŁAJCZYK

Introduction: archaeology and prehistory in primary school texts

What Polish schoolchildren learn today about prehistory depends chiefly on the history syllabus laid down in the national curriculum, and this in its turn depends greatly on the textbooks currently in use. It is these textbooks that shape teachers' attitudes towards prehistory and how to present it to children. It is, therefore, of some importance that the textbooks currently in use in different countries be compared and analysed from the perspective of prehistory. Some initial attempts to do so have already been undertaken by assessing the illustrations used in textbooks in Europe (Mikołajczyk in press).

The following lines introduce a lesson on prehistory in a primary history text book currently in use in primary schools in Poland (Koczerska & Wipszycka 1985):

> The history of humankind is very old, certainly going back further than we can really imagine. The history of Poland covering a period of over one millennium, seems, with reason, to be very long and eventful. Just think, our ancestors appeared three million years ago . . .

The textbook is used by the fifth class (12 to 13 year olds). One of its chapters is called 'Life in most ancient times' and the first topic discussed there is on 'Nature and people', under the subheadings: 'The earliest people', 'The discovery of fire', 'The first tools', 'Man as hunter', 'Tents and dugouts' and 'Collective life'. The chapter ends with two questions: 'Explain why scholars studying the distant past call the oldest period in the history of humankind the period of "chipped stone"' and 'Talk about the discoveries and inventions discussed in the above chapter'.

The term 'chipped stone period' as opposed to the 'polished stone period' is typical of the anachronistic vocabulary used in school textbooks. In Polish the term 'chipped stone period' suggests something outdated, primitive, and inconvenient. It reflects the pejorative attitude prevalent in the presentation of the earliest prehistoric periods to schoolchildren and reveals the lack of a real understanding of the goals of a school textbook.

The next chapter in the book is devoted to the 'beginnings of agriculture, husbandry, handicraft and trade'. The children are taught about 'early farming', the transition from 'hunting to husbandry', the 'slow development in people's life', 'early trade', 'the first settlements', 'the casting of copper and bronze', 'the casting of iron' and 'craftsmen'. This chapter also ends with a series of questions: 1) 'Why did the people domesticate animals?'; 2) 'How did the domestication of the dog facilitate the life of primitive people?'; 3) 'What was the significance of smelting metals for people?'; 4) What objects were made of copper and bronze and what objects of iron? Which were better?' The text is illustrated throughout with black and white drawings of ape-like people making fire, examples of flint implements, objects made from bone and antler, dugout cottages, stone age settlements surrounded by palisades, blast furnaces for smelting iron ore and primitive weaving.

Prehistory next appears in this textbook in Part 8, Chapter 13 entitled 'On the Amber Route' (pp. 127–9). It is separated from the previous section by courses on the history of Egypt, the Near East, Greece and Rome. In 'On the amber route', the study of the cultural and commercial relations between the Roman empire and Barbarian Europe focuses almost entirely on the territory of modern-day Poland. There is a map showing the amber route and pictures of two ornaments from Polish excavations. The children are asked: 1) 'What goods were brought by the merchants to Polish territory in exchange for amber and furs?'; 2) 'What should you do if you ever find an antiquity or if you discover that someone you know has found one?'

The next mention of archaeology occurs in Part 11, Chapter 4: 'What do we know about our ancestors?' (p. 161). This covers the Pre-Slavs, Slavs from the Bronze and Iron Ages, Slav migrations to the west, south and north and the pagan faith of the Slavs. Slavic prehistory is illustrated with drawings of the Biskupin settlement, the Swietowit temple on Ruggen, an early medieval wooden idol excavated in Great Poland and a map of the Slavic migrations. The questions set are: 1) 'What peoples were neighbours to the Slavs?'; 2) 'Where did the Slavs live in the first millennium BC?'; 3) 'Of what was the Biskupin fort constructed?'; 4) When did the Slavs begin their migrations and what territories did they occupy?'; 5) 'What was the chief deity of the Slavs?'; 6) 'When were the Slav deities worshipped?'

Another book used by the fifth class introduces a course on the plastic arts thus: 'The term "Prehistoric Art" means all those pieces of art which have survived until today, usually covered by a layer of earth that has built up slowly over centuries and millennia' (Stopczyk 1982, pp. 24–9).

'When did art begin at all?' asks the book, and answers itself (Stopczyk 1982):

One thing is known for sure: the first pieces of art were . . . stone spears, axes and knives . . . perhaps already [being made] before 400 000 BC or a little later, anyway in times we can scarcely even imagine. We usually call this period the period of chipped stone (for as you will remember, tools were at that time chipped off blocks of stone) or the palaeolithic period.

Here we have two contemporary primary school textbooks published for use in Polish schools, one on history and the other on plastic arts, illustrating the element of archaeology present in the education of children of 12 to 13 years. It is clear that the archaeological element is almost marginal. Archaeology occurs on only 12 pages, taking up just 5 per cent of the entire contents of books that cover the period of antiquity through to the early Middle Ages up to the 13th century. In contrast Egyptian history alone also constitutes about 5 per cent, Greek history about 17 per cent, Roman history about 20 per cent, and early medieval Poland about 29 per cent.

The place of the past in the primary school curriculum

At present there is a general tendency to reduce the amount of history included in the curriculum because of constant pressure from the technical disciplines. State commissions have been set up to discuss the issue and we are frequently being informed, even in the daily papers, about new cuts in the amount of history taught in schools. This tendency seems most damaging to the study of the distant past and reflects the overall changes taking place in the Polish education system. The continued presence of archaeology has been interpreted as an indication of the government's anxiety over the possible influence of the Church in education and the growth of a biblical explanation of the origins of humankind and early civilization. This standpoint, however unofficial, deters the education authorities from completely obliterating archaeology and prehistory from the school curriculum. Relations between the communist government and the Church are, as always, very complicated and difficult.[1] In the past the religious side of the story has always also been included. Teachers are obliged to accept that what they teach always has a political and religious dimension. The dispute over history textbooks and their content has a long tradition in Poland and during the early 1980s many of the contentious aspects of that dispute again came to the fore. The debate continues. In the remainder of this chapter I confine myself to exploring how archaeology and, particularly, prehistory is presented to children outside school.

Museum lessons

The only institutions engaged in teaching about prehistory apart from schools are archaeological museums. This chapter uses the Archaeological and Ethnological Museum in Łódź as an example (see also Mikołajczyk 1986). The chapter concentrates on what is provided on a regular basis to help schoolchildren increase their knowledge of prehistory and to encourage teachers to use the museums by ensuring that what is offered corresponds to what is taught in the classroom.

Łódź museum has archaeological exhibitions constantly accessible to visitors. During 1979–86, 829 topics were presented to an audience of 33 545, the largest part of which was made up of children on school visits (Mikołajczyk 1987). However, the education project at the museum at Łódź needs the teachers' support since without their interest in bringing the children to the museum the project would reach only a few people. Individual visitors are, of course, also sought and have their place, but they cannot be compared with contacts with teachers, which result in whole classes of children visiting the museum to strengthen and broaden their knowledge of the prehistoric past.

Some teachers' reports on museum projects

In order to test their responses, teachers were asked to write reports on lessons held in the museum. Three reports on lessons given to children of the fifth class are presented here.[2]

'HOW OUR ANCESTORS LIVED'

This lesson had three major aims: a) To teach the children about the surviving monuments, material culture, and living conditions and customs of the Slavic people; b) to teach them respect for monuments and to encourage an awarness of culture outside school; c) to develop the children's skill in observation, help create historical imagination and a capacity to draw conclusions, and enrich their historical vocabulary.

The visit to the museum took the form of a lesson using a film entitled *The 2500-year-old Pre-Slavic defensive settlement at Biskupin*, followed by a discussion. The children were invited to the museum cinema where the teacher explained the aims of the visit and told them about the topics covered in the film they were about to see and on which they should concentrate.

The children then visited the exhibition. 'Prehistory of Central Poland' where they saw pottery, bronze and iron tools, and weapons and ornaments made of bronze, iron, horn, and glass. The museum officer explained various points, including the different sites on which prehistoric items have been found. She explained how the evidence shows likely contacts between the Slavs and the Roman Empire and indicates something of Slav customs, burial rites, artistic skills, and aesthetic sense. She then answered the children's questions. The teacher afterwards recapitulated and summarized the lesson for the children and asked them questions to test their understanding. The conclusion that was drawn from the lesson was that there was archaeological evidence for the Slavs having practised agriculture, husbandry, fishing, and hunting: that they produced tools, clothes, weapons, and ornaments; and that they maintained commercial links with the Romans. The question set for homework was: 'What new words have you learnt during the museum lesson?'

'EXCAVATION AS A SOURCE OF KNOWLEDGE ABOUT
THE LIFE OF OUR ANCESTORS'

During this lesson the children visited the same exhibition and saw the same film. Each child was then given a sheet of paper with the following questions: 'Which of the exhibits you have seen tells you about: 1) the beliefs; 2) the dwellings; 3) the occupations; 4) the skills of our ancestors?'

As in the previous lesson the teacher described the two main aims of the lesson. These were cognitive – to learn about the archaeological exhibits relating to the Slavs and about the museum as a scientific institution – and educative – to grasp the link between the knowledge presented in the textbooks and its historical source.

The class was divided into four groups, each of which began its tour of the first part of the exhibition at a different point. This took 15 minutes, after which the guide in each group asked individual children to point out exhibits showing something about the houses, occupations, skills and faith of our ancestors, thus bringing together the information received in the classroom and in the film, and that which could be gleaned from looking at the artefacts on display in the exhibition. The children's responses revealed their excitement and enthusiasm for the subject and the museum visit in general.

The second part of the exhibition, which moves on to the Iron Age, helped the children to see the technological and cultural changes that occurred in prehistory. They could easily identify the tools and glass artefacts that were new at that time and see the improvement in the precision of the manufacture and aesthetics of the objects. These observations led them to conclude that the standard of living has been rising for centuries, as a result of improving skills and practical knowledge, and communication with other peoples. The visit to the museum enabled the children to revise their class lessons and fixed the material in their minds. They learnt that there are real historical and prehistoric sources besides their textbooks, to be found in films and exhibitions, and they were able to explain the significance of archaeological investigations. In their homework they had to describe their impressions of the museum.

'THE INFLUENCE OF THE ROMAN EMPIRE ON THE LIFE OF THE SLAVS'

The children had already learnt something of the trade that existed between the Roman Empire and Slavic territory in the past from some additional school literature, including a story called 'The merchants are coming'. The aims of the museum lesson were cognitive – to make some aspects of Roman and Slavic cultures more familiar to the children using material from excavations – and educative – to encourage the children's interest in archaeology and museum exhibits in addition to teaching them such terms as 'museum', 'archaeology', 'excavation', 'historical source', 'urn', and 'stronghold'.

The children visited a permanent exhibition entitled 'The history of money' which shows the Amber Route connecting the Roman provinces with the Baltic coast. Roman coins from the first centuries AD illustrate the commercial links that existed with the Empire. Roman imports excavated from settlements and cemeteries dating from the 1st to the 4th century AD were presented as further evidence of these links. The children also saw slides of other Roman artefacts found in the area of Barbarian Europe that resembled those they had seen in the showcases.

After the children had covered the main topic of the lesson they went on to discuss why archaeologists so carefully collect the material about our prehistoric past now on display in the museum. The children knew that material from excavations is evidence about our past, about a way of life, a past culture, and that such material is the primary source of knowledge about prehistory.

Follow-up work and the effect on school grades

The above reports all show a very positive attitude towards the role of the museum in the teaching of prehistory. Moreover, the teachers were convinced that the visits resulted in improved school grades.

The first of the lessons, 'How our ancestors lived', was followed up in school by a discussion on the visit and by checking the homework and testing the knowledge gained at the museum. The children were asked to explain the words 'museum', 'archaeology', 'custodian', 'stronghold', 'spinning wheel', 'barrow', and 'urn', and they were asked to describe the 'occupations' and 'handicrafts' of the Slavs. The grades achieved were very high: 8 children out of 27 got very good, 7 good, and 12 fair. This showed an improvement on previous grades for historical subjects.

The second lesson on 'Excavation as a source of knowledge about the life of our ancestors', was followed up with questions set for homework concerning the chronology and geography of Slavic prehistory. The best grades were achieved by the children who answered the questions dealing with the various functions of different tools and other objects they had seen in the exhibition and the significance of various sites to Slavic culture. Six children got very good, 10 good, and 14 fair. The grades obtained by other children from the same year who had not visited the museum were lower.

The third lesson, 'The influence of the Roman empire on the life of the Slavs' resulted in drawings and descriptions of the archaeological objects observed in the museum. The drawings were displayed around the classroom and the children compiled a vocabulary of the new words and wrote reports on the visit.

In all three of the above examples teachers expressed their satisfaction at what had been achieved through their visits. They felt that they had enriched the children's historical vocabulary, had advanced their knowledge of prehistoric Slavs, had improved their individual grades, and had positively influenced the development of their historical imagination and aesthetic sense and generally raised their personal levels of cultural awareness (Gamulewicz 1984, pp. 24–36).

A museum officer's perspective

Another report on school visits to the museum has been written by museum officer Ewa Kurylak. She reported on two lessons given in 1987 entitled 'Life in the Stone Age', one attended by children from the 4th class and the other by children from the 5th class.

The 4th class group consisted of 30 children and one teacher. First they were shown round part of the permanent archaeological exhibition about the Stone and Bronze ages. The children answered the questions successfully although they were still repeating the same mistakes that occurred in their textbooks. The visit, however, did reinforce the knowledge gained in the classroom. The main problem with the visit was that there was only one teacher for 30 children as opposed to the three really necessary for such a trip. As a result, discipline was poor and the children were noisy. On the other hand, the layout of the exhibition cases does allow for all members of such a large group to see whatever exhibit is under discussion.

The children were able to see and touch various artefacts such as flint and stone implements. They were excited about being allowed to handle the objects and commented both on the raw materials and the function of the objects. They were so enthusiastic that they drew some of the objects and sites that they had seen (Fig. 21.1a–e). They even wanted to go on to see the temporary exhibition, although this had not been planned as part of the visit.

Having been round the exhibition the children went to the museum cinema for a colour film entitled *Strongholds and settlements* which gives only a very basic idea of the kind of archaeological sites in the area and concentrates on the famous site at Biskupin.

The teacher was pleased with the visit although she had taken groups to the museum before and felt that some museum officers were better at dealing with children than others. This may well be because of a tendency in some of the archaeologists employed by the Educational Department to use overly scientific language, as well as their variable pedagogical abilities. However, even after the visit the teacher failed to notice errors concerning

a   b

   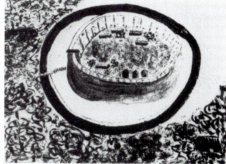

c   d

Figure 21.1 Children's drawings
inspired by the archaeological objects
and sites seen in the Archaeological and
Ethnological Museum in Łódź.
(a) Reconstruction of a Mesolithic camp
by a river, (b) clearing the forest,
(c) barrow, (d) stronghold, (e) 'jugs
where human ashes were put, swords,
prehistoric knives'.

e

the prehistoric past in the textbooks, and she did not opt to widen the archaeological component of her teaching in line with the museum displays that advanced knowledge beyond that available in the textbook.

The second group consisted of 27 children from the 5th class accompanied by two teachers. These children were better-disciplined and were well prepared for the lesson. They answered the questions perfectly and were able to talk about the issues not included in the textbooks. They too were given objects of stone and flint to handle. At first they could not determine the function of the tools but after having had them explained they could describe their functions without making mistakes. They also saw the temporary exhibition although this was not included in the original pro- gramme. The teacher felt museum visits to be a perfect way to fix know- ledge about prehistory learnt in school firmly in the children's memories. She uses the museum regularly.

Museum lessons in archaeology and ancient history mainly attract primary schoolchildren. However, although they are accepted in primary schools as being generally useful, in the 1980s only 79 out of 124 primary schools in Łódź regularly brought children to the Archaeological and Ethnographical Museum. A few more schools from the surrounding areas (Zgierz, Aleksandrów, Nowosolna, Wiśniowa, Góra, Koluszki) also used the museum. Only 798 of the approximately 20 000 children who were in the 4th and 5th classes in 1984 attended classes in history and only 1198 those in prehistory. The figures for 1985 were a little better: out of a total of 21 066, 967 attended history lessons and 2292 prehistory lessons. In 1986 still more attended: out of a total of 22 381, 1199 attended history lessons, and 3518 prehistory.

Museum activities for secondary school children

Secondary schoolchildren do not visit the museum as frequently as younger ones. Only 11 out of 30 schools in Łódź use the museum, although a few other secondary and technical schools from the surrounding areas (Zgierz, Aleksandrów, Konstantynów) do so as well.

Holiday activities

As far back as 1958, the museum introduced a new way to make prehistory and archaeology more accessible to schoolchildren; the museum invited them to take part in archaeological investigations, including excavations. About 1000 children take part in these excavations organized in 40 two-week periods. Children attend nearly all of the museum's current excavations in central Poland, including those of the megalithic tombs in Sarnowo and the 16th-century defensive manor in Wojstawice. Children also assist in field-walking projects linked to some of these excavations.

In addition the museum invites scouts from their nearby camp for a few hours each day to join the excavation of a late Bronze Age–early Iron Age cemetery. Such invitations are always accepted and the excavations form the basis for frequent discussions with children about the nature of prehistory.

Conclusion

Since archaeology is not a separate subject in the Polish school curriculum, basic knowledge about prehistory has to be included within courses on world and Polish history and supported by archaeological museums closely cooperating with the schools. This would seem to be the main way in which we can ensure that something of our prehistoric past is taught through, for example, textbooks, museum exhibitions, and films. Even if the capacity of museums to shape young people's imaginations is limited, we are convinced that they can, and should, be constantly trying, in close association with schools, to improve individual attitudes towards archaeological remains and the protection of monuments.

Note

1 In August 1989, after this book had gone to press, a new Polish government was formed under a non-communist leadership.
2 The subjects most frequently offered by Łódź museum to schoolchildren in 1986 were the following: 1. The beginnings of the Polish state (21 lessons); 2. The peoples of Black Africa (16 lessons); 3. The life of the Slavs (15 lessons); 4. Life in the Stone Age (15 lessons); 5. The art of Egypt (14 lessons); 6. Life of the Pre-Slavs – Biskupin (14 lessons); 7. The art of Rome (13 lessons); 8. South America and Mexico (13 lessons); 9. The culture of Ancient Greece (11 lessons); 10. The culture of Ancient Rome (11 lessons). The following archaeological subjects were covered: 1. Prehistoric art (10 lessons); 2. Archaeology as a source of knowledge about the past (5 lessons); 3. The contacts between the Slavs and the Roman Empire (5 lessons); 4. Archaeological investigations in the Łódź area (1 lesson).

References

Gamulewicz, M. 1984. Wykorzystanie zbiorow archeologiczuych w procesie nauczania historii. In Roła muzeum w procesie dydaktyczno – wychowawczym. Zbiory muzealne pomoca w nauczaniu historii, A. Mikołajczyk (ed.), 24–36. Łódź.
Koczerska, M. & E. Wipszycka 1985. Historia. Swiat przed wiekami. Warsaw.
Mikołajczyk, A. 1986. On the didactic presentation of the past in the archaeological museum: some retrospective considerations. In Archaeological 'objectivity' in interpretation. World Archaeological Congress, Vol. 3 (mimeo).
Mikołajczyk, A. 1987. Muzeum Archeołogiczne i Etnograficzne w Łódźi w latach 1979–1986 i jego prace badawcze. Builetyn Informacyjny Zarzadu Muzeow i Ochrony Zabytkow. Łódź.
Mikołajczyk, A. in press. Prehistory and archaeology illustrated in history textbooks in Europe.
Stopczyk, S. K. 1982. Wydawnictwa Sckolne i Pedagogiczne. Plastyka 5, 24–9. (Warsaw)

22 Rediscovering Rome's hidden past

STEFANO MAMMINI

This chapter is based on my own experience in the field of education over the past few years. It deals with two main subjects: the city of Rome, with particular reference to its cultural heritage (archaeology, art, and museums), and the students of the Scuole medie, whose ages range between 10 and 18. I chose to work in this area as a result of my archaeological studies and an interest in education which has resulted in my work with the Società Cooperativa Archaeologia.

The knowledge of our past, of the way in which our culture has developed, of our history and of history in a broader and transnational sense, is knowledge of inestimable value. It is vital not only in order to promote a real appreciation of what remains of the past (for example, monuments and churches), but also in order to make it easier for us to understand the causes and effects of events that take place in modern society.

Only by increasing this knowledge can we hope to involve and interest the so-called general public in the innumerable problems that hinder the preservation and protection of our cultural heritage. In Italy, for example, the restoration of the marble reliefs that decorate Trajan's Column (Fig. 22.1) is currently seen as a problem that concerns only archaeologists and restorers, not as one that involves the Italian people as a whole. If Italy's cultural heritage is to be preserved, the Italian people must be made aware of its importance and of the problems involved in its preservation. This can most successfully be achieved through the education of the young, who tend to be more receptive and open to new ideas than adults. A group of adults, for instance, will diligently follow a guided visit or a lecture without asking for any clarification, in order not to appear impolite in front of the expert, or for fear of seeming less cultured than the other members of the group; a group of children, however, will question and comment.

The Roman situation

Paradoxically, Rome and its past appear more complex and chaotic to those people who live there than to the many tourists who consume it from the windows of the inclusive tour coaches. This is because, slowly but surely, the people of the city have become hardened and indifferent, an attitude that springs from the superabundance of the remains of the past. Since the Middle Ages Rome has developed and modernized its appearance, thanks to

Figure 22.1 Restoration work in progress on the extraordinary reliefs that ring Trajan's Column. The preservation of such Roman monuments should be an issue of national concern. (Photograph by G. Binns.)

continual reconstruction and reutilization of the ancient city. For many centuries, therefore, the Romans have lived with the Rome of the consuls and of the emperors, giving rise to an uninterrupted process of interaction between the modern and the ancient city, which still continues today. As a result, many of the people who live in Rome do not perceive the major ancient monuments as anything special or out of the ordinary. These

Figure 22.2 Neglected grandeur: modern Romans tend to disregard the overfamiliar ruin of the Colosseum. (Photograph by David R. Harris.)

monuments have become slowly transformed into nothing more than a backdrop for the city, or at least simply as architectural or artistic phenomena having no more importance or value than the more modern or more anonymous historical structures. Thus awareness and perception of the past have been lost, despite the abundance of its spectacular remains. Perhaps the most striking example is the Colosseum (Fig. 22.2). The area surrounding

the difference between the two. The first stage is to encourage people to use their eyes: discussions in the classroom are always accompanied by slides and the level of understanding achieved in the classroom is tested during subsequent guided visits or excursions. Visits to the same archaeological sites or museums and city tours on different occasions can concentrate on different aspects or periods of the past. It is also hoped that visits will later be possible to the Società's excavation in the Via della Consolazione (the north-western part of the Roman Forum).

On the whole schoolchildren seem to find it quite difficult to filter and memorize information when it is presented in this way as all too often they have fallen into a routine of being told exactly what work (either in the class or at home) they must do. For this reason methods must be found to make the subject as attractive as possible. Another problem is that although adopting the teaching methods used by the teachers of regular subjects makes it easier for children to learn, this carries with it the risk that the expert is seen as being no more interesting than them. In this respect we have learnt how effective the use of a videorecorder can be. The immediacy of the message, and the familiarity with television, make it a very direct and successful form of communication.

Much more work must be done if we are to succeed in spreading a wider knowledge of Rome and its past. Only by doing this can we encourage Romans to take an interest in the restoration and conservation of the monuments around them, an interest which, as I have already stressed, is an essential starting point for the preservation of Rome's cultural heritage. It is vital to pay special attention to the younger generation, so that in Rome and elsewhere we can begin to hope for a gradual and widespread rediscovery of the past about which too little is understood.

Acknowledgements

I would like to thank Catherine Nightingale for the help she has given me in translating and editing this chapter.

References

Carandini, A. and Pucci, G. 1978 L'archeologia oggi. In *La difesa del patrimonio artistico*, Milan: Mondadori.

Castagnoli, F., C. Morselli & E. Tortorici (eds) 1982. *Progetto per lo scavo di un settore dei Fori di Cesare e di Nerva*, Rome: De Luca Editore.

Dondero, I. & M. Mele in press. Relazione sull'attivita didattica della Soprintendenza Archeologica di Roma. In *Roma Archeologia e Progetto: Atti del Convegno, 23–28 May 1983*.

Lamberti, R. 1982. Problemi di didattica della storia. In *La storia: fonti orali nella scuola*, 53–65. Venice: Marsilio Editori.

Mammini, S. & F. Rovis. 1986. La ricostruzione dei siti archeologici tra esigenze scientifiche ed esigenze didattiche. *Pact News* **17**, 87–93.

Matera, V. & M. Sanfilippo 1982. La Cooperativà e la scuola. *Scuola e Notizie* **14**, 27–31.

Pascolini, A. 1978. *Ostia. Ritorno in un'antica citta*. Rome: Armamdo Editore.

Rovis, F. & M. Sanfilippo 1985. Esperienze di sensibilizazione archeologica nell 'area romana: un bilancio. *Pact News* **16**, 53–5.

23 New Archaeology, New History – when will they meet? Archaeology in English secondary schools

PHILIP PLANEL

The initial constraints

The teaching of archaeology in English secondary schools (ages 11 to 16) in practice means the teaching of history. This is neither desirable nor, in the long term, necessary; it is dictated by subject specialism within secondary schools, particularly in the upper school (14 to 16). In primary education, by contrast, all the teachers in a school can participate in an archaeology project and bring their own specialist interests to bear on the work in hand (Stone 1986).

Occasionally, when history in the lower school is taught within a humanities course, contact is made with a geography teacher. Depite the rapidly increasing role of science within professional archaeology, archaeology does not feature in school science curricula, and this at a time when many schools are beginning to study environmental science, a subject very amenable to archaeological input.

A further constraint – even in schools where the chronological gallop from the origins of the human species to the Korean War has been abandoned – is that where prehistory is taught at all it is always in the first year. In the next two years the children, with almost Napoleonic certitude, will become medievalists. This developmental approach only serves to reinforce the view that prehistory equates to 'primitive' and medieval equates to 'more civilized'. History syllabuses inspected in 16 Hampshire schools by Her Majesty's Inspectorate of Schools were all chronological in format (HMI 1983).

In 1984 a questionnaire on the use of archaeology in schools was sent to all 107 secondary schools in Hampshire (Stone 1984). Of the 50 that responded, 36 included some study of archaeology within another subject and while 24 of the schools visited museums, only 2 ever visited monuments and 2 excavations. Yet 32 of the schools said they would like to be visited by archaeologists. Thus, despite the constraints of the secondary curriculum, it is clear that considerable scope exists for archaeology in secondary schools in Hampshire.

Archaeology is seldom taught as a separate subject at school level. However, until recently there were separate archaeology examinations for the General Certificate of Education (GCE) and the Certificate of Secondary Education (CSE). These have now been replaced by the more skills-oriented General Certificate of Secondary Education (GCSE). However, only one school in Hampshire followed a GCE archaeology 'O' level and has taken up the GCSE archaeology course, and this school is in the independent (non-state-funded) sector. The course is taught within a classics department.

The curriculum revolution

History teachers are now eager to bring archaeology into the classroom. This has come about for a number of reasons.

History teachers have been in the forefront of the curriculum reform movement that has transformed the teaching of many subjects at secondary level in the last two decades (Coltham & Fines 1971). The main thrust of the curriculum reform has been pupil participation or 'active learning'. History teachers can therefore no longer teach history as 'received truth chronologically arranged'.

The New History

Out of the curriculum revolution came the 'New History', incorporating skills-based learning, an evidence-based curriculum and, in common with other subjects, a clear set of educational objectives. A teacher (Jones 1983, p. 30) takes up the story:

> New History ... sprang from the enthusiasm and idealism of the curriculum developers urging a concentration upon the essentials of the subject, an examination of the processes of historical research (albeit at an elementary level), a reaching after the excitement of discovering for oneself in contrast to a dreary ramble through well trodden ways in English History.

Traditionalists, meanwhile, complained that history teachers should teach history and not train historians, that content had been thrown to the winds, and that children were leaving school without the contextual historical framework in which to situate themselves in contemporary English society (Deuchar 1989).

Archaeology as evidence

History teachers realized that evidence-based work could mean a good deal more than handling primary documentary sources, and began looking around for further categories of evidence, which often included fieldwork and standing remains – archaeology. In this respect history teachers were ahead of the majority of their academic colleagues, and still are.

The New Historians, born of the curriculum revolution in schools, should be distinguished from the New Historians of the French *Annales* school. For, despite the great strides made in the interpretation of evidence by the latter group the evidence base is still overwhelmingly documentary. *Montaillou* (Le Roy Ladurie 1975) is an exception; it carries two photographs of the contemporary town and a brief topographical descripton. *Le carnaval de Romans* (Le Roy Ladurie 1979) is closer to the norm; it is only in the course of the narrative that we discover Romans to be a walled town surrounded by 'ramparts' and 'fosses' (Le Roy Ladurie 1979 p. 25). We are never privileged to discover the disposition of the *quartiers* of the town or the relationship of Romans to the surrounding villages and countryside, nor whether any elements of modern Romans survives from the late 16th century – there are no detailed maps or plans. It appears that these 'New Historians' give no more than passing attention to material evidence from the past and the additional data it could provide.

From the early 1970s, a teacher-led centralized curriculum project and a prime mover in evidence-based history, the Schools Council Project, made considerable use of archaeological evidence in preparing material for history teachers. A forward-looking syllabus, History 13–16, led to the acceptance of a new GCE 'O' Level/CSE examination. By 1980, 512 British schools were embarking on this examination course and many teaching packs were available, although it was made clear that the Schools Council Project was 'essentially a piece of curriculum development and not a ready-to-use package' (News from Schools Council History 1980). By 1985, 850 schools were entered for the Schools Council history examination (Schools Council Report 1985). The Schools Council no longer exists but its influence is still felt. Indeed it has been said that, with reference to Schools Council work in history, 'the Schools Council Project is the bedrock of most of the thinking that has gone into the development of GCSE' (Canon 1986, p. 1).

Part of the Schools Council examination assessment involves coursework, and part of this coursework is a 'history around us' component in which a historical 'site' has to be investigated 'personally'. Such a course component is an obvious opportunity for the use of archaeological information within a history syllabus.

Since the late 1960s there has been a revolution in archaeology. However the New Archaeology and the New History have not yet been formally introduced. The use of archaeology in schools still leans towards a very traditional approach.

Archaeological content, even in so-called evidence-based history textbooks (and there is now no shortage of these), is relegated to providing ancillary evidence to the historian. Even sadder is the fact that this evidence is usually outdated, often by two or more decades. Saddest of all, some of the 'evidence' is clearly wrong, being often based on outdated secondary sources and inadequate research. One suspects that it is often only the visual impact of archaeological plans and artists' illustrations that wins them a place in these textbooks.

However, these are only symptoms of a malaise. The kernel of the issue is that historians and history teachers have not yet accepted that archaeology, in bringing meaning to the past, has a number of unique pedagogical advantages.

There are exceptions: some individual schools and teachers have been prepared to use highly original methods to interpret the past; from drama, through experimental archaeology to analysis of modern rubbish – 'we are what we throw away'. Acting on the premise that archaeology provides the sole evidence for most of the human past, one history teacher developed a project for mixed ability classes in the lower school, involving both field-work and documentary research (Reid 1982). Teachers at Soar Valley College (Leicester) have included archaeology in an integrated humanities course, carefully evaluating archaeological input in the light of clear educational aims and objectives (Croft 1983). By and large, however, we are still confronted in schools with an archaeology that is concerned with the mechanistic problem of 'piecing together the past', with techniques, typologies, chronology, provenance all to the fore; any levels of inference, problem-solving and interpretation remain almost unknown.

Even writers for the Schools Council, and writers of Schools Council derived work, seem to have a very limited understanding of archaeology. We read that children 'will have developed their understanding of the concept of evidence by . . . using relics – the accidental remains from the past – as evidence' (Boddington & Dawson 1987). There is nothing accidental about the archaeological record. This might seem a minor point but it is symptomatic of an attitude. The existence of relics has to do with land use and social organization in the past, land use and ecology in the intervening period and land use and attitudes towards preservation in our own times. All these processes are deliberate, not accidental, and all are legitimate grounds of enquiry in schools, especially in humanities course involving geography and history. The deposition, modification and survival, or disappearance, of 'relics' is very much the province of archaeology in schools.

There is, in any case, a problem in the use of the word 'relic'. 'Relic' is not a satisfactory description of an archaeological site, or standing remains, which are, in any case, only one part of productive, cultural, or religious systems. Archaeologists have found that they have to move out of sites and into a wider landscape to give meaning to their data; teachers will have to follow them.

Can New Archaeology deliver the goods?

Conceptual links between New Archaeology and New History (as practised in schools) are explicit. As Flannery (1967) points out, 'New Archaeology is concerned with 'culture process' as well as 'culture history'. There are more specific British links. As Jones (1986) remarks, 'GCSE assesses process rather than product. Process, after all, is the essence of historical experience'. Renfrew (1983) and Binford (1983) make the point at greater length:

> The task of archaeology is not simply a matter of piecing together the past – as if the bits and pieces, the material data, could be fitted together in some painless way to make a coherent picture, as soon as they are dug up. The real task is, on the contrary, a challenge and a struggle – a sustained struggle to devise meanings and interpretations which can be related to the finds, the data, in a coherent and justifiable way. (Renfrew 1983)

> Archaeologists are not digging up the past. Observed facts about the archaeological record are contemporary, they do not in themselves inform us about the past at all. The archaeological record is not made up of symbols, words or concepts, but of material things and arrangements of matter. The only way we can understand their meaning – if you will, the way in which we can state the archaeological record in words – is by knowing something about how these material things came into being, about how they have been modified, and about how they acquired the characteristics they have today. (Binford 1983)

New Archaeologists are continually asking themselves whether they are asking the right questions of their data.

It is important to incorporate recent theoretical approaches within archaeology into archaeology in the classroom, without expecting children to read difficult theoretical books. The debate within archaeology has led to interesting departures in archaeological method. The search for 'meaning' in interpreting the archaeological record is exciting and, if we accept Bruner's (1963) axiom that at all levels children should be taught in a way that is intellectually honest, there can be no reason for excluding children from this activity.

In marked contrast, archaeological evidence in recent school text books is often used to buttress untested, untestable, or, quite simply, invalid hypotheses; the Myceneans built Stonehenge, beakers mean Beaker Folk, Beaker Folk mean 'invasions'. In addition, the underlying assumptions are usually the assumptions of a settled, 'civilized', society – our own. For example, in explaining the transition from hunter-gathering to farming, a march of civilization is often implied; the transition to farming is inevitable and even beneficial. This can lead to misreading of the archaeological record. What evidence do we have that nomads have ever become settled of their own volition? On a more general level, what evidence do we have that early humans set themselves problems, such as the domestication of plants and animals?

Figure 23.1   Children investigating a cemetery. (Photograph by Mike Corbishley.)

How do we know we are teaching the 'right stuff'?

Recently there have been several influential reports by HMI that should be of considerable use to evidence-based history teachers working in schools. The 1977 HMI Report, *Curriculum 11–16* offers general guidance, suggesting eight areas of experience that children should have access to: aesthetic/creative, ethical, linguistic, mathematic, spiritual, physical, scientific, social politics (HMI 1977).

More specific is the recent report, *History in the primary and secondary school years* (HMI 1985). This tackles the questions of historical empathy, a concept that looms large in all New History syllabuses and a concept of interest to all archaeologists. Can we imagine what it was like to be prehistoric? Can we 'step into the shoes' of our forefathers? Ought we to try? The report concludes (HMI 1985, p. 3): 'Empathising is not the same as identifying with, still less sympathising with, people in the past; it is simply a word used to describe the imagination working on evidence, attempting to enter into a past experience while at the same time remaining outside it'.

Figure 23.2 The past around us: schoolchildren record the remains of Southampton's medieval walls. (Photograph by Philip Planel.)

Enough pedagogical reference points, then, do exist for those who are concerned with making archaeological evidence available to school children, whether they are trained teachers or not.

It has been observed that with guidance schoolchildren can participate in original research about the past even in the lower secondary school (ages 11 to 13). This has been exemplified in work on recording a Southampton

Figure 23.3   Visits to sites can make the past come alive: schoolchildren observed the 'discovery' of this medieval wall as Victorian masonry was removed.

graveyard which is shown in Figure 23.1 (Hill & Mays 1987). Children have responded to authentic experiences whether it be a visit to an impressive field monument of the Neolithic, the handling of an artefact, or participation in original research.

When children leave the classroom, as they do in many projects with an archaeological component, the scope for development, in both the project and the individual pupil increases greatly, and is full of pleasant surprises. Pupils of 15 and 16 years old, who were working on a 'history around us' study of Southampton's walls for their GCE 'O' Level, were able to see, while they were drawing a section of the walls, workmen removing Victorian masonry from the base of the wall (Fig. 23.2). They were able to observe before them features of medieval buildings that had never been recorded (Fig. 23.3).

The Southampton walls project was suggested by a local school and took a conventional theme, the study of a defended perimeter, as the 'history around us' component of the Schools Council examination. The project attempted to marshall as many categories of evidence as possible to interpret the priorities and practice of medieval wall-builders. By studying archaeological reports, the walls themselves, documentary sources and prints and photographs, the students were able to question whether the walls were built well, whether defence or status was the main criterion, whether the walls served to include as well as exclude. The project revolved around a key historical event, the French raid on Southampton in 1338, and the extent to which this raid exposed weakness in the defence (Planel 1986).

School projects with an archaeological component are capable of unlocking the historical imagination, in the widest possible sense of the word 'historical' (the GCSE definition of history is 'history is primarily concerned with recreating mankind's past' [GCSE National Criteria 1985]). This is of great importance for children from new urban or suburban areas where, in their normal lifeways and environment, they experience an almost complete discontinuity with the past.

Problems in the field

In interpreting an historical site to schoolchildren it is often the case that the remains, as presented to the public generally, do not satisfactorily account for the chasm in meaning between what can be seen today and what once existed. There is almost universal failure in the literature to account for the processes of survival and destruction that explain the actual state of a site. Well-manicured lawns, interspersed with cement-capped foundations bearing legends such as 'Norman Tower', carry few messages between the modern visitor, child or adult and the past (Fig. 23.4). Field trips to historical sites are of little value without considerable input before and after fieldwork, aimed at overcoming such presentational difficulties.

When presenting a site such as the multiperiod (Iron Age to Medieval) Old Sarum to 12-year-old children, one of the problems is that of situating the site within a natural and human landscape, and within a constantly changing ecology. Old Sarum has changed as much in the last hundred years – as a result of excavation and removal of earth, vegetation, and trees – as it

24 'Well in the Neolithic ...': teaching about the past in English primary schools in the 1980s

WENDY RICHARDSON

In 1987–8 education was probably more often on the lips of English politicians, in the minds of the English public, and written about by English journalists than ever before. Legislation is under consideration that will sort out the supposed ills of current educational practice, ushering in a new system that will fit English children better to cope in the modern world and better supply the needs of modern society. A National Curriculum is being implemented, and all children will be required to study certain subjects labelled Core and Foundation Subjects (Department of Education & Science 1989). Other subjects will be optional and will have to fight for a proportion of the time allowed for optional subjects. The decision on whether subjects are to be included in the foundation group (and are therefore deemed to be necessary and relevant) and which are designated optional (and therefore less relevant, useful, and important) is agitating concerned groups nationwide.

Archaeology is not included. This came as no great surprise to anyone concerned with education about the past in schools or to academic archaeologists. The subject has never been included. It is taught in a few secondary schools as an examination subject for pupils aged between 14 and 18 (Planel, Ch.23, this volume). It is taught in a number of university departments. It is not taught officially in any college of higher education (the institutions in which most British teachers receive their professional training), although one or two enthusiasts manage to sneak a little into history courses. It is very difficult for archaeology graduates to find places on teacher training courses, their university degree not being seen as relevant. As there is no teaching of archaeology at present there is no relevance. And so it goes on.

In September 1987 one of the first offshoots of the 1986 World Archaeological Congress took place. A conference was held in Southampton entitled Archaeology Meets Education (AME) (Richardson 1989). It was attended by teachers, museum staff, and archaeologists from all over the British Isles. Much discussion centred on the proposals for a national curriculum and it was decided that a message from the conference be sent to the Secretary of State for Education, asking him to take advice from such bodies as the

Council for British Archaeology before finalizing the National Curriculum proposals (Ucko 1989). It was pointed out that without the help of archaeological knowledge our children's understanding of their past would be restricted to a narrow aspect: the last two thousand years.

Without special reference to archaeology in the Core and Foundation subjects, it seems hardly likely that the present situation will change. If the subject has but a tenuous foothold in a 'free trade' situation, it is hardly likely that it will find a niche in the scrabble for a bit of the non-foundation time.

Such exclusion would seem to be a pity since in recent years some very interesting archaeological work has been going on in schools, especially in the primary sector (for children aged 5 to 12 years). Interested teachers in many parts of the country have been awakened to the use of archaeology as a tool with which to attain some of the aims of primary education. As long ago as 1931 the Hadow report on primary education suggested that 'The curriculum is to be thought of in terms of activity and experience rather than of knowledge to be acquired and facts to be stored' (Hadow 1931). This message took a long time to percolate through, but by the 1960s it had begun to shape teaching practice, and primary schools were theoretically free to devise interdisiplinary courses, aimed at providing opportunity for learning through experimentation and personal development through broadening experience and awareness. The new practices gained respectability through the findings of a number of English and European reports (Thomas & Majult 1963, Plowden 1968, Her Majesty's Inspectorate 1978).

Much traditional book-based learning continued. History was taught (and is still taught in many schools) as a series of discrete topics, starting with the caveman in some anonymous place in the world, then jumping to Egypt and on to Rome. At that point in time 'real' history teaching can begin. Names and dates can be stuffed into and regurgitated by pupils with good short-term memories, just as they can stuff in and regurgitate capes and bays, and botanical and zoological tags, all of which is good, easily testable material.

The 1960s also witnessed the popularization of the work of cognitive psychologist Jean Piaget. Piaget separated cognitive development into four stages which he attributed to certain ages (e.g. Piaget 1953). The end of Piaget's second stage, and his third coincide with English primary education. His second stage can be described as relating to those actions that are intuitive and subjective and are a result of the child's perception of immediate experience. During the third stage, known as the stage of 'concrete operations', the child begins to make explanations of the perceived world in quantifiable, spatial and physical terms. Classifying, organizing, and seeing relationships between things or events are characteristics of this stage. The testing of ideas is done by trial and error. The making of hypotheses, generalization from the particular, assumption, and deductive thinking are the characteristics of the final stage, known as the stage of 'formal operations'.

A general acceptance of these theories led to a quiet revolution in the classroom. Environmental studies began to make strong headway, with an emphasis on first-hand exploration and experience, and nature study and geography took to the open air. History suffered. It nearly disappeared. Teaching from a book about events that were remote in both time and space did not appear to fit the notion of 'concrete operations'. Local history started to make a mark, but it proved difficult to exploit. Few in primary teaching had the expertise to search the environment for concrete evidence of the past, and the experts were slow to come forward to offer help.

Even in revolutionary classrooms, history teaching remained, on the whole, book-bound, but attempted to become child-centred. Work was undertaken in topic or project form but information would, at best, be gathered from a variety of secondary sources or, at worst, copied in chunks from one source. Often the quality and accuracy of sources available to teachers and pupils left much to be desired. Prehistory was especially badly served. Where actual evidence was called upon it was dressed in fantasy. The club-swinging grunter-groaner surrounded by half-naked cringing women and children was a frequently proposed inhabitant of the prehistoric scene.

It was against this background that a number of teachers and archaeologists began to voice their concern and to cooperate in ventures aimed at proving that with experience of material remains and involvement in archaeological method children could achieve understanding of the past, both remote and nearer in time. In fact it made little difference to the children whether the past they were studying was 100 or 10 000 years away. It was all a long time ago. Through investigation of the artefacts made and left behind by the peoples of the past, by visits to the sites, and by experiments which explored ancient work methods, children were enabled to piece together the past, and to develop a sense of the sequence of events if not the duration of time which, the further we move from the present, remains an elusive concept even for most adults.

In Hampshire, under the auspices of the Department of Archaeology at the University of Southampton, a team was set up to bring together schoolteachers and archaeologists (Stone 1986). Before the team was set up a survey had established a need for expert input if archaeology was to be accepted as a useful educational tool (Stone 1984). Teachers wanted help. They wanted to be shown where and how to get their hands on relevant material and how to use it to advantage.

In cooperation with the team a project was arranged to introduce older primary schoolchildren to prehistory (see Fig. 24.1) (Richardson 1987). The project left teachers impressed by the possibilities inherent in the approach and left children with a thirst for more. All the children involved said that the project should be repeated every year for other children. Most of them thought that they had worked harder and learned more than in any other project. Post-project testing indicated a high level of retention of new knowledge. For example 82.2 per cent understood the function of West Kennet Long Barrow, and all but one of the children correctly ascribed the Avebury monuments to the Neolithic (Richardson 1987).

Figure 24.1 'Hands-on' archaeology: primary schoolchildren cook bread made from flour they have ground using prehistoric technology.

However it was not only in factual knowledge that the children had gained. They learned about the use and interpretation of a number of different types of evidence and began to use their understanding in one area to elicit understanding in others. It was a remark made by a child a year after the project that prompted consideration of the changing attitude towards learning about the past that this and other similar projects seemed to be bringing about. The remark was made during an interview for local radio. The subject under discussion, chosen by the interviewer, not the children, was preconditioning for gender roles or, as it had been put to the children, what makes girls do girly things and boys act like heroes!

The conversation had ranged over pink and blue baby clothes, toy cars versus Cindy Dolls, and on to sport. The question of strength was under discussion, and various theories were being put forward to explain these differences when one girl said it: 'Well in the Neolithic . . .' She went on to draw upon her understanding of Neolithic society. She was quickly joined and helped in her thinking by others. They attempted quite spontaneously to examine their knowledge of an even more distant past, for clues to explain the greater strength of the male, and soon established as a possible theory the differing roles that would be thrust upon man and woman in hunter-gatherer times, due to the physical requirement that the female keep the young with her. They supposed that strengths established during this long period would have predetermined roles by the Neolithic.

It was a long and complicated argument, put forward with great relish. They delighted in their ability to theorize, and enjoyed finding evidence to support their ideas. Such occurrences, although not common, were happening now and again. When questioned about their learning the children were very positive.

In an attempt to discover whether this reaction and subsequent discussion had been brought about by the teaching method, a small enquiry aimed at ascertaining the attitudes towards the past and the way in which it is taught was carried out among a group of 80 children aged 14 from two secondary schools. Their views were then compared with those of a group of 64 primary school children aged between 10 and 11.

The older children were at the beginning of their penultimate year of compulsory education, and had all been taught history. They had just made choices on whether or not to abandon further studies in any subject other than English and mathematics, although they had been encouraged to maintain a broad base and to include both humanities and sciences. Slightly less than half of them (36) had chosen to continue to study history and to take public examinations in it.

Despite the relatively high take-up of history as an option only 18 per cent of the 80 pupils thought that history would be important or useful to them in their future, although 66 per cent said that they had found it interesting. There was no clear division of opinion regarding usefulness or importance between those who had chosen to continue to study history and those who had given up. Asked what they hoped to gain from their continued studies of the past, 15 (41 per cent) of the 36 said 'more knowledge', one mentioned 'understanding', one spoke of 'broader horizons', and one hoped to understand present tensions in Europe better because of his study of the past. Among them were seven who thought that history would be one of the three subjects that they would study between the ages of 16 and 18, but even they could find little use for the subject. They expected that they might become historians or archaeologists, or teachers of the subject, but had no idea that their study might in some way be of benefit to them in any wider context.

The whole group was asked to recall the sources from which they had learnt history. An astonishing 51 per cent did not know or did not understand the question. Those who did respond mentioned books (32), teacher (21), visits (7), films (6), and worksheets (5). The group continuing to study history showed a greater awareness of the nature of historical source. To the question 'From where does our historical knowledge come?', they answered books (11), teachers (5), the oral tradition (7), material evidence (9) documents and written evidence (6). Although four who had given up history had done so because it was too difficult, those who were to continue its study saw it as an easy subject. Ranked with English, French, mathematics, and physics, it was seen by 31 per cent to be the easiest subject and by another 28 per cent as being the second most easy.

Their attitudes are of course a reflection of general public attitudes towards the past, as well as a reflection of what may have happened in their schooling. When questions were asked about the past in a context outside school work they acknowledged the need for it to be protected. Asked to consider the usefulness of institutions to the nation, they ranked museums well above cinemas, sports halls, concert halls, and art galleries, and just above libraries. It is this almost instinctive desire to hang on to the past, for nonscientific reasons, that promotes public outcry at any proposal that threatens a local monument, and causes outrage if it is suggested that charges be made for entry to national museums. We feel we have some form of common ownership over the relics of the past. The past belongs to us, and even if we do not take much notice of it we want someone to keep it properly for us.

Those who were to continue to study history were asked what they thought might be done to encourage others to follow suit. It was by far the most thoughtfully answered question. The following list is gathered from their comments. They asked for more learning at first hand, finding out for yourself, site visits, doing things, plays, stories, creative work, realistic films and television, digging, people talking of their own experiences, local studies, individual studies, a broader view, pointing the difference between now and the past. They asked for less sitting and listening, and writing.

The younger group of children had been involved over a period of two or three years in historical studies that included all the elements requested by the older pupils. Through careful questioning during and after studies their teachers had tried to ensure that a broad view had emerged, and that the expression of an opinion was valued, especially if it could be supported with evidence as well as feeling. Stories had been used to illustrate the work of archaeologists and historians as well as the content of the study. Dramatic improvizations, sometimes based on evidence uncovered, had helped sort out ideas that the children were forming. On one occasion, during a stormy re-enactment of a mid-19th-century council meeting to debate the need for a new drainage system, councillors were accused of wicked self-interest. The names of families living just 100 m from the council chamber and dying from cholera were quoted, alongside the date of the laying of the foundation stone of the new council chamber. The children had got their facts from searches in the archives and visits to the sites. Both sides could put them to good purpose.

When this group was asked: 'Why are children taught about the past?', they too thought first of future employment, but there were struggles to express something more. The words 'change', 'difference', 'how things evolved', and 'comparison', were used by 22 per cent of them. One said, 'because a lot of things that happened in the past affect life today'. Another said, 'because it tells us how things got where and how they are'. Altogether 81 per cent were able to express some opinion.

One project on the 20th century, which had used film, witnesses to events, artefacts, visits to museums and archive searches, had ended with a dramatization in four parts. The children had chosen four topics to represent the century: 1912 and women's emancipation, the 1930s and the impact of the motor car, life in an air raid shelter in the 1940s, and a very 'high tech' Winchester in the 1980s. Their plays were recorded on video, and six months later were played back to them. They were asked to recall the project and what they had learnt from it. Listed below are some of the questions they were asked, and a sample of their responses.

What do you remember most about your work on the 20th century?

'I remember the plays most because they had so much information in them.'
'I remember mainly about the war because it was tragic.'
'I remember the industrial jobs.'
'I remember the Second World War and the conditions.'
'How tough it was then and how hard on poor people.'

What was the most important thing you learned?

The lives of different types of people.
How life has changed.
How much things have improved.
How well people managed without technology.
The speed of change in this century.
That the world has changed in some places but not in others.
'I think the most important bit was the research.'
Women going out to work and getting the vote.
How countries are controlled.

What do you think were the most important changes during the century?

Jobs and votes for women.
Conditions in cities.
Advent of car/plane/computer/telephone.
Educational opportunities.
Changing attitudes to work.
Changing attitudes to people.
Changing sorts of government.

What do you think was the purpose of this study?

To learn how life has changed.
To understand life today.
To look back and think.
To help us improve things by comparing with the past.

These children appear to be struggling to make real use of their studies of the past, and to be taking on board the beginnings of understanding of such complex concepts as power, government, and money. They are beginning to see that where people are in time, and the consensus of opinion of that time, affect their actions. It is the combination of experience and activity with the archaeological method and the availability of (sometimes photo-copied) archival material that has, as the older pupils predicted, enabled these children to engage with the past.

At the Archaeology Meets Education Conference there were contri-butions from a teacher and from an archaeologist who had worked together but who saw the combination of archaeology and education from quite different viewpoints. It was a visit to Butser Ancient Farm, an experimental Iron Age project (Reynolds 1979, 1989) that set the imagination of a Dorset teacher of craft, design, and technology (CDT) going. As a result, his school grounds now boast a round house 6.5 m high and 9.2 m in diameter. This house is the second to be built, the first house having burnt to the ground shortly after its completion (Keen 1986). Not only has the building of the house involved the children in the school, it has become a focal point within the community, and weekends and summer evenings see village families gathered round to help in construction. The house is in an enclosure with bank and ditch, animal houses on a smaller scale than the main house have gone up, soay sheep are kept, an iron smelting pit is under construction, and pits are dug for storage of clay and for any other purpose that can be conceived as this is a favourite activity of the children (see Fig. 24.2) (Keen 1989).

Why have they built the complex? Originally conceived as something much more exciting to make than the models and small-scale works that were predominant in their CDT lessons, the house gave opportunity for planning, investigation of evidence, consideration of materials, develop-ment of tools, measurement, understanding of structures, and cooperative working. A wider knowledge of the environment has been achieved in many ways. Reeds are gathered for thatching, a local wood is coppiced to provide the right sort of spars, geological investigations are required to find supplies of clay. The local farmers have been contacted about husbanding the sheep and in order to acquire the necessary ingredients for the daub, although the second time round it was an animal that was acquired and the materials were produced at base. The project is never ending. Soft sandstone is brought back to the site from visits to the coast and is carved. Art classes happen in and around the house, and decorative elements are added for a while. It is envisaged that the completed house will offer opportunity for sleeping out. Perhaps just being in a round house will stimulate new

Figure 24.2 Children build their own round house based on information gained from local excavations of Iron Age sites (Cranborne Middle School, Dorset).

perceptions. Exciting things may happen there.

Though careful investigation of Iron Age method was incorporated, with the assistance of several archaeologists and in particular those from Butser, the main aim of the project was not to teach prehistory. The project is a perfect example of the way in which interdisciplinary action can provide not only excellent quality, but also considerable breadth in the curriculum. Not least amongst the learning achieved will be considerable respect for the people of the past, their skills and their ingenuity. From it may develop an understanding of relationships between mankind and the environment both in the past and now.

It was a worry that archaeological quality was being sacrificed to provide educational breadth that brought the director of the Butser project to the AME conference. Under pressure to provide public access to the site, he was disinclined to provide a sort of Disneyland, where the day tripper might pretend to be something he was not. He questioned the value of dressing up and playing at making pots or cakes in search of empathy with a society so clearly different from our own. Instead he proposed that children become involved in the real work of the project, the careful observation and analysis of growth and decay in the plants, the animals, the structures. He told of a seed-growing experiment undertaken by one local school, which had allowed the children genuine participation in the project, brought them face-to-face with real science as it was happening, and at the same time taught them method and skills (Reynolds 1989). It is hard to imagine a more exciting way to learn than through sharing in real research.

Archaeology, standing as it does at the crossroads between the humanities and sciences is uniquely fitted to offer both the specialization and the cross-fertilization that education for the 21st century requires. It is also especially suited to the primary years since it incorporates experience and activity, as recommended by Hadow (1931). No special place is needed for it in the curriculum. It will not be necessary to devise benchmarks in archaeology for 7-year-olds, but unless its potential contribution is officially recognized and clearly stated, the little that is about will disappear.

In his autobiography, R. G. Collingwood, archaeologist and philosopher, describes the role that history must play in the future:

> It seemed to me nearly as certain as anything in the future could be, that historical thought, whose constantly increasing importance had been one of the most striking features of the nineteenth century, would increase far more rapidly during the twentieth; and that we might very well be standing on the threshold of an age in which history would be as important for the world as natural science had been between 1600 and 1900. If that was the case (and the more I thought about it the likelier it seemed) the wise philosopher would concentrate with all his might on the problems of history, at whatever cost, and so do his share in laying the foundations of the future. (Collingwood 1939, p. 87)

Collingwood's archaeological experience had led him to serious reappraisal of question and answer which he saw as a mighty tool for discovery. He saw that archaeology, in discovering new evidence, was doing more than fill in the gaps: it was restructuring historical knowledge. It provided the means with which orthodoxies might be challenged. Old questions were being asked again because new questions had been answered. In coming to understand, he argued, we proceed from the unknown to the known. The same techniques he found could open up thinking in any area. If we are prepared to accept Collingwood's argument about thinking, should we not choose it as a way of leading our children towards an organization of their learning that will begin to help in the formulation of their understanding of the past?

References

Collingwood, R. G. 1939. *An autobiography*. Oxford: Clarendon Press.

Department of Education & Science 1989. *The National Curriculum: from policy to practice* London: DES.

Hadow. 1931. *Report of the Consultative Committee on Primary Schools*. London: HMSO.

Her Majesty's Inspectorate 1978. *Survey of primary schools in Britain*. London: HMSO.

Keen, J. 1986. Hot remnants. *Remnants* **2**, 13–14. London: English Heritage.

Keen, J. 1989. Learning through doing – a middle school explores Iron Age life. *CBA Education Bulletin* **6**, 12–16.

Piaget, J. 1953. *The origin of intelligence in the child* London: Routledge & Kegan Paul.

Planel, P. 1990. New Archaeology, New History – when will they meet? Archaeology in English secondary schools. In *The excluded past: archaeology in education*, P. Stone & R. MacKenzie (eds), Ch. 23. London: Unwin Hyman.

Plowden, B. 1968. *Children and their Primary Schools* London: HMSO.

Reynolds, P. 1979. *Iron Age Farm: The Butser experiment*. London: British Museum.

Reynolds, P. 1989. Butser Ancient Farm: an extraordinary classroom. *CBA Education Bulletin* **6**, 27–32.

Richardson, W. 1987. Bones, pots and boomerangs. In *Degree, Digging, Dole, our future*, S. Joyce, M. Newbury, and P. Stone (eds), 69–77. Southampton: University Archaeology Society.

Richardson, W. (ed.) 1989. *CBA Education Bulletin* **6**. (Papers presented at the Archaeology Meets Education Conference, Southampton 1987.) London: CBA.

Stone, P. G. 1984. Unpublished research. University of Southampton.

Stone, P. G. 1986. Even older than granny? The present state of the teaching of the past to children of 8–12 years. In *Archaeological 'objectivity' in interpretation*. World Archaeological Congress, Vol. 3 (mimeo).

Thomas, J. and Majult, J. 1963. *Primary and Secondary Education – modern trends and common problems*. Strasbourg: Council for Cultural Cooperation.

Ucko, P. J. 1989. Telemessage to the Secretary of State for Education. *CBA Education Bulletin* **6**, 2. London: CBA.

25 Archaeology in the Toronto school system: the Archaeological Resource Centre

KAROLYN SMARDZ

Archaeology combines many of the modes of active and integrated learning that are the focus of modern educational theory. At the same time, an enhanced popular perception of the importance of archaeology can only benefit a profession long starved of public funding, and whose major resource is diminishing at an alarming rate in the face of rapid urban and suburban development in many parts of the globe. Yet it is only recently that there has been a coordinated effort on the part of archaeologists, at least in North America, to encourage appreciation of the past through participation in excavation, analysis, and heritage conservation on the part of the public in general, and preuniversity students in particular.

Archaeology in the school system

Archaeology's role in education

With archaeology, and particularly field archaeology, educators have a unique opportunity to involve students in the actual process of research. Unlike almost any other exercise to which students are exposed at the preuniversity level, archaeological excavations may be viewed as actual scientific experiments. What is more, they are experiments that can be conducted only once. Every site is destroyed by the very technique used in its exploration.

The educational impact of outdoor, experiential education has long been recognized. By taking students out of the classroom, by putting them in the site context for a hands-on excavation programme, and by allowing them to discover and handle actual artefacts, students of any age can participate in the recovery of new information about heritage. It should perhaps be noted at this point that sites used for education need not be undisturbed, nor even particularly old. The objective is to teach students how archaeologists acquire their information, and to increase their appreciation for the past through their involvement in its discovery. This can be done on sites that have been widely disturbed and where artefacts date even as late as the early

20th century. However, one important criterion in maintaining student interest is the expectation of a high artefact yield. That the objects recovered happen to be sherds of pop bottles is considerably less important that the fact that each child during the programme has 'found something'. Personal involvement, coupled with the fact that students are 'really doing archaeology', provides an educational experience that few traditional teaching methods can emulate. Participating students are aware that there is a relevance to their work that goes far beyond the simple purpose of educating them. This conviction, reinforced at all phases of the programme, instils a sense of pride in the careful execution of various duties entailed in digging, recording, and cataloguing.

Modern education has moved far beyond the point where the child is viewed as the passive recipient of facts and figures. In 1980 the Ontario Ministry of Education described its conceptual approach to the student as follows:

> Recognising the diversity of individual abilities and interest, the Ministry views the learner as an active participant in education who gains satisfaction from the dynamics of learning. The concept of the learner as a mere processor of information has been replaced by the image of a self-motivated, self-directed problem-solver, aware of both the processes and uses of learning and deriving a sense of self-worth and confidence from a variety of accomplishments . . . Thus, the very goals of education flow from the image of the learner for whom the direction is being provided. (Ontario Ministry of Education and Ontario Ministry of Colleges and Universities 1980, pp. 2–3)

Across the curriculum a model of Cognitive-Skills-Development is being applied in order to involve students, of all ages and in all subject areas, in the stages inherent in information gathering, assimilation, and interpretation for the purpose of drawing conclusions on which generalized applications and theories can be based. Archaeologists will be struck by the direct correlation between this model and the processes they undertake in archaeological research:

Cognitive-Skills-Development Model

1	FOCUS	Limit, direct, or define a problem or issue
2	ORGANISE	Select or develop a visual presentation, chart, or organiser for the focus
3	LOCATE	Identify, find, and use reliable, relevant sources of information
4	RECORD	Summarise and translate information
5	EVALUATE/ ASSESS	Determine the validity, appropriateness, significance, and accuracy of information
6	SYNTHESISE/ CONCLUDE	Observe relationships in and draw conclusion(s) from information

7 APPLY   Predict, generalise, compare and decide, basing these fomulations on the conclusion(s)

8 COMMUNICATE   Express information and ideas, and describe the cognitive processes involved

(Ontario Ministry of Education 1986, p. 12)

At the same time, traditional barriers between class-taught subjects are being eroded; integrated approaches are used in elementary and intermediate education, and are beginning to find their application at the senior secondary level as well.

Archaeology provides the teacher with a pursuit tailor-made to the needs of the modern educator, because of its uniquely multidisciplinary character, its suitability for active learning programming, and the potential of the study for meeting the requirements of the Cognitive-Skills-Development Model. Not only are skills borrowed from a variety of disciplines demonstrated in the field and laboratory situation, but the student is also offered the opportunity to practise these skills in the service of a particular – and socially significant – function, the unearthing of information about the past.

Whose responsibility is it?

Archaeologists world-wide are faced with diminishing funds for research and salvage ('rescue') projects, and with a quite incredible rate of destruction of prehistoric and historic sites. Political support, legislation and, of course money, are urgently required to alleviate this crisis. But most members of the general public are not aware that the situation is so critical, and, if they are, have been provided with little reason why they should care. It is not enough for archaeologists to tell them that heritage sites are 'important' – not everyone is intrinsically convinced of that truth. It is incumbent upon 'someone' to teach the average taxpayer why funding and supporting archaeological projects is of paramount importance: it is, to be blunt, necessary to market archaeology to the consumer. This is as true of archaeological sites, essentially invisible underground, as it is of historic buildings and monuments which are a familiar and often beloved element of the local landscape. In order to achieve this necessary level of public awareness people who are not archaeologists, historians, or museologists must be made to feel both that they have a stake in the conservation of heritage resources, and that they can and should be effective in helping to ensure it.

Public education and archaeology

The obvious way of encouraging popular support is through public education. There are many ways of implementing public education programmes in archaeology, ranging from simple mounting of a display, to encouraging visits to sites that are restored or still under excavation, to the operation of full-scale 'public archaeology' sites, where people actually take part in the excavation. The more involved people feel in the issue, the more they feel it is *their* heritage resource that is endangered, and the harder they will fight to preserve it from destruction.

Archaeologists have a vested interest in making people who are not archaeologists feel that saving sites is important. Yet to a large extent the responsibility for heritage education has been left to the classroom teacher. Such educators are best equipped to teach, far better than archaeologists, for they are trained and dedicated to the purpose. But what tools and support are they being provided with to carry out this task?

A great deal has been said about having more archaeology put into the average classroom curriculum. This is certainly desirable. But it is asking a great deal to expect the average educator to have intensive knowledge of this one subject, which in many institutions is not even included in the list of disciplines that makes one eligible for teacher's certification. Nor are most archaeologists sufficiently up-to-date or even interested in pedagogical theory to be of much help in the matter.

In order to get archaeology taught in school archaeologists are going to have to begin by learning something about how to teach their own subject. And they are going to have to cooperate with teachers and educational consultants, who can instruct them in how children of different ages learn. No matter how hard the person trying to teach is working, if the students are not learning, there is no teaching going on (McKenna 1988).

Through cooperation between educators and archaeologists, students can be exposed to the best that both professional groups have to offer: the most up-to-date techniques and information, offered in a planned pedagogical context, by people whose objective, at least partially, is to teach them.

By presenting archaeology as a means for involving students in actual research, for introducing them to the practice of skills gleaned from a multiplicity of disciplines, and for giving new life to studies about the past, the archaeologist can both serve the needs of the educator and help alleviate the desperate plight of our endangered heritage resources.

Archaeology and education in Toronto

In Canada, through the creation of the Archaeological Resource Centre (ARC), the Board of Education for the City of Toronto has taken a leading role in the development and implementation of archaeological curricula at the elementary, secondary and general interest levels. (In Canadian education, 'general interest' refers to noncredit courses offered through departmens of continuing and adult education.)

Archaeological participation programmes are available to students throughout the system, but in addition the Board has on its permanent staff a team of seven professional archaeologists who have the complex task of conducting archaeological research projects in which students from the age of 9 to 90 can take part.

The Board's involvement in archaeology came about as a result of long-term efforts on the part of educators and a small group of archaeologists to bring this subject into the Toronto public education system. The seeds for this institution's innovative and, to date, unique commitment to archaeological education were sown in 1982, when a dozen or so secondary-school students volunteered to participate in excavations at the site of Fort Rouillé, as part of the City of Toronto's Sesquicentennial celebrations.

The experiment was so successful that in the following year the Board cooperated in the excavation of another site, this time offering a full-credit Field School course as part of its Summer School programme. A credit is normally awarded for a course lasting an entire academic year. In Summer School, students have the option of taking an intensive programme of three or more hours of class time per day over a six-week period. The Field Schools of the Archaeological Resource Centre consist of a period of classroom instruction coupled with a participation session devoted to excavation, laboratory work, field trips, and archival research on a daily basis for six weeks. The response from teachers, students and parents to the course was such that the programme was again offered in 1984, as it has been every year since then.

At the same time requests from many teachers for class field trips to the site resulted in experimentation with hands-on excavation sessions being provided to school groups in the autumn of 1984. The popularity of these field trips was, quite literally, overwhelming. Students were thrilled to have the chance to reach out and touch 'something really old'. The supervising archaeologists were pleasantly surprised by the care and attention to detail displayed by even young children when they were cautioned that what they were doing was part of an actual research project, and that they had to be 'really, really careful'. And teachers were struck by the direct curriculum relevance of archaeology in the light of changing Ministry of Education guidelines for the social sciences.

In the spring of 1985, the Toronto Board of Education applied for and received a grant of $241 758.19 from the Ontario Ministry of Culture and Communications. This grant system was initiated in order to improve cultural facilities of various kinds throughout the province and was not a normal source of funding for archaeology. However, the Board's plan demanded the development of a fully equipped facility. As such, the Archaeological Resource Centre was eligible for the provincial grant. The funds were requested for the purpose of creating the first year-round archaeological education facility within a North American public school system.

The site, carefully chosen as a pilot project for both its heritage research potential and its suitability as an educational focus, was the home and business that had belonged to an escaped slave couple from Kentucky who began Upper Canada's first taxi business. The Thornton Blackburn House

Site was the first Black heritage site excavated in the Province of Ontario, and received more media attention than any other archaeological project in Canadian history, with the exception of the Fortress of Louisburg in the 1970s. It was a most auspicious beginning for public education archaeology in Toronto.

The mandate of the Archaeological Resource Centre may be defined as follows:

a) to offer students and interested members of the general public an oppor-
    tunity to experience first-hand the important role archaeology plays in
    heritage conservation;
b) to conduct research into the material and archival evidence of Toronto's
    historic past following a comprehensive long-range research design; in
    North America, 'historical archaeology' is *specifically* post-contact with
    Europeans.
c) to serve as a resource facility housing artefacts, a computerized data base,
    instructional media materials, and other reference information for use by
    teachers, students, and researchers.

The ARC staff have, to date, developed programmes for use in primary grade classrooms where early childhood skills such as sorting and matching are carried out using buttons, modern coins, and animal bones; classes in artefact identification in respect to form and function which are applicable to intermediate skills levels in hypothesizing and organizing; and programmes in field archaeology relating to the older students' development of decision-making and causal analysis skills (Ontario Ministry of Education 1986, p. 11) They have also organized a plethora of subject-oriented classes ranging from maths skills used in archaeological cartography for learning-disabled students to artefact conservation methods for chemistry students and computer-use in archaeology for senior grades. This extreme flexibility in application to many parts of the curriculum makes archaeological programming a highly relevant resource that is greatly in demand within the Toronto school framework.

It has always been our contention that proper supervision coupled with a highly structured system for all work carried out by students and volunteers can guarantee the maintenance of excellent research quality. Further, partici-pating students are actually of great help in the process of excavation and analysis. With proper instruction and a 1:6 supervisory ratio, even very young students are able to carry out some of the simpler tasks normally required of archaeologists. At the risk of destroying the mystique of the profession, washing pottery is well within the scope of a 9-year-old (see Fig. 25.1).

The work of the Archaeological Resource Centre to date bears out this contention. Protecting the resource while operating educational pro-grammes simply requires the presence, constant vigilance, and complete commitment of a highly qualified instructional and supervisory staff,

Figure 25.1   Young students from Toronto take part in excavation.

together with a system of excavation and recording designed with the exigencies of educational archaeology in mind. The Centre is five years old (Smardz 1989). It operates a six-month field season each year on a site of historic significance located in downtown Toronto. Winter months are spent at the facility, where day field trips in archaeology and related disciplines, cooperative education programmes, independent study courses, and a variety of night school classes are offered. Also included are courses geared for special education, various disabled, senior citizen, and English-as-a-Second-Language students. Some 12 000 students take part in archaeology courses on an annual basis. All programmes, with the exception of credit and adult courses, are offered in English and French.

Excavations are operated within the boundaries of the City of Toronto and are accessible by public transportation. The full costs for the operation of courses, excavations, research, analysis, conservation, display, reporting, and publications are borne by the Toronto Board of Education, supplemented wherever possible by a variety of grants available for heritage studies and student summer employment. The programmes are operated within the firm legal restrictions applied to archaeological excavation in the Province of Ontario. Each excavation is licensed on an annual basis by the provincial Ministry of Culture and Communications. Under the 1974 Ontario Heritage Act the licensing system requires that all excavation be conducted under the supervision of qualified archaeologists and result in the production of a competent archaeological site report before the next year's licence is issued. Each report is reviewed by the Ministry's Archaeological Committee, to ensure that professional standards are maintained.

Our research design calls for the excavation and analysis of sites relating to Toronto's 19th-century heritage (Jamieson et al. 1988). Specifically, the Centre is interested in researching domestic, commercial, and light industrial sites occupied by immigrants to the 19th-century city. Prior to the founding of the Centre, the brief archaeological history of Toronto had included the excavation of upper-income domestic sites, public institutions, and the military establishments of Fort Rouillé (French, founded 1751) and Fort York (British, founded 1790s). Hence the Centre's work is doing much needed work filling in a lacuna in the record, leading to the creation of the first archaeological data base for the City of Toronto.

Sites are chosen on the basis of their provision of data for the continuing research outlined above, but also for their potential suitability for the operation of educational programmes. In general, these are not salvage situations, nor are the sites extremely sensitive or unique from an archaeological perspective. This is not a hard-and-fast rule, however. The O'Sullivan Inn excavated in 1987 was slated for redevelopment. The excavation was conducted with the permission of the development company. However, it was a case where sufficient time could be allowed for the rather slow excavation to be expected in highly structured student-oriented projects.

The O'Sullivan Inn excavation is an excellent example of the impact on the general populace of well-publicized educational archaeology programmes. For the first time in Ontario an archaeological excavation was conducted in response to the demands of the local community. Aware that development of the site was imminent, the East Toronto and Beaches Historical Society launched a petition aimed at the Toronto Historical Board, demanding that an archaeological excavation, with public involvement, be carried out. Such enthusiasm could hardly be refused; the excavation project was jointly operated by the Toronto Board of Education and the Toronto Historical Board.

Often sites are located on schoolyards in the city centre. This has obvious logistical advantages; classrooms and sanitary facilities are close at hand. But it is also significant from a research point of view. Schools were usually built in areas of high population density, and on land that was relatively inexpensive to purchase. Thus, domestic, commercial, and small industrial sites found on schoolyards are admirably suited to furthering the stated research goals of the Centre (Jamieson et al. 1988). Such sites are also often well preserved because of the presence of an asphalt cap on the playground overlying the remains of demolished structures. A final benefit, unforseen but quickly becoming apparent in the first season's excavation, was the possibility that the dearth of available information about immigrant children's leisure activities during the 19th century in Southern Ontario might be overcome. Data produced by the Archaeological Centre may help increase our knowledge in this area.

Half-day programmes for school groups

During spring and autumn the Centre offers seven half-day programmes per week. These are offered in the site context, and are open to classes from Grade 4 (age 9 or so) through to adult. It has been found that students below the age of 9 generally have insufficient comprehension of the chronological passage of time to understand the significance of stratigraphy. Nor do small children possess the stamina or eye–hand coordination necessary for archaeological excavation in the site context.

The programmes consist of an audiovisual-aided presentation focusing on the goals and methods of historical archaeologists in an urban site situation. The talk emphasizes the fact that students are 'really being archaeologists' for the day, and that they have to be very, very careful, since a 'site is destroyed in the process of digging it' and if they make a mistake, the archaeologists in charge 'can't fix it, the heritage information will be gone forever'. 'This is not an educational exercise – it's an archaeological excavation' is an assertion made repeatedly throughout the students' time on site.

Following the introduction, students are divided into groups of six under the supervision of an Archaeological Resource Centre staff member. Equipment is distributed and students are each assigned an excavation unit. They are instructed in mapping (planning) techniques, using forms specially designed for this purpose, artefact retrieval methods, and the proper screening (sieving) of all dirt removed from each unit. All artefacts are mapped *in situ*, a practice that helps ensure the proper recovery of data as well as reinforcing the need for slow, careful excavation.

. Throughout the active part of the programme, instructors discuss the significance of interesting objects recovered. After the excavation session, students clean up their units, replace the equipment that they have used in their buckets, and gather around two archaeologists bearing display cases full of previously excavated artefacts. They are then introduced to the ways in which archaeologists identify artefacts and discuss how recovered materials can help in dating and interpreting the site. At the end of the period students are thanked for their help in saving Toronto's heritage and are presented with a site button as a souvenir of their day on the dig.

In case of poor weather, a 'rainy day programme' is put into operation. In this case, students learn how to clean and catalogue artefacts in the site laboratory (depending upon the age group of the students the objects used may be surface scatter or refuse; this is not pointed out to the participants!).

The impact of these programmes on students is immense. Children and adults alike respond well to being told that what they are doing is of vital importance. The sense of responsibility generated in each group by its supervisor produces an astonishingly high quality of excavation on the part of even those students who seem only marginally interested when they first arrive and although the Centre deals largely with inner-city school students, supervisory staff experience almost no discipline problems on site.

Two further points should be borne in mind. First, few students of any age respond positively to a completely unstructured learning environment. In the field context, the classroom situation cannot be duplicated. However, a clear, comprehensive plan for each day's lessons will ensure a good educational experience for the students, as well as providing a reassuringly organized system for the staff to follow. It is not suggested that secondary-school field education programmes be operated with a supervisor to student ratio higher than 1:6, which in Ontario is the maximum ratio allowed for a public archaeology project. In field schools, a 1:4 ratio seems to be most effective, at least when dealing with teenagers.

Second, sufficient good-quality equipment should be provided. Much teaching time is lost if students are forced to wait to use a line level, or to sharpen their trowels before beginning to excavate. Camera and transit equipment should be both simple to operate and durable. Recording systems, too, should be clear and comprehensible to nonprofessional excavators. In our case, we have developed a colour-coded system of forms contained in three-ring binders for each unit. They consist of layer/feature forms (summaries of the findings of each layer or feature), daily record forms, plan view forms and object forms (small finds record sheets). The colour coding not only helps the students, but also provides a quick reference for supervisors gathering specific layer data for interpretation purposes.

Summer field schools and volunteer programmes

During the summer months two credit courses are offered, the Grade 11 and 12 Archaeological Field Schools. In addition, the site is opened to the general public and invitations are issued through the media for special interest groups, charity organizations, and individuals to take part in half-day archaeological programmes. These programmes are offered free-of-charge as a public service. Visitors are provided with a free guided tour, and a special trailer fitted out as a display unit contains a frequently updated exposition of site findings for the benefit of regular visitors, of whom there are many. Even experienced volunteers are required to take part in a half-day educational programme (similar to that described for the school groups above) to ensure their familiarity with ARC excavation and recording systems. The Ontario Archaeological Society has recently initiated a programme entitled 'Passport to the past', whereby volunteers throughout the province can acquire stamps attesting to their participation and experience in specific archaeological tasks and all ARC programmes are eligible for such accreditation.

Field school students are divided into groups of no more than four to each staff member. Each is assigned an excavation unit for the entire course session, and is fully responsible for its excavation and recording. Specific skills are taught, first in the classroom and then in the field, by staff members expert in their execution, on a rotating basis throughout the course. The objective is to ensure that all students receive instruction in the basic techniques applied by professional archaeologists in the site situation. In addition, at least one laboratory session per week provides sufficient time for processing artefacts recovered in each unit; the laboratory period includes intensive instruction in artefact cleaning, cataloguing, and identification, using manuals provided for this purpose.

Students are also accompanied on field trips to sites of archaeological or historical significance at intervals throughout the course. An important component of the programme is a visit to the libraries and archives where the major primary documentary material relating to Toronto historical archaeology is available.

The final assessment for field school students is based on a formal examination, and on submission of a 'mini-site report' based on data recorded from each student's excavation unit. Students are required to undertake all the steps required of historical archaeologists to this end including archival research about the site and its environs, a description of the stratigraphy complete with plans views and profiles drawn up by the student, analysis of artefacts found in each layer and feature, and basic interpretation of finds in the unit. This has been found to be a remarkably successful means of assessing student comprehension at each phase of the course presentation, and it also provides a real learning experience in its requirement for the application of learned skills.

The field schools have proved a popular and remarkably effective course of study in the Toronto school system. Several students have enrolled in both courses in successive years (the Grade 12 course, for 17-year-olds, has a slightly more research-oriented curriculum based on independent study than does the earlier one). Although the programme is not aimed at indoctrinating students into taking archaeology at university, it should be added that two have recently applied to do so, and that one of the students on the 1983 programme has graduated with a degree in archaeology and is currently an employee of the Archaeological Resource Centre.

Winter programmes in the centre

Over the winter months, the staff of the Centre conduct a wide variety of educational programmes. In addition, the analysis and interpretation of the preceding season's excavation is undertaken with a view to the production of a final site report.

Since no other programme of this type is available, archaeologists at the Centre also work with educational consultants and teachers to design new curriculum packages relevant to Ministry of Education guidelines. This includes the development of various types of instructional media ranging from videos to crossword puzzles for use by the classroom teacher as introductory or follow-up materials relating to a class field trip to the Resource Centre.

HALF-DAY FIELD TRIPS FOR SCHOOL GROUPS

Seven half-day field trips are offered for Grade 4 students through to adults throughout the winter months. These are conducted in the Centre's classroom facilities, and provide a wide range of educational experiences in archaeology and related disciplines. All programmes are participatory. In developing hands-on curricula we were confronted with the fact that the classroom curriculum in use in Ontario schools is flexible at each grade level, so it is difficult to predict the degree of previous knowledge in a given subject area which visiting classes might have acquired.

The Centre has twenty half-day programmes currently in use, and an average of five more are being developed and implemented annually. Each is created with a view to curriculum relevance at all school levels. Thus 'Science and archaeology' designed for 10 to 12 year olds is also modified and upgraded as 'Scientific dating methods' for 16 to 18 year olds. In addition, individually designed half-day programmes will be provided for classes with special requirements. In this way, the facility serves not only as an educational centre with a core set of course offerings, but also offers an infinite number of programmes devised to meet 'market demand'.

Half-day courses include such topics as 'Ontario rock art', where students learn about the role art plays in a non-technological society, and produce their own versions on pieces of old roofing slate; 'Native foodways', in which the class makes and eats a Native Iroquoian dish called 'sagamite'; and 'The archaeology of early Toronto', where actual artefacts from various sites are used to illustrate economic, social, and technological development in the 19th-century city. The course also exposes students to the use of historic maps from various periods to define cultural and ethnic areas of immigrant residence.

Each programme is taught by two archaeologists. Although the proportion of specific programmes varies depending upon bookings, most staff members teach no more than three half-days a week. This allocation of time allows for the completion of other duties assigned to these individuals, such as curriculum and instructional media developments, the public education and relations campaign, and teaching other courses of study.

Cooperative and independent studies programmes

At some of the secondary schools in the Toronto system students have the option of engaging in practical employment in a subject area of their choice as a way of earning credit hours. The 'Co-op' programme relies on the fact that many companies, government institutions, libraries, and the like can find a place for a willing worker who is interested in learning how to perform specific tasks. The ARC participates in the Board Cooperative Education programme, and provides individually designed courses of study relating to the area of the student's interest. Such a student might undertake the cleaning, cataloguing, data entry, and research leading toward analysis of a specific artefact category. Another project might include archival and land-titles office research for the next season's planned excavation site. Independent studies programmes operate in a similar manner, but require the production of an extensive report on the part of the student.

Night school classes

The ARC first offered a general interest programme for adults in night school in 1986. There are currently four courses offered, including 'Introduction to archaeology', 'Ontario prehistory', 'Classical archaeology' and 'The archaeology of the ancient Near East'. Many of the students return year after year for further instruction, and a small corps of artefact-washing volunteers have been developed through the night school archaeology enthusiasts.

Archaeological analysis and reporting

In addition to providing a comprehensive range of classes in archaeology and related disciplines, the staff of the Centre is responsible for conducting research and analysis of each site's recovered data for the purposes of annual report production and each staff member has an average of between 15 and 20 hours a week to devote to these tasks. This ensures that the site reports are completed to professional standards and that the conclusions drawn from the research results can be disseminated to the general public in the form of booklets, handouts, lectures and displays.

Public, promotion and access

The ARC performs a community outreach function in respect to archaeological education which goes far beyond the classroom walls of Toronto Board of Education schools. One of the staff members is an experienced public relations officer in addition to having archaeological training. The work of this individual has been invaluable in bringing archaeology to the public eye, and has to a great extent been responsible for the success of ARC.

Throughout the year, the staff of the Resource Centre presents public lectures on Toronto archaeology to heritage, special interest, and educational groups. A portable 'Exposystem' unit is used for mounting combined photographic, information panel, and artefact displays at public locations throughout the city, as well as at archaeological and historical group events and conferences. Sites and the Centre itself are open to the public daily, and guided tours are arranged for visitors. The permanent facilities contain library, slide, and film collections as well as a budding historical artefact reference collection. These resources are available for use by researchers on request.

Each season opens with a 'Heritage open house', at which the various heritage groups operating in the Toronto area are invited to put up displays and distribute information to visitors. The site opening is an occasion for speeches and ribbon-cutting festivities by prominent personages and the media are invited. Press packages with photos are sent out in advance to ensure proper coverage of the event. Journalists are also contacted at intervals throughout the dig season to encourage newspaper, radio, and television coverage of the public education programmes in progress. The response to date has been tremendous.

Spin-off projects by the media have gained national recognition for the involvement of Toronto school students in heritage conservation. The Thornton Blackburn House Site was the focus for a 22-minute documentary video produced by journalism department students of Ryerson Polytechnical Institute in Toronto. The video, *Makin' Free*, won the Canadian Broadcasting Corporation's Telefest Award for best documentary in 1986.

Conclusion

'Educational archaeology' is a relatively new speciality, but one whose benefits for both students and archaeologists have only now begun to be realized. The experience of the Toronto Board of Education in developing the Archaeological Resource Centre has been extremely positive, and it is hoped it will provide a positive model for programmes that may be initiated elsewhere. Fundamental to the ethos of the Archaeological Resource Centre is the notion that the operation of educational programmes in archaeology requires that archaeologists become, if they are not already, dedicated professional educators. It is an unfortunate fact that far too many field schools in the past have been operated for the express purpose of obtaining both labour and funding for 'getting the site dug'. Archaeologists in charge have had a great sense of responsibility towards the salvage of the resource, but little commitment to the students taking part in the so-called educational component.

The staff of the Archaeological Resource Centre believe our children must be made to feel that it is their own heritage they are helping to preserve by taking part in archaeology programmes. Only through increased public awareness will fewer sites be destroyed, fewer historical buildings torn down, and more people become active in the conservation process. The preservation of heritage resources can no longer be regarded as the province of a small group of underfunded professional archaeologists.

The archaeological community in Ontario is becoming increasingly aware of the necessity of conducting public education programmes in archaeology. A recent colloquium conducted by consulting archaeologists in Ontario resulted in the following resolution: 'Be it resolved that recommendations concerning an educational component be required in the Master Plan reports' (Hodge & Stewart 1988). A 'Master Plan' is the heritage conservation element in an environmental assessment conducted prior to development in a community or county.

The Toronto programme is a pioneering venture in bringing archaeology into the public milieu. It is our sincere hope that through the various programmes offered at the Archaeological Resource Centre a new generation of Torontonians will grow up thinking that archaeology in general, and heritage conservation in particular, is a normal and important part of their everyday lives.

References

Hodge, P. & W. Stewart. 1988. Unpublished letter to D. Munro (Ontario Minister of Culture and Communications), 20 October 1988.

Jamieson, D. et al. 1988. The Archaeological Resource Centre of the Toronto Board of Education. Unpublished manuscript of Ontario Ministry of Culture and Communication, March.

McKenna III, G.1988. Sharing the responsibility. Unpublished kenote address to the BEST conference. Toronto. November.

Ontario Ministry of Education and Ontario Ministry of College and Universities 1980. Issues and directions: the response to the final report of the Commission on Declining School Enrolments in Ontario. Toronto.

Ontario Ministry of Education (OME) 1986. Curriculum guideline: history and contemporary studies Part A: policy and programme considerations.

Smardz, K. 1989. The Toronto Board of Education Archaeological Resource Centre: an update. Unpublished paper given at the First Joint Archaeological Congress. Baltimore, 7 January.

Appendix 1

B.A. IN HISTORY (ARCHAEOLOGY OPTION)

COMBINATION OF COURSES

First year: Two Papers for Examination:
(1) Introduction to Archaeology
(2) Sources in African History

Second Year: Four Papers for Examination:
(1) African Prehistory
(2) Archaeology Laboratory (including compulsory field work)
(3) History of Kenya to the Present
(4) Physical Geology (GEY S 150) and Historical Geology (GEY S 153)

Third Year: Four Papers for Examination:
(1) One Archaeology Area Course (except African Prehistory)
(2) Themes in East African History OR one second-year Regional Survey (e.g. West Africa or South-Central Africa or North Africa, whichever is available)
(3) Geomorphology (Geography C 315)
(4) Dissertation

(Source: University of Nairobi Calendar, 1981–82, p. 162.)

Appendix 2

B.A. IN HISTORY (ARCHAEOLOGY OPTION)

COMBINATION OF COURSES

First Year: Two Papers for Examination:
      C 131 History of Kenya to the Present
      C 132 Introduction to Archaeology

Second Year: Four Papers for Examination:
      C 23B African Pre-History
      C 23D Archaeology Laboratory (including
          compulsory field work)
      I 151 External Earth processes
      One History Course

Third Year: Four Papers for Examination:
      C 23C One Archaeology Area Course
      C 330 Themes in East African History OR Regional
          Surveys of Africa
      C 315 Geomorphology
      C 332 Dissertation

N.B. Students take a total of 8 papers during their second and third years – 4 in the second year and 4 in the third year.

(Source: University of Nairobi Calendar 1984–85, p. 361.)

Index